Human Biological Diversity

HUMAN BIOLOGICAL DIVERSITY

An Introduction to Human Biology

Daniel E. Brown

Boston   Columbus   Indianapolis   New York   San Francisco   Upper Saddle River
Amsterdam   Cape Town   Dubai   London   Madrid   Milan   Munich   Paris   Montréal   Toronto
Delhi   Mexico City   São Paulo   Sydney   Hong Kong   Seoul   Singapore   Taipei   Tokyo

VP, Editorial Director: Leah Jewell
Editor in Chief: Dixon Musslewhite
Publisher: Nancy Roberts
Editorial Assistant: Nart Varoqua
AVP/Director of Marketing: Brandy Dawson
Senior Marketing Manager: Laura Lee Manley
Marketing Assistant: Pat Walsh
Managing Editor: Maureen Richardson
Project Liaison: Shelly Kupperman
Senior Operations Manager: Nick Sklitsis
Operations Specialist: Cathleen Petersen
Manager, Visual Research: Beth Brenzel

Photo Researcher: Lee Scher
Manager, Rights and Permissions: Zina Arabia
Image Cover Permissions Coordinator: Karen Sanatar
Image Interior Permission Coordinator: Annette Linder
Manager, Cover Visual Research & Permissions: Jayne Conte
Cover Designer: Margaret Kenselaar
Cover Art: Diana Ong/Superstock
Full-Service Project Management/Composition: Leo Kelly, Macmillan Publishing Solutions
Printer/Binder: Hamilton Printing Company
Cover Printer: Coral Graphics Services, Inc.
Text Font: 10/12 Minion

Credits and acknowledgments borrowed from other sources and reproduced, with permission, in this textbook appear on page 321.

Library of Congress Cataloging-in-Publication Data

Brown, Daniel E.
    Human biological diversity : an introduction to human biology / Daniel E. Brown. – 1st ed.
      p. cm.
    Includes bibliographical references and index.
    ISBN-13: 978-0-13-045571-0 (alk. paper)
    ISBN-10: 0-13-045571-7 (alk. paper)
      1. Human biology—Textbooks.   2. Human evolution—Textbooks.   3. Physical anthropology—Textbooks.
      I. Title.
  QP36.B868 2010
  612—dc22

                                                         2009026678

10 9 8 7 6 5 4 3 2 1

Prentice Hall
is an imprint of

www.pearsonhighered.com

ISBN 13: 978-0-13-045571-0
ISBN 10: 0-13-045571-7

To Annie Yu Brown

whose support made this book possible.

CONTENTS

Preface   xiii

Chapter 1   Introduction   1
    Chapter Summary   6

Chapter 2   Concepts of Evolution   7
    A Brief History of Evolutionary Ideas   7
        Ideas About Time   7
        The Great Chain of Being   9
    Scientific Approaches to Evolution   9
        Lamarck's Theory of Evolution   10
        Darwin's Theory of Evolution   11
    Types of Evidence for Evolution   13
        Creationists vs. Evolutionists   13
        Adaptation   15
        Paleontology   19
        Biogeography   19
        Comparative Anatomy   20
        Comparative Embryology   23
        Artificial Selection   23
        Other Evidence for Evolution   23
    Chapter Summary   24

Chapter 3   Genetics and Microevolution   26
    The Chemical Basis of Life   26
        Proteins   26
        Nucleic Acids   27
        Duplication of DNA   30
        Direction of Protein Synthesis   31
    Genetics   32
        Sexual Reproduction   33
        Mendelian Genetics   34
    Microevolution   40
        Introduction to Population
            Genetics   40
        Forces of Evolution   43
    The Synthetic Theory of Evolution   46
    Chapter Summary   47

Chapter 4   Molecular Genetics, Genomics, and Human Genetics   48

A Closer Look at Chromosomes   48

   Characteristics of Chromosomes   48

   Chromosome Mapping   51

   Epigenetics   53

Extrachromosomal Genetics   55

   RNA Processing   55

   Mitochondrial DNA   57

   Chloroplast DNA   58

Tracing Genetic Variability and Function   58

   Genetic Variability   58

   Understanding Gene Function   59

   A Brief Look at Quantitative Genetics   61

Human Genetics and the Human Genome   62

   Family Studies in Human Genetics   62

   The Human Genome   63

   The Human Genome Project   63

   The Next Step?   64

Chapter Summary   65

Chapter 5   Macroevolution and Taxonomy   66

Taxonomy   66

   Species and Speciation   66

   Taxonomic Units above the Species Level   71

Macroevolution   74

   Some Highlights in the History of Life: An Anthropocentric View   74

   The Human Journey   81

   Macroevolutionary Processes   86

Chapter Summary   87

Chapter 6   "Race" and Human Variation in Physical Traits   89

Race   89

   Race, Population, and Ethnic Group   90

   Clines Versus Clumps   90

   A Short History of Western Race Concepts: Ancient   91

   A Short History of European Race Concepts: Modern   93

Phenotypic Characteristics of Human Variability   96

   Nature Versus Nurture   96

   Human Pigmentation: Skin Color   97

Human Pigmentation: Hair and Eye Color   102

Hair Form   104

Epicanthic Eyefolds   105

Body Size and Shape   105

Head Form   108

Dermatoglyphics   109

Skeletal and Dental Variation   110

Age Differences in the Skeleton and Teeth   110

Sex Differences in the Skeleton   110

Individual Variation in Skeletal
and Dental Features   111

Race and Intelligence   112

What Is Intelligence?   112

IQ and Heredity   113

Population Differences in IQ   113

Patterns of Human Variability   114

Chapter Summary   115

Chapter 7   Genotypic Traits and the Tracing of Population Affiliations   116

Genotypic Traits Traditionally Used in Human Biology   116

Blood Groups: The ABO System   117

The MNSs Blood Group Systems   120

The Rhesus (Rh) Blood-Group System   120

Hemoglobin Variants   122

Glucose-6-Phosphate Dehydrogenase Deficiency   127

Genetic Traits from Contemporary Molecular Biology Used
in Human Biology   127

Major Types of Molecular Genetic Studies Used
in Human Biology   128

Uses for Human Molecular Genetics Studies   128

The Genetic History of Homo Sapiens   129

Genetics and Human Migrations   132

Genetic and Disease Risk   140

Genetics and the Notion of Race   140

Chapter Summary   141

Chapter 8   Demography: Populations, Reproduction, and Mortality   142

Population Ecology   142

Population Growth   142

Population Ecology: Concluding Remarks   146

Demography of Human Populations 147
  Fertility and Fecundity 147
  Mortality 150
  Migration 153
Human Population Growth 155
  Population Increase 155
  Human Population Structure 156
  Implications of Growth 157
Chapter Summary 160

Chapter 9 Life Span: Growth and Development 161
The General Pattern of Human Growth 161
  Prenatal Growth 161
  Growth after Birth: General Patterns 165
Growth of Specific Body Parts 169
  Development of Differential Systems 170
  Development of Selected Other Systems 172
Growth after Birth: Population Differences 175
  Environmental Effects on Growth 175
  Genetics and Population Growth Differences 178
Growth and Development: A Final
  Consideration 179
Chapter Summary 179

Chapter 10 Life Span: Aging and Senescence 181
The Biology of Senescence 181
  Aging at the Cellular Level 181
  Superficial Changes During Senescence 186
Theories of Senescence 188
  Mechanistic Theories of Senescence 188
  Evolutionary Theories of Senescence 190
  Selected System-Specific Senescence Theories 192
  Conclusion: Theories of Senescence 192
The Human Population Biology of Senescence 193
  Population Differences in Life Span 193
  Sex Differences in Senescence 196
  Population Differences in Diseases Associated
    with Senescence 196
  Conclusion 200
Chapter Summary 200

Chapter 11 Human Adaptability to Physical Stressors   201

Limiting Factors, Tolerance, and Environmental Physiology   201

Law of Tolerance   201

Environmental Physiology   202

Human Adaptability   204

Adaptation to Cold and Heat   206

Thermoregulation   206

Cold Adaptation   208

Heat Adaptation   212

Hot-Dry Macroenvironments   212

Warm-Humid Environments   214

Conclusion to Thermoregulation   216

Adaptation to High Altitude   216

Behavioral and Cultural Adjustments to Hypoxia   217

Biological Adaptations to Hypoxia   218

Population Differences in Adaptability to High-Altitude Hypoxia   219

High Activity Levels   221

The Requirements of Work   221

Behavioral and Cultural Adjustments to High Workloads   221

Biological Adaptations to High Workloads   221

Adaptive Consequences of Work Capacity   224

Conclusion   224

Chapter Summary   224

Chapter 12 Human Adaptability to Biological Stressors   226

Malnutrition   226

Food versus Nutrients   226

Types of Nutrients   227

Protein-Calorie Malnutrition   227

Protein Deficiency   228

Protein-Calorie Malnutrition: Total Undernutrition   229

Micronutrient Deficiencies   233

Vitamin Deficiencies   233

Electrolyte and Mineral Deficiencies   236

Overnutrition   238

Conclusion: Malnutrition   238

Infectious Disease   238

Host-Parasite Relationships   239

Vector-Borne Diseases   240

Direct-Contact Diseases   242

Diseases Due to Intimate Contact 244

Poor-Sanitation Diseases 247

Conclusion: Infectious Diseases 249

General Conclusion: The Impact of Biological Stressors on Human Biology 249

Chapter Summary 250

Chapter 13 Human Biology in the Modern World 251

Possible Reduced Selective Forces 251

The Accumulation of Minor Genetic Problems 252

Reduced Selection Due to Medical Interventions 254

General Stress 256

The Nature of General Stress 257

Adiposity and Obesity: Are We Eating Ourselves to Death? 262

The Obesity Epidemic 262

The Causes of Increased Adiposity 263

Pollution: The Fouling of the Environment 268

Air Pollution 268

Water Pollution 269

Solid-Waste Pollution 270

Pollution and Human Variation 271

Conclusion 272

Chapter Summary 272

Chapter 14 Human Biological Variation: A Look to the Future and Some Final Thoughts on Ethics 274

Human Biology in the Future 274

An Individual-Level View of Future Human Biology 274

The Future of Human Population Variability 275

Final Thoughts on the Ethics of Human Biology Research 277

Prevention of Harm to the Individual Participant 277

Prevention of Harm to Communities 279

What Is Normal? 280

Chapter Summary 282

Glossary 283

References 296

Credits 321

Index 323

PREFACE

Human biology is a fascinating field, integrating the study of anthropology and biology as a means to better understand our extraordinarily complex species. A human individual is a puzzling mix of behavior, values, genetics, physiology, and more, while a population of humans is all the above, plus the peculiarities that social life and inter-individual diversity add to this mix. Our brains appear to be hardwired to identify differences among individuals, and this sometimes prevents us from also appreciating the incredible similarity among all people. An understanding of human diversity promises to bring with it tolerance for—or even admiration of—human differences, and this surely can only lead to a reduction in the bigotry and provincialism that has caused much misery through the ages.

It has taken many people to bring this book to completion over the several years that I have busied myself with it, finding time to work on it around the interstices of my day job. I want to thank the great patience of my editor and publisher, Nancy Roberts, who must have often wondered if this was a project without end. I also am grateful to the other editorial people who aided me during this process, including Nart Varoqua, Leo Kelly, Paula Bryant Bonilla, and Mayda Bosco. I appreciate the thoughtful advice of the reviewers: Sunil K. Khanna, Oregon State University; Mark A. Rees, University of Louisiana at Lafayette; Lynnette Leidy Sievert, University of Massachusetts Amherst; Trudy Turner, University of Wisconsin-Milwaukee; Linda Taylor, University of Miami; Baron Pineda, Oberlin College; and Robert Anemone, Western Michigan University.

Many colleagues have contributed to the text, serving as sounding boards, informal editors, and long-suffering friends. I thank the several anonymous reviewers who found many errors of fact or tone, and whose comments greatly improved the text. Special thanks go to colleagues Lynnette Leidy Sievert, Craig Severance, Lynn Morrison, Ron Amundson, Brooke Thomas, Joel M. Hanna, Ralph Garruto, Michael Little, and Gary James for their aid and support. My thoughts are with the late Paul Baker and Charles Hoff, who provided inspiration. I also thank my colleagues who allowed me to include them in profiles of human biologists, allowing readers to get a sense of the field's breadth. I find their research to be among the most exciting that takes place in the discipline, although there are many others who could have been included as well. Others provided photos or moral support, and I really appreciate my good fortune to work in an academic discipline where mutual support, rather than vicious competition, is the norm.

My greatest thanks go to my son Aaron and daughter Elena (who contributed some of the drawings contained in the book), who put up with their absentee father on many occasions, but most of all to my saintly wife Annie Yu Brown, to whom this book is dedicated.

Human Biological Diversity

CHAPTER 1

Introduction

We can quickly pick out visual differences in the people around us. We recognize individuals easily despite meeting hundreds or even thousands of people every day. (Putting names to the individuals is a separate, more difficult skill.) The presence of this ability in all humans, save for those with severe brain damage, and its early development in infants suggest that it is hardwired in our brains—that is, it is an ability we obtain at birth through our biology, as opposed to something we learn. It is also an ability found in related species such as chimpanzees (Parr et al. 2000). While our recognition is based mostly on facial characteristics, we can also pick out other bodily traits in identifying differences among people. This ability to identify individuals is crucial to our species's considerable sociality and thus may be considered as an adaptive trait. Whether it is adaptive or not, the trait implies an ability to rapidly focus on *differences* in individuals that allows such identification to take place.

Our ability to discriminate between individuals can also be used to distinguish between groupings of people. We develop the ability to distinguish males from females (usually), elders from children, and, most important for the purposes of this book, to create other categories based on often subtle differences in facial shape, skin color, eyelid structure, and a host of other characteristics. Many of these latter categories persist over time, with parents and children retaining some similarities, although also showing differences. Thus some, but hardly all, of the variability we use to distinguish people is inherited.

This focus on human diversity is formally studied in the discipline of **anthropology**, which considers the variation of people in biology and **culture**, and over both space and time. Culture, as used by anthropologists, is defined as an organization of "conventional understandings, manifest in act and artifact, that characterizes societies" (Redfield 1941, p. 132) The definition shows that culture is more than a group of behaviors, it is an organized set of understandings about the world, both social and natural. Thus, culture includes values, behaviors, expectations, and materials, with these all being passed down through learning from generation to generation.

Anthropology is traditionally divided into four subdisciplines. **Cultural anthropology** examines the variation in human culture throughout the world in present (or near-present) times. Cultural anthropologists have recognized the incredible complexity of human behavior and the values that underlie this behavior. They have observed that patterns of behavior, understandings, and values are passed down through learning from generation to generation. **Archaeology** is the subfield of anthropology that studies cultures of the past, primarily through examination of the materials that these peoples have left behind. **Anthropological linguistics** is the subfield that focuses on human language and its connections with other aspects of culture. Finally, **biological anthropology** is a subfield of anthropology that studies human biological variation in space and time. **Human population biology**, in turn, is a branch of biological anthropology that studies the biological diversity of contemporary humans, and this subfield forms the subject matter of this text.

Our visual recognition of individuals occurs mostly on an unconscious level—usually we simply glance at the person, and memories of previous encounters occur to one degree or another. Human population biology is the scientific study of the variation in humans that permits individual recognition, focusing on the specific features that we use to discriminate among people and, particularly, groups of people. This study requires considerations beyond the unconscious—discovering in an objective way what variation exists and what it means. A major question that arises is whether the groupings of people that we construct are natural categories of people, or more arbitrary divisions. For instance, we often focus on skin color, but our groupings would be quite different if we based categorization on how tall people are, or how large their ears are, or any number of other traits. Supposed categories that represent natural, biologically based groups of humans are traditionally termed "**races**." A major issue for human biologists in the early twenty-first century is whether human diversity in fact conforms to a classification of people into races, and, if so, how that categorization can be made. Evidence will be presented in this book that shows that humans, in fact, do *not* form large regional groupings that fit the traditional concept of races. We must also remember that our hardwired skill at detecting very minor differences in individuals—even permitting the distinguishing between pairs of identical twins by their friends and family—may lead us to overlook the greater similarities that unite all people. The text will also differentiate between the broad-scale groupings designated as races from the smaller units that correspond to biological **populations**, which are groupings within sexually reproducing species that interbreed frequently and thus tend to be more closely related to members of the population than to members of the species from other populations.

The importance of understanding the scientific basis for race is hard to overestimate. Racially based conflicts rage in many areas of the world. Many people are denied basic rights due to perceived membership in a given race. Racial profiling, where police stop and search people based on "racial characteristics" (how they look), is common in many areas of the United States in these early years of the twenty-first century. It is easier for people to mistreat others if those others are seen as being innately different, which can quickly be interpreted as being innately inferior. If the differences are believed to be permanent and hereditary, a perception of sub-human status in comparison to these other people can ensue.

The horrors of Nazism received support from pseudoscientific theories of human variation that justified the attempted annihilation of certain ethnic groups in Europe. Scientists must not retreat from establishing good scientific understanding of human diversity in order to avoid the issue, or surely poor science will triumph again. There are many examples of poor science in contemporary times that allegedly find evidence for the inferior status of certain human races. It is the responsibility of human biologists to rebut fallacious theories and the false conclusions drawn from them. The study of evolutionary biology has taught us that diversity is actually beneficial to a species, and therefore we can argue that the scientific study of human diversity will actually permit us to celebrate our differences instead of deploring them.

During the first half of the twentieth century, human population biology was primarily a descriptive science (Baker 1988), and attempts to categorize humans into races were a major focus of the discipline. Beyond categorization, human biologists described the ways in which people differed in physical features, examining characteristics from skin color to facial shape to blood type. This study was greatly influenced by the field of population biology, in which the diversity of all species was studied. Population biology developed from Charles Darwin's writings and is closely integrated with evolutionary biology.

Beginning in the 1950s, human biologists began shifting their focus from simply describing human diversity to attempting to understand the naturalistic, causal processes for this variation. These attempts linked human biologists with others in the biological sciences from ecologists to population geneticists to molecular biologists. The International Biological Programme, a major attempt to understand biological ecology in various **biomes** (that is, major types of environments) that lasted from 1964 to 1974, involved many biological disciplines, including human biology. This program stimulated consideration of human populations as part of larger ecosystems, and also motivated scientists to begin examining human populations much as they studied populations of other species. The program included intensive research projects focused on the understanding of processes involved in human biological variability.

Today, human biologists have many different specialties—from human molecular genetics to international health to environmental physiology to growth and development to nutrition—but a common perspective: the understanding of the causes and consequences of the "natural" variability of *Homo sapiens*. In fact, these specialties overlap considerably. Human biologists interested in human biological adaptability to high altitude environments work with geneticists in search of specific genetic variations that may aid people in dealing with the low-oxygen pressures found at these altitudes. Understanding population differences in the prevalence of a given disease often entails understanding of environmentally based physiological and nutritional issues for specific populations.

It is impossible to understand human biology without also reckoning with human behavior and culture. Our behavior and our values shape our biology in many ways. There is also strong evidence that our culture is in many ways influenced by our biology as well. Thus, humans cannot be understood simply as biological—or simply as cultural—beings; we are biocultural organisms, where biological and cultural characteristics are integrated in a complex, and sometimes inextricable, manner. The biocultural viewpoint will therefore play a prominent role in this introduction to human biological diversity, although our focus will necessarily remain on biology.

Human biology is a very broad field, and as our knowledge of specialties within the field grows, it becomes increasingly difficult for any one person to be able to understand the entire field in great depth. Human biologists are noted for taking a broad view, however, and they often work in interdisciplinary teams when attempting to deal with complex issues of human variability. The intent of this book is to provide a general introduction to basic concepts of the field as a whole and to illustrate some of human biology's great breadth, as well as give an inkling of the field's depth through a few extended examples. An attempt to illustrate what it is like to actually be a human biologist is made through the inclusion of a few profiles of selected scientists who have made careers in the field. Each chapter has a summary section that briefly reviews the major points made in that chapter.

Chapter 2 provides an introduction to evolution. In fact, an understanding of variability in humans or any other species is impossible without a basic understanding of biological evolution. The evolutionary process is what produces variability among biological organisms and provides a theoretical understanding for how—and perhaps even why—biological variability exists. The chapter covers scientific theories for the mechanism of how evolution occurs and also the types of evidence for the existence of evolution.

Chapter 3 covers the basics of the science of genetics. Human biologists must also have an understanding of the mechanism by which biological traits are passed down through generations and how changes can appear over time. This entails learning the fundamentals of genetics, which is the science of biological inheritance. The chapter covers the cellular processes involved in biological reproduction, and then goes through the basic ideas of genetics. Next, the chapter covers population genetics and the process of "microevolution," in which the genetic basis of biology changes over time.

Our understanding of genetics is undergoing a revolution as we learn details of the biochemical basis for heredity. This aspect of genetics is covered in Chapter 4. Some of the exciting new genetics discoveries will be included here, although chances are great that major new discoveries will come to light before this book can be printed. We are chasing a moving target, and while that can be frustrating for a textbook writer, it is symptomatic of the excitement from ongoing discoveries that marks human population biology.

In Chapter 5, the focus will be on a longer-term view of evolution, concentrating on "macroevolution," or evolutionary events that occur over millions of years. Topics covered include taxonomy, the way in which living organisms are categorized by biologists, which involves the tracing of evolutionary relationships among species. The process of speciation, in which new species appear, will be described. The chapter then will trace the history of life briefly, with a focus on illustrating how some species are related, and also will discuss evidence for the loss of species through extinction.

Chapter 6 will examine the concept of "race," arguing that the evidence shows that the common notion of biological races does not apply to modern humans. Some of the history of ideas about races will be explored, along with discussion of the impact of these ideas on relationships between peoples. The chapter will go on to explore some of the common "phenotypic" traits (generally, characteristics that are externally apparent in organisms), such as skin color and body form that have been used to characterize races. The chapter will conclude with a brief rebuttal of fallacious ideas about supposed racial differences in intelligence.

Chapter 7 continues the study of population differences among humans, applying genetics to the study of human variability. The chapter examines human characteristics for which the genetics are fairly simple and well understood, and uses the geographical distribution of these characteristics to better understand the underlying reasons for human biological variation. The chapter describes such classic genotypic traits as ABO blood types and hemoglobin variants, as well as describing the results of studies using recent molecular techniques to uncover variation in mitochondrial DNA, Y chromosomes, and molecular studies of nuclear DNA. Applications of these studies for understanding the general level of human genetic diversity, for tracing human migrations, and for understanding the relationships among human populations will be reviewed.

In Chapter 8, we will turn to the study of human populations: their size, growth, structure, and the factors that influence population characteristics. The chapter begins with an overview of population ecology, including notions of the opposing forces of reproduction and environmental resistance, and also examines the age and sex structure of populations. Next, these principles are applied to human populations, and topics examined include fecundity and fertility, mortality, and migration. The chapter concludes with a look at human population growth from both global and regional perspectives, and examines variability in human demography in different populations.

The next part of the book will focus on the human life span, from processes of growth in childhood to processes of aging in the elderly, and how these processes are related. Chapter 9 focuses on growth and development, describing the great variability in growth patterns among individuals and populations and also investigating some of the reasons for this variability. Chapter 10 examines aging and senescence, and the focus again is on the variability found in these processes among humans.

Chapters 11 through 13 explore another major issue of human biology: how humans adapt to the environments in which they live. An attempt will be made to answer the question: do some aspects of human population differences derive from their need to adapt to specific environments? Chapter 11 discusses how humans cope with physical stressors in the environment, from temperature extremes to the low oxygen levels found at high altitude. These coping strategies include behavioral and cultural responses, such as manufacturing clothing and shelter, as well as biological responses, such as sweating, shivering, and hyperventilation.

Chapter 12 covers how humans cope with two types of challenges that come with living on food chains: eating and being eaten. Nutritional studies encompass a complex of behaviors, including obtaining nutrients, defining what food is, sharing food, and dealing with times of scarcity. There are biologically based responses to malnutrition that are reflected in human biological variation. The chapter also covers how our species copes with infectious diseases, both biologically and behaviorally.

In Chapter 13, attention is paid to the special circumstances to which humans must adjust in modernized conditions. Most of our lives today are spent in conditions far removed from those faced by the foraging bands of hominids on the African savanna. The rapidity of the changes in our environment may overstep our evolutionary ability to adapt. The new environment includes increased psychosocial stress, elevated body fat, and exposure to high concentrations of various pollutants. The result is high rates of heart disease, diabetes, and cancer. An understanding of human biological variability is an important aspect of our attempts to understand these challenges.

Finally, we'll take a brief look at what the possibilities are for the future of human biology, both at the individual and population level. Some of this discussion is fanciful; foretelling the future is always a risky business.

PROFILE 1
Catherine Panter-Brick

Catherine Panter-Brick is an anthropologist whose research creates new interdisciplinary perspectives for evaluating human health, bridging the fields of biological, social, and medical anthropology, as well as public health. She focuses her work on critical risks to health and well-being across key stages of human development, giving special attention to the impacts of poverty, disease, malnutrition, and social marginalization. She has directed more than twenty interdisciplinary projects in Afghanistan, Ethiopia, the Gambia, Nepal, Niger, Pakistan, Saudi Arabia, Tanzania, and the United Kingdom.

To examine trade-offs between subsistence work and reproductive responsibilities among hard-working Nepali women, she combined classical methods of observation and measures of energy balance with pioneering data collection on reproductive hormones. Seasonal changes in physical activity, dietary intake, body weight, and breastfeeding behavior altered hormonal profiles—changing reproductive ability across the year in different ways for women of different ethnic groups. Thus, behavior and biology were finely attuned to social and environmental conditions.

An important goal of her research is to situate human biology in careful descriptions of society and ecology. This includes borrowing research techniques from different disciplines, testing hypotheses in new settings, working with different comparison groups, and examining the impact of different social stressors or social disruptions on human well-being. For example, Dr. Panter-Brick's research has refined our understanding of psychosocial and physiological stress for populations facing very challenging conditions. She has evaluated mental health, risk, and resilience among homeless street children in Nepal, a refugee population in Pakistan, and schoolchildren in war-affected areas such as Afghanistan. This work has broad significance for understanding the impact of social, economic, and political adversity on health and behavior. It also has implications for developing effective health interventions. Her project in the Gambia is a good example of working with local communities to identify culturally compelling reasons for participation, motivating behavior change by mobilizing households to repair torn mosquito nets to reduce risks of childhood malaria.

Professor of Anthropology at Durham University in the United Kingdom, Catherine Panter-Brick has co-edited many books to bridge research and teaching practice and to foster interdisciplinary understanding on issues relevant to human biology and society. These include *Hunter Gatherers*; *Abandoned Children*; *Hormones, Health and Behaviour*; and *Biosocial Perspectives on Children*, all published by Cambridge University Press. Her most recent book is *Health, Risk and Adversity*, published by Berghahn Books. She has been director of the Biosocial Society, serves on the editorial board of a number of journals, and is senior editor of medical anthropology for *Social Science & Medicine*.

While human biologists all have specialties, they also like to see themselves as being generalists—never losing a view of the forest while studying the trees. Any attempt to understand our species's variability is embedded within concepts taken from evolutionary biology. This field seeks to understand the diversity of all life and how it arose. It is a field that has been surrounded by controversy based on objections from some religious organizations, but it is also a field that has become nearly universally accepted by the scientific community. We must turn first to this subject before making any attempt to explain human biological diversity.

CHAPTER SUMMARY

This book provides an introduction to the investigation of human biological variability. This field of study is based within the broader study of evolutionary biology. Therefore, topics covered include evolutionary theories, genetics, and biological taxonomy. After these general topics have been covered, they will be applied more specifically to our own species, with chapters covering human genetics, race (once considered a form of human taxonomy), human demography, the human lifespan, human adaptability to stress, nutrition and infectious disease, modernization, and a brief consideration of possible changes in human biological variability in the future. While the focus is on biology, humans are biocultural organisms, and consideration will be paid to the effects of human behavior and values on the biological processes that lead to our species diversity.

CHAPTER 2

Concepts of Evolution

The term evolution literally means "unfolding." For our purposes, the term refers to the development of populations of living organisms and the changes in their form with time. This change refers to populations, not individuals. Individuals grow and develop, age and die, but they do not evolve. It is change that occurs over generations, not within a single lifetime, that defines the evolution of a population of living organisms.

A BRIEF HISTORY OF EVOLUTIONARY IDEAS

Ideas about evolution in the form of scientific theories started at least a generation before Charles Darwin presented his theory. In fact, Darwin's grandfather, Erasmus Darwin, wrote poetry about evolution. Charles Darwin's major contributions were that he presented an enormous amount of evidence that evolution had in fact occurred, and he devised a logical, naturalistic explanation for how evolution took place. Ideas about change over time have a much longer history. An understanding of some of these ideas necessitates a brief look at concepts of time, for we can hardly understand changes over time if we do not understand what time itself represents.

Ideas About Time

Is time linear, stretching in a single line from some point in the past to another point in the future? Or is time cyclical, moving at a stately pace in circles, ever repeating? How long has time existed, and how long will it go on? There are divergent views on these profound questions within Western culture, and there is far more diversity when we view ideas across cultural boundaries. Actual definitions of time will not be addressed; this is a topic that warrants too much of our time. Rather, we will consider only general ideas about the nature of time.

WESTERN IDEAS. The Greco-Roman tradition, although itself quite diverse, may in general be characterized as a belief that time was cyclical (Lloyd 1976). Each cycle began with a golden age of simplicity, followed by slow but inevitable degeneration, then a cataclysm of fire and flood, and finally intervention of the deity (or deities) and the start of the next cycle (Bury 1932). This general view of the nature of time was retained in the Judeo-Christian tradition, with the exception that the idea of multiple cycles had to be discarded, since it contradicted the belief in a single creation. Thus, the Greek idea was replaced with a concept of time that was basically one long cycle. In this cycle, the golden age coincided with the Garden of Eden. The degeneration was equated with the fall from grace and the succeeding decline in human circumstance. One need only read through the "begats section" of the Bible to note that the human lifespan, for one example, had declined markedly with time. The cataclysm and intervention was represented by the Apocalypse, Second Coming, and Final Day of Judgement.

The Judeo-Christian view of time also suggested that, for all time since the Creation, there was a steady degeneration of the world. This view has been termed the **Idea of Decline**. Thus, for much of the past 2,000 years of Western history, there was a notion that the general condition of the world, and of time, included an inexorable decline. This decline went beyond the human condition to include all aspects of Creation. Because the decay was inevitable, there was nothing that an individual could do to stop it; decline was seen as an inevitable condition of the universe.

The Judeo-Christian view of time also included notions about the duration of the cycle. The cycle began with the Creation as described in Genesis and stretched into the future until the Apocalypse. While there was some debate as to the actual time since the Creation, most agreed with figures of about 7,000 years or less. One famous computation, published in 1650 by James Ussher, Archbishop of Armagh, was that the Creation occurred in 4004 B.C., based upon generation times listed for patriarchs in the Bible (Eiseley 1959). This date was further refined by John Lightfoot, the vice-chancellor of Cambridge, to 9 a.m. on the Sunday morning of October 23, 4004 B.C. (Bowler 1989), although some controversy exists over Lightfoot's actual computation. Ideas about the duration of the world until the Apocalypse varied even more, with a strong contingent believing that the Apocalypse would arrive with the millennium (1000 A.D.). Predictions for the world's demise have had to be corrected when these days have come and gone without a discernable Second Coming, and no clear agreement has been reached by either contemporary Jewish or Christian scholars about when, or even if, the Final Judgement Day will arrive.

CONTEMPORARY WESTERN VIEWS OF TIME. Contemporary views of time in Western culture are highly complex, with time seen by physicists, after Einstein, as one element of space-time. There is great unanimity among scientists concerning the notion of **deep time** (Gould 1987). That is, time is seen as stretching over an immense span, on the order of twelve billion years or more. Time is seen to have begun with the "Big Bang," a singular event in which all space and time was created at a single point, and since then space has steadily expanded. Interestingly, there is some disagreement among cosmologists as to whether time is linear or cyclical. To the majority, time is generally viewed as linear and asymmetric (that is, there is a single-pointed "arrow" to time, with distinct differences between past and future). Scientists who hold this view believe that space will continually expand, though at an increasingly slower pace, for eternity, with increases in entropy and the eventual decay of protons leading to chaos. Others, in the minority, believe that the universe's expansion will eventually slow to a stop, followed by a general contraction back to a single point. The contraction may then be followed by a new Big Bang that would start the enormous cycle over again.

In recent times, beginning in the Renaissance but not becoming generally popular until the eighteenth century, Western views of the nature of time changed in a different way, as the notion of Decline was superseded by the **Idea of Progress** (Bury 1932), the belief that the world improved steadily over time. This remarkable reversal in world view, understandably, took time to occur. Progress, like the older idea of decline, was thought to be an integral part of the natural world, as evidenced by the adage that "you can't stop progress." Progress thus came to be conceived as a part of the asymmetry of time.

SOME NON-WESTERN CONCEPTS OF TIME. The notion of time as being linear appears to be a characteristic of contemporary Western culture but not necessarily a commonly held notion in all cultures. Cyclical views of time's nature may be more common. Many of these views are related to natural cycles, such as seasonality. Among Bantu speakers in Africa, for instance, time has aspects both of cycles – repeated days, months, seasons, initiation ceremonies, repetitive dynastic names, and so forth – and of non-repeatability. Thus, time may be seen as more of a spiral than a simple repetitive cycle (Kagame 1976). Traditional Indian notions of time involve much greater durations of temporal cycles. Each cycle, or *mahayuga*, consists of four stages, or *yuga*. Each stage is shorter, and more degenerate, than the preceding one, echoing the Western Idea of Decline. Time span, however, is quite long: the fourth, and shortest, of the stages, termed the *Kaliyuga* and considered to be the point in the cycle at which we exist today, lasts for 432,000 years (Pocock 1964). Thus the Hindus traditionally had a notion of deep time; in fact, the cycles were thought to be infinite in number.

In a study of the Hopi language, Whorf (1950) noted that the language contained "no reference to time, either explicit or implicit" (p. 378), a statement that some feel is exaggerated (e.g., Malotki 1983). Instead of using time designations, the Hopi divide the world, necessarily expressed here in Western language, between "objective" and "subjective" forms. Objective elements include what is observable to the senses, both past and present, with the latter two not distinguished. The subjective form

> embraces not only our future, much of which the Hopi regards as more or less predestined in essence if not in exact form, but also all mentality, intellection, and emotion. . . . It is the realm of expectancy, of desire and purpose, of vitalizing life . . . a dynamic state, yet not a state of motion . . . (Whorf 1950, p. 380).

Whorf notes the great difficulty of discussing Hopi concepts of time using English. Language reflects its speakers' concepts of time; thus, in the Hopi language, there are no tenses for verbs.

The Great Chain of Being

Another important concept that influenced theories of evolution stemmed from Western conceptions of the nature of the creator of the universe. Greek philosophers such as Plato, as well as Biblical writings, espoused the notion that God is perfect, the ultimate good. Plato also noted that a perfect being could not be envious of other things; in fact, perfection would in a sense require the creation of other things. Since God is the ultimate in perfection, the world must be fully stocked with all possible things, because God could not begrudge existence to anything (Lovejoy 1957).

Aristotle introduced another element to this concept: the notion of continuity. While Aristotle did not believe that all living organisms could be graded into a single continuous arrangement, he did discuss the gradual transition from inanimate to animate forms, and the continuity between, for example, plants and animals seen in some marine organisms. From his ideas, later scholars conceived the idea of a *scala naturae*, a "scale of nature" that was a continuous gradation of

FIGURE 2-1 The Great Chain of Being.

all living forms (Figure 2-1). The concept of continuity, added to the notion of all possible things having been created, led to the idea that all beings formed a continuum – an invariant, linear gradation called the **Great Chain of Being** (Lovejoy 1957). From this theory we get the familiar idea of the "missing link" – if a gap should be found between two kinds of being, or links on the chain, this must be filled by something in between, since God created everything. Thus, there could not be any missing links.

SCIENTIFIC APPROACHES TO EVOLUTION

An important notion in all early formulations about biology was the concept of the immutability, or fixity, of species. The idea of immutability of species was a major element in the Great Chain of Being. Species were seen by European scholars as having been created by God, with no significant changes in their form occurring since the creation. In fact, the idea of changes in species was heretical, as it questioned God's perfection.

Around the time of the Enlightenment, early attempts were made at using scientifically based investigations of evolution, and these referred to all biological organisms, not just humans. Scientific generalizations were devised in an attempt to understand the information that was being obtained by naturalists, including information on living organisms throughout the world and data from the emerging science of geology. Fossils of organisms in the past were observed to be different in their structure from that of living organisms. Additionally, naturalists noted that, in general, the older the fossils (where this could be determined), the greater the difference in form from contemporary life.

Lamarck's Theory of Evolution

The best known of the early scientific theories of evolution was made by Jean-Baptiste de Lamarck (in several publications, the main summaries of which were published in 1802 and 1809). His theory combined the common notions of progress and the Great Chain of Being. Lamarck believed that organisms, over generations, tended to move, or progress, up the scale of nature. That is, succeeding descendants of an organism that held a given position on the scale would evolve into the types of organisms in higher positions on the scale. These higher positions were left vacant because descendants of organisms that had been at these higher positions had in turn evolved to still higher levels of the scale. The lowest positions on the scale were renewed through the action of spontaneous generation, in which lowly organisms developed from inanimate matter (Ruse 1979; Corsi 1988).

What made Lamarck's theory of scientific importance (in today's terms) is the mechanism he postulated for the evolutionary movement toward higher forms. This mechanism can be summarized into five steps:

1. All organisms have needs caused by conditions in the environment.
2. These needs lead to different habitual behaviors (for example, a duck will strive to swim better, a giraffe will stretch its neck to get top leaves off trees, etc.).
3. As a result, there will be a **differential use of body parts**, with some parts used more, some less than others.
4. **Theory of use and disuse**:
   a. Those parts used more will improve (become bigger or better in some way).
   b. Those parts used less will deteriorate (become smaller or worse in some way).
5. Inheritance of acquired characteristics: the changes in body parts will be passed down through inheritance to descendants.

In other words, individuals are born with an instinct to adjust to environmental changes which (somehow) leads to a need to behave like organisms higher up the scale of life than they are. This behavior results, through differential use of body parts, in changes in body structure with some parts improving and others deteriorating, leading to a structure more like that of organisms on higher links of the Great Chain of Being. The changes in body structure will then be inherited by the organism's offspring, with these modifications constituting evolutionary change.

Lamarck's ideas were clearly based on the general ideas present at the time, including notions of progress and the Great Chain of Being, but also based on observations of changes in individual organisms. For instance, muscle changes can clearly be related to use and disuse; weight training leads to the muscular enlargement associated with bodybuilding, while prolonged inactivity leads to muscular atrophy. Other body parts are influenced by use: alcohol clearance by the liver speeds up in those who frequently imbibe alcohol, allowing them to "hold their liquor" – at least until liver function drops precipitously due to alcohol-induced pathology. There is even some evidence that mental functions improve, or at least decline more slowly, in elderly people who actively engage in cognitive tasks compared with age mates who do not. In contemporary terms, the theory of use and disuse is considered problematical, however, as there are frequent examples where excessive use of body parts leads to damage rather than improvement.

The major problem with Lamarck's theory is in the final step of his mechanism. In general, bodily changes incurred during an individual's lifetime are not passed to offspring through inheritance. For instance, a bodybuilder cannot pass on his muscular development to his offspring through biological inheritance. In Lamarck's time, our current ideas about the mechanism for inheritance, involving the passing of genes from parents to offspring in reproductive cells, was unknown. Thus, Lamarck's theory, while brilliant in many respects, is not correct.

Darwin's Theory of Evolution

The great Darwinian revolution, as can be seen, did not consist of introducing the concept of evolution, but rather made the concept widely known (but not necessarily understood) throughout the world. Darwin's major contributions were in marshaling an enormous amount of evidence that evolution had, in fact, occurred (the "fact" of evolution) and in devising a naturalistic mechanism (a "theory" of evolution) for how evolution worked.

Darwin's theory, first presented along with a similar paper by Alfred Russel Wallace in 1858 (and, in full form, in *Origin of Species* published in 1859), is quite different from that of Lamarck. The main principles of the theory involve biological populations, variability, and reproductive success. The mechanism is based on five premises:

1. Offspring resemble parents (but not exactly) due to **inherited** traits.
2. **Variation** exists among all populations of living organisms.
3. All organisms have the innate ability to **overpopulate** their environments.
4. There is a "struggle for existence," or **competition**, among individuals because of overpopulation.
5. The organisms who compete best (based on individual variations) will have more success at reproducing themselves; that is, there will be **natural selection** of the "fittest" organisms.

The mechanism is commonly termed "the theory of evolution by natural selection." It basically states that the variation that exists in all populations provides differential means of competition for survival and reproduction. Those varieties best able to handle the competition (that is, the fittest) will leave more offspring than other varieties. Since, through inheritance, offspring resemble their parents, the successful varieties will grow in number over generations. This change in the population's makeup constitutes evolutionary change.

This simple and elegant mechanism has many implications for an understanding of evolutionary change. It is worthwhile to take a closer look at each premise in the theory.

OFFSPRING RESEMBLE PARENTS. We now know the mechanism for inheritance, which is explained by the modern science of genetics. In Darwin's time, familial resemblances were known, but the mechanism for how this occurred was unknown. Darwin concurred with the general belief of his time period that inheritance occurred through the *blending* of traits from the mother and father in the offspring, accounting for the observation that offspring often seemed to represent a mix of parental characteristics. This belief in blending inheritance did not readily account for offspring taking on characteristics that were different from both parents. Darwin knew and wrote about "sports of nature" (now termed major mutations), but more subtle forms of genetic change were not well known at the time. In fact, the greatest weakness of Darwin's theory is that it states that while variation exists in all populations, there was no explanation for how *new* variation might be created. Moreover, natural selection, as described in his theory, would tend to eliminate variation over time as the less fit varieties would not be reproducing offspring like themselves.

VARIATION. This is an empirical statement. All populations of living organisms contain a great deal of variation (particularly, but not limited to, sexually reproducing species). Much work by natural historians in Darwin's time period showed this, and Darwin's own work on the biological variability of barnacles, as well as his observations when he served as a naturalist on the voyages around the world of the ship HMS Beagle, supported this observation. Now, with our ability to observe molecular variation in organisms, we have learned that there is much more variation than previously realized.

OVERPOPULATION. A tendency for populations to increase to the point of overpopulation is also an empirical observation. Darwin took this idea in part from Thomas Malthus, the great economist, who discussed overpopulation in reference to humans. Malthus noted that human populations tended to increase geometrically, while resources increased only arithmetically. Thus, there was always a danger of population size exceeding resources. This excessive growth would only be stopped by disease, famine, or war in the absence of "moral restraint." Darwin, and many previous biologists, had shown that this same tendency existed in *all* populations of living organisms. For sexually reproducing organisms, overpopulation will ensue if females are able, on average, to reproduce more than two offspring, while, for asexual forms, individuals need to average more than one offspring. In fact, all biological species are able, under proper conditions, to reproduce much faster than these minimal criteria for increase.

COMPETITION. The notion of competition, particularly for resources, results directly from overpopulation. Since there are too many organisms (or, at least, the potential for too many) to be supported by environmental resources, not all organisms survive or are successful at reproduction; they will therefore compete for what resources are available (food, water, mates, living space, and so forth). While Darwin stressed a "struggle for existence," contemporary biologists emphasize that competition does not have to involve violence. In fact, it can be quite passive.

NATURAL SELECTION. Natural selection results from competition. It is the varieties in a population that are competing, and some varieties will do better than others (presumably because they are better adapted for the given environmental conditions). The competition, and the selection, is based on **reproduction**. Those organisms that leave more surviving offspring are the ones who have been selected (as they leave more organisms for the next generation). Thus, varieties that are better adapted will tend to predominate in a population, and the population will change with time. Natural selection therefore refers to a **differential reproductive rate**. The "survival of the fittest" doesn't necessarily mean fighting or killing; some individuals simply don't find a mate, or are unsuccessful in raising offspring for a host of reasons (lack of food, unsuccessful defense against predators, etc.). In the term natural selection, "selection" refers simply to the differential reproductive rate, while "natural" refers to the fact that the circumstances that lead to selection come from nature – the population of organisms and their surrounding environment. Darwin contrasted "natural selection" from "artificial selection" that humans perform by breeding animals and crops.

The major scientific flaw in the theory was in its inability to account for how new variability entered populations. It was not until 1903, with the rediscovery of Gregor Mendel's work on inheritance, that an explanation could be found. The integration of Mendel's work, which led to the study of **genetics**, with Darwin's theory did not occur until the 1930's, when the modern, synthetic theory of evolution was devised. More details on genetics and the synthetic theory will be given in Chapter 3. First, let us turn from Darwin's mechanism for how evolution occurs to his overwhelming evidence that evolution had in fact occurred. This evidence is voluminous, so we will confine ourselves here to recounting some of the major *types* of evidence for evolution with no attempt to adequately detail specifics.

TYPES OF EVIDENCE FOR EVOLUTION

There are two basic kinds of observations that biologists make that relate to evolution: evidence for whether evolution (that is, change in biological organisms over generations) has indeed occurred, and evidence for a particular *mechanism* for how that change took place. Obviously, arguments for mechanisms of evolution are irrelevant if evolution has not occurred.

Creationists vs. Evolutionists

Many individuals are still unconvinced that evolutionary changes have occurred, and this has led to great controversies in religious and educational communities, particularly in the United States.

The primary combatants in this controversy are evolutionary biologists ("evolutionists") on the one hand, and members of some religious groups, primarily certain Christian fundamentalist and Jewish orthodox sects ("creationists"), on the other. Many Jewish and Christian groups have endorsed evolutionary ideas as being compatible with their beliefs. In fact, creationism as a tenet of some Christian sects did not arise until the 1920s (Numbers 1992). Creationists believe that the description of Genesis in the Old Testament of the Bible is literally true. This entails a belief in a single creation, with no significant change thereafter. Creationists are split into "old earthers" and "new earthers" according to whether or not they accept geological evidence for deep time. Creationists believe that evolution is "only a theory" that is unproven and should not be considered fact.

There is often an imbalance in the arguments: evolutionists usually provide objective evidence for whether evolution has occurred, and creationists attempt to discredit the evidence. Creationists generally do not provide naturalistic evidence for their Genesis-based theory of creation, relying on Biblical quotations for support. An unspoken assumption of creationists is that if evolutionary views are falsified, that automatically implies that their Biblically based view is correct. However, creationists must also account for the hundreds of other documented creation stories found in religions throughout the world.

A frequent point of confusion in the arguments is a muddling of two issues: the *presence* of evolution (that is, a change in biological organisms over generations) and the *mechanism* for how evolution occurs. Biologists generally perceive that an enormous preponderance of evidence exists that evolution has occurred. They then seek an improved general explanation (that is, a theory) for the mechanism of how this occurrence took place. Thus, when evolutionary biologists argue about improved theories for how evolution occurred, creationists may mistakenly believe these are disagreements about *whether* evolution has occurred. In fact, there are no such disagreements among evolutionary biologists.

A more recent attack on evolution from creationists involves the notion of **intelligent design** (ID). This idea states that the presence of complexity in living organisms means that they could not have appeared through chance events, but rather must have been designed by an intelligent creator.

PROFILE 2
A. Roberto Frisancho

Roberto Frisancho is a human biologist who studies how people adapt to stressful environments. Dr. Frisancho was born and raised in Cusco, Peru. Before attending college he went to the Tour Guide School of Cusco, where he learned English, French, and Portuguese and, combining these with the Spanish and Quechua that he originally spoke, became a successful tour guide of Cusco and the renowned Inca site of Machu Picchu. He later graduated from the National University of San Antonio Abad in Cusco. He won a Fulbright Fellowship and enrolled in the Pennsylvania State University in the United States where he earned his doctoral degree in anthropology and became a faculty member at the University of Michigan. He has conducted research on how people have adapted to high-altitude hypoxia in the Andes, and his work demonstrates that developmental adaptations to high altitude are an important aspect of how native peoples cope with this stress. Based on this research, he proposed the conceptual framework of "developmental adaptation," which posits that adult biological traits are byproducts of adaptation made by the organism during the period of growth. The notion of developmental adaptation has been validated by studies conducted throughout the world and by current research in both epigenetics and the long-term effects of early development. His research has also explored the importance of nutritional problems for human adaptation and evolution. Studies on growth and development have been a major concern in Dr. Frisancho's research. Along with his research in basic science, he has provided human biologists and health workers with a uniform reference in the form of anthropometric standards to determine the growth and nutritional status of children and adults. He has studied critical periods of growth, both for adaptation to high-altitude hypoxia and for variation in risk for chronic diseases later in life, including obesity and type 2 diabetes.

Dr. Frisancho has also studied ethnic disparities in hypertension (high blood pressure) risk, particularly in African-derived populations. His research focuses on the genetic and environmental factors that contribute to the high risk for hypertension in individuals from these populations.

He is the author of many books in anthropology and human biology, including *Humankind Evolving*, *Human Adaptation and Accommodation*, *Human Adaptation*, and *Anthropometric Standards for the Assessment of Growth and Nutritional Status*. Dr. Frisancho is the Arthur A. Thurnau Professor of Anthropology, Research Professor at the Center for Growth and Development at the University of Michigan, and Honorary Professor of Anthropology of the National University of San Antonio Abad of Cusco, Peru.

Proponents of ID state that some traits are "irreducibly complex," meaning that they could not have been built up from simple characteristics (Behe 2002). Evolutionary biologists, on the other hand, have had a long history of demonstrating that various complex traits could indeed have arisen through natural selection, with constituent parts, in some cases, originally adapted for other purposes (Miller 2002).

There isn't sufficient room in this text to deal with the issues of creationism and ID in depth; students are encouraged to read more about them. Some excellent references include: Godfrey 1983, Numbers 1992, National Academy of Sciences 1999, and the April 2002 issue of *Natural History* magazine, among many others. An important point to consider is the fallacy of an argument made by some creationists that there is a dichotomy between religion and evolution. Many biologists are devout Christians and scientists who are convinced that evolution has occurred (Miller 2000).

Several types of evidence for evolution were available to Darwin. This evidence demonstrated that organisms had in fact changed over time, and that mechanisms that Darwin suggested for evolution did in fact cause biological change. The types of evidence, as we characterize it here, include: adaptation, paleontology, biogeography, comparative anatomy, comparative embryology, and artificial selection. Two types of evidence unknown to Darwin are comparative biochemistry and genetics. The evidence for the occurrence of evolution could easily fill libraries; in this text, we will simply outline these major types of evidence to give a flavor of the nature of the evidence.

Adaptation

Each organism has a set of traits that makes it capable of dealing with its environment. In Darwin's theory of evolution, these adaptations are viewed as being the result of selection. The examples of adaptations in living organisms are as extensive as the range of biological studies that have been carried out. Just a few examples will be noted here to make the point, and they will focus on visual tricks used by animals to aid in survival and reproduction.

CONCEALMENT. Various adaptations are seen whereby animals avoid predation through concealment. A classic example is the presence of **countershading** in fish. Many fish tend to be dark dorsally (on their backs) and light-colored ventrally (on their bellies). The dark dorsal side is seen by a potential predator that swims above the fish, and thus the dark shade blends into the ocean (or other body of water) floor. The light ventral side is seen by a predator swimming below the fish, and therefore the light shade blends into the lighted water surface. Some animals, such as chameleons, can change their colors or shading to match the environment.

A classic case of adaptation by blending into the environment involves the British moth *Biston betularia.* These moths are found in two major varieties in nature: light and mottled and dark colored (see Figure 2-2). The moths often rest on tree trunks, and they suffer from predation from visual-based hunting by birds. The light and mottled variety blends in better with the tree trunks on which they often rest, and the dark form therefore suffers higher rates of predation. The dark variety is therefore rarer than the light form. However, during Britain's Industrial Revolution, soot from air pollution darkened tree trunks in many areas. In these areas, the dark form blended in better with the tree trunks, and therefore the lighter varieties suffered greater predation, with dark forms becoming more common in these areas. With progress in the cleanup of Britain's air pollution has

A   B

FIGURE 2-2 Two varieties of *Biston betularia,* one light and mottled and the other dark colored, shown against two backgrounds: **A.** a tree trunk that is light colored and **B.** another that is darkened by soot.

come bad news for the dark varieties of moths: they are now less well concealed and more commonly eaten by birds than their lighter conspecifics.

MIMICRY. Other animals blend into their environment by taking on a similarity in form with other organisms. For instance, some insects take on the forms of plants (or parts thereof). These include stick insects (relatives of grasshoppers that are long and resemble twigs) and the leaf butterfly *Kallima* (Figure 2-3) (Simpson et al. 1957).

Another kind of adaptation to predation is the ability of some butterflies to retain high levels of chemicals in their bodies that predators find to be toxic. For instance, Monarch butterflies consume milkweed that contains cardiac glycosides that are noxious to many animals, including potential predators like insectivorous (insect-eating) birds (Futuyma 1983). Simply being unpalatable is insufficient; an organism must *look* unpalatable to a visually directed predator to prevent an attack. Thus, unpalatable butterflies like the Monarch have adapted to be brightly colored: this "warning coloration" reduces the level of predation they must endure. This type of adaptation has been taken a step further among butterflies: the various unpalatable species of butterfly in the same region tend to look alike. This form of mimicry, termed "Müllerian mimicry" for the naturalist Franz Müller who first described it, allows predators to receive a consistent warning about which butterflies to avoid (Stebbins 1966).

Things can become yet more complex. While the unpalatable butterflies have adapted to predation pressure, what is to become of the more tasty species of butterflies in the region? If varieties of the tasty species arise that look similar to (that is, mimic) the unpalatable forms, these varieties will tend to be more successful at avoiding predation, and thus be selected. This form of mimicry, termed "Batesian mimicry" for the nineteenth-century British naturalist Henry Walter Bates, leads to selection of individual butterflies belonging to palatable species (such as the Viceroy butterfly) that look like unpalatable ones. This, in turn, creates problems for the unpalatable species, as predators mistake their coloration for that of the tastier forms. Hence, varieties of unpalatable forms that differ in

FIGURE 2-3 The leaf butterfly *Kallima*.

coloration from their more tasty neighbors will be selected over time. In other words, there are selective pressures for the unpalatable species to evolve in such a way as to become distinctly different in appearance from palatable forms, while palatable forms are selected to mimic the unpalatable species. Since the evolution of one form is affecting the evolution of other forms, this is termed a case of **coevolution** (Gilbert 1983). The example shows that evolution is a process; selection continues as the environment changes, and, in fact, evolutionary changes can give rise to the very environmental changes that lead to continued selection.

A HUMAN EXAMPLE: HIGH-ALTITUDE ADAPTATION IN TIBET. Adaptations are found among humans as well as other organisms. One example can be found among people living in Tibet. At high altitude, the air is literally thin, with atmospheric pressure about 60 percent of that at sea level at 4,200 m (about 14,000 feet elevation). Because the air is thin, less oxygen gets into one's lungs with each breath, and therefore the entire body becomes **hypoxic** (having too little oxygen). This has an important effect on pregnancy and child birth. Infants born at high altitude weigh significantly less than do infants born at sea level, and this is true even when careful comparisons of mothers' ages, weights and other variables are considered. Since infant mortality is closely tied to birth weight, infant mortality rates are higher in high-altitude locations.

People have been living on the high-altitude Tibetan plateau for more than 25,000 years (Moore et al. 1998) and have apparently evolved adaptations to the harsh conditions found there. Native Tibetans have significantly heavier infants than do the recent Chinese migrants to Tibet, apparently because they are better able to increase blood flow to their fetuses by diverting flow to the uterine artery (Moore et al. 2001). More on high-altitude adaptation by humans can be found in Chapter 11.

IMPERFECT ADAPTATIONS. Stephen J. Gould (1980) has noted that in attempting to provide evidence for evolution by the presence of adaptations, it may be more useful to cite examples of *imperfect* ones. Perfect adaptations can also be used by creationists as evidence for the presence of a beneficent and intelligent Creator. Adaptations that appear to be a makeshift combination of traits that only partially work are a better example of what may occur as a result of natural selection. According to Darwin's theory, selection works on the variations that happen to be present in a population. If a variety of organism, however imperfect, can out-compete other varieties, its features will be passed down to future generations. This opportunistic nature of natural selection is a hallmark of Darwinian evolution, and it is evidenced by the very imperfect living world we observe around us.

One example of an imperfect adaptation given by Gould (1980) is the panda's "thumb." Actually, it is not a thumb at all, although it looks a lot like one: it is a modification of a wrist bone, the radial sesamoid. This false thumb does not work very well, at least compared with the human thumb, but it does serve its purpose of helping pandas strip leaves off of bamboo stalks. The panda's true thumb is, as in all other species in the bear family, much like its other fingers (Figure 2-4). It therefore appears as if the panda has six fingers.

Another example derives from Darwin's work with orchids. He demonstrated that structures that originally functioned as a simple flower petal became variously adapted in different orchid species to insure cross-fertilization.

A final example can be found in a very curious condition of human anatomy. The tube that connects the testes to the urethra (see Figure 2-5) travels quite a distance up the abdomen, loops across the ureter (the tube that carries urine from the kidney), then travels back down the abdomen to the urethra, which is located close to the testes where this tube originated (Williams 1996). This is surely an inefficient arrangement. Williams (1996) has shown that this can be explained by observing the anatomy of the early ancestors of mammals, in which the testes are located high up in the abdomen. The testes descended to a position outside the abdomen proper in mammalian evolution, allowing for lower temperatures in these reproductive structures. In the many generations in which the testes descended there was selection for lengthening the connecting tube which was "hung up" on the ureter, as opposed to a change that would have redirected the route of the tube around the ureter.

FIGURE 2-4 The hand skeleton of the
panda showing the false "thumb."

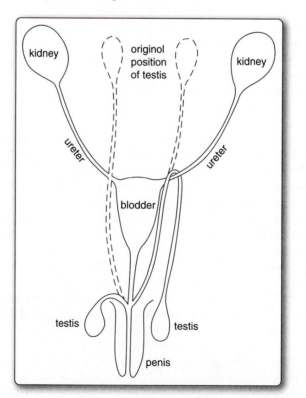

FIGURE 2-5 Diagram of the male reproductive system showing that the descent of the testes has resulted
in a "looping" of the male reproductive tract around the ureter.

Paleontology

Fossils are visible traces of organisms that lived in the past and therefore provide direct evidence for earlier life. Paleontology, the scientific study of fossils, is a very broad subject covering a vast amount of information. It is impossible to fairly represent this massive information here; university libraries and museums are crowded with the results of paleontological research (Figure 2-6).

We may make a few basic generalizations from this body of scientific work. Perhaps the most important is that the more recent a fossil is, the more likely it is to resemble living organisms. By contrast, the older the fossil, the less likely it is to resemble a living form. This is what one would expect from an evolutionary process in which changes are continual over long periods of time.

Another generalization refers to the so-called "gaps" in the fossil record. These are not nearly as wide as creationists claim, and what gaps exist are narrowed as paleontological work continues. There is, in fact, a great deal of evidence for "intermediate forms." However, the possibility exists that forms are not completely continuous. Small gaps that are found in the fossil record may be due to processes involved in long-term evolutionary change. The **theory of punctuated equilibria** (Eldredge and Gould 1972) states that evolutionary change does not occur at a steady rate; it tends to occur in periods of very rapid change ("punctuations") interspersed with periods of relatively slow change ("equilibria"). Because of this pattern of evolution, some intermediate forms would be quite rare compared with forms that lived during the much longer periods of equilibrium, and therefore the fossils of these rare forms are unlikely to be found.

Biogeography

Biogeography is the study of the distribution of living organisms on the earth. The basic point about biogeography is that living organisms are distributed unevenly in the world. The unevenness of the distribution is due to several factors, the most obvious of which is adaptation. Organisms are found in places for which they are adapted. Polar bears are not ordinarily found in the tropics, and arboreal (tree-living) tropical monkeys are not found on the treeless arctic tundra.

The adaptive factors that affect distribution of organisms is often divided into those due to abiotic ("not living") factors, such as temperature, soil type, and the like; and biotic ("living") factors, such as predation, food, sociality, and so forth (Simmons 1979).

Ecological conditions are not sufficient to explain the distribution of plants and animals. There are many examples of widely separated places with similar climates, soils, etc., that have widely different fauna and flora (such as deserts in central Australia versus the U.S. Southwest). Thus, similar environments do not necessarily mean similar organisms. On the other hand, organisms often share structural

FIGURE 2-6 Photograph of a fossil Coelurosaur.

similarities with organisms in the same general region of the world, even though these similar organisms might live in very different kinds of environments. The marsupials of Australia present a clear case of structural similarity despite their adaptations for quite dissimilar environments within the continent of Australia. Another, more focused, example is the honeycreepers of Hawaii (Figure 2-7). The honeycreepers have adapted to many different habitats in Hawaii, but all these birds share basic structural similarities, suggesting that they were derived from a single ancestor but changed to adapt to the diverse habitats found in the Hawaiian Islands.

Islands are of special interest to biogeographers, because the organisms found on them had to derive from elsewhere. Continental islands, those located close to a major continent, have organisms on them that are undoubtedly derived from the continent, although sometimes with some minor local variation. For example, Britain's fauna is basically that of the European continent.

Oceanic islands, located far from continents, are quite different in their biota (defined as the totality of animal and plant life in a region). Island organisms are usually composed of species that are derived from nearby marine life or that are capable of long transport from distant lands such as birds, saltwater-tolerant reptiles, or plants that reproduce through wind-borne seeds or spores. Fresh water fish on oceanic islands are closely related to nearby saltwater fish forms and not closely related to freshwater fish in other places. In the vast span of geological time, it is possible that rare events, such as organisms being carried long distances in storms or on "rafts" of vegetation, may have occurred. If so, these rafting events are unlikely to have occurred repeatedly over short periods of time. The recent movement of humans to oceanic islands has greatly changed the distribution of organisms, because the people, sometimes inadvertently, have transported organisms with them. Many oceanic islands are faced with ecological disruption from these introduced species.

Comparative Anatomy

Many organisms tend to parallel the basic structure of other organisms in great detail. This similarity in structure can be seen on a general scale with comparisons of similar species, such as dogs and wolves, tigers and lions, and so forth. Comparisons of detailed structure also show great correspondences in organisms that superficially do not appear to be so similar. For instance, the underlying anatomical structure of bat wings, human arms, and seal flippers are very similar in structure

FIGURE 2-7 Honeycreepers in Hawaii showing a radiation from a single ancestor on the isolated Hawaii islands.

(Figure 2-8). The question is: why should structures with such different functions share so many structural characteristics? The similarities may be explained if the different organisms have a shared ancestry, with the descendants of this ancestor developing some differences over time due to selection for different environmental circumstances. Evolution, as already noted, can be viewed as opportunistic: selection acted on what variation existed in the ancestral population, and thus later changes are built upon a common basic structure. These similarities in anatomy that are based upon common ancestry are termed **homologous structures**; they involve similarity in form but not necessarily in function.

HOMOLOGOUS VS. ANALOGOUS STRUCTURES. A different form of anatomical similarity is sometimes found when comparing different species of organisms: superficial similarity with marked differences in underlying structure. Examples include the wings of birds, flying fish, and insects, respectively (see Figure 2-9). This type of similarity in anatomy, termed **analogous structures**, involves body parts that differ in structure but have similar functions. Analogous structures arise due to independent selection for similar needs in species with different ancestry and thus derive from quite different ancestral body forms. There are only so many shapes that a wing can have and still permit flight, or for a flipper to have and allow efficient aquatic locomotion. Thus, evolutionary selection will lead to the development of structures with similar superficial form, but the underlying differences illustrate the differing ancestral pathways to derive the structure.

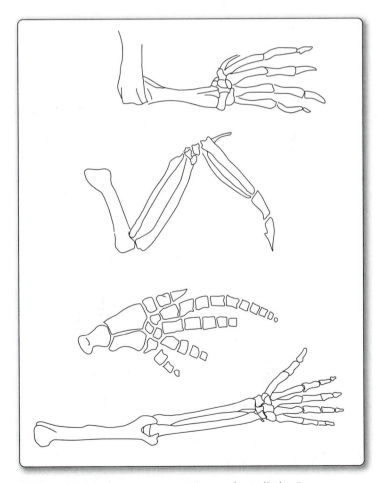

FIGURE 2-8 Homologous structures in vertebrate limbs. From top to bottom: forelimb of lizard, bird's wing, whale's flipper, human arm.

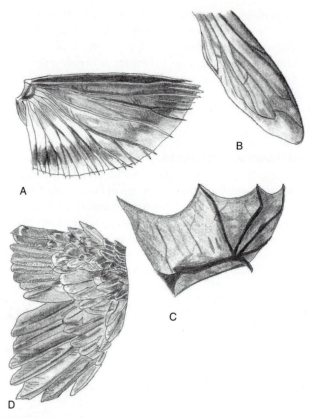

FIGURE 2-9 Analogous structures: animal wings. Clockwise from top left: **A.** flying fish, **B.** insect, **C.** bat, and **D.** bird.

VESTIGIAL STRUCTURES. Organisms also frequently have **vestigial structures**: body parts that have no apparent function, but are similar in form to structures in other species that do serve important purposes. These structures may have served a purpose in ancestors, but evolutionary changes in the organism have made them outmoded. One interesting example is found in humans: "goose bumps," the bumps that appear on the skin when people are cold or frightened. In furry animals, goose bumps make the animal's hair stand up. This is adaptive in cold weather, where the hair fluffs out and then serves as a better insulator. The fluffing out of fur also makes the animal look larger and provides its skin with some protection, an adaptive advantage when another animal is deciding whether to fight it or prey upon it. Hence, mammals get goose bumps both when cold or when highly emotional, with a familiar case being found in cats that are about to fight. In cold or frightened humans, goose bumps do cause our hair to stand on end, but our relative lack of hairiness has taken away the traditional adaptive functions of insulation or protection. Instead, goose bumps, if they have any function, now are used as a source of communication with other humans.

Another example of vestigial structures in humans is our third molars, or so-called "wisdom teeth." Fossil evidence of human ancestors shows that these ancestors had larger jaws than contemporary humans do. As the jaw got smaller in human evolution, the third molars simply did not fit in the mouth as well. Many people suffer from impacted, or even infected, third molars. Thus, selection would seem to work against these now mostly functionless molars; perhaps descendants of contemporary humans will never develop third molars at all. In fact, normal human variation includes people who do not develop third molars; perhaps these individuals represent the future of humanity.

Comparative Embryology

During embryonic stages of organisms, natural selection may be considered to act somewhat differently than it does later in an organism's life cycle. Embryos are usually protected in some way from the environment, whether inside eggs or a mother's body, so structures may be present that could not be present in free-living organisms. The development of individual organisms is, in most species, a quite complex process in which structures develop in a progression, sometimes arising from other structures but always developing in relation to other body parts. Because of the nature of development (to be discussed in more detail in Chapter 9), small changes in organisms during early development can lead to major changes in the adult organism, since developmental changes build upon the early changes. Major changes in adults usually leave the individual poorly adapted, since most features found in organisms have stood the test of time; sudden major changes are usually for the worse.

Sometimes structures are present in embryos that hark back to ancestral forms. These early structures, if changed much, will lead to maladaptive changes in adult organisms. Selection thus tends to be conservative, inhibiting changes in embryonic structures. Therefore, structures found in ancestral organisms may be retained in some form in the embryos of living species. A classic example is the presence of gill slits in the human embryo (Figure 2-10). The gill slits eventually are transformed during development into other structures, specifically part of the middle-ear region in humans, but their early presence gives evidence of the fishy ancestry of the human species.

Artificial Selection

Artificial selection refers to the changes in organisms caused by breeding under human direction. Artificial selection demonstrates that biological change in organisms over generations can be achieved by a selection process, and thus is an important type of evidence for Darwin's mechanism for evolutionary change.

There are many cases for evolutionary change due to human intervention, whether the human activity is purposeful or not. Purposeful breeding includes the diverse dog breeds, each with special characteristics that people value, whether speed, fighting ability, various hunting skills (pointing, retrieving, and so forth), or simply appearance. Dairy cows are a remarkable human invention: they approximate walking udders, machines that convert grass into milk. Surely no dairy cow could survive without human aid, and therefore it is highly unlikely that natural selection would have produced such an improbable animal.

Humans have also bred plants, particularly for use as food. The remarkable changes to the corn (maize) plant over the past few thousand years have resulted from human selection for larger kernels and ears (Figure 2-11). These changes have made corn a better food supply for people but at the expense of the loss of the corn plant's ability to reproduce itself without direct human help.

Human activities have sometimes accidentally led to changes in other organisms. The moth *Biston betularia* discussed earlier experienced changes in numbers of dark versus light forms as a result of adaptation to changes in the environment caused by humans. In the past century, the spread of antibiotic use by humans has led to the evolution of antibiotic-resistant forms of bacteria.

Other Evidence for Evolution

There are two other kinds of evidence for evolution: the science of heredity, or genetics, which documents how biological changes are passed down through generations; and comparative biochemistry, which illustrates the kinship of living organisms based upon their chemical similarity. We will take up these kinds of evidence in the next chapter, where we will explore the mechanisms of inheritance and evolution in greater depth.

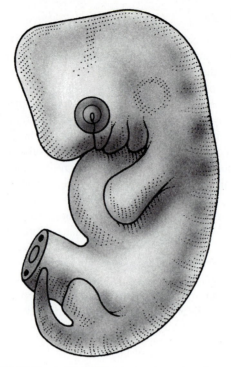

FIGURE 2-10 Five-week-old human embryo showing vestigial gill slits.

CHAPTER SUMMARY

The concept of evolution, or the change in life forms over large periods of time, is a very old one both in Western culture and in other cultures throughout the world. Current ideas about evolution are informed by scientific, empirically based approaches that incorporate objective evidence for "deep time," the incredibly long period available for evolution to occur on the earth, and for changes in living populations. We can infer the relatedness of living things from observations of their biological structure and function in the present, and we can also directly observe these connections through our study of the fossil record.

Darwin provided an explanation for how evolution occurs, through a simple process in which the natural variation in populations of living organisms and the propensity for overpopulation leads to competition among the varieties for the ability to survive and reproduce. The competition leads to a differential reproductive rate among the varieties, with some varieties having more offspring than others. Over time, certain varieties will disappear, while others will increase in frequency, leading to biological change in populations. Finally, the inclusion of new variation through mutations allows selection to continue over the generations.

Several major types of evidence for evolution are present. They include the study of adaptations, imperfect though these adaptations may be, that provide evidence for past selection for organisms that can survive and reproduce successfully. Paleontology, the study of fossils, provides direct evidence for change over time in living organisms. Biogeography, the distribution of living things in the world, shows that organisms are adapted to specific environments, and that regional similarities exist between species that may have adapted to different, specific environmental conditions. The science of comparative anatomy shows the close similarity in structure of evolutionarily related species, with these

FIGURE 2-11 Corn cobs from approximately 4000 B.P. and modern times.

structural similarities present even in organisms that have adapted for very different environmental conditions. Similarly, comparative embryology shows great resemblance in structure and developmental processes between different species, even if they have quite different adaptations as adult organisms. Artificial selection, in which humans can breed animals and plants to create very different forms, provides evidence that differential reproduction caused by selection actually does lead to profound biological changes. The next chapter deals with the actual mechanism for inheritance of characteristics, genetics, and how this process can lead to biological change over time. The biochemical similarities between organisms, even those as distantly related as viruses and people, provide yet another type of evidence that evolution has occurred and still takes place.

CHAPTER 3

Genetics and Microevolution

Darwin's mechanism for evolution provides an explanation for how variation within species changes over time, but it does not explain how *new* variation is created and passed down to descendent generations. Our understanding of the nature of variation and inheritance has increased dramatically in the past century, particularly in the last half of the twentieth century, during which our understanding of the molecular basis of biology greatly expanded. Our knowledge is increasing at an ever-faster pace during the early years of the twenty-first century. We have learned that biological processes and structures are determined by the underlying chemistry of life, and that what is passed down through inheritance is a set of chemical blueprints for the body plan of living organisms.

THE CHEMICAL BASIS OF LIFE

The chemicals that make up living organisms are familiar to us from basic concepts of nutrition: we need to ingest the chemicals of life, or their precursors, in our food. Thus, major types of biochemicals, or macronutrients, include **carbohydrates** (sugars and starches), **fats**, and **protein**. Also included are the nucleic acids, namely DNA and RNA, that are the materials from which genes, the units of inheritance, are made. In addition to these major constituents of living organisms, there are many chemicals classified as micronutrients, including vitamins, minerals, and electrolytes (salts). To add to the complexity, different types of biochemicals can join together, forming such materials as glycoproteins (combinations of carbohydrates and proteins) and lipoproteins (combinations of fats and proteins). While most details of biochemistry exceed the bounds of this book, we will look more closely at two important biochemicals: proteins and nucleic acids.

Proteins

From a functional standpoint, the proteins are arguably the most important single type of biochemical. In fact, the term "protein" derives from the Greek word *proteis,* meaning of highest importance (Armstrong 1989). Among other functions, proteins are important structural constituents of body tissues. They direct chemical reactions, such as what occurs during the digestion of food or the building of complex biochemicals from smaller molecules, through their role as **enzymes** (molecules that guide or assist chemical reactions). And proteins control most communication between body cells through their roles as hormones and neurotransmitters.

PROTEIN STRUCTURE. Proteins vary quite a bit, but they are generally large molecules made up of many atoms of carbon, hydrogen, oxygen, nitrogen, phosphorus, and sulfur. There are regularities in protein structure which simplifies our understanding of their chemical makeup. Proteins are made up of subunits termed **amino acids** that are linked together in long chains. There are 20 different kinds of amino acids found in the proteins of living organisms. The thousands of different proteins take on their individual characteristics based on the number, type, and order in which these amino acids are linked together. The shape of a protein, which determines its function, results from the folding of the amino acid chain due to secondary interactions between nonadjacent amino acids that can lead to the formation of quite complex shapes.

When we eat a meal containing protein, our digestive enzymes direct chemical reactions in which the proteins are broken down into their constituent amino acids. These amino acids then are used in constructing proteins in our own bodies. We are, in a sense, what we eat, but in a more important sense we are much more than that. We eat the constituents of our proteins, but it is the **order** in which those constituents are combined that determine what kind of proteins is found in our bodies.

PROTEIN FUNCTION. A protein's structure, therefore, depends on its amino acid sequence. A protein's function, in turn, depends on its structure. It is the shape, distribution of electrical charges, and size of a protein that determine how it acts in organisms. Proteins control much of how body function occurs, and, therefore, the ordering of amino acids may be viewed as one of the most critical aspects of the biochemical basis of life.

Nucleic Acids

Nucleic acids are of two major types: DNA and RNA. DNA is found in long strands which, in many organisms (eukaryotes, referring to organisms comprised of cells that have nuclei), is confined to the nuclei of body cells. Other organisms, like bacteria (prokaryotes, or "pre-cells"), do not have nuclei, and therefore their DNA occurs more generally throughout the interiors of cells. Our discussion here will focus on eukaryotes, a group which includes humans as members. DNA is combined with protein material to form **chromosomes**, long, linear structures found in cell nuclei that can be seen with microscopes (Figure 3-1). RNA molecules are found both inside and outside the nuclei of cells and take several forms. (Students should explore beyond the basic outline provided here, starting with any of the many textbooks on molecular biology and genetics, such as Schleif, 1993 or Klug and Cummings 2000.)

FIGURE 3-1 Large chromosomes from the salivary gland of a fruit fly.

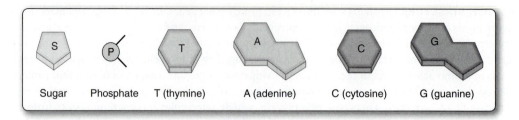

FIGURE 3-2 The constituents of DNA. DNA is made up of a sugar (deoxyribose), a phosphate group, and a nucleotide base. There are four nucleotide bases: adenine, thymine, guanine, and cytosine.

DNA STRUCTURE. DNA, like protein, is a large, highly complex molecule. Also like protein, it is made up of subunits that simplify our understanding of its structure. In the case of DNA, the subunits are termed **nucleotides**, relatively small molecules composed of a sugar (deoxyribose), a phosphate group, and a nucleotide base. These subunits form a strand of linearly connected nucleotides. The DNA molecule is a double-stranded helix, where two separate strands of nucleotides are wound around each other in a shape similar to a corkscrew. There are four types of nucleotides, distinguished by the presence of one of four nucleotide bases. The four bases are adenine (A), cytosine (C), guanine (G), and thymine (T) (see Figure 3-2). DNA is a linear chain made up of linked nucleotides, as shown in Figure 3-3. Again, as with proteins, it is the order in which the types of nucleotides are linked in the strands that determines DNA structure.

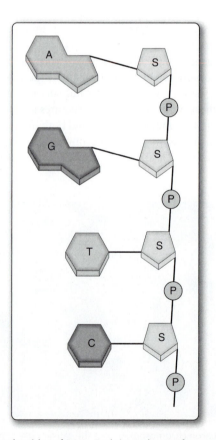

FIGURE 3-3 The four nucleotides of DNA, Each is made up of a sugar, a phosphate, and one of the four nucleotide bases. Nucleotides are linked together to form DNA chains.

DNA FUNCTION. DNA is much less diverse in shape and function than are proteins. A major function of DNA is to direct the order in which amino acids are linked in protein construction. **It is the order in which nucleotides are linked in DNA that determines how amino acids are ordered in proteins.** It is the order of nucleotides in DNA that is inherited during reproduction: this constitutes the information used to construct an individual in a new generation of organisms.

The order of nucleotides determines protein synthesis through the **genetic code**. The code consists of the ordering of three successive nucleotides, or triplets; each of these triplets codes for a single amino acid, or is used as "punctuation," directing the coding machinery to where the code for a given protein begins and ends along the DNA chain. Each stretch of DNA that codes for a specific protein is termed a **gene**, which serves as the basic unit of biological inheritance. Figure 3-4 shows the genetic code.

For DNA to function as the unit of inheritance, it must be able to accomplish two major feats: it must be able to be duplicated, so genetic instructions can be passed from parent to offspring during the process of cell division, and it must direct protein synthesis. Both abilities of DNA are based on its chemical structure.

DNA triplet codes	RNA triplet codes	Amino acid
CGA, CGG, CGT, CGC	GCU, GCC, GCA, GCG	Alanine
GCA, GCG, GCT, GCC, TCT, TCC	CGU, CGC, CGA, CGG, AGA, AGG	Arginine
TTA, TTG	AAU, AAC	Asparagine
CTA, CTG	GAU, GAC	Aspartic acid
ACA, ACG	UGU, UGC	Cysteine
CTT, CTC	GAA, GAG	Glutamic acid
GTT, GTC	CAA, CAG	Glutamine
CCA, CCG, CCT, CCC	GGU, GGC, GGA, GGG	Glycine
GTA, GTG	CAU, CAC	Histidine
TAA, TAG, TAT	AUU, AUC, AUA	Isoleucine
AAT, AAC, GAA, GAT, GAC, GAG	UUA, UUG, CUU, CUA, CUG, CUC	Leucine
TTT, TTC	AAA, AAG	Lysine
TAC	AUG	Methionine
AAA, AAG	UUU, UUC	Phenylalanine
GGA, GGG, GGT, GGC	CCU, CCC, CCA, CCG	Proline
AGA, AGG, AGT, AGC, TCA, TCG	UCU, UCC, UCA, UCG, AGU, AGC	Serine
TGA, TGG, TGT, TGC	ACU, ACC, ACA, ACG	Threonine
ACC	UGG	Tryptophan
ATA, ATG	UAU, UAC	Tyrosine
CAA, CAG, CAT, CAC	GUU, GUC, GUA, GUG	Valine
ATT, ATC, ACT	UAA, UAG, UGA	STOP code

FIGURE 3-4 The genetic code. Each three nucleotide unit codes for a single amino acid or as "punctuation" for marking the beginning and end of genes that code for a protein.

Duplication of DNA

As noted, the structure of DNA is somewhat more complex than a simple chain of nucleotides. DNA is a double nucleotide chain, in which the two chains, or nucleotide strands, are linked by weak chemical bonds between the nucleotide bases of each chain. Only specific nucleotides will bond together in each chain: adenine will only bond with thymine, and cytosine will only bind to guanine, as shown in Figure 3-5. Thus, if one chain has the following order of nucleotides (using only their first letters to simplify things):

A–G–C–T–G–T–T–A–C–G . . .

then the second, attached chain of the DNA molecule will have the following order of nucleotides:

T–C–G–A–C–A–A–T–G–C . . .

That is, the order of nucleotides in one of the chains *determines* the order of nucleotides in the second chain. The second chain is termed the **complement** of the first, and each of the corresponding nucleotides that bond to each other in the double chains is, similarly, a complement of each other.

For DNA to duplicate itself, the double chains are separated (with the help of enzymes) and each chain "grows" a new chain. The order of the new chains is determined by the nucleotide order of the original chains. The result is two molecules that are identical in structure (see Figure 3-6).

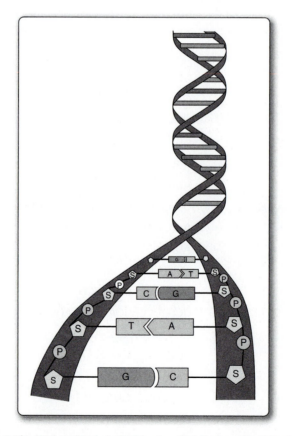

FIGURE 3-5 The DNA molecule is double-stranded. Each nucleotide attaches to its complement: adenine binds to thymine, and cytosine binds to guanine. The ladder-like shape of the molecule is twisted, forming a double helix.

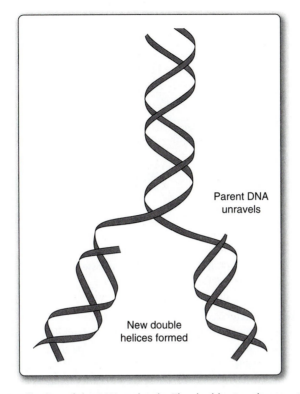

Parent DNA
unravels

New double
helices formed

FIGURE 3-6 Duplication of the DNA molecule. The double strands separate, then each strand connects with complementary nucleotides to form two identical molecules.

Direction of Protein Synthesis

DNA directs protein synthesis through the genetic code, with each triplet of nucleotides in one of the DNA chains coding for a specific amino acid. The process is actually much more complicated than that. While we need not be concerned with too much detail, a brief sketch of the process is in order.

MESSENGER RNA. The first step in the process occurs with the coding of messenger RNA (mRNA) from the DNA. RNA is a chemical similar to DNA. It also is made up of nucleotide subunits, but these have a somewhat different makeup. RNA nucleotides are made up of a different sugar (ribose) connected to a phosphate group and to a nucleotide base. RNA also has four types of bases: adenine, cytosine, and guanine as in DNA, and a different base, uracil, replaces thymine in RNA.

In the coding of mRNA from DNA, termed **transcription**, a portion of one of the DNA chains is separated from its complement, and it directs the construction of an mRNA molecule by the linking of complementary nucleotides. This is similar to the process of DNA replication, but RNA nucleotides are used in mRNA construction, with adenine's complement being uracil.

RIBOSOMES. The next step in the process of protein synthesis is the transport of mRNA from the nucleus where it was constructed to the site where proteins are formed in the extranuclear region of the cell. These sites are found at the **ribosomes**, small particles composed of RNA material ("ribosomal RNA") and proteins.

TRANSFER RNA. The process of protein synthesis occurs through the action of yet a third form of RNA, termed "transfer RNA" (tRNA). Transfer RNA contains a series of nucleotide bases that form

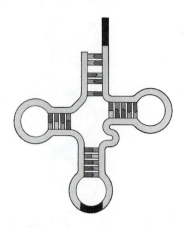

FIGURE 3-7 Diagram of the transfer-RNA molecule.

a particular shape, often characterized as a cloverleaf (Figure 3-7). One portion of the molecule chemically attaches to one, and only one, particular amino acid, while another portion of the molecule displays a specific triplet ordering of nucleotides. Each type of tRNA, which is attached to its particular amino acid, also attaches to the complement of its triple ordering of nucleotides located on the mRNA molecule. The mRNA acts as a sequence of triplet nucleotides termed "codons," with each codon attaching to the complementary triplet nucleotides on specific tRNA molecules; the tRNA's triplets are referred to as "anticodons." As protein synthesis occurs, particular tRNA molecules with attached amino acids are linked up to the mRNA based upon chemical bonding of codons to anticodons. The amino acids attached to each of the tRNAs link with amino acids on neighboring tRNAs, thus forming a protein chain (this process is summarized in Figure 3-8). The process in which the sequence of nucleotides on mRNA is converted into a sequence of amino acids on a protein molecule is termed **translation**.

DNA actually does more than direct protein synthesis. Each chain of DNA contains the information for constructing thousands of different proteins. The DNA also contains information coded in the order of its nucleotides and working in conjunction with protein-based enzymes in the cell nucleus. This information directs which parts of the DNA molecule will be used, and at what times, in producing which proteins. This process is the molecular basis of genetic science.

Virtually all organisms share the same genetic code. In fact, DNA from nearly any organism can be placed into the cells of any other, and the cellular protein synthesis will faithfully produce the identical protein that would have been made in the cells of the original organism. Thus, human genes can be placed in bacteria, and the bacteria will begin to produce the human proteins coded for by those genes.

A few exceptions have been found to the universality of the genetic code. For example, most organisms read the mRNA triplet CUG as coding for the amino acid leucine, but in species of the fungal genus *Candida* this sequence codes for the amino acid serine. Thus, the genetic code appears to be subject to natural selection, and, in fact, there is evidence that the standard code (listed in Figure 3-4) minimizes mistakes that can be made during protein synthesis (Freeland and Hurst 2004).

GENETICS

Genetics is the science of biological inheritance. It explores how biological traits are passed from parents to offspring and how variation can occur in such traits. Genetics must therefore concern itself with reproductive processes in organisms.

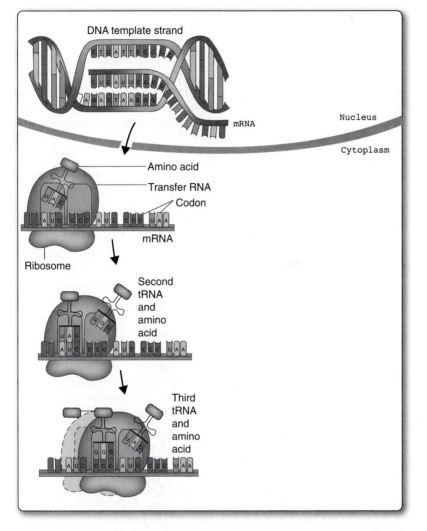

FIGURE 3-8 Protein synthesis. The messenger RNA molecule is transcribed from the allele on the DNA molecule, and the messenger RNA molecule is then translated into a string of amino acids.

Sexual Reproduction

When reproduction occurs, DNA—in the form of long chains that make up chromosomes from both parents—is combined in offspring. Different species of organisms have different numbers of chromosomes. In general, these chromosomes are paired: each chromosome has a second chromosome in the same cell that is similar, although not necessarily identical, to it. One of each pair of chromosomes stems from each of the individual's two parents, and the paired chromosomes are said to be **homologous** to each other.

There are two basic means of cellular reproduction (and hence of inheritance) in biology: **mitosis** and **meiosis**. Mitosis is simply the process by which a single cell divides into two cells, each with very similar characteristics to the original cell. Meiosis, on the other hand, is a special process in which cells divide to form reproductive cells (formally termed "gametes").

MITOSIS. Cell division, in which one cell splits into two daughter cells, is part of a larger process termed the "cell cycle." The initial phase of the cell cycle, occurring during the interval between divisions, is termed the "interphase." Towards the end of the interphase, in what is termed the "S phase," DNA is synthesized, eventually leading to a replication of each chromosome. There are two periods, occurring just before and just after the S phase, termed "G1" and "G2" respectively, in which no DNA synthesis occurs. Immediately after the G2 phase, **mitosis** is initiated. Mitosis is the process of cell division. In this process, the original cell divides into two "daughter" cells, each of which has a copy of every chromosome (Figure 3-9). Unless something in the process goes awry, each cell will possess the exact same number and type of chromosomes, with the precise order of nucleotides identical in each. After the mitotic division occurs, the daughter cells enter the interphase period of the cell cycle.

MEIOSIS. A different process of reproduction occurs when reproductive cells are formed. Each individual contains a given number of pairs of chromosomes, with the members of the pairs stemming from the organism's two parents respectively. If this individual were to pass all of its chromosomes to its offspring, and if its mate were to do the same, the offspring would end up with four of each type of chromosome instead of two and would possess double the chromosome number of its parents. By the next generation, cells would have quadrupled their chromosome number, and so on, until cells would be bursting from the myriad chromosomes inherited through the generations. Obviously, this does not occur. In fact, offspring nearly always retain the same number of chromosomes as each of their parents.

To conserve the correct chromosome number in offspring, specialized cells are used during reproduction that have only half the normal number of chromosomes—one of each chromosome pair. These cells are termed **gametes** and exist in two types: sperm (in males) and eggs (in females). The process by which gametes are produced is termed **meiosis** (see Figure 3-9), and it involves DNA duplication, much as occurs during mitosis. In this case, however, two cell divisions occur, yielding only one of each pair of chromosomes in the resulting cells. When two gametes combine in sexual reproduction, the resulting organism thus possesses two chromosomes in each pair, and chromosome number is conserved.

Mendelian Genetics

Many of the principles of biological inheritance were understood long before our recognition of the molecular basis for genetics. Several general principles were discovered by the Austrian monk Gregor Mendel. A major principle of genetics derived from his work is that inheritance of traits from parents occurs through inheritance units (genes) that act as if they are particles, solid structures that largely keep their forms through the generations. This challenged the prevalent idea at the time, shared by Darwin, that inheritance units acted more like a fluid, with blending of traits from the mother and father. Mendel also originated the idea that genes came in pairs, one from each parent. These pairs refer to similar stretches along homologous chromosome pairs that code for the same protein.

ALLELES VS. LOCI. The stretches of DNA that code for the same type of protein may not be exactly alike. There may be one or more differences in the nucleotide sequence along the chain. Nevertheless, the proteins that are produced from these differences will be similar, although not identical. To distinguish between the *types* of genes and the specific sequence that may make up the gene, geneticists use specialized terms. An **allele** refers to the specific sequence of DNA that makes up a gene. A **locus** (plural: loci) refers to the general position on the chromosome (or the homologous chromosome having the same sequence of loci) where that gene is located. In that position, specific nucleotide sequences may be somewhat different, but they code for the same type of protein. An individual receives one allele from each of its parents at each locus. If his or her parents have different alleles at a given locus from each other, that individual will possess two different alleles at the

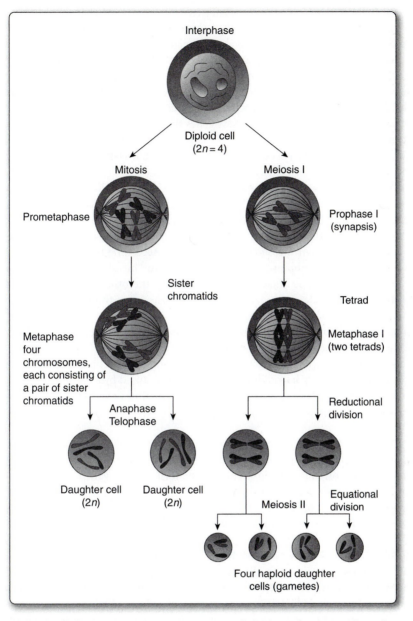

FIGURE 3-9 Mitosis and Meiosis. In mitosis, one cell divides to form two cells, each with a full complement of DNA (diploidy). In meiosis, a fertilized gamete divides twice to form four cells with half the usual amount of DNA (haploidy).

same locus. Basically, all individuals within a species share the same loci, but the specific alleles that are present at each locus differ among individuals.

While Mendel did not have information about alleles and loci, he did understand that multiple forms of many genes existed. He formulated three general principles to understand the repercussions of particulate, paired genes in inheritance. These principles have incorrectly been termed "laws," but all have exceptions and complications. These principles of Mendel deal with dominance, segregation, and gene assortment.

PRINCIPLE OF DOMINANCE. If an individual's two alleles at a locus are identical (a condition referred to as being **homozygous**), all forms of protein coded for by the alleles will be identical. Thus, the individual will "show" the biological trait created by that allele's function. For instance, the allele may code for a protein that acts as an enzyme in some biochemical pathway. If the individual has an allele that makes an alternate form of the enzyme, the biochemical pathway may not operate in the same way as it would with the "normal" form of the enzyme. For example, biochemical pathways enable organisms to synthesize proteins that act as coloring agents in skin, hair, feathers, or other structures. Should the individual possess genes that coded for enzymes that do not function properly, it may not be able to manufacture the coloring agent and therefore will not exhibit the color in the relevant body part. This explains the variation that Darwin noted in all living species; the variation stems from different alleles at specific loci.

What happens, however, if an individual has two different alleles at a locus (a condition referred to as being **heterozygous**), the different alleles arising due to differences between its parents at the given locus? In the above example, if the individual has one allele that codes for the properly working enzyme and one that codes for the enzyme that does not work well, will they show the color, show part of the color, or not show the color at all? According to Mendel, the individual will either show the color or not; halfway measures (similar to "blending") will not occur. In other words, the effects of one of the alleles will *dominate* over the other. This concept is termed the **Principle of Dominance**, and, as noted, has exceptions. Deleterious traits (those that are bad for the individual) may be either dominant or recessive.

A human example of a dominant genetic trait occurs with Huntington's disease, which is a fatal neurological ailment caused by brain-cell degeneration in selected areas of the brain. Huntington's disease is passed on in families, and it usually only becomes apparent in middle age after the individual has already had children. The disease is caused by a variant allele that is lengthened due to a repeated sequence of three nucleotides many times over, and this allele is dominant over the "normal" allele (Walker 2007).

PRINCIPLE OF SEGREGATION. The second principle of Mendel, the **Principle of Segregation**, states, in modern terms, that the paired genes in an individual separate (that is, segregate) from each other in a random fashion during meiosis (during the formation of gametes). In other words, if an individual is heterozygous at a given locus, there is an equal chance of its passing either of its alleles at that locus to any one of its offspring, but in all cases only one of the alleles will be passed on. While this principle is usually valid, there are occasions where segregation does not occur.

PRINCIPLE OF INDEPENDENT ASSORTMENT. The **Principle of Independent Assortment** refers to the idea that whichever one of an allele pair at a locus goes into a gamete (through segregation) has no effect on which of *another* pair of alleles at a different locus will go into that gamete. In modern terms, this principle works for chromosomes. Individuals have several paired chromosomes with one member of the pair stemming from each parent. When meiosis occurs, as noted earlier, only one of each pair will be in a given gamete. If, for instance, for one chromosome pair the chromosome from the individual's father is placed in the gamete, which of the chromosomes from a different pair will be in the same gamete? Mendel's answer would be that there is an equal chance for the second pair of chromosomes in the gamete to have either the one derived from the individual's father or from its mother. That is, the placement in the gamete of one member of each pair of chromosomes occurs independently of the placement of members of other chromosome pairs.

From this discussion one can see that Mendel's principle that genes are inherited independently does not always hold true: what if the genes are found along the same chromosome? Alleles on the same chromosome are usually passed down together, a phenomenon termed **linkage**. However, linkage does not always occur for alleles on the same chromosome. During meiosis, duplicated pairs of chromosomes actually wrap around each other, forming **chiasmata** where they overlap. Physical

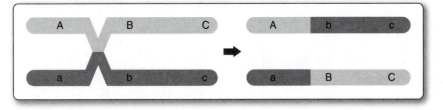

FIGURE 3-10 Crossing over of genetic material between homologous chromosomes during meiosis.

switching of parts of DNA strands between these chromosomes can occur at the chiasmata in a process termed **crossing over** (see Figure 3-10). In this way, alleles once on the same chromosome can wind up separated with one allele on the other chromosome of the pair.

GENOTYPE AND PHENOTYPE. From Mendel's principles rises a distinction between what alleles an individual possesses (termed the individual's **genotype**) and what the results of having those alleles are in terms of how the organism looks or functions (termed the individual's **phenotype**). An individual who is homozygous at a given locus, for example, for alleles that code for a protein that is a brown-colored pigment found in the iris of the eye, would clearly show the trait of having brown eyes. Another individual who is heterozygous at the same locus, with one allele coding for a brown pigment but the other allele coding for a protein which does not have a color, may show the trait of having brown eyes if that allele is dominant over the non-pigment allele. Thus, two individuals showing the same trait (that is, having the same phenotype) may have a different underlying set of alleles at that locus (and thus different genotypes).

CONSEQUENCES OF MENDEL'S PRINCIPLES. There are ramifications of Mendel's principles. Knowledge of dominance, segregation, and independent assortment allows prediction of what offspring will probably be like, both genotypically and phenotypically—that is, if the genotypes of the parents are known.

Classic examples stem from Mendel's studies of inheritance in pea plants. He discovered many traits that could be explained by his principles of inheritance. One such trait is the texture of seeds in the pea plant: some plants have smooth seeds, while, in others, the seed surface is wrinkled (Srb et al. 1965). He established types of pea plants over many generations such that all in one group were smooth-seeded and all in another group were wrinkled-seeded (that is, both groups were homozygous, but for different alleles). When he cross-bred plants from the two groups, he discovered that all their offspring were smooth. In modern terms, the offspring were all heterozygous, and the "smooth allele" is dominant over the "wrinkled allele," thus the phenotype of all the offspring was smooth. When he crossbred the offspring to form a third generation, he found that the third generation contained both smooth- and wrinkled-seeded individuals, with the smooth individuals outnumbering the wrinkled ones by a margin of about three to one. This can be understood by making up a grid to show what the odds of inheriting various allele combinations would be (Figure 3-11). Each parent, by the principle of segregation, would have a 50 percent chance of passing either of its alleles to its offspring. Thus, the third generation plants would have a 25 percent chance of getting a smooth allele from each parent, a 25 percent chance of getting a wrinkled allele from each parent, a 25 percent chance of getting a smooth allele from its father and a wrinkled allele from its mother, and a 25 percent chance of getting a wrinkled allele from its father and a smooth allele from its mother. These chances of getting alleles from each parent result in 25 percent of the genotypes of the third generation organisms being homozygous for the smooth allele (with a smooth phenotype), 25 percent of the genotypes being homozygous for the wrinkled allele (with a wrinkled phenotype), and 50 percent of the

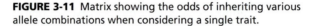

Ss x Ss, where S = smooth allele and s = wrinkled allele			
		Father's Alleles	
		S	s
Mother's Alleles	S	SS	Ss
	s	sS	ss

Genotype ratios: SS = 0.25
                  Ss = 0.50
                  ss = 0.25

Phenotype ratios: Smooth = 0.75
                   Wrinkled = 0.25

FIGURE 3-11 Matrix showing the odds of inheriting various allele combinations when considering a single trait.

genotypes being heterozygous for the two alleles (with a smooth phenotype, due to dominance of the smooth allele over the wrinkled one). Thus, the three-to-one ratio of phenotypes in the third generation is what one would expect from Mendel's principles.

Things get a bit more complicated when more than one trait is considered at a time. Due to the principle of independent assortment, the traits should be inherited independently of each other. Figure 3-12 shows a grid that follows the inheritance of alleles from both the wrinkled-smooth locus, and alleles from a second locus with two different alleles, one leading to a yellow-colored cotyledon on the pea plant (yellow) and the other leading to a green-colored cotyledon (green), where the yellow allele is dominant (Srb et al. 1965). If parents that are both heterozygous for both traits (and thus have a phenotype that is both smooth and yellow) are mated, a variety of phenotypes and genotypes are produced. Experiments have shown that these varieties are indeed produced from such a union and in approximately the proportions predicted by Mendel (and as shown in the grid).

SEX CHROMOSOMES. Among the chromosome pairs, there is a special pair referred to as the **sex chromosomes.** The sex chromosome pair is different from the other pairs in that these two chromosomes do not contain the same loci. In mammals, one of the chromosomes is considerably longer than the other; the long chromosome is termed the "X" chromosome, and the small one is termed the "Y." Females have two X chromosomes, while males have one X and one Y. The sex of offspring is thus determined by whether the father passes down his X or his Y chromosome through his gamete; the mother always contributes an X because she has no Y chromosome.

The X chromosome has many more loci than the Y chromosome, and the traits determined by the alleles at these loci, therefore, are often different in males and females; females have two alleles but males only one for these traits. In short, this makes males more vulnerable to the ill effects of a nondominant (termed **recessive**) allele on the X chromosome that codes for a poorly made protein. Females would need to inherit two copies of a recessive allele for its effects to be seen in the phenotype. A classic example in humans is one form of red-green color blindness in which the alleles for the trait are resident on the X chromosome, and the allele for normal color vision is dominant to the allele that codes for color blindness. As expected, this form of color blindness is more common in males than females.

COMPLEX TRAITS. Many physical traits of organisms are not determined in a simple manner by alternate alleles at a single locus. In fact, most traits result from the action of many proteins acting together during the development of an organism and thus are influenced by many loci. Such traits

SsYy x SsYy, where S = smooth allele and s = wrinkled allele;
Y = yellow allele and y = green allele

Father's Alleles

Mother's Alleles		SY	Sy	sY	sy
	SY	SSYY	SSYy	SsYY	SsYy
	Sy	SSyY	SSyy	SsyY	Ssyy
	sY	sSYY	sSYy	ssYY	ssYy
	sy	sSyY	sSyy	ssyY	ssyy

Genotype ratios: SSYY = 1/16 (0.06);
SSYy = 2/16 (0.12);
SsYY = 2/16 (0.12);
SsYy = 4/16 (0.25);
SSyy = 1/16 (0.06);
Ssyy = 2/16 (0.12);
ssYY = 1/16 (0.06);
ssYy = 2/16 (0.12);
ssyy = 1/16 (0.06)

Phenotype ratios: Smooth and Yellow: 9/16 (0.56);
Smooth and Green: 3/16 (0.19);
Wrinkled and Green: 3/16 (0.19);
Wrinkled and Green: 1/16 (0.06)

FIGURE 3-12 Matrix showing the odds of inheriting various allele combinations when considering multiple traits.

are **polygenic**. To further complicate matters, many proteins affect more than one physical trait in an organism; for instance, some enzymes are involved in several different biochemical pathways. The condition where an allele codes for a protein with multiple effects is termed **pleiotropy**.

As if the effects of polygenic and pleiotropic inheritance were not difficult enough to unravel, geneticists are faced with yet another challenge: traits are also affected by environmental forces. For instance, while an organism may have several alleles that affect aspects of its ability to store fat tissue on its body, if that organism is not able to obtain sufficient food, then the proteins involved in facilitating fat storage will not be able to function. In fact, for many complex traits, one of the first tasks of the geneticist is to determine to what degree the trait is caused by genetics (termed the **heritability** of the trait) versus environmental factors. In formal terms, heritability is a measure of the proportion of variance in a trait that is determined by genetic variation.

MUTATIONS. Knowledge of how genetic traits are passed through different alleles on chromosomes tells us much about the mechanics of inheritance. Knowledge of dominance helps explain some of the differences between offspring and parents: traits produced by having two recessive alleles on the chromosome pair may be seen in offspring of parents who were both heterozygous and thus showed the dominant phenotype. However, we have not yet answered one of the major problems faced by Darwin: how does *new* variation occur?

Truly new variation stems from creation of new alleles at a locus. These new alleles come about from changes in the order of nucleotides along the stretch of DNA comprising the locus. One way in which changes occur is due to chemical or physical damage to the chromosome. New ordering of DNA may also occur through errors in the process of duplicating DNA during mitosis and meiosis, with errors in the latter process being passed down to offspring. Since DNA chains contain millions of nucleotides, even a very efficient duplication process is likely to include some errors. Thus, noncomplementary nucleotides may be incorporated in a chain, or a few nucleotides may be omitted, or extra nucleotides may be inserted during the duplication process. Any of these errors are termed **mutations**.

Mutations are due to changes in the order of nucleotides because of substitutions, deletions, or insertions of nucleotides. Remembering that codons are triplets of nucleotides that code for a single amino acid in a protein chain, mutations that change only one triplet have a smaller effect than those that change several. This difference in effect is shown if we use as a model for the genetic code a phrase written in the English language using only three-letter words:

The boy and his dog ran for fun.

If a substitution mutation changes the "y" in "boy" to a "t":

The bot and his dog ran for fun.

the meaning of the sentence can probably be deduced. However, if the "t" is inserted before the "y," the sentence becomes more difficult to discern:

The bot yan dhi sdo gra nfo rfu n.

Similarly, deletion mutations of single nucleotides (letters) also cause a "frame shift" mutation that destroys the meaning of all succeeding triplets:

The boa ndh isd ogr anf orf un.

Mutations seem to occur at random intervals due to errors during duplication, but their frequency may be enhanced by environmental elements that cause an increase in mistakes. These environmental elements include radiation and assorted chemicals that affect DNA. One chemical that has a strong mutagenic (that is, producing mutations) effect is mustard gas, which was manufactured for use in chemical warfare and led to severe injuries in the people who were exposed to it (Novitski 1977). Because of the serious concern about the effects of potential mutagens on humans, a common standardized procedure known as the Ames test is carried out for examining chemicals, using a sensitive strain of the bacterium *Salmonella typhimurium* to derive an estimate of the mutation rate caused by the chemical compound. Some mutagens only become activated after they have been partly metabolized by the human liver, and, therefore, the Ames test includes a procedure in which mammalian liver extract is incubated with the compound (Klug and Cummings 2000).

MICROEVOLUTION

In the study of evolution, scientists have focused on different time scales. Major biological change over long periods of time, as can be seen in changes in structures from the fossil record, is termed **macroevolution**, a topic that will be discussed in Chapter 5. Smaller-scale changes, such as generational differences explained by Mendelian genetics and mutational events, are termed **microevolution**. We will confine ourselves to the latter here.

Introduction to Population Genetics

In understanding microevolutionary processes, we must move our focus from the individual to the population of which that individual is a part. At this level of analysis our concern turns to the

PROFILE 3
Rebecca Cann

Dr. Rebecca L. Cann is a geneticist and human biologist who has revolutionized our perspective on modern human evolution. Her groundbreaking research comparing the mitochondrial DNA (mtDNA) of people from around the world showed that modern humans have little genetic diversity compared with many other primate species, suggesting that we are all descended from a single ancestor in the recent past. Since mtDNA is passed down through the maternal line (it is passed down through egg cells), the ancestor of modern humans can be traced to a hypothetical single small population of Homo sapiens, and, in simplified form, to a single woman who has been termed "the Mitochondrial Eve." In fact, this individual would be the ancestress to whom a direct line of matrilineal inheritance can be traced (that is, at each generation, at least one daughter would have had to be born and in turn to have given birth to a daughter). Dr. Cann's research also showed that there is more genetic variation in Africa than in the rest of the world, which implies that our oldest ancestry stems from Africa.

Dr. Cann's research has focused on the use of genetics to understand the migration and dispersal of human populations throughout prehistory and into the present. Much of her research has focused on the movement of people into the Pacific Islands and on the population dynamics of these peoples, including the sharp drop in population size for many groups during the period of initial contact with Western and other outside populations that brought devastating epidemics of infectious disease.

Dr. Cann has also studied another group that has faced recent population decline due to infectious disease—endangered Hawaiian native birds. Her research examines the genetics of the birds and of their parasites, in particular that of Avian malaria.

Dr. Cann is Professor of Genetics and Molecular Biology at the University of Hawaii at Manoa.

---

frequencies of alleles at given loci. That is, in a biological population there may be several different alleles at a given locus, even though any individual can only have one (if homozygous) or two (if heterozygous) of those alleles.

FREQUENCIES. Knowledge of how common or rare any given allele is (termed the **allele frequency**; usually expressed as a percentage) allows prediction of the likelihood that any individual will have one or two of those alleles (and thus one can predict the **genotype frequency**, or the likelihood of a given allele pair in a given individual). Furthermore, from the genotype frequency one can predict the likelihood of any given phenotype being present in an individual (termed the **phenotype frequency**).

HARDY-WEINBERG EQUILIBRIUM. Determining allele and genotype frequencies requires knowledge both of genetics and how to calculate probabilities. What one observes is the phenotype frequency; the other frequencies must be inferred.

In a simple genetic trait determined by a single locus with two alleles, one dominant over the other, one can observe two phenotypes in the population, the dominant phenotype (determined by the product of the dominant allele) and the recessive phenotype (determined by the product of the recessive allele in individuals homozygous for that allele). Individuals with the dominant phenotype may have either of two genotypes: homozygous for the dominant allele or heterozygous. Individuals with the recessive phenotype, however, only can be of a single genotype: homozygous for the recessive allele.

The probability that an individual will be homozygous for the recessive allele is equal to the chances of receiving the recessive allele from one's father *times* the chance of receiving the recessive allele from one's mother. The chances of getting the recessive allele from one's father, if we do not know specific information about a given family, is equal to the proportion of alleles in the population that are recessive, with this being equal to the allele frequency of the recessive allele. We can designate the allele frequency of the recessive trait by the letter q. Similarly, the chance of getting the recessive allele from one's mother is also equal to the population frequency of the recessive allele, which is q. This calculation is based on the principle of probability, which states that the chances of two independent events occurring together are equal to the probability of the first event times the probability of the second event. Therefore, the probability of being homozygous for the recessive allele, which is equal to the phenotype frequency of the recessive trait, is $q \times q$, or q^2.

Once we know the genotype frequency of the homozygous recessive (q^2), we can easily compute the other values of the allele and genotype frequencies of the population. The allele frequency of the recessive trait (q) is equal to the square root of that trait's genotype frequency (q^2). Since there are only two alleles at the locus, the allele frequency of the dominant trait (designated by the letter p) must be equal to the remaining proportion of alleles in the population; that is: $p + q = 1$ (or $p = 1 - q$). Thus we can calculate both allele frequencies. The genotype frequency of the dominant trait is similarly calculated by the chances of getting the allele from one's father (p) times the chance of getting the allele from one's mother (p), or p^2.

Finally, one can calculate the heterozygote's genotype frequency, but here one must be aware that there are two ways of being a heterozygote: one could have received the dominant allele from one's father and the recessive allele from one's mother, or the recessive allele from one's father and the dominant allele from one's mother. In both cases, the odds of getting the dominant allele from a parent are p and the odds of getting a recessive allele are q. The genotype frequency of the heterozygote is therefore $[p \times q] + [q \times p]$ (allowing for both ways to be a heterozygote), which equals $2pq$.

As an example, suppose we wish to find out the allele and genotype frequencies of the locus for PTC taste sensitivity, a trait found in humans where the majority of people are sensitive to the bitter taste of the chemical phenylthiocarbamide (PTC) ("tasters") while a minority are not sensitive ("non-tasters"). PTC is a synthetic compound not found in nature, but the ability to taste PTC is thought to be related to the ability to detect other bitter compounds, and this trait may have helped its possessors to avoid ingesting toxic substances. While the trait is actually dependent on multiple alleles, in general the non-taster category is based on a recessive allele, meaning non-tasters are homozygous for the "non-taster allele." Among Europeans, approximately 28 percent of people are non-tasters (Kim and Drayna 2004). Thus, in this case $q^2 = 0.28$. From this, we can compute that $q = 0.53$ approximately (the square root of 0.28), and therefore $p = 0.47$. The genotype frequencies are therefore (when rounded up): for the homozygous dominant $0.47 \times 0.47 = 0.22$; for the homozygous recessive $0.53 \times 0.53 = 0.28$; and for the heterozygote $2 \times 0.47 \times 0.53 = 0.50$.

The above mathematical formulation for computing allele and genotype frequencies is termed the **Hardy-Weinberg equilibrium** in honor of the two people who independently devised it. This relationship is useful in studies of genetics in populations, but a close look reveals that it is based on several assumptions, which might not always be true. These assumptions are that natural selection is not working against one of the phenotypes (which would then be present in smaller proportions than predicted), that mutations are not occurring that change the alleles, that there are no alleles coming from other populations into the one under study (in the above example, one must assume that non-Europeans are not migrating into the population), that chance events (particularly if the population is small) do not lead to slightly different proportions than one would predict, and also that random mating is occurring in the population. Violation of any of these assumptions would lead to a change in the proportion of alleles, and of genotype frequencies, over time. **This change over time in allele frequencies represents evolutionary change.** The factors involved in the assumptions, therefore, are termed **evolutionary forces**.

Forces of Evolution

The major evolutionary forces are selection, mutation, chance (or genetic drift), and gene flow. The first three can lead to changes in the allele frequencies of an entire species, while gene flow can change allele frequencies in populations within a species. Non-random mating can affect the ratio of homozygotes to heterozygotes in a population.

SELECTION. From a genetic perspective, natural selection can take several forms. In each case, a given phenotype is more successful than others, with the variation in phenotypes based upon genotype differences. If selection is against the dominant phenotype, individuals that are homozygous for the recessive allele will be more successful at reproduction, and thus the frequency of this genotype (represented by the value q^2 in the Hardy-Weinberg equilibrium) will increase. If q^2 increases, then so does the value of q. Therefore, in this case, selection leads to an increase in the frequency of the recessive allele in later generations.

Selection against the recessive phenotype leads to less success at reproduction for the homozygous recessive genotype, or a *reduction* in q^2. This, in turn, means a decrease in the frequency of the recessive allele in later generations.

Selection against both homozygotes, and, therefore, in favor of the heterozygote, only will occur when dominance is not present or is not complete. Here, selection against both alleles when found in homozygous individuals is balanced by selection in favor of the alleles when they are found in heterozygous individuals. Just how the balance will be found between these opposing forms of selection will depend on just how much selection is occurring against each type of homozygous individual. Should selection against each of the homozygous genotypes be identical, an equilibrium allele frequency of 0.5 for each allele might eventually exist in the population; however, if selection is greater against one of the homozygous genotypes, a balance in favor (that is, a frequency greater than 0.5) of the other allele will be reached. Similar considerations are applicable to a case where selection *against* the heterozygote occurs.

TYPES OF SELECTION. The effect of selection on complex, polygenic traits has also been studied. In brief, complex traits usually exist as a gradient of values in the phenotype instead of simply as one of two absolute values. For instance, populations of humans show a range of stature (total body height), not simply one height or another. Different types of selection (shown in Figure 3-13) include: that in favor of one extreme end of the gradient (termed **directional selection**), that in favor of the middle range of the gradient (termed **stabilizing selection**), and that in favor of both extreme ends of the continuum (termed **diversifying selection**). For example, imagine a population species when numbers are reduced. A species that has enjoyed a large population size for millennia may go through a population bottleneck for a short time period and, as a result, experience allele frequencies that have been affected greatly by genetic drift. Such a bottleneck leads to a loss of rare alleles because they are unlikely, by chance, to be found in the individuals who live through the bottleneck. Thus population bottlenecks are also referred to as "genetic bottlenecks."

A species that seems to have gone through a population bottleneck recently is the cheetah (O'Brien et al. 1986). Cheetah populations have very little genetic variability as a consequence. This has alarmed wildlife conservationists, who fear for the long-term viability of the cheetah species.

A special case of a genetic bottleneck occurs when a small number of individuals start a new population of a species, for instance, if storm-blown birds establish a population on an oceanic island far from the continent on which they originated. In such a case, the new population is likely to have fewer alleles at many loci than occurs with other genetic bottlenecks, since the alleles present are only those that were present in the founders of the new population. This sort of evolutionary force, termed the **founder effect**, may have acted on isolated human populations in the Pacific that stem from small colonies; an example is the human population of Pitcairn Island, descended from seamen on the H.M.S. Bounty and their Polynesian wives (Refshauge and Walsh 1981). Many of the crew of the British ship *Bounty* mutinied against their captain (Bligh) in 1789, and after setting him and some loyal crew adrift in a lifeboat, sailed for Tahiti where they took women aboard who then sailed with them to a small, unsettled, and uncharted island later called Pitcairn's Island, where they hid from the British authorities. They had children and established a small population that at the beginning of the twenty-first century totals approximately 50 people.

ASSORTATIVE MATING. The Hardy-Weinberg equilibrium discussed earlier is based on the assumption that random mating occurs in the population. If there is a tendency for organisms with similar physical attributes to seek each other as mates, than any alleles that may underlie these traits will tend to cluster in the population. In other words, homozygotes will be produced at a greater rate than predicted. On the other hand, if opposites attract, heterozygotes will be produced in greater frequency than predicted by the equilibrium. Certainly individuals are more likely to find mates from within their population or from near neighbors than from distant populations, and this will tend to increase matings with individuals who are genetically similar.

Non-random mating patterns are termed **assortative mating** and can be both positive (mating more likely with individuals of similar phenotype, and thus more likely to be carrying the same alleles) or negative (mating with dissimilar individuals). There have been many instances of positive assortative mating in humans; a clear case occurs in marriages within castes in India, leading to allele frequency differences between castes (Brues 1977). An example of negative assortative mating is found in European populations, where red-haired people marry each other less frequently than would be expected by chance (Harrison et al. 1964).

The Synthetic Theory of Evolution

The modern, synthetic theory of evolution is derived from a synthesis (thus its name) of understandings from the science of genetics merged with Darwin's theory of evolution. In simple terms, the theory can be described by restating Darwin's theory (as outlined in Chapter 1) in genetic terms, again with five steps:

1. Individual organisms pass their alleles to their offspring, with alleles remaining intact. Offspring of sexually reproducing organisms inherit half of each parent's alleles, one at each locus, but also may obtain mutations that create new alleles.
2. Genetic variation exists among all populations of living organisms, with variation derived from segregation and independent assortment of alleles, and from mutations.

3. All organisms have the innate ability to **overpopulate** their environments.
4. There is a "struggle for existence," or **competition**, between genetic varieties because of overpopulation.
5. The organisms that compete best will have more success at reproducing themselves; that is, there will be **natural selection** of the "fittest" organisms, with these organisms more likely to pass their alleles on to future generations. This leads to changes in allele frequencies.

These steps are only somewhat changed from those listed in Chapter 2 to describe Darwin's theory, but the notions of genetics as the mechanism of inheritance and of mutations as the means of creating new variation in populations have been added.

In this theory, evolution may be defined by genetic changes in a population over time; over short time periods, evolutionary change is defined as changes in allele frequencies. Complexities accompany the theory. Natural selection occurs at the level of the individual organism, which is a collection of thousands of genetic loci, each possessing two alleles (with the exception of those on the X and Y chromosomes in males). Thus, a wonderful new mutation may occur but never be added to a population because it took place in an individual who had poorly adapted alleles at other loci. Also, selection acts on an individual's phenotype, which is complexly and incompletely related to the individual's genotype. A given phenotypic feature of an individual may stem from the actions of several loci (polygenic traits) and/or be also affected by environmental circumstances. Evolution itself is a characteristic of populations; individuals do not evolve. Thus, evolution is a complicated process that occurs on many levels, including molecular, organismal, and population levels. These levels are not easily reducible to each other, making it very difficult to make predictions from the theory (Lewontin 1974; Slobodkin and Rapoport 1974). (This difficulty in making predictions is a hallmark of theories in biological sciences.) Despite these difficulties, the synthetic theory of evolution is a well supported one, explaining the diversity of life on earth.

CHAPTER SUMMARY

Biological inheritance occurs through the transmission of DNA from parents to offspring. DNA is the chemical constituent of genes. The DNA is made up of four subunits, termed "nucleotides," and the order in which nucleotides appear determines how genetic traits are transformed into the ordering of the amino acid subunits of proteins. The order of amino acids, in turn, determines the structure and function of proteins, and this determines the development of biological traits in living organisms.

Variation in nucleotide order in DNA creates the variation that occurs in biological populations, although observable variation is due to a complex interplay of multiple genes and environmental conditions. Evolutionary change occurs through changes in DNA sequences over time, and this change is driven by the evolutionary forces of selection, mutation, and genetic drift. The modern, synthetic theory of evolution combines the scientific principles of genetics with Darwin's theory of evolution through natural selection.

CHAPTER 4

Molecular Genetics, Genomics, and Human Genetics

The previous chapter introduced basic concepts of genetics. The recent revolutionary advances in molecular biology, however, have vastly increased our knowledge well beyond these basic concepts. We now can sequence long DNA chains, actually observing the specific nucleotide sequences that lead to changes in alleles, and then follow up with studies of the effect these changes have on protein structure and function. We have come a long way towards bridging the gap between explanations of genotype and phenotype in individual organisms.

In the past, scientists recognized phenotypic differences between organisms, and then labored, often for years, in an attempt to identify the genetic basis of these differences. Currently, our ability to work with DNA is so advanced that the process is often reversed: first genetic differences are recognized, and then scientists must work to discover what phenotypic variation is related to the genetic differences. In this chapter, we will take a broad look at some of this new knowledge of genetics, knowledge that has given us the ability to control inheritance in many organisms.

A CLOSER LOOK AT CHROMOSOMES

Characteristics of Chromosomes

CHROMOSOME STRUCTURE. Chromosomes are, in essence, long strands of DNA that contain many alleles, strung out like pearls on a string (Figure 4-1). In actuality, chromosomes are much more complex structures than this. DNA in chromosomes combines with several forms of protein. In eukaryotic organisms, the protein-DNA complex exists in a dispersed form in cells during much of the cell cycle, with this form termed **chromatin**. During replication of DNA, whether in mitosis or meiosis, the DNA-protein structure coils up into a tight form, condensing into the distinct structures that are termed chromosomes. Chromosomes are microscopic structures. But if completely uncoiled, the DNA in each human cell containing forty-six chromosomes would stretch about six feet in length (Klug and Cummings 2000). It is the coiling that permits so much information to be contained in such a small structure.

Prokaryotes such as bacteria have chromosomes that are somewhat different than those found in eukaryotes. Bacterial chromosomes are circular, and the total amount of genetic material in bacteria tends to be much less than in eukaryotes, usually with only a single chromosome present. Plasmids, which are small, linear, or circular DNA molecules, may also be present in bacteria, but their presence varies from individual to individual even within the same species.

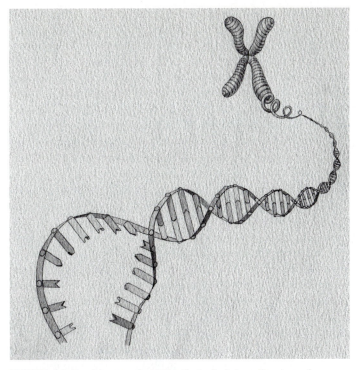

FIGURE 4-1 Double-stranded DNA that winds together to make up the chromosome.

CHROMOSOME STRUCTURE AND FUNCTION. When chromatin is tightly looped, its DNA cannot function as a template for either replication or protein synthesis. An important aspect of chromosome structure is that it can change to expose the DNA sequences necessary for cell function. The crux of the issue is how the correct sequences can be made available at just the right times. These changes allow the specific DNA sequences making up alleles to become available for transcription, and they form a fundamental means of controlling gene regulation in the cell (Alberts et al. 2002).

REGULATORY REGIONS OF DNA. Certain segments of DNA molecules do not function directly as codes for protein synthesis. Instead, they form regulatory regions that initiate or end DNA transcription of chromosome segments, in some places regulating transcription of a single allele, and in others controlling transcription of multiple alleles. The regulatory DNA sequences function in concert with **gene regulatory proteins**. These proteins bind to the DNA at the regulatory sites by "recognizing" specific nucleotide sequences, with the recognition due to chemical complementarity of the protein and DNA surfaces. Surface features of the DNA molecule are caused by specific nucleotide sequences (Alberts et al. 2002). The protein, once bound, changes the conformation of the chromosome, uncoiling DNA segments to permit transcription. There are several types of regulatory proteins, based on their three dimensional structures, the specific means of attachment to DNA, and on the presence or absence of specific additional atoms, such as zinc. From this classification come such exotic names for gene regulatory proteins as helix-turn-helix proteins, ß sheets, isoleucine zippers, and zinc fingers.

SPECIAL FEATURES ON CHROMOSOMES. Chromosomes of eukaryotic organisms have special segments that differ in structure from the rest of the molecule. These specialized regions occur at each end of the chromosome, as well as at a region somewhere in the middle. The two end regions of the chromosome are termed the **telomeres**. Chromosome ends require a special structure because of the details involved in DNA duplication. As one approaches the end of a chromosome during replication, the very ends of the DNA molecule will not be duplicated, due to the mechanics of enzymatic processes involved with the forming and stitching together of the complementary DNA strand (see Brown 1999 or other advanced genetics texts for a fuller explanation).

Telomeres have an unusual nucleotide sequence, consisting of a thousand or more repeated copies of a sequence of six nucleotides (TTAGGG). Multiple copies of a short sequence of nucleotides in a DNA molecule, such as occur in the telomere, are referred to as **tandem repeats** (see Figure 4-2). When the chromosome is duplicated, one or more of the tandem repeats in the telomere will not be replicated because of the mechanical difficulty in copying the very end of the chromosome, and the resulting chromosome is slightly shorter than the original. Repeated duplications during an organism's life will lead to steady shortening of its chromosomes, and this progressive shortening may be an important factor in the cellular aging process.

A special enzyme, termed "telomerase," that is composed of both RNA and protein, can act to reverse the shortening process (Greider and Blackburn 1996). One segment of the enzyme's RNA has the complementary sequence (AAUCCC) to the end terminal repeat sequence of the telomere. This RNA sequence is used as a template for adding copies of the TTAGGG tandem repeat to chromosome ends, thus reversing the shortening process. Bacterial chromosomes are circular, and therefore telomeres are not present. As a result, there is no special need for replication near their ends, and hence no telomerase is present.

Another special region of chromosomes is the **centromere**. This is the segment, sometimes near the chromosome center, that attaches to the fibers that make up mitotic and meiotic **spindles** during cell division. The fibers serve to move homologous chromosomes into separate daughter cells during the segregation process of cell division. The centromere also connects the two homologous chromosomes until they finally are pulled apart by the spindle fibers. Centromeres are located

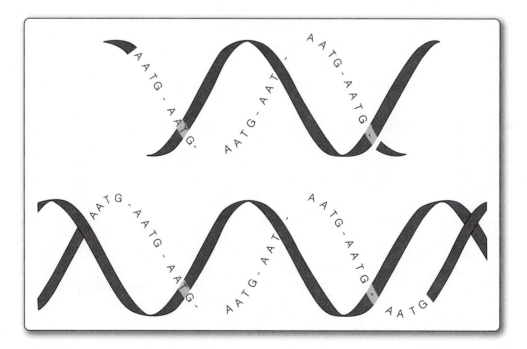

FIGURE 4-2 Variants of the short tandem repeat TH01 that repeats the sequence AATG multiple times.

at a fixed position on any given chromosome. In early studies of chromosomes, classification was based on where on the chromosome the centromere was located. For instance, if the centromere was near the center, the chromosome was termed "metacentric." If the centromere was located near either end, the chromosome was termed "telocentric."

OTHER TYPES OF REPEATED DNA SEQUENCES. The repeated sequences that characterize telomeres are also found in other sections of the DNA molecule. Approximately five percent of the human genome is made up of highly repetitive DNA sequences, and there is another considerable proportion taken up by moderately repetitive DNA sequences. These repetitive sequences vary from short repeats of six or so nucleotides in length (as found in telomeres) to over 100 nucleotides. The repeated segments are found between alleles on the DNA chain, but also sometimes *within* alleles, and are referred to as **minisatellites**. A different group of repeating sequences is usually only two or three nucleotides long and its members are referred to as **microsatellites**. There is often a great deal of variability in the number of repeats within these minisatellites and microsatellites among individuals within the same population. Still more exotic are **transposable sequences**, or transposons, which are segments found repeatedly along the DNA molecule, but these repeated segments are not necessarily situated right next to their copies; they may be dispersed throughout the genome. The transposable sequences are mobile and can move to different locations within an individual's genome, moving both within a chromosome and onto other chromosomes. The transposable sequences are copied, either through direct copying of DNA, or by producing mRNA, which is reverse-transcribed to DNA through the action of an enzyme termed "reverse transcriptase." The best known of these transposable sequences is termed the "*Alu* transposon," which is common among primates, including humans. *Alu* transposons are typically about 300 nucleotide bases long, and more than one million of these sequences are found in any human's genome (Dagan et al. 2004; Xing et al. 2007). Other important types of mobile DNA elements for human biology include SVA and LINE1 elements (Xing et al. 2007).

Chromosome Mapping

Each chromosome contains many genetic loci along its length in a characteristic order. Finding the relative, and absolute, locations of the various loci on the chromosome allows a map to be constructed of each chromosome.

LINKAGE MAPs. Early attempts at mapping involved studies of crossing over of alleles during meiosis. Alleles on the same chromosome are linked to each other, and thus cannot assort independently, in contradiction to Mendel's third principle. However, the process of crossing over during meiosis does permit alleles to be exchanged with the alleles at the same loci located on homologous chromosomes. The further apart two alleles are on the same chromosome, the greater the chance that a crossing-over event will occur between them on the chromosome, and therefore result in the two alleles being separated onto homologous chromosomes. The method, then, examines the degree of linkage between loci on the same chromosome. By careful study of the crossing over rate that leads to the separation of previously linked alleles, general maps of distances between loci on chromosomes can be constructed.

In fact, crossing over often occurs several times along the lengths of chromosomes during meiosis. By examining the frequencies at which several different alleles are linked or become unlinked with other alleles on the same chromosome, one can compile the order of the loci at which the alleles are located. However, multiple crossovers may occur between two alleles (see Figure 4-3). Because of this, distance between alleles may be underestimated, and the underestimate becomes greater for alleles that are widely separated on chromosomes because there is more chance for multiple crossing-over events between them (Klug and Cummings 2000).

LINKAGE MAPS OF THE X CHROMOSOME. Linkage maps of the X chromosome can be formed in much the same way as maps are derived for autosomal (non-sex determining) chromosomes, but

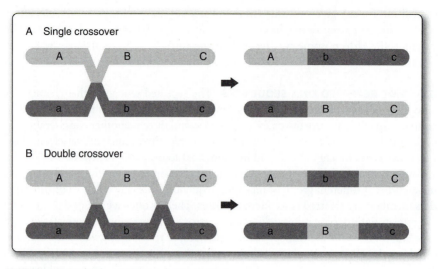

FIGURE 4-3 Multiple crossovers during meiosis.

one difference should be noted: no crossing over between homologous chromosomes will occur in males, who only have one X chromosome. Thus, crossing over will only occur in females. On the other hand, observation of the effects of crossing over in females are made easier due to the fact that X-linked recessive traits always are observable in the phenotypes of their male descendants.

MAPPING BY MEANS OF RFLPs. Certain enzymes exist, referred to as "restriction endonucleases," that recognize specific DNA nucleotide sequences and split the DNA molecule into two pieces at that site. Several restriction endonucleases have been identified that recognize different nucleotide sequences. If the enzymes are combined with a chromosome, they will cleave the DNA molecule into several pieces. Identical chromosomes would be cleaved in exactly the same places by the restriction endonucleases, and thus each chromosome would be divided into the same number of pieces that are also the same length. However, if one chromosome has a mutation that changes one of its nucleotides such that the nucleotide sequence now is not recognized by one of the enzymes, the chromosome will not be split at that site, and thus, after incubation with the restriction endonuclease mixture, will have one fewer piece. One of the pieces will be longer, incorporating what would be two pieces in the non-mutated chromosome. Alternatively, a mutation could change a nucleotide sequence such that it is now recognized by a restriction enzyme where it hadn't been previously, leading to an extra cleavage, yielding one extra DNA piece compared to the non-mutated chromosome. These differences in DNA molecules that are detected through the use of restriction enzymes are termed **restriction fragment length polymorphisms** (or RFLPs; see Figure 4-4). By use of different mixtures of restriction enzymes that yield similar or different DNA fragment lengths of chromosomes, it is possible to develop general location maps of specific mutations on the DNA chain, at least for mutations that affect the recognition site of a restriction endonuclease.

One of the restriction endonucleases is termed Alu, and this endonuclease was used when the first *Alu* transposon was discovered. Thus, the transposon was named for the restriction endonuclease.

MICROSATELLITES IN MAPPING. Because microsatellites are scattered at numerous places throughout the DNA molecule, they have been used as genetic markers for mapping purposes. The microsatellites are fairly easily detected using modern molecular genetics techniques, and their frequency and variability make them useful mapping tools.

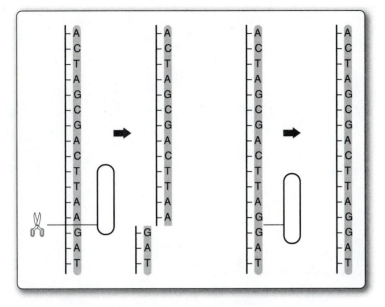

FIGURE 4-4 A restriction fragment length polymorphism. On the left, a restriction endonuclease cuts the DNA molecule after the sequence TAA; on the right, a DNA molecule that has substituted a single nucleotide, with a G for an A to form the sequence TAG, is not cut by that restriction endonuclease.

DNA SEQUENCING. The most direct way to map chromosomes is to actually discover the entire sequence of nucleotides that make up the DNA molecule. Because of the millions of nucleotides that make up any chromosome, sequencing whole chromosomes was thought to be nearly impossible. Development of rapid sequencing instruments and scaling up of laboratories into industrial-scale operations have made sequencing possible, and sequencing of the entire genome of several species of organisms, including humans, has been achieved. This remarkable accomplishment took considerable resources, including time, personnel, and money. However, now that general sequences for several species exist, it is possible to focus on small areas of chromosomes where individual nucleotide sequence differences exist and to actually map genetic variations between individual organisms within the same species.

It is impractical to directly sequence DNA molecules that are too long, so, in practice, sequencing efforts are carried out on segments of chromosomes. Often, these small chromosome sections are derived from restriction endonucleases. However, once the segments are sequenced, a difficult next step is to order the segments, so as to derive the entire chromosome sequence. This can be accomplished if different restriction endonucleases are used to break the chromosome into different segments, using overlapping portions of the segments to enable ordering.

POLYMERASE CHAIN REACTION. The ability to do large-scale sequencing, or to use RFLPs to map large areas of chromosomes, is dependent upon the availability of large amounts of DNA. One methodology, the polymerase chain reaction (or PCR), has transformed our ability to use DNA. The technique is based upon DNA's ability to replicate itself. The PCR is, in a sense, a production method for rapid DNA duplication (see Figure 4-5).

Epigenetics

Some of the features of an organism's phenotype are caused not by the order of nucleotides in their DNA, which defines genetic effects on the phenotype, but rather by processes involved in gene

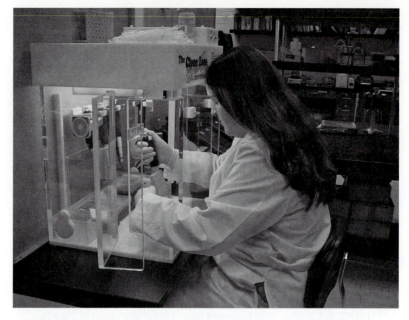

FIGURE 4-5 Photo of a molecular geneticist carrying out DNA sequencing.

expression. This quasi-genetic effect on phenotypic expression is termed **epigenetics**. A major process involved in epigenetic effects is methylation.

METHYLATION OF DNA. Methyl groups are small molecules consisting of a single carbon atom chemically bonded to hydrogen atoms. When methyl groups attach to the nucleotides of a given allele, they usually stop the expression of that allele. Thus, methylation of DNA controls which genes function at any given time within a cell. If there is either too much or too little methylation, or methylation in the wrong places of the genome, the cell's genetic activity functions inappropriately. This can lead to various problems, including the development of cancer (Pray 2004).

IMPRINTING. Differential methylation patterns can be inherited. For instance, it is normal for there to be differences in methylation of alleles inherited from one's father and mother, respectively. One example of this occurs with the insulin-like growth factor II gene, for which the maternally derived alleles are often methylated. This means that usually only the paternally derived alleles are active for this gene.

Imprinting is particularly interesting because it opens the possibility for Lamarckian inheritance: acquired characteristics (that is, methylation) of the parent can be passed down to their offspring through epigenetic mechanisms.

IN UTERO EFFECTS. There is another means by which non-genetic traits can be inherited in humans. If development of the fetus is impaired by an environmental factor (poor nutrition, infectious disease in the mother, etc.) the offspring's reproductive system can be affected. This usually has a greater effect on females, because their reproductive requirements are much more elaborate than that of males, although defects in sperm formation in male offspring of deprived mothers has been seen in experimental studies on rats, with these problems persisting for several generations (Anway et al. 2005). A daughter whose reproductive system development was impaired will have a greater chance of herself having an impaired daughter because of her condition, and this can continue for many generations. Maternal effects in early development can also make offspring more susceptible to diseases later in life, and this in turn can affect their reproduction, leading to effects in later generations.

A human example of a multiple generational epigenetic inheritance occurred due to a famine in the Netherlands during World War II. Women who were exposed to the famine in late pregnancy gave birth to small babies, and these babies had a high risk of developing diabetes later in life. The daughters of the women exposed to famine in turn had smaller infants, and this third generation is also at greater risk for diabetes (Stein and Lumey 2000; Gluckman et al. 2007).

EXTRACHROMOSOMAL GENETICS

Not all genetic processes occur in the cell nucleus, let alone on the chromosomes themselves. DNA is present in other eukaryotic cell structures, and the translation of RNA during protein synthesis occurs outside the nucleus. In addition, the messenger RNA (mRNA) molecule in eukaryotes must undergo processing before it is able to guide the translation of amino acid chains. Gene expression, the process by which a given sequence of DNA nucleotides leads to the production of a specific gene product, can be quite complex.

RNA Processing

Transcription of the DNA molecule into a complementary messenger RNA occurs within the cell nucleus. The mRNA is then transported out of the nucleus through pores in the nuclear membrane to ribosomal sites, where the mRNA information is translated into a chain of amino acids. The straightforward process of DNA transcription into messenger RNA, and translation of the mRNA into an amino acid chain (described in the previous chapter) is actually a better description of what occurs in prokaryotes than the process in eukaryotes, in which the process has become more elaborate.

INTRONS AND EXONS. Eukaryotes are more complex in many ways than prokaryotes. One important example is the presence of non-coding sections of DNA *within* the chromosomal locus for alleles. Thus, instead of a simple stretch of DNA nucleotides that, after transcription into mRNA, yields a sequence of triplet codons that specify the order of amino acids in a given protein, the mRNA that is transcribed from DNA in eukaryotes has within its length one or more sequences of nucleotides that do not specify amino acids. These stretches of non-coding mRNA are referred to as **introns**. The coding portions of the mRNA are referred to as **exons** (see Figure 4-6). Introns are quite variable in length, although they tend to be longer than exons, with introns averaging about 3,000 nucleotides in length, compared to only 150 or so nucleotides for each exon (Zorio and Bentley 2004).

The initial transcribed mRNA, which includes introns, is commonly termed "pre-mRNA." The introns must be precisely spliced out of the pre-mRNA molecule and the exons stitched together before the mature mRNA can be properly translated into a chain of amino acids. This splicing involves a highly complex procedure that occurs at a massive cellular structure termed the **spliceosome**, and involves several RNA molecules combined with protein (forming ribonucleoprotein complexes) (Nilsen 2003). The spliceosome is in part made up of small RNA-protein units termed **s**mall **n**uclear **r**ibo**n**ucleoprotein **p**articles (snRNPs). The RNA on the snRNPs attaches to specific mRNA base sequences at the boundary between exons and introns. These connections indicate where to splice out the intron (see Figure 4-7).

OTHER mRNA PROCESSING. There is yet another layer of complexity found in eukaryotic mRNA processing. Each pre-mRNA includes more than one exon, and it is possible for processing to result in the splicing of only some of the exons into a completed mRNA. Alternative splicing of the same pre-mRNA can lead to completed mRNAs that code for different proteins. This means that more

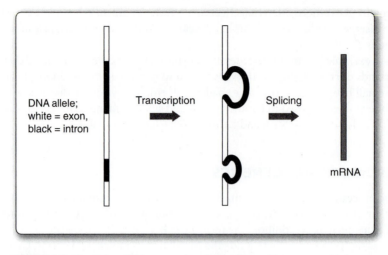

FIGURE 4-6 Messenger RNA processing: DNA allele with exons and introns; the introns are spliced out in the processing of mRNA.

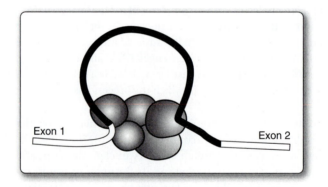

FIGURE 4-7 Messenger RNA processing in more detail. The gray spheres represent small nuclear ribonucleoprotein particles (snRNPs) that make up the spliceosome.

than one protein can be derived from the same gene, but the specific protein produced depends upon how the RNA processing is carried out. In fact, it has been estimated that approximately 35 percent of human genes undergo alternative splicing, with about 60 percent of gene products resulting from the alternative splicing, allowing about 35,000 genes to code for nearly 100,000 different proteins (Zorio and Bentley 2004; Black 2003).

WHY THE COMPLEXITY? The increased complexity in the protein synthesis process of all eukaryotes raises the question: why? Bacteria have gotten along nicely for over three billion years without a need for introns or for the complexities of RNA processing. There have been many explanations proposed; one suggestion being that the greater complexity of eukaryotes in general has necessitated a more complicated process for converting DNA sequences into the amino acid chains that comprise proteins, allowing multiple proteins to be derived from a single gene. This greater efficiency in the encoding of information on DNA would permit organisms to have smaller amounts of DNA in their nuclei.

WHEN THINGS GO WRONG. A process as complex as the conversion of pre-mRNA into mature mRNA inevitably exhibits occasional errors. There is evidence for a "surveillance" process that evaluates mRNA for mistakes, confining and eventually destroying defective mRNA molecules before they can reach the ribosomal translation site (Vasudevan and Peltz 2003). Despite this surveillance mechanism, errors in processing can occur, and these errors can lead to phenotypic consequences for the individual organism.

Mutations to chromosomal DNA can affect sites recognized by the spliceosome mechanism, leading to aberrant splicing and thus incorrect mRNAs. Of greater consequence is a mutation that leads to an alteration in a protein or ribonuclease component of the spliceosome itself, as this may lead to errors in many different proteins due to improper processing of pre-mRNA (Faustino and Cooper 2003).

An example of the first kind of mutation occurs in the disorder termed "familial isolated GH [growth hormone] deficiency type II" that is a dominantly inherited condition found in humans. The result of this condition is short stature (Cogan et al. 1994). The growth hormone gene usually contains five exons, and there is some amount (5 to 10 percent) of alternatively spliced mRNAs. In this disorder, there is an increased amount of alternative splicing of one of the exons.

An example of a human disorder related to a mutation in an element of the spliceosome itself is retinitis pigmentosa, a disease characterized by the degeneration of the retina and eventually leading to total blindness (Faustino and Cooper 2003). There are several forms of retinitis pigmentosa, involving at least three different proteins that form part of spliceosomes.

Mitochondrial DNA

Eukaryotes have other structures in their cells besides the nucleus. These structures are termed **organelles**. A particularly important organelle is the mitochondrion (the plural form is mitochondria), which serves as the cell "powerhouse." (see Figure 4-8). It is the site where aerobic metabolism takes place, involving many different enzymes that are involved in the breakdown of

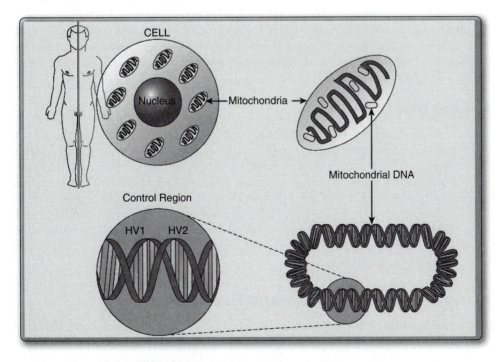

FIGURE 4-8 Mitochondria are organelles in cells. They contain DNA.

foods such as glucose (a simple sugar) into water and carbon dioxide, with the release of energy during the metabolic process. It has long been recognized that mitochondria contain their own DNA, with the DNA coding for several proteins, many involved with metabolism, as well as possessing elements necessary for replication, transcription, and protein synthesis. Mitochondria have thus been characterized as semi-autonomous organelles within the cells of eukaryotes (Saccone et al. 2000).

Mitochondria also produce their own ribosomes and some of their own transfer RNA, therefore containing their own protein-synthesis apparatus (Burger et al. 2003). However, many of the proteins that make up the mitochondria are actually coded for by alleles on nuclear DNA.

ORIGINS OF MITOCHONDRIA. Mitochondria apparently are derived from bacteria, and they may represent an ancient parasitic invasion of eukaryotic cells by bacteria that later became a cooperative mutual relationship in which the two organisms became dependent upon one another. This idea has been called the **endosymbiotic theory** (Margulis 1971; Gray et al. 1999).

MITOCHONDRIAL DNA. The DNA of mitochondria resembles that of bacteria much more than it does eukaryotic nuclear DNA. In most eukaryotes, mitochondrial DNA is found in a single chromosome, and this chromosome has long been thought to be circular, like bacterial chromosomes. However, the mitochondrial chromosome often maps as a linear structure, and it shows some features similar to eukaryotic nuclear DNA, such as short terminal repeats near its ends (Burger et al. 2003).

One important feature of mitochondrial DNA is that there are lower rates of recombination (exchange of DNA from one complementary DNA to another due to crossing over) than are found in nuclear DNA. In fact, at one time it was thought that recombination did not occur at all in mitochondrial DNA because chromosomes are not paired, as is true for nuclear DNA. Another important feature of mitochondrial DNA is that it is predominantly passed down maternally. This maternal inheritance happens because there are far more mitochondria in the mother's egg than are passed down through the father's sperm during reproduction. This has important implications for inheritance. An individual can trace his or her mitochondrial DNA back over generations to a single female ancestor (one's mother's mother's mother's mother's [etc.] mother). For nuclear DNA, one has two direct ancestors that are one generation removed (one's parents), four ancestors that are two generations removed (grandparents), eight ancestors after three generations (great grandparents), and 2^n ancestors after n generations. (Overlapping of ancestors will reduce the actual number of ancestors as one goes back in time.)

Chloroplast DNA

Separate DNA molecules are also found in the chloroplasts that are present in plant cells. These cellular organelles contain chlorophyll, the pigment used in photosynthesis that permits plants to produce sugars and other energy sources from sunlight. Like mitochondria, chloroplasts are thought to derive from endosymbiosis, in this case between a photosynthetic bacterium and a eukaryotic plant cell that acted as its host (Howe et al. 2003). Chloroplast DNA is usually found in a single circular chromosome, and it contains many fewer genes than are found in independent bacteria. It appears that, again like the mitochondrion, the chloroplast has lost DNA after its endosymbiotic relationship began with a eukaryotic host, with some of the necessary alleles now present in the plant's nuclear DNA.

TRACING GENETIC VARIABILITY AND FUNCTION

Alleles on chromosomes, and the messenger RNA coded by the chromosomal DNA, can now be identified quite readily through the use of sophisticated molecular techniques. It is also possible to detect differences in the alleles that are found at given loci on homologous chromosomes. It is, then, crucial to understand the functional implication of these differences for the organism.

Genetic Variability

It is interesting to characterize the degree of variability present in populations for genetic differences, and also to understand the functional consequences of the variability. Differences in an allele are referred to as **polymorphisms** [poly = many; morph = form].

SINGLE NUCLEOTIDE POLYMORPHISMS (SNPs). The simplest form of variation in an allele is an individual point mutation that leads to a change in a single nucleotide in a stretch of DNA. These **single nucleotide polymorphisms** (or SNPs, pronounced "snips") represent a substitution of one nucleotide for another. SNPs are found in large numbers throughout the genome of eukaryote species and can act as markers for chromosome mapping, as well as marking degrees of similarity between individual organisms, whether within the same species or from different species.

OLIGONUCLEOTIDE HYBRIDIZATION ANALYSIS. Oligonucleotides are short stretches of single-stranded DNA that can be synthesized in laboratories. Conditions can be set up in the lab so that a given oligonucleotide will only hybridize (pair up) with a complementary oligonucleotide if each nucleotide in the sequence matches with its homologue (A with T; G with C). If there is even one difference in the homologous oligonucleotide sequence, hybridization will not occur. One will have therefore identified a difference between the two chains, suggesting the presence of a SNP. Thus, this method of analysis can be used to identify two alleles at a given locus that differ by a SNP (Brown 1999). The hybridization analysis can be used to observe the number of SNPs over a given stretch of DNA (Pennisi 1998).

DNA CHIPS. A small square of silicon, less than a square inch in area, can be constructed that carries a matrix (an array with several rows and columns) of oligonucleotides attached to it in a given pattern. This silicon square is called a DNA chip. DNA of interest in a sample can be labeled with a chemical that causes fluorescence and then combined with the chip. Where the DNA in the sample hybridizes to one of the oligonucleotides on the chip, it will attach and be visible by examination of the chip with a fluorescence microscope (see Figure 4-9). Using this DNA chip technique, many SNPs can be detected in a single step (Wang et al. 1998).

OTHER ALLELE DIFFERENCES. Not all allele differences are due to single nucleotide differences, as are found in SNPs. Insertion and deletion of nucleotides can occur, and these can involve more than one nucleotide, including entire alleles or even longer stretches of chromosomes.

Understanding Gene Function

After genetic variability has been identified, the greater question is to understand the nature of the variability's functional consequence for the individual organism, and perhaps also for the population as a whole. A SNP is simply a single nucleotide difference in the DNA molecule; the consequence of such a difference can have little effect, or it can be a matter of life and death for an organism. Traditionally, in order to understand the consequences, geneticists need to map the SNP to a given allele and then trace what difference, if any, the DNA change has for the structure of the protein produced by the allele. Finally, geneticists have to be able to detect what functional change in the organism the altered protein causes. Using contemporary techniques, it is actually sometimes easier to do the final step, assessing the functional effects of a given SNP, than it is to trace specific changes in protein structure.

GENE INACTIVATION. Traditionally, gene function has been assessed in organisms by finding mutations at the locus in question and observing the effects of the mutation. Where the mutation is great enough that the allele loses its function entirely, the importance of that gene product for the overall functioning of the individual organism can be judged. A technique has been developed to inactivate a specific gene and then culture cells that contain the inoperative DNA to observe the

FIGURE 4-9 Photograph of a DNA chip. Light squares indicate where hybridization has occurred.

effects on phenotype caused by the absence of an allele that is normally operational. Much of the experimentation using this technique has been done on yeast, which are simple eukaryotic organisms. Yeast organisms are a far cry from humans, however. Although, obviously, this kind of experimentation cannot be done in humans, it is useful to experiment with a mammalian model. It has become common to use so-called "knockout mice" (mice who have a gene "knocked out" of function) to trace the effects on phenotype of a given allele's absence. Homologous alleles in humans (based primarily on similarity of nucleotide sequence) are assumed to have a similar function.

An organism's phenotype encompasses many things, so it is not always a simple process to identify the phenotypic effect of inactivating a given gene. If inactivation leads to death, particularly if the death occurs in a fetal stage, it may be quite difficult to identify just what caused the death. On the other extreme, gene inactivation effects may be quite subtle. The effects may also vary depending upon the environment an organism lives in.

RNA INTERFERENCE. Geneticists have been able to use another technique to stop the expression of selected genes in an organism. This mechanism is referred to as **RNA interference**. Research originally carried out with plant cells showed that the presence of long, double-stranded RNA molecules sets off a strong, general cessation of DNA transcription into mRNA and subsequent translation of mRNA into proteins (Duxbury and Whang 2004). Later work with mammalian cells showed that introduction of short segments of double-stranded RNA (21-23 nucleotides long) suppressed gene expression in a much more specific manner. This gene suppression in the presence of double-stranded RNA is thought to be a natural antiviral response by organisms, since many viruses employ RNA instead of DNA as their genetic material and at some stage of their infection make double-stranded RNA (Downward 2004).

Geneticists can use this antiviral response to cause silencing of specific genes in an organism by creating double-stranded RNA molecules that match the sequence of codons of mRNA transcribed from the organism's own alleles. The organism's cellular response will cause it to stop all protein synthesis from that allele, and thus one can observe changes in phenotype due to inactivation of a given gene.

There are potential practical applications of RNA interference, as well. For instance, it is all too common when the body is fighting cancer for malignant cells to become resistant to multiple anti-cancer drugs. In part, this can be caused by the cells adapting to the drugs through accelerated production of P-glycoprotein, a chemical that transports drugs out of cells, by increasing the protein synthesis rate from the gene that codes for this chemical. RNA silencing techniques are being developed to stop this accelerated synthesis of P-glycoprotein, and thus reduce the cancer cell's resistance to standard drug therapy (Lucentini 2004).

GENE OVEREXPRESSION. Another means to understand the effects of a gene is to observe what occurs when gene activity is greatly increased. A common means to do this is to insert multiple copies of the allele into the organism's cells along with (or next to) a regulatory section of DNA that will promote transcription. The idea is that the allele's effects will be readily apparent in the individual because of its great activity. However, one must be mindful that such overexpression is not natural to the organism, so at least some of the phenotypic change observed may be due to this abnormality (Brown 1999).

A Brief Look at Quantitative Genetics

In fact, most characteristics of organisms that can be observed in the phenotype are due to the action of multiple genes, combined with the effects of many environmental factors. A measure of the degree of importance of genetic versus environmental factors on any given characteristic is expressed as the heritability of the characteristic, as noted in the previous chapter.

BASIS OF QUANTITATIVE GENETICS. The basis for quantitative genetics is the notion that several alleles can impact a single characteristic in differing ways, and the action of these multiple alleles can lead to traits that seem continuous in variation (such as difference in body height), as opposed to discrete (such as blood types). For instance, supposing that three different loci (A, B, and C), each with two possible alleles (Aa, Bb, and Cc, respectively) are involved in determining some trait, then there are 27 possible allele combinations:

AABBCC, AaBBCC, aaBBCC, AABbCC, AaBbCC, aaBbCC, AAbbCC, AabbCC, aabbCC,

AABBCc, AaBBCc, aaBBCc, AABbCc, AaBbCc, aaBbCc, AAbbCc, AabbCc, aabbCc,

AABBcc, AaBBcc, aaBBcc, AABbcc, AaBbcc, aaBbcc, AAbbcc, Aabbcc, aabbcc.

If each allele makes a somewhat different contribution to the trait, there will be 27 categorical states that an individual can have regarding the trait. Allowing for environmental effects, a phenotypic trait influenced by these three loci could appear to be continuous. If there are additional loci, or if more alleles are present at each locus, the possible genetic combinations increase significantly. Thus, continuous traits can be explained by the effects of discrete, multiple polymorphic loci, and therefore basic Mendelian genetics concepts can be used to explain these traits.

HERITABILITY. The degree to which variability in a quantitative trait is caused by genetic versus environmental effects is assessed by the **heritability index** (H^2). The heritability index is a measure of genetic contribution to variability in the phenotypic trait, within the range of environmental circumstances that is present for the studied population. H^2 will differ for the same trait if the range of environmental circumstances changes. Actually, the variance in the phenotypic trait is a result of the sum of three factors: that due to the genetic variance, to the environmental variance, and to the interaction between genetics and environment. In general, H^2 near 1.0 signifies a trait whose variance is primarily due to genetics, whereas H^2 near 0.0 signifies a trait whose variance is primarily caused by environmental conditions.

HUMAN GENETICS AND THE HUMAN GENOME

The study of human genetics is very difficult in comparison to the study of most other species. Humans are long-lived and slow-reproducing organisms, usually having only one offspring at a time, making it difficult to observe the effects of varying conditions on offspring. It is also both abhorrent morally and impossible in practice to perform mating experiments on humans. This eliminates our ability to take advantage of many major genetic methods for understanding, characterizing, and mapping the genetic basis of human traits. Human geneticists attempt to make use of **natural experiments**, where natural conditions occur in circumstances that allow for some control over factors that may otherwise affect the traits of interest. Still, progress on the study of human genetics has been made, to the point where "human genetic variation" was named the "Breakthrough of the Year" for 2007 by the journal *Science* (Pennisi 2007).

Family Studies in Human Genetics

Study of traits that run in families provides evidence for genetic input into these characteristics. However, human geneticists must attempt to distinguish familial influences on traits from strictly genetic influences. Some traits may run in families (that is, are familial) due solely to shared environmental conditions among family members, while other traits common to family members may be due to strong genetic input.

TWIN STUDIES. A major means for separating environmental from genetic influences within family members is the study of the degree of concordance (individuals having the same characteristic) of traits based on the degree of genetic relatedness. For instance, siblings (brothers and sisters) are more genetically similar (sharing genes from their two parents) than first cousins (sharing genes from two of their four grandparents). However, in many populations, siblings also share a more similar environment than do first cousins, who may live in a different household. A better means of measuring concordance is comparing identical twins (monozygotic twins, who share 100 percent of their genes) with fraternal twins (dizygotic twins, who share the same proportion of genes as do any pair of brothers and/or sisters). Here one assumes that each type of twin shares the same general environment and that any greater concordance one finds among the monozygotic twins is due to genetic causes. This may not always be the case; because monozygotic twins look so much more alike than fraternal twins do, they might be treated more similarly (and thus have more equal environments) than are dizygotic twins.

A better scenario is to compare monozygotic twins raised apart. Here, one can observe the effects of differing environments on the same overall genetic blueprint. Unfortunately, this situation is fairly rare, and therefore studies making use of this technique are difficult and small in scale. Another difficulty with all twin studies is that twins actually have shared an intrauterine environment (although each twin may have had somewhat differing conditions depending on variations within the womb) and thus have a greater shared environment during development than singleton people. Thus, twins may be a special case, making projections from results of twin studies to all of humanity suspect.

A classic example of the use of twin studies to attempt to understand the heritability of a human trait has been work on alcoholism. This affliction has variously been considered an individual weakness, an environmentally caused disease, or a genetically based affinity. Most studies that have compared monozygotic twins with dizygotic twins have tended to show greater concordance among monozygotic twins, suggesting that there is a genetic component to alcoholism (Kaij 1960; Loehlin 1972), although equivocal results were found in a large study of twins in Finland (Partanen et al. 1966), in which stronger alcoholism problems were observed to have greater concordance in monozygotic twins than was true for those with milder alcoholism problems. Part of the difficulty is the imprecise, or at least differing, definition of alcoholism in various studies.

ADOPTION STUDIES. Yet another method for differentiating between environmental and genetic contributions to human traits is to study adopted children, comparing concordances between the children and both their biological and adopted parents. Traits with a strong environmental component are likely to be more concordant between children and adopted parents, while traits that are primarily due to genetic influences will have greater concordance among children and their biological parents. Adoption studies related to alcoholism have generally shown greater concordance between children and their biological parents compared to with their adopted parents (Cloninger et al. 1981). These studies also suggest that different forms of alcoholism have differing heritability, with a form of the affliction found chiefly in males that has an early onset and an association with behavioral problems having greater heritability than other forms of the disease.

The Human Genome

The **genome** refers to the total genetic information in an organism: the total of all DNA in each cell. The incredible suite of molecular techniques available to scientists today permits a view of the entire genome of organisms. In the past, understanding of any given gene and its role in an organism's structure and function was a life's work. In fact, full understanding of the effects of any single gene is still a daunting enterprise. However, we can now observe all the genes present in a species and attempt to understand the interactions of all the individual genes, including the workings of RNA processing, that lead to an individual organism's total phenotype and to the variability between individuals in the species.

The sequencing of all of the DNA in several species, including humans, is now complete. Geneticists are working to identify each individual allele that makes up the genome and what proteins these alleles code for.

Advances in genomics can lead to important medical breakthroughs. Gene therapy is an intriguing possibility, with treatment of genetic disorders (perhaps due to a given allele's malfunctioning) occurring through the insertion of working genes into human cells. There are still difficult challenges to overcome before gene therapy lives up to its promise, primarily in finding means of transporting genes into the cells without causing unintended negative consequences (Friedmann 1997). On the opposite track, therapeutic advances may be possible through halting of detrimental gene activity. RNA silencing methods are one possible approach to the problem.

The Human Genome Project

One of the incredible achievements of modern molecular genetics has been the completion of the sequencing of the entire human genome. Because of the sheer size of the undertaking— there are about three billion nucleotides in human nuclear DNA—advances in developing laboratory robots to automate the sequencing project, and even advances in the information technology to allow handling such huge data sets, were required to complete the Human Genome Project. Now scientists—must determine which sequences are parts of alleles and which are outside the alleles, which are exons and which are introns, and so forth. Still more difficult will be assigning functions to each of the alleles. From an anthropological standpoint, the project's greatest value will be in allowing a clearer view of the degree of genetic variability among humans—both on the individual and population level. Identification of the SNPs that are present, and the rates at which these variants are present in given populations, will permit greater understanding of the relationships among populations and even permit estimates of the time scale of human diversification. It has been estimated that about 15 million SNPs may be present in the human genome; as of 2007, approximately three million had been charted and placed on a genetic map of human SNPs termed the "HapMap." We will take up the topic of human genetic variation again in more detail in Chapter 7.

PROFILE 4
J. Koji Lum

Dr. Koji Lum is a human geneticist and anthropologist who uses molecular genetics as a tool to understand both the history of human migrations and population interactions in the past, and the intersection of genetics and disease in the present. One area of his research explores the prehistory and origins of Pacific Island peoples. His work on mitochondrial DNA (mtDNA) has provided evidence that both Polynesians and Micronesians have a shared ancestry with people from Southeast Asia. He also has examined mtDNA of Native American peoples from Ecuador, and in peoples of south India and Southeast Asia, and these studies have increased our understanding of the complex population dynamics of these regions. Dr. Lum has also studied the genetics of the animals and parasites that people have brought with them on their migrations.

Another aspect of Dr. Lum's research involves study of the genetics and ecology of malaria in human populations, both in Africa and particularly in the Pacific Islands. He has examined archived blood samples of Pacific Island peoples from several decades ago to note genetic changes in malaria parasites that are related to resistance to chloroquinine, an important anti-malarial drug. His research has also shown that spread of malaria on individual islands in the Pacific archipelago of Vanuatu is primarily due to movement of the disease's mosquito vectors, while the spread of malaria between islands is primarily due to the movement of people. Genetic studies have shown that mosquitoes travel only short distances on a given island, and this finding has implications in Vanuatu for mosquito control, and thus malaria control.

Dr. Lum is Associate Professor of Anthropology and Biological Sciences and Director of the Laboratory of Evolutionary Anthropology and Health at Binghamton University. His research interests also include study of ancient DNA, use of DNA in forensics, polymorphisms of neurotransmitters and their connection with behavior, and molecular evolution.

The Next Step?

Perhaps the next major step to be taken in genetic research is a deeper exploration of the actual protein products produced by the genetic process. This has led several scientists to point to the science of **proteomics** as the next frontier in molecular biology research (Ezzell 2002). In proteomics, studying the complete network of proteins in an organism (the "proteome") will permit understanding of how this network controls cellular and organismal functions. Right now, our understanding of protein structure trails our sophisticated knowledge of DNA and RNA structure, and our techniques for studying proteins on the molecular level are also much more poorly developed. Still, the incredible advances in molecular biology have revolutionized our ability to understand how organisms, including humans, survive, function, and reproduce.

CHAPTER SUMMARY

The human genome is more than a simple string of genes that each code for a specific protein. The majority of human DNA does not code for proteins at all. The genome consists of portions of DNA that are transcribed into messenger RNA and later translated into protein chains (these parts of the DNA are termed "exons"). The genome also consists of long stretches of repeated sequences of DNA between genes, stretches of non-coded DNA within genes (termed "intervening sequences," or "introns"), and areas that function as regulatory regions where enzymes attach and determine which genes are transcribed into messenger RNA at what time.

Genes can be mapped as to which chromosome they are located on, as well as where they are located on the chromosome. Mapping has been done through studies of crossing over, where alleles on one chromosome become exchanged with the matching allele on a homologous chromosome during meiosis. Chances of crossing over increase with distance along a chromosome. Mapping can also be done through the actual sequencing of the nucleotides on a chromosome. The polymerase chain reaction, in which many copies are made of a given stretch of DNA, allows sequencing of large stretches of the genome. In many species, including humans, the entire genome (at least of a single individual) has been sequenced.

When variation exists among alleles at a given locus, the locus is said to be "polymorphic." The simplest type of polymorphism is a SNP, or single nucleotide polymormorphism. Other polymorphisms can include differences in alleles due to substitution, deletion, or duplication of one or more nucleotides. Gene function can be discerned by means of inactivation of alleles at a given locus and observing the organism for the effects caused by the absence of the gene's activity.

Many traits are influenced by multiple alleles (so-called "polygenic traits") that interact to produce a given phenotype. Some traits are passed down through generations that are not due to the sequence of DNA nucleotides, but rather to "epigenetic" phenomena, such as methylation of DNA that affects the regulation of what genes are transcribed at what time, and events that occur *in utero* that affect the individual's later reproductive processes. Traits are also influenced by environmental effects, and thus an organism's phenotype is a product of the interaction of multiple genes, the environment, the interaction between the environment and genes, and epigenetic effects. A measure of how much of a population's phenotypic variability is attributable to genetics as opposed to environmental phenomena is termed "heritability," with a range from 1.0 (entirely due to genetics) to 0.0 (entirely due to environment).

Human genetics is no different from other mammals' genetic processes, or much different from any eukaryotic organism. However, it is more difficult to discern details of human genetics because of the long lifespan of humans, the immorality of conducting breeding experiments with our species, and the great influence of behavior on all of our phenotypic traits. Geneticists derive estimates of heritability from observing traits that are passed down in families, by studying identical twins who share the same genome, and by comparing adopted versus biological offspring. The Human Genome Project has succeeded in determining the entire sequence of the human genome. Information from this project serves as the basis for improving our understanding of human genetics, from tracing ancestry of individuals to understanding the genetic basis of many diseases.

CHAPTER 5

Macroevolution and Taxonomy

Microevolution, as we have seen, occurs due to changes in allele frequencies from one generation to another. Macroevolution, however, encompasses processes that often take thousands of generations, resulting in major changes in the average phenotypes of populations. These processes can be quite complex, incorporating long-term microevolutionary processes, but additionally involving other considerations, such as major extinction events. These other considerations may be systematic, but they may also be somewhat random. A full consideration goes well beyond the bounds of our concern with human biology, but some basic concepts are relevant. First, however, a discussion of how organisms are classified is warranted.

TAXONOMY

Even a superficial observation of living organisms reveals many impressive similarities among all living things. They all share nucleic acids and proteins as their building blocks; they all have (or use, in the case of viruses) cells as major constituents. We can also easily see that organisms can be divided into groups that share basic characteristics, such as unicellular versus multicellular organisms, and, among the latter, plants, fungi, and animals. Evolutionary biologists have shown that many of these similarities are due to common ancestry: descent from a single population of organisms. Darwin referred to this as "descent with modification." Thus, all animals are believed to have descended from a single population, and similarly, all plants derive from a common ancestral population. Still further back in time, one would find a common ancestor for all multicellular organisms, whether plant, fungus, or animal.

Biologists have attempted to classify organisms according to their similarities, intending the classification to show "natural" groupings. This classification is termed biological **taxonomy** and is particularly associated with the monumental work of Linnaeus in the eighteenth century. Since Darwin's time, this "natural" grouping is presumed to show similarity of descent. Much as in a family tree, close relatives (siblings who share common parents, first cousins who share common grandparents) are distinguished from more distant relatives (second cousins who share common great-grandparents, third cousins who share common great-great-grandparents, and so on).

Species and Speciation

SPECIES. For biologists, the fundamental unit of taxonomy is the **species**. The species represents a grouping of organisms within which individual organisms can interbreed (independent of human intervention) and produce fertile offspring. Familiar species receive common names by people and these species are usually quite easily recognized: humans, cows, pigs, cats, dogs, oak trees, morels, and so on. Sometimes we do not distinguish separate species as easily, grouping many insect species into "cockroaches," many plant species into "grass," and so forth. A closer look at the organisms in these categories usually allows biologists to distinguish different species. There are cases, however, where even a closer look yields problems in distinguishing closely related species.

Horses and donkeys are seen as separate species, but they do sometimes interbreed, yielding female jennies or male mules. These offspring are usually infertile, though, and from this result we can see that horses and donkeys are indeed separate species. There are cases where it is even more difficult to distinguish species, especially when considering sibling species and "semispecies."

SIBLING SPECIES AND "SEMISPECIES." Some species are so similar in general appearance that even detailed observation fails to distinguish them. However, mating experiments or biochemical tests will allow such species to be separated into groups. These closely related species are referred to as **sibling species**. An example cited by Edward O. Wilson (1992) is the protozoans traditionally classified into the three species *Paramecium aurelia, P. bursaria, P. bursaria* and *P. caudatum*. Observations of mating behavior have shown that there are actually at least 20 species of these protozoans. Sibling species have also been well studied among the genus of fruit flies so dearly loved by geneticists, *Drosophila*. A clear example is found in the two species *D. pseudoobscura* and *D. persimilis*. These two species appear to be identical. Eventually, however, workers found subtle differences in the anatomy of the male genitalia, although females remain structurally indistinguishable. The species can be identified by mating behavior: hybrid males are sterile (Dobzhansky 1970).

Semi-species are even more closely related. They consist of populations that partially interbreed and produce many hybrid individuals (Wilson 1992). This is fairly common among plants that rely on wind pollination, where pollen from distant populations may reach the flower of an organism from a closely related species. In fact, the oak trees noted earlier as comprising an easily recognized species are actually comprised of several semi-species (Whittemore and Schaal 1991). Understanding why species do not necessarily come in easily recognized packets, but rather sometimes seem to blend together, requires knowledge of how new species are created, a process termed **speciation**.

SPECIATION. Speciation refers to the creation of new species. In the traditional view, two steps are required:

1. Complete **geographical isolation** of biological populations. During isolation, genetic differences in the separated populations build up due to the microevolutionary processes of mutation, natural selection, and chance events (genetic drift).

2. Development of **reproductive isolation**. The genetic differences between the separated populations build up, eventually getting to the point where genes won't pair up properly during meiosis, or where any other difference develops that prevents fertile hybrids from being produced. These differences are such that if the geographically isolated populations come together again, little or no intermating occurs. In fact, reproductive isolation defines different species. Moreover, once geographic isolation ends, competition between the two new species would ensue, as they presumably would remain similar enough to overlap in their resource needs.

This traditional model of speciation is referred to as **allopatric speciation** because it requires geographic isolation (allopatric = "of different countries") and is illustrated in Figure 5-1. It is considered to be one form of a speciation type termed **cladogenesis** (literally, creation by splitting) because it results in the creation of two species from an original single species.

FIGURE 5-1 Allopatric speciation. In this example, a species of bird resides on a continent, but some individual birds are blown in a storm to an island. After time, the bird populations on the continent and island become reproductively isolated, resulting in speciation.

Biologists have debated whether speciation can occur without complete geographic isolation. In recent times, evidence has accumulated that speciation can indeed occur when total geographical isolation is not present. This is termed **sympatric speciation** (sympatric = "of the same country"), and is another form of cladogenesis. There are several possible ways for sympatric speciation to occur, including:

1. Seasonal isolation. For instance, if one population is only reproductively active in early spring, and another population of the same species changes such that reproductive activity occurs later in the spring, the populations will not interbreed even though they live in the same area. Alexander (1968) gives credible evidence that this situation has occurred in at least one species of North American cricket in the genus *Gryllus. G. veletis*, the northern spring cricket, breeds from May to July, while *G. pennsylvanicus* breeds from July to October. Alexander postulates that they derive from an ancestral, tropical species that moved into northern regions requiring seasonal breeding and overwintering in juvenile and/or egg stages, because soon after hatching the early instars are not cold resistant. Some individuals developed adaptations for fall breeding and overwintering in a nymphal (juvenile) stage of development, while others developed adaptations for spring breeding and overwintering in the egg stage of development. The differences in breeding stages led to reproductive isolation between the two adaptive types, leading to what has been termed "allochronic speciation" (allochronic = "of different times").

2. Other timing differences. Cicadas provide a particularly interesting example. The so-called periodical cicadas of the *Magicicada* genus are insects that live underground as nymphs in a pre-reproductive state for either 13 or 17 years. They emerge and live as adults for approximately three weeks, during which time reproductive activity occurs. Adult females lay eggs, which soon hatch into nymphs that burrow into the ground, remaining there for another 13 to 17 years before emerging. There is evidence that 13-year cicada species in the U.S. Midwest have recently derived from 17-year cicadas due to changes in the timing of their life cycle (Simon et al. 2000). This is another example of allochronic speciation.

3. Habitat isolation. If one population adapted to a **habitat** that was slightly different from that of other populations of a species (and developed different ecological requirements, thus developing a different ecological **niche**), then the populations would effectively be isolated, even though they resided in the same general area. For instance, many insect species are highly specialized in interacting with the type of plant species on which they live. If some individuals move onto neighboring plant species and evolve adaptations to that new species, they could rapidly speciate, even though they live in proximity to each other (Wilson 1992). This has apparently occurred among fruit flies in the genus *Rhagoletis*, the species of which are highly specialized to live on different species of fruit trees. *R. pomonella* lives on hawthorn trees in North America but was observed in the mid-nineteenth century to have moved into European-derived apple trees. Furthermore, in the 1960s, *R. pomenella* began to be found on cherry trees. The fly populations on apple trees have apparently achieved "incipient species" status, becoming reproductively isolated, in part, from the populations residing on hawthorns (Feder et al. 1988; Filchak et al. 2000). The trees that these flies inhabit differ in the season in which their fruit matures, providing the possibility for allochronic speciation as well as habitat separation.

4. Speciation could occur within a widespread polytypic (literally "many types," or having much variability) species in which intermediate varieties in the species' range die out, leaving range extremes that are reproductively isolated. An improbable example would occur if all dog breeds except chihuahuas and great danes died out, leading to the sudden appearance of two different dog species. The frog species *Rana pipiens* provides a better example. It has a range from Canada to Central America, and its northern populations adapt better to cold temperatures (Moore 1949; 1950). Populations of the species also show distinct seasonal differences in breeding dates at different points in its geographical range. Populations of *Rana pipiens* in Canada have breeding seasons in May or June, while populations further south in New York breed in April, and populations in Georgia and Florida breed year-round. Hybridization experiments (Porter 1941) showed that nearby populations mated successfully, as did populations from distant areas but similar latitudes (such as Vermont and Wisconsin), but hybrids between populations from widely different latitudes were much less successful (Dobzhansky 1970). If middle-latitude populations should become extinct for any reason, speciation of *Rana pipiens* into northern and southern species would result.

ADAPTIVE RADIATION. There is a special kind of speciation that occurs when a population of organisms contacts a whole series of possible living arrangements. For example, go back to the scenario shown in Figure 5-1 in which a bird species is blown onto an island that previously contained no birds. The birds will tend to get rapid specializations for each type of ecological niche available on the island, leading to habitat isolation and speciation into a number of new species. This occurs very rapidly in evolutionary time and is referred to as an **adaptive radiation**. It may be viewed as simply a number of cladogenesis speciation events that occurs in a relatively short period of time (in geological terms). The term "adaptive radiation" may overemphasize the importance of adaptation in these periods of rapid diversification, but the term is common in evolutionary biology and so will be used here. A classic example of an adaptive radiation occurred among Hawaiian honeycreepers. These birds, named for the way they "creep" or flutter about while in search of food, are noted for having divergent bill shapes that complement their diverse food sources (see Figure 2-7). It is believed that a single species was introduced to Hawaii seven or eight million years ago, and then underwent an adaptive radiation, with currently 26 species extant (Freed et al. 1987; Johnson et al. 1989; Feldman 1994). Many more species existed in Hawaii before humans first arrived.

RAPID DIVERGENT EVOLUTION IN OVERLAPPING INCIPIENT SPECIES. One important point should be kept in mind: no matter what manner by which speciation by cladogenesis occurs, if the two new species have overlapping ranges, there will be very strong selective pressures to avoid interbreeding. This is because those who interbreed have, by definition, much lowered reproductive success. Thus, one might expect to find very rapid divergent evolution once speciation occurs.

There are several isolating mechanisms found between similar species with overlapping ranges. A major one involves various forms of behavioral isolation. Commonly, species develop differences in mating behavior (that is, behavior that is directly or indirectly related to the choosing and convincing of potential mates). As a result, the two species are not sexually attracted. The classic examples are birdsongs and various forms of mating displays.

Another isolating mechanism is termed "mechanical isolation." Species develop changes in the structure of the genitalia or flower parts such that sex is difficult or impossible. This is especially common in plants, where behavior has less of an impact on mating.

When mating does occur, different species remain reproductively isolated in other ways. There may be fertilization problems. For example, sperm from one species might not be able to penetrate the egg of the other species, or sperm cannot survive in females of the other species, or pollen tubes won't form in the correct shape to allow fertilization of the other species. If fertilization does occur, offspring are usually nonviable. In this case, offspring don't survive (or rarely survive) to reproductive age. Often, since genes pair up poorly, maladaptive recessive traits appear, or traits are poorly coadapted. If offspring survive, they may be infertile, as in the case of mules. This may be due to gene-pairing problems, making it difficult for meiosis to occur properly so as to produce functional gametes.

Finally, there may be cases in which some offspring are reproductively viable, but the bad effects of hybridization take a few generations to manifest themselves. This delayed effect of hybridization is termed **hybrid breakdown**. The first generation may appear to function well, or at least not be totally selected out, but later generations do more poorly. An example of this is found among duck species, where hybrids are completely fertile, but, nevertheless, hybridization is rare in nature (Mayr 1970). Hybrid breakdown may be due to the genetic phenomenon of crossing-over, where after a few generations several genes from the different species may be situated on the same chromosome. Then, since an individual only passes one of each pair of chromosomes to its offspring, the offspring may have a mixture of genes from the two ancestral species such that neither of the ancestral species provides at least one of each gene pair. If the genes are poorly coadapted, they may not function properly. For instance, one can imagine a scenario in which one gene might produce substance A in the body, while a second gene produces substance B. A and B react chemically to form some necessary substance C. If there are slightly different forms of A and B in the two species, such that one species's A will not react properly with the other species's B, then substance C won't be formed, and the organism cannot survive.

It is apparent that the more time and/or energy an individual places in reproductive activity with individuals of another species, the greater the selective disadvantage for that individual, since the reproduction is bound to be unsuccessful. Thus, behavioral or mechanical isolating mechanisms usually evolve quickly when similar species have overlapping ranges. This happens because those mechanisms are much more advantageous for reproductive success than the other processes noted here.

ANAGENESIS. It is also possible for speciation to occur simply as a result of changes in a species that build up over time. In this case, there is no splitting into two species. Rather, one species simply develops enough change over time such that evolutionary scientists judge that its descendants would not mate with the ancestral forms even if it were possible to get them together. Unfortunately, since time machines do not exist, there is no way to do a mating experiment. Instead, evolutionary scientists resort to observing biological structure. If the structure of descendants is as different from that of their ancestors (based on fossil evidence) as the differences seen between individuals in two different but closely related species in the present, it is assumed that speciation has occurred. This type of speciation where no "splitting" occurs is termed **anagenesis**.

EVOLUTIONARY SIGNIFICANCE OF SPECIES. Because the species represents a reproductive unit, with all successful reproduction occurring within the boundaries of the species, a species can be variously viewed as: a reproductive community, a genetic unit, and an ecological unit (since the individuals share basic adaptive traits that are codified in their shared genetic heritage). As a result, species may also be viewed as the primary unit of evolution. As noted in Chapter 2, individuals do not evolve, it is species that evolve.

Taxonomic Units above the Species Level

While species form the primary unit of biological taxonomy, several other units, or **taxa** (singular: taxon), are commonly used by biologists. Again, the primary basis for taxonomy is evolutionary relatedness, and these taxa reflect that relatedness.

GENERA. A group of closely related species is placed into a single **genus** (plural: genera). Genera represent species that have speciated relatively recently (based on geological time) from a common ancestor. A classic example among mammals is the grouping of dogs and wolves into the genus *Canis* (*familiaris* and *lupus*, respectively).

FAMILIES. Families are composed of collections of related genera that have shared a common ancestry a bit further back in time; among mammals this is often in the range of 15 to 20 million years or so. Examples include the dog family, which contains dogs, wolves, coyotes, foxes, etc.; and the cat family, which contains cats, lions, tigers, leopards, cheetahs, jaguars, and so on.

ORDERS. Orders are groups of families that trace ancestry to a common ancestor that speciated further back in time (in mammals this is typically about 65 million years ago or so, but there is much variability). Examples include rodents, carnivores (which include dogs, cats, bears, hyenas, weasels, badgers, raccoons, and so on), and primates.

CLASSES. Classes are groupings of related orders that share common ancestry. Often, classes also share special basic adaptations. Ages of classes are very variable (for example, fish—Pisces—are a much older taxon than mammals), but the degree of diversity within them is usually about the same. Classes are often formed from a past adaptive radiation. Examples include mammals, birds, reptiles, and fish.

PHYLA. Phyla (singular: phylum) are groups of classes that share a common ancestor. Phyla are usually fairly old in evolutionary terms (on the order of 500 million years or older). Organisms in a phylum usually share basic structural traits. Examples of phyla among animals include chordates (a phylum that includes all of the vertebrates as well as some other organisms), arthropods, and mollusks.

KINGDOMS. Kingdoms are the highest taxon. Biologists traditionally recognize a total of five kingdoms: Monera (that is, precells, also termed "Prokaryotae"), Protoctista (or Protista), Animals, Plants, and Fungi (Margulis and Schwartz 1988). Kingdoms are made up of evolutionarily related phyla. Many biologists believe, based on genetic comparisons, that living organisms are better divided into three major groupings: Bacteria, Archaea, and Eukaryotes. Archaea are a group of organisms that traditionally were included as a type of bacteria in the Monera kingdom. They are genetically quite distinct from other bacteria, however, and have more in common with the Eukaryotes ("true cells," or those organisms, including multicellular forms, that have organelles such

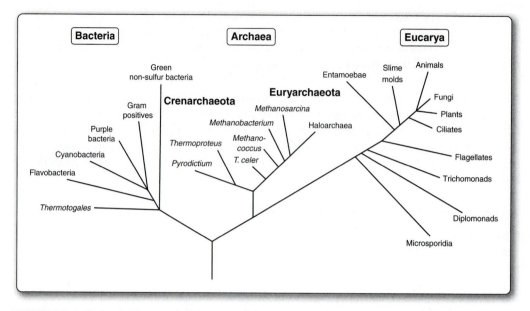

FIGURE 5-2 A phylogenetic tree of major taxonomic groupings of organisms, based on ribosomal RNA comparisons.

as nuclei, mitochondria, Golgi bodies, etc. within their cells, and include the traditionally named kingdoms of Protoctista, Fungi, Plants, and Animals). Figure 5-2 (above) shows a phylogenetic tree of all living organisms, based upon comparisons of ribosomal RNA sequences.

TWO TAXONOMIC EXAMPLES: PEOPLE AND DOGS. As examples of taxonomic classification, here are the taxa in which humans and dogs, respectively, are placed:

	People	**Dogs**
Kingdom:	Animalia	Animalia
Phylum:	Chordata	Chordata
Class:	Mammalia	Mammalia
Order:	Primates	Carnivora
Family:	Hominidae	Canidae
Genus:	Homo	Canis
Species:	Sapiens	Familiaris

As can be seen, dogs and people share the same kingdom, phylum, and class, since both are mammals. They are in different orders of mammals, however, and thus are placed in different orders, families, genera, and species.

INTERMEDIATE LEVELS OF TAXONOMY. Taxonomy is intended to be a tool for biologists, allowing categorization of species into groupings that reflect their relative degree of relationship to each other. It is often useful for biologists to make intermediate categories in order to further detail degrees of relatedness. In the Primates order, taxa include the suborder, which consist of major groupings within the order as a whole, and superfamilies, which are groups of related families within each suborder. Humans, for instance, are placed in the Anthropoid suborder, which includes monkeys and apes as well as humans, and the Hominoid superfamily, which includes only the apes and humans.

SUBSPECIES OR RACES. One of taxonomy's intermediate categories meriting separate discussion is the **subspecies**. This is a unit within a species, intended to identify populations or population clusters that differ in genetic makeup from other populations or population clusters. Here, the genetic differences are not sufficient to lead to reproductive isolation, and thus range overlap will lead to intermating and production of fully viable offspring. A subspecies is therefore usually based upon geographic isolation that permits differences in allele frequencies to develop between populations. Once range overlap occurs, the subspecies's differences are rapidly reduced due to intermating. Thus, subspecies may be ephemeral, disappearing over time, or, with extended geographic isolation, they may be the precursors to new species.

Humans are spread over most of the earth's land surface. Until recently, most human travel took a long time. In particular, human populations were partly isolated by oceans, deserts, and mountain chains. These barriers slowed gene flow between populations. There has been much controversy over whether human subspecies, or biological races, exist. This topic merits special consideration and will be explored in the next chapter. A more general controversy within taxonomy will be addressed here: should common ancestry be the only criterion for the classification of living organisms?

TAXONOMY DEBATES. One would not think a field as apparently straightforward as taxonomy would generate passionate debate, but that is just what has occurred among taxonomists in deciding whether common ancestry should be the sole criterion for classification. Some biologists answer unequivocally "yes." Others believe that general structural similarities should be a major consideration. The debate is actually more complex.

Some taxonomists, termed **cladists**, believe that all taxa should include collections of species that share a common ancestor; the taxon (termed a **clade**) contains all descendants of the common ancestor, but no organisms that did not share the common ancestor. This seems to get at the root of evolutionary relatedness, but there are problems. How can we tell which organisms are descendants of a common ancestor? Unlike with human family trees, we cannot rely on written records in family Bibles or parish registers. In fact, biologists rely on structural similarities (including DNA sequences) to deduce common ancestry. Furthermore, not just any structural similarity is useful: only homologous traits, as opposed to analogous traits, are of value. But how can one tell the difference between a homologous similarity and an analogous one? Fossil sequences are of great value here, but they are not always available, and rarely, if ever, are they complete. Thus, while the goal is classification by common descent, in actuality classification is based largely on structural similarities.

There is another interesting problem: strict use of cladistic principles leads to some nonintuitive situations. For instance, studies of the fossil record have led paleontologists to believe that, at an early date (the Devonian period), fish split into cartilaginous and bony forms (Chondrichthyes class and Osteichthyes class, respectively). Land vertebrates, including amphibians, reptiles, birds, and mammals derived from a common ancestor among the bony fish. Based on this evolutionary history, how would one group the following three forms into which two "go together" into the same clade: shark, trout, and human? The answer is that humans and trout are grouped together, while sharks are in a separate clade. Thus, our common term "fish" is not a proper clade, as it includes forms with distant common ancestors (sharks and trout) but excludes forms with more recent common ancestors (people, with trout). In another example, "reptiles" is not a proper clade, as it includes forms that have more distant common ancestry (turtles and lizards) and excludes forms that have more recent common ancestry (birds, with lizards).

Other taxonomists believe that, since structural similarity is the basis for most classifications, taxa should reflect structural similarities. They would argue, for instance, for keeping reptiles and birds as separate taxa.

MACROEVOLUTION

Although there are differences in approaches to taxonomy, in general, the biological classification system attempts to approximate major macroevolutionary events that have occurred in the history of life. For example, by placing animals and plants in separate kingdoms, biologists state their belief that these organisms shared a common ancestor long ago, followed by a speciation that occurred between a population that later gave rise to all living plants and a population that later gave rise to all living animals. In fact, evolutionary biologists have managed to reconstruct much of the basic nature of the evolutionary history of life on earth, primarily based on fossil evidence. Much is still unknown or in dispute, but basic trends are well understood.

Some Highlights in the History of Life: An Anthropocentric View

What follows is a very abridged summary of some key findings in the study of the history of life. The view is very anthropocentric (human centered) as it predominately focuses on events related to our own species's evolutionary history. This approach should not lead readers to believe that the history of life depicts a Great Chain of Being leading to humans. One could easily use a clam-centered approach to the history of life, or a fungus-centered approach. In fact, a text on the history of life would usually attempt to avoid a focus on a specific taxonomic group.

ORIGIN OF THE EARTH. The earth itself is approximately 4.5 billion years old, believed to have formed at the same time as the sun and other planets from the gravitational "condensation" of a gaseous nebula. At the time of its formation, the earth was quite hot. Hot enough, in fact, that the gases—principally hydrogen and simple hydrogen-based molecules such as ammonia and methane—that made up its original atmosphere probably moved at fast enough speeds to escape earth's gravity and thus were lost. As the earth cooled, it developed a secondary atmosphere made up of gases given off from volcanic activity, including water vapor, nitrogen, and carbon dioxide. The early solar system was very dynamic, featuring many small bodies orbiting the sun. This activity led to many collisions, and these collisions between earth and early comets contributed material to the planet, including water. As further cooling occurred, condensation of water vapor and resulting rainfall joined forces to change the atmosphere's composition and create the oceans. Carbon dioxide was dissolved in the rainwater and eventually combined with other materials, forming rocks such as limestone. Free oxygen would have been absent (or nearly so) in the early atmosphere, and in fact only appeared within the past two to 2.5 billion years or so (Margulis 1982).

Figure 5-3 shows an abbreviated view of the geologists' major divisions of the earth's geological and evolutionary history. The largest divisions in geological time are termed "eras," and these large time spans are divided into geological "periods." Geological periods are further subdivided into epochs, particularly for the most recent periods.

EARLIEST LIFE. The oldest rocks known on earth today are about 3.8 billion years old, and the oldest known fossils are also from that time period. Thus, life began at least 3.5 billion years ago on an earth that was quite different, particularly in its atmospheric makeup, than it is today. Life itself has had an effect on the earth's development. For instance, oxygen is a byproduct of photosynthesis. This byproduct, over the course of hundreds of millions of years, accumulated in the atmosphere. By about 2.5 billion years ago, there is evidence for rocks containing ferric iron (and having a rusty look), suggesting that our atmosphere's oxygen levels were increasing (Price 1996).

The earliest evidence for life consists of microfossils (microscopic-sized fossils of bacterial cells) and stromatolites (layered rocks that result from fossilization of layers of microbial mats, which in turn are combinations of bacterial filaments and sediments). The bacteria in the stromatolites apparently engaged in photosynthesis, as they are found in proximity to the earliest rocks banded with ferric iron (McAlester 1968), a sign of the oxygen given off during photosynthesis.

Era	Period	Epoch	Millions of years ago (est. start of time unit)	Major events; first appearances
Cenozoic	Quaternary	Holocene (Recent)	0.01	End of last Ice Age; origin of agriculture; first cities and states
		Pleistocene	1.6	Homo sapiens
	Tertiary	Pliocene	7	Hominid line
		Miocene	23	"Age of Apes"
		Oligocene	35	Catarrhines
		Eocene	56	Modern looking primates
		Paleocene	65	Mammalian radiation
Mesozoic	Cretaceous		145	Age of Dinosaurs
	Jurassic		208	
	Triassic		245	
Paleozoic	Permian		290	Mammal-like reptiles
	Carboniferous		362	Seed, bearing plants; reptiles
	Devonian		408	Land vertebrates
	Silurian		439	Placoderms
	Ordovician		510	Agnathans
	Cambrian		570	Animal fossils common
Precambrian*			4,500	Origin of earth, of life, and of multi-cellular life

FIGURE 5-3 The major divisions in the earth's geological history.

* The Precambrian Era, by far the longest unit of geological time, is often subdivided, for instance into Hadean, Isuan, Swazian, Randian, Huronian, Animikean, Riphean, and Sinian Eras (Harland et al. 1990). The Sinian Era is further subdivided into two Periods, and the most recent Period is divided into two Epochs; the most recent Epoch in the Precambrian, beginning 590 million years ago, is the Ediacara.

ORIGIN OF THE EUKARYOTES. The invasion of an early form of Eukaryotic cell by a bacterium, as noted in the endosymbiotic theory of Lynn Margulis (1970), may have been a crucial step in the origin of Eukaryotes, which differ from Prokaryotes in the possession of organelles such as mitochondria, among other basic differences. As noted, in contemporary Eukaryotes, mitochondria have their own DNA, which is thought to be a vestige of the invading bacterium's separate genome. This **endosymbiotic** theory of the origins of Eukaryotic cells has been expanded to also include the origins of other cellular organelles, such as chloroplasts.

MULTICELLULAR LIFE. It was only after the origin of Eukaryotes that complex multicellular life evolved. The gradual increase in atmospheric oxygen permitted the evolution of aerobic metabolism, a more efficient energy use in organisms, and was therefore a necessary but not sufficient reason for the origins of multicellular organisms. The earliest extensive fossil evidence for multicellular organisms comes from the Ediacaran fauna (570 to 590 million years old), named for a rock formation in Australia. The Ediacara organisms were soft-bodied forms that are structurally quite different from the forms that followed soon after in the Cambrian period. It is with the Cambrian period, beginning about 570 million years ago, that we find fossils that resemble many of the major phyla of contemporary organisms (Gould 1989). These include sponges, brachiopods, annelid worms, arthropods, echinoderms, crustaceans, and brachiopods (Price 1966). It has been termed the Cambrian "explosion" because of the seemingly sudden appearance of many fossils of multicellular organisms. It appears that the explosion was principally due to the origin of hard parts in multicellular organisms, as opposed to the origin of multicellular organisms themselves, with the hard parts (such as shells) evolving as an adaptation to predation (Vermeij 1987; Freeman and Herron 2004) and/or due to a possible sudden increase in calcium carbonate in ocean waters, allowing shell material to become readily available (Raup 1991). The hard parts greatly increased the chances for fossilization, thus vastly increasing the number of fossils that we can find. The Cambrian period marks the beginning of the Paleozoic ("old life") era, which lasted until about 220 million years ago.

EARLY VERTEBRATES. The earliest known (or suspected) chordate, which is the phylum that contains vertebrates as a subphylum, is a single species found in the early Cambrian, *Pikaia gracilens,* although there is some controversy as to whether this fossil is actually a chordate (Price 1996). It is not until in the next geological period, the Ordovichian, that the first fossils recognizable as vertebrates are found. These are the Agnatha, or jawless fishes, represented today by such species as the lamprey and hagfish, but whose earliest fossils date back nearly 500 million years. It was about 100 million years later, in the late Silurian and early Devonian periods, that the fishes had a major adaptive radiation, becoming both more diverse and more common. A major group of fish that appeared at this time was the Placoderms, jawed fish that included large, heavily armored genera such as Dinichthys (see Figure 5-4).

Placoderms declined in numbers by the late Devonian, about 350 million years ago, being replaced by the two modern fish classes: Chondrichthyes (the cartilaginous fish, including sharks and rays) and Osteichthyes (the bony fish). It is from the latter that the first land vertebrates, the amphibians, evolved in the late Devonian period (McAlester 1968), about 350 million years ago.

REPTILES AND BIRDS. Reptiles, like amphibians, are land vertebrates, but they have adapted more completely to life on land. Amphibians must live in water during part of their lives—primarily to reproduce and develop as juvenile forms. Reptiles can live their entire lives outside of water, in part due to the evolution of the amniote egg, which can be laid, and hatched, on land (Romer 1970). Reptiles evolved from amphibian ancestors in the late Carboniferous period, about 300 million years ago. The reptiles rapidly diversified during the next geological period, the Permian. At the end of the Permian, there is evidence for a major upheaval among living organisms: many species became extinct in a short time period. This mass extinction, as it is termed, did not cause reptiles to diminish. In fact, it was after the Permian, in the Mesozoic era, that the reptiles became the dominant life on land and included such forms as dinosaurs, ichthyosaurs, flying reptiles such as pterosaurs, as well as ancestors of modern-day lizards and snakes, turtles, and crocodiles.

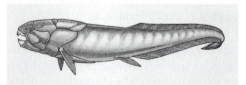

FIGURE 5-4 The Devonian Placoderm Dinichthys, which reached thirty feet in length.

Another mass extinction event occurred at the end of the Cretaceous period, which also marked the end of the Mesozoic era. At this time, approximately 65 million years ago, many reptile species became extinct, including all dinosaurs. However, many biologists believe that one branch of dinosaur persisted. These biologists believe that one type of dinosaur evolved into a new kind of vertebrate: the bird.

MAMMALS. While it is certain that mammals arose from reptilian ancestors, it is difficult to identify precise ancestry, in part because the main differences between mammals and reptiles, such as the presence of hair, mammary glands, and improved control over internal body temperature, are not discernable in the fossil record. One adaptation found in mammals is useful in identifying fossils: tooth structure. Mammals, who have greater dietary energy needs related to body heat control, tend to eat smaller and more digestible food items, whereas reptiles often swallow their food whole and then spend long inactive periods while digestion takes place (McAlester 1968). Mammalian jaws and teeth have become adapted for the better processing of food, including the development of different basic tooth forms, such as incisors, canines, and molars.

During the Triassic, several lineages of mammal-like reptiles developed jaws and teeth similar to those seen in later mammals. It is conceivable, therefore, that modern mammals derive from several separate reptile ancestors and thus are not a true "clade." Clearly, by the late Triassic period about 200 million years ago, mammals had evolved. The early mammals were all quite small compared to most reptiles of the time (such as dinosaurs) and also were less common.

Mammals remained relatively small and uncommon until the end of the Cretaceous period. The mammals then rapidly diversified into most of the modern orders recognized today, with this adaptive radiation occurring after the demise of the dinosaurs. Comparison of DNA sequences in modern mammalian orders suggests that the classes separated millions of years before the mass extinction at the end of the Cretaceous (Gibbons 1998). Many paleontologists disagree, noting that 15 of 18 placental (mammals that have placentas, allowing them to give birth to well-developed live offspring) mammalian orders are first seen in the fossil record in a 16-million–year period immediately following the Cretaceous extinction event (Archibald et al. 1999).

PRIMATES. One of the mammalian orders that first appears in the fossil record in the time period immediately after the Cretaceous extinction event is the Primates, the order that includes humans. Species in the Primates order are characterized as having relatively large brains, short snouts, forward-facing eyes, and grasping digits, the latter allowing most primate species to be arboreal (tree-living). There has been much controversy about which fossil species should be assigned to the Primate order in this early time period. For instance, a major group of mammalian fossils, termed "Plesiadapiformes," was long considered a type of early primate from the Paleocene and Eocene epochs, a time period in the Tertiary period that immediately followed the Cretaceous extinctions. Further study of the fossils led some paleontologists to conclude that these fossils probably were ancestral to a different group of living mammals, the flying lemurs, and not to primates (Kay et al. 1990). However, study of more recently discovered fossils have led other paleontologists to assign the plesiadapids to the Primate order (Bloch and Silcox 2001). The difficulty in identifying early primates may be because the order has retained a fairly general body structure. Figure 5-5 shows the taxonomy of living primates.

The earliest primate fossil forms that resemble modern organisms occur in the Eocene epoch, approximately 50 million years ago. There were two main families of primates present at that time, Adapids and Omomyids. The Adapids are characterized as having fairly long snouts relative to other primates. In general, they share many resemblances with modern lemurs. Omomyids tend to have shorter faces, as well as other features that resemble modern tarsiers and anthropoids. This seems to represent an early division of primates into two major groupings, sometimes termed "semiorders": the strepsirhines (literally "turned noses," referring to the complex nose structure—sometimes

Order				Primates					
Semiorder	Strepsirhines			Haplorhines					
Suborder	Prosimians		Tarsiers	Anthropoids					
Infra-Order	Lorises	Lemurs		Platyrrhines		Catarrhines			
Superfamily				Ceboids		Carcopithecoids	Hominoids		
Family	Lemurids	Indriids		Cebids	Callitrichids		Hylobatids	Pongids	Hominids
Subfamily	Lorisines, Galagines	Lemurines, Cheirogaleines		Cebines, Aortines, Callicebines, Saimirines, Pithecines, Alouattines, Atelines		Cercopithecines Colobines			
Selected Common Names	Lorises, Bushbabies	Lemurs, Ruffed Lemurs	Indris, Sifakas	Tarsiers	Squirrel Monkeys, Capuchins, Spider Monkeys	Marmosets, Tamarins	Colobus, Langurs, Mangebeys, Baboons	Gibbons, Siamangs	Orangutans, Gorillas, Chimpanzees, Bonobos	Humans

FIGURE 5-5 Taxonomy of the living Primates.

FIGURE 5-6 A living strepsirhine: the ring-tailed lemur.

referred to as a "doggy nose"—that includes moist membranes covering the nostril area, a structure found widely among mammals) and the haplorhines ("simple noses" referring to primates that lack the moist membrane in the nostril area). Modern strepsirhines include lemurs and lorises. Modern haplorhines include tarsiers and anthropoids. See Figures 5-6 and 5-7.

ANTHROPOIDS. Anthropoids are a suborder of primates that include monkeys, apes, and humans (see Figures 5-8, 5-9, and 5-10). The origins of Anthropoids are somewhat obscure, but fossil finds in the 1980s and 1990s have pushed back the fossil record into the late Eocene epoch, about 37 million years ago (Kay et al. 1997). Earlier fossils have sometimes been identified as Anthropoids, but the

FIGURE 5-7 A living haplorhine: the tarsier.

FIGURE 5-8 An anthropoid from Central America: *Brachyteles arachnoides*, the woolly spider monkey.

fragmentary nature of the remains makes their classification controversial. Anthropoids, as a group, have traits that represent exaggerated primate evolutionary trends with larger brains, more overlapping vision, and shorter snouts than other primates.

Living Anthropoids are divided into two infra-orders: the platyrrhines ("flat noses") that live in South and Central America and the catarrhines ("narrow noses") that live in Africa and Asia. The two groups apparently diverged soon after Anthropoids evolved and have been geographically isolated on separate continental masses for millions of years. The platyrrhine fossil record is very sparse, although a few forms are known from the late Oligocene and early Miocene (Martin 1990). These early fossils resemble early anthropoids from the Late Eocene in Africa, leading some researchers to believe the platyrrhines may have originated and undergone an early diversification in Africa before arriving in the New World via a crossing of a then-narrower Atlantic Ocean by "rafting" on drifting pieces of vegetation (Takai et al. 2000).

FIGURE 5-9 An African monkey: *Cercopithecus aethiops*, the vervet.

FIGURE 5-10 A Hominoid: the chimpanzee, *Pan troglodytes*.

The catarrhines in turn are divided into two superfamilies, the Cercopithecoids, or Old World monkeys, and the Hominoids, or apes. The earliest catarrhines are known from the beginning of the Oligocene epoch, particularly from fossils discovered in the Fayum, a locality in what is now Egypt. There are some disagreements about what fossils may be ancestral both to platyrrhines and catarrhines, but there is much agreement that by the early Oligicene there is a separate catarrhine

FIGURE 5-11 Fossil cast of *Aegyptopithecus zeuxis*, center, an early catarrhine fossil from the Oligocene epoch, compared with skulls of modern lemur (left) and modern catarrhine (macaque, right).

clade, represented by such fossils as *Aegyptopithecus* (Figure 5-11). *Aegyptopithecus* was fairly small, on the order of 15 pounds as an adult, with a long snout and small brain relative to modern catarrhines. It may have been ancestral both to Old World monkeys and Hominoids (for example, Jurmain et al. 2005).

During the Miocene epoch (seven to 23 million years ago), evidence exists for numerous and diverse Hominoid species. Hominoid fossils dating from this so-called "Age of the Apes" have been found in Africa, Europe, and Asia. The Miocene epoch was a time of climatic change in much of the Old World, particularly Africa. Early Miocene times were wetter and warmer than they are today, with rain forests widespread from central Africa to East Asia. During the Miocene, much of Africa and west Asia became drier and cooler, with rain forest giving way to tropical grasslands, or savanna, by the late Miocene. Hominoid forms mirror this climatic change somewhat: all early Miocene Hominoids were apparently adapted for arboreal niches, while in the later Miocene some forms were adapted for terrestrial life.

The Human Journey

The human evolutionary path is reflected in our taxonomy, which groups us with our closest relatives. We are therefore animals (that is, related to all other animals), vertebrates, mammals, primates, anthropoids, and Hominoids. Our species's evolutionary history can be traced back to the origins of life on the planet, but for our purposes it commences with the speciation from our common ancestors, chimpanzees and bonobos, some five to ten million years ago in East Africa.

EARLY HOMINIDS. It is in the Pliocene epoch that hominid, or human family, fossils are first observed, although the beginnings of the hominids may date back to the late Miocene. Very incomplete fossils are known from five to eight million years ago that may be early hominids, but it is not until about 4.5 million years ago that clear evidence for hominids is found (Jurmain et al. 2005). Fossil hominids from this early time period have almost all been found in the East African Rift Valley, an area stretching from Tanzania in the south to Ethiopia and Eritrea in the north that is characterized by much active volcanism, earthquakes, and geological faults. An exception is a skull found in Chad, to the west of the Rift Valley (see Figure 5-12), that has been provisionally dated at

FIGURE 5-12 Fossil cranium of an early hominid from Chad, approximately six to seven million years old

approximately six million years old (Gibbons 2002). Other remains from about six million years ago have been found in the Tugen Hills of Kenya. These fossils, said to belong to a species called "Millennium Man" because they were first discovered in the year 2000, represent numerous bones from several individuals and include both limb bones and teeth. They represent an intriguing mixture of ape and human features, including stout thigh bones indicative of bipedal walking and thick-enameled molar teeth indicative of a terrestrial animal's diet, with forelimbs that indicate an arboreal climber (Aiello and Collard 2001; Senut et al. 2001).

ARDIPITHECUS RAMIDUS Beginning in 1997, fossil remains from Ethiopia dated between 5.2–5.8 million years old have been unearthed. These consist of feet, hand, and arm bones, as well as a jaw with teeth. The remains, placed in the species *Ardipithecus ramidus*, also have both chimpanzee and human-like features. Like all remains from these times, there is great controversy over whether the given species represents an ancestral hominid (occurring after the speciation of the ancestors of humans and chimpanzees, respectively, but descended from the line leading to humans) or an ancestral chimp. Some have suggested that the types of characteristics most commonly found in the primate fossil record, namely cranial and dental remains, may not be ideal for use in reconstructing evolutionary relationships (Collard and Wood 2000). However, it should not be surprising that as remains are found closer in time to the most recent common ancestor of chimpanzees and humans, it becomes increasingly difficult to distinguish the two evolutionary lines from each other.

AUSTRALOPITHECUS Fossils also placed in the *Ardipithecus ramidus* species are known from about four million years ago, as are remains from another species, named *Australopithecus anamensis*. The fossils show some hominid features, such as adaptations for bipedalism. Much more is known about hominid fossils beginning about 3.5 million years ago: nearly complete skeletons and fossilized footprints give unambiguous evidence for bipedalism in fossils that are assigned to the species *Australopithecus afarensis* (see Figure 5-13).

Within the past 3.5 million years, until recent times, there is also abundant evidence for a great deal of variation in hominid forms, with two or more species present at any one time. Thus, the contemporary situation of only a single species extant, and that one exhibiting relatively little biological variability, is unusual. Starting nearly four million years ago, early hominids showed considerable variability, sufficient for most paleoanthropologists to assign multiple species to the family (Kimbel

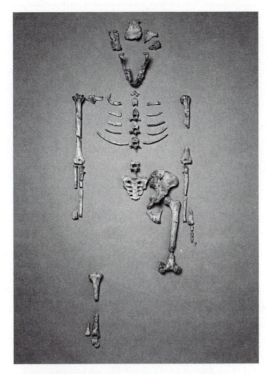

FIGURE 5-13 Skeleton of "Lucy," a nearly complete specimen of *Australopithecus afarensis*.

et al. 2006). In the following two million years, bipedalism was perfected, including a lengthening in leg size yielding a larger stride length, and teeth became more adapted to a coarse terrestrial diet. By two to 2.5 million years ago, there is very good evidence for hominids (often grouped into the genus *Australopithecus*) throughout East and South Africa, represented in different species, including robust and gracile forms (some separate these forms into separate genera). The robust (that is, strong, muscular) species possessed large jaws, huge molar teeth, and powerful muscles to move their jaws. The gracile (that is, weak, less muscular) species possessed moderate-sized jaws, smaller (but still fairly large) molar teeth, and smaller jaw muscles. In both forms, brain size was closer to that of great apes than to modern humans, and body size was small.

HOMO HABILIS One species of gracile hominid differed from the rest in possessing larger brain size, and because of this has been classified as the earliest known member of the human genus *Homo*. Still, brain size was less than half (averaging somewhat less than 700 cm^3) of that found in modern humans (see Figure 5-14). It is probably not coincidental that the oldest stone tools are found when early *Homo* appeared, and this gives the species its name: *Homo habilis* ("handy man"). While other hominids were present where the tools are found, it is likely that they were made, and used, by early *Homo*. These forms are found in several habitats, but adaptations to life on the tropical grasslands (termed **savannas**) are evident (Reed 1997).

PLIO-PLEISTOCENE HOMINIDS. In summary, the earliest known hominids (the evolutionary line that diverged from the lines leading to the modern great apes) lived in open woodlands and had adaptations for both terrestrial and arboreal life. Their canine teeth were somewhat smaller than those found in living great apes (but considerably larger than in modern humans), but these earliest hominids' molar teeth were relatively large, with evidence for adaptations to chewing terrestrial

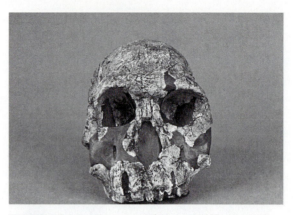

FIGURE 5-14 Fossil cranium of *Homo habilis*, specimen KNM-ER 1470.

foods. Bipedalism was present in the early hominids but not perfected. Brain size was similar to that of the great apes (measured by the cranial capacity at below 450 cm^3, compared with an average of about 400 cm^3 for contemporary chimpanzees and about 1,325 cm^3 for modern humans), and the face protruded forward (a condition termed **prognathism**). In essence, we closely resembled our ape cousins except for our tooth morphology and a transition to walking on our back legs. General body size was considerably smaller than found in modern *Homo sapiens*.

HOMO ERECTUS. By 1.8 million years ago, a new form of *Homo* appeared. The main difference between this form and earlier ones is that the new species was much larger, approximately the size of modern humans. This new species is termed *Homo erectus*, although some paleoanthropologists assign a separate species, *Homo ergaster*, to African forms (Wood 1992; Gilbert et al. 2003). It, like its ancestors, was fully bipedal, and its average cranial capacity (about 1,000 cm^3) was larger, although this increase was somewhat in proportion to its larger body size. The skull shape was similar to earlier forms, a generally long, low brain case, with some—but reduced— prognathism.

What truly distinguished *Homo erectus* from earlier species was its range: within a hundred thousand years of its earliest evidence in East Africa, the species had migrated throughout much of the Old World, with fossils found in what are now China, Indonesia, Russia, and Western Europe, as well as throughout Africa. The widespread distribution permitted geographical variation to evolve, with distinctive biological traits found in East Asian and Western forms.

HOMO SAPIENS. *Homo sapiens* evolved from *Homo erectus*. These early forms (termed "archaic *H. sapiens*") also were spread through much of the Old World. Archaic *Homo sapiens* were similar in form to *H. erectus*, except they had much larger brains, overlapping in size with that of modern humans. Like their ancestors, this species showed distinct geographical variation. One form, the Neanderthals from Europe, is often classified as a separate species.

Fully modern-looking *Homo sapiens* appear approximately 100,000 years ago in Africa. The main difference in form between them and archaic forms is the shape of the skull. In modern *H. sapiens* the skull is dome shaped, taller and shorter in profile, and the jaw is reduced in size, with much less prognathism. In general, modern forms are more gracile than archaic ones. Overall, modern *Homo sapiens* extends a general tendency for humans to become more infantile in appearance compared to their common ancestors with apes. This is a characteristic that biologists term **pedomorphism**. Modern humans share characteristics with infant or juvenile great apes, or at least more so than we do with adult apes.

PROFILE 5

Ivy L. Pike

Ivy Pike is a biological anthropologist whose research seeks to ask questions that are equally relevant to our understanding of the evolution of human reproduction and to social inequality. To blend these interests, her work has focused on women's health in marginalized communities of East African camel and cattle herders, emphasizing pregnancy. Pregnancy requires considerable investment of energy resources from the mother. A woman's ability to meet the demands of reproduction is structured by the circumstances of her social and physical environment, including the nature of her workloads and levels of social support. How a woman meets the energetic challenges of pregnancy has direct implications for her and her children's health and survival. In the herding communities in which Dr. Pike works, women experience seasonal patterns of lower nutrition and higher disease burdens that are linked to livestock productivity and severity of workloads. These seasonal nutrition patterns have been linked to a highly seasonal pattern of conceptions and births, as well as to the outcomes of pregnancies. These findings suggest important links among the social environment that patterns food availability, gender roles, and workloads; a harsh physical environment; and women's reproductive experiences.

Another research focus for Dr. Pike includes women's psychosocial coping and health as the pathway for understanding who thrives in difficult circumstances. This research includes examining the impact of poverty and rapid social change on the mental health of Datoga herders of Tanzania and the psychosocial impact of increased armed AK-47 raiding of livestock among Turkana herders of Kenya. Her current project extends an interest in the impact of violence and endemic warfare by examining how armed livestock raiding has impacted wealth/poverty and health in three adjacent herding communities—the Turkana, Pokot, and Samburu—which have a long history of raiding one another.

Dr. Pike is Associate Professor of Anthropology at the University of Arizona and serves on the Editorial Board of the *American Journal of Human Biology*.

There is increasing evidence that modern *Homo sapiens* migrated out of Africa and totally or largely replaced the archaic forms that were living in Africa and the rest of the Old World. There is some controversy as to whether—or to what extent—archaic forms may have interbred with moderns. The small genetic variability in today's human population, and some evidence for considerable genetic differences from Neanderthals (Hebsgaard et al. 2007; Noonan et al. 2006), suggests that few, if any, genes from the archaic forms have persisted in our contemporary population.

This brief survey of evolutionary history is necessarily a "bare bones" account that leaves out much of the fossil record's richness. As with much science, the devil—and the most interesting issues—is in the details. This does, however, give students of human biology a framework for understanding major events in the history of life.

Macroevolutionary Processes

In examining the history of life, a major question in evolutionary biology can be addressed: are there special processes in macroevolution that are not simply long-term consequences of microevolutionary processes? For instance, a basic tenet of microevolution is that selection acts only on individual organisms. However, some scientists (for example, Gould 2002) believe that selection can act on whole species, and it is this process that defines many of the features of macroevolution. Our brief and biased (toward humans) overview of the history of life does not provide enough detail to answer these questions, but a closer look at some basic concepts of macroevolution may help.

TEMPO AND MODE IN EVOLUTION. In assessing the evolutionary record, a major question concerns the *rate* at which evolution occurs (Simpson 1944). This is not a simple question, as it is not obvious what is to be measured to derive such a rate, much less how to actually do the measurement. Ideally, one would measure the average rate of genetic change over time (for example, the average number of nucleotide base changes in a species per year), but the usual fast breakdown of DNA makes this impossible for most of the fossil record. It has become possible to extract DNA from fairly recent fossils. Therefore, in some cases, direct measurement of the rate of DNA change over time is becoming a reality for relatively recent evolutionary time. One other possible measure of evolutionary rate is some quantization of structural change over time, although it is unclear how this could be done. An example would be a measure of cranial capacity, which is an approximation of brain size, in hominid species over time. This example presents some of the problems with this approach, as only a single characteristic is used, rather than an appraisal of how fast the whole organism has evolved.

An alternative measure of evolutionary rate is the number of speciations, or some other measure of the number of clades formed, in a given evolutionary line over a certain period of time. Simpson (1944) compared rates of appearance of genera in three disparate evolutionary lines: horses, chalicotheres (ancient horse-like mammals), and Triassic ammonites. He noted that there were a similar number of new genera per million years for horses and Chalicotheres, but that ammonites had less than a third the number of new genera per time. He therefore concluded that horses and chalicotheres evolved faster than ammonites.

Besides attempting to estimate the simple rate of evolution, it is also interesting to note changes in the evolution's rate over time. Thus, evolutionary biologists are interested both in the velocity and acceleration of evolutionary change. This can be boiled down to a simple question: does evolution occur gradually and steadily, or does it occur at different rates? Some evolutionary scientists have postulated that evolution moves in fits and starts, occurring very quickly for short periods, followed by long periods of relatively little change (Eldredge and Gould 1972). This notion, called the theory of punctuated evolution, has received some support from studies of the fossil record, as noted in Chapter 2.

EXTINCTION. The other side of the coin from speciation is the loss of a species, termed "extinction." Actually, a species can become extinct in two ways: by transformation through anagenesis into a new species, or by termination without descendants. It is the latter type of extinction that we refer to here. In fact, extinctions are a normal part of the history of life, and involve either species or higher taxa. Raup and Sepkoski (1982), for example, calculated a "background" level of extinctions in marine animals of between one and eight families per million years.

MASS EXTINCTIONS. Raup and Sepkoski (1982) also recognized several time periods when the rate of extinctions increased markedly. Three in particular stand out: the Late Permian, dated at 253 million years ago, when the extinction rate rose to 14 families per million years, and fully 96 percent of species are believed to have become extinct in a short period of time; the Late Triassic period,

213 million years ago, when the extinction rate rose to 16 families per million years; and the Late Cretaceous, 65 million years ago, when the extinction rate rose to 16 families per million years, including the loss of all dinosaur species (Price 1996).

There have been varied explanations for these periods of mass extinctions, from asteroid impacts with the earth to unusually voluminous volcanic activity, to rapid climatic change. Whatever the cause or causes, these are unlikely to be related to typical adaptive concerns of biological organisms that are considered in microevolutionary studies of natural selection. Rather, these events can be viewed as externally driven phenomena that have a critical effect on the makeup of earth's biota. Not only are many taxa missing after these events, but these events are followed by rapid radiations of surviving taxa. Most notable of these circumstances was the rapid radiation of mammals that occurred after the Late Cretaceous mass extinctions that wiped out the dinosaurs.

SURVIVORS. Species that are more likely to survive extinction events share some characteristics. Species that are too narrow in their ecological requirements appear to be at greater risk, while those species that are not highly specialized are more likely to survive (Slobodkin and Rapoport 1974). This is partly due to the general rule that non-specialized species are more widely distributed throughout the world than are specialists, being less "picky" about their surroundings. Thus, when a catastrophe strikes one region of the world, a widely distributed species is more likely to have at least some of its individuals survive. Ironically, in the short-term, species are rewarded for becoming specialized, as they become highly effective and efficient at getting needed resources from a given environment. It is when the environment changes, and changes relatively rapidly, that the less specialized but perhaps more adaptable species are at an advantage.

Some evolutionary biologists have stated that the differential survival of species constitutes a separate evolutionary force termed "**species selection**" that functions, at least to some degree, independently of natural selection, as the latter acts only at the level of the individual organism (Gould 2002). This notion is quite controversial, however. A scientist has referred to evolution as a combination of "chance and necessity" (Monod 1971). This principally refers to the random (chance) nature of mutations versus the more directed nature of natural selection (necessity) that acts upon the mutations. However, the notion of species selection adds to the chance elements that direct the way in which life's history has unfolded. Was it the chance event of an asteroid impact that wiped out the dinosaurs in the Late Cretaceous and opened the way for the diversification of mammals, including the evolution of humans? The events in the history of life are contingent upon what has occurred previously. Since chance elements have a role in directing these events, the organisms present today on earth are here, in part, due to caprice rather than clear adaptation processes.

CHAPTER SUMMARY

Biologists classify living organisms based on their evolutionary relationships to each other, with an attempt to group together organisms with a close common ancestor. Taxonomy's basic unit is the species, defined as a group of organisms that are capable of reproducing with each other. Other taxonomic units, based on increasingly distant common ancestry, are the genus, family, order, class, phylum, and kingdom.

Speciation, the creation of new species, occurs either through splitting, a process termed "cladogenesis," or through change in a single line of evolution over time, a process termed "anagenesis." Cladogenesis is generally thought to occur due to geographic isolation (allopatric speciation) but also can occur without large spatial separation (sympatric speciation).

Study of the fossil record has allowed an understanding of the history of life. Within a billion years of the earth's creation 4.5 billion years ago, there is evidence for life in the form of bacterium-like organisms. Evidence for multicellular life does not appear until within the past one billion years. Vertebrates first appear as marine organisms, with the first land vertebrates occurring within the last

400 million years. Mammals were relatively uncommon until the dinosaurs disappeared approximately 65 million years ago. The human species is relatively new on the evolutionary scene: modern *Homo sapiens* appears to be no older than 200,000 years. Our species is characterized by bipedalism, large brains, small jaws and teeth, and uniquely complex social behavior.

When observing macroevolutionary events, other processes besides the microevolutionary forces of selection, mutation, and genetic drift become important. These forces include major geological events that have caused mass extinctions. These mass extinctions seem to have been caused by processes that are distinct from normal selective forces, and therefore the history of life appears to have been shaped, in part, by processes beyond natural selection alone.

CHAPTER 6

"Race" and Human Variation in Physical Traits

People have been fascinated by the physical diversity of humans long before they developed any appreciation for genetics and the modern scientific understanding of heredity. In the terms of modern genetics, the traits that make up human physical diversity are phenotypic: observable variations for which the precise genetic basis may or may not be understood. Today, human biological variation is explained through our notions of evolution and genetics, but many other theories for the origins of these differences have been entertained. Formal studies of human physical diversity have explored descriptions (the "what") of the variable traits, as well as the theoretical underpinning for the "how" and "why" of these traits.

RACE

Because there is a geographical distribution to many of the variable traits used to describe human differences, there has been a tendency to use the traits to classify humans into geographical variants, or "**races**." In a modern biological sense, races can be seen as subspecies, a grouping of populations within a species that are thought to have a much closer shared ancestry within the race than with populations that are grouped in other races. Earlier notions of race were quite different from ideas based on modern biological taxonomy. Both modern and early ideas about race should be distinguished from the idea of **racism**: the notion that humans classified into a given racial grouping are inferior to people in some other grouping. In this chapter, evidence will be presented that the biological notion of race does not correspond to the distribution of human biological variation: humans simply do not "lump" into the large regional units that correspond with the biological concept of subspecies. Therefore, in the textbook, the word race will be placed in quotation marks upon its first mention in each chapter, in order to signal that the concept does not have biological utility in our species. However, there are very real consequences to the idea that human races exist; the twenty-first century is still confronted with the legacy of racism that has been a major part of Western history. The wonderful book by C. Loring Brace (2005) entitled *Race Is a Four-Letter Word* does full justice to this important discussion. It should be used as a reference by all students interested in human variation or the use of race as a means of dividing our species.

Race, Population, and Ethnic Group

In current times, it is common to classify human groups in terms of populations, ethnic groups, or races. In fact, there is much confusion about what these terms actually mean. An **ethnic group** is defined as a collection of people who believe they share a common history, culture, or ancestry (Scupin 2006). In some cases, ethnic groups match nationalities, particularly among immigrant groups whose recent ancestors stemmed from specific countries, such as Italians and Irish in the United States. In many other cases, ethnic groups do not match nationalities and may include tribal or religious groupings within nations. It is usually cultural differences that characterize ethnic groups as opposed to perceived biological differences, and specific religions, language, values, cuisine, or other customs are emphasized in determining who are members of the ethnic group and who are outsiders.

In biology, **populations** are groupings of organisms within a species that interbreed frequently, usually sharing a geographical area. There is, therefore, a tendency for greater genetic similarities among individuals within populations than in individuals from different populations of the species. **Human populations** are often synonymous with cultural groups, implying both cultural and reproductive inclusiveness, although gene flow between populations is universal. The usual high degree of gene flow between human populations blurs the populations' genetic distinctiveness.

In common usage, race is an ambiguous term that sometimes is used interchangeably with either population or ethnic group. The term "race" is imbued with the notion that there are biological attributes that separate one race from another, with this concept more commonly found in the United States than in other Western countries (Brace 2005). Biologists use the term race to refer to major geographic subdivisions of a species, and it is in this context that the term has been used in this text.

A major question that human biologists have asked is: do human biological races exist? It is a difficult question to answer, because it depends on the way in which races are defined. As noted, definitions of race differ greatly, at least in common usage, ranging from notions of **ethnicity** that encompass cultural differences among human groups, to strictly biological differences that equate with the term "subspecies" used for other organisms.

If the term "race" is restricted to mean a major geographical, and biologically based, categorization of the human species, then we will see that the data (presented in this chapter and the next) show that human races *do not* exist. In other words, while humans vary, and human populations show biological differences, the amount of variation *within* any human population is much greater than the average variation *between* large geographical groupings of populations. Also, individual populations do not "clump" well into larger geographical groups; certainly not when the traditional division of humans by continent of ancestry is used. However, to quote a noted human biologist: "While the concept of biological race remains untenable when applied to modern humans, the biological dimensions of ethnicity should not be ignored..." (Jackson 1992, p. 125). Human biological diversity has important implications even though traditional ideas about biological races are false.

Clines Versus Clumps

If human races did in fact exist, one would expect to find that human traits show geographic discontinuities. That is, one would expect to find easily recognizable borders between one geographic race and another. The results of studying human biological variation, as noted in this chapter and the next, indicate that humans do not show these strict borders. Instead, the geography of human variation generally exhibits a gradient of change over distance: characteristics (whether measured as average values or frequencies of occurrence) change slowly over geographic distances, a feature referred to as "clinal distribution," or simply as **clines**. The human biologist Frank Livingstone stated in 1962: "There are no races, there are only clines" (Livingstone 1962, p. 279), and it has taken many of his colleagues many decades to understand the truth of this statement.

The idea of race goes far back in time, and thus many ideas about race have little to do with modern scientific ideas about ancestry. In fact, it was not until the twentieth century that scientific notions of race became common. Until then, the term race had broad meaning, referring to geographic regions, national origins, skin color differences, even differences between peoples based on religion or social class (Barkan 1992).

A Short History of Western Race Concepts: Ancient

As noted in the previous chapter, population variation has long been a hallmark of our species, even more so in the past than in current times. In fact, multiple hominid species coexisted in the past. There surely was recognition of these differences where geographic overlap occurred. We have no means of understanding what early hominids thought about variability between groups, whether of species or races, although there has certainly been much speculation about the interactions between modern Homo sapiens and **Neanderthals**, both in scholarly writings and the popular media. We must go to written records from the historic era to obtain clear evidence for how people characterized human variation.

ANCIENT VIEWS OF RACE. Paintings from ancient Egypt depict people who vary in skin color, from quite light to dark. This is not surprising, as Egypt lies midway between Europe and sub-Saharan Africa and was likely in contact with people of diverse skin color. It is difficult to make too much of this, however, as much of Egyptian art was based on conventional depictions of different people based on gender, social class, and national origins, with these conventions changing over time (Bard 1996). For instance, skin tones of females were usually depicted as being lighter than those of men. Today, and quite probably in ancient times, there is a gradient in skin color in Egypt, with average coloring being darker in southern regions (Brace et al. 1993). According to the Greek author Flavius Philostratus from the third century A.D., people from the southern border region of Egypt were intermediate in skin color, falling between the more northern Egyptians and the Ethiopians (cited in Snowden 1983). Whatever the actual diversity in skin color that existed in ancient Egypt, there is no evidence for racism based on skin color, as is made explicit in the text of the *Great Hymn to the Aten,* which has been ascribed to Akhenaten (1379–1362 B.C.), and marriage between people of distinctly different skin colors was apparently fairly common (Snowden 1996). In fact, racism was not a major concern in other ancient Western societies, including the Greeks and Romans (Snowden 1983).

THE GREEK MYTH OF PHAETHON. A well known Greek myth relates the misadventure of Phaethon, son of Helios, the sun god. Phaethon took off on his father's sun chariot, lost control of the powerful horses that pulled it, and bounded through the sky, rushing close to earth in some places, scorching the ground and creating deserts. One place that he flew low over was Ethiopia, and "it was then, so they believe, that the Ethiopians acquired their dark color, since the blood was drawn to the surface of their bodies. . . ." (Ovid, Metamorphoses, Book II, 227–271).

GREEK HUMORAL VIEW OF HUMAN VARIABILITY. An ancient Greek notion about the natural world, from the Hippocratic tradition, is that it was made up of four basic elements and associated humors. These humors were blood, phlegm, bile (or "choler") and black bile (or "melancholer") (see Figure 6-1). The balance of these humors in people accounted for differences in physical form, personality, behavior, and health. People who lived in areas with a preponderance of one of the humors would have a different balance of these elements, leading to physical differences in appearance from other people, as well as differences in common health problems (see, for example, Dubos 1965). Thus, for the Hippocratic school of thought, racial variation in humans was environmentally caused.

BIBLICAL VIEW OF RACES. The Bible makes no direct mention of human races. There is mention of the three sons of Noah, and that their descendants populated different areas of the earth. In many commentaries, the three sons are stated to have given rise to the three major races of humanity: Asian (Shem), African (Ham), and European (Japheth). These commentaries also often include

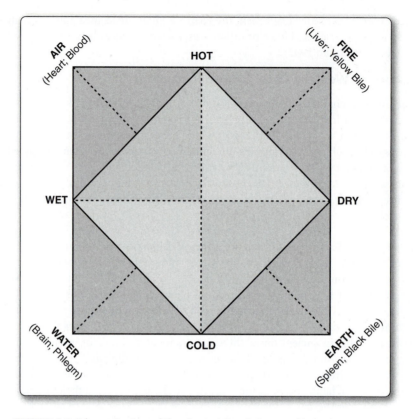

FIGURE 6-1 Schematic view of the classical Greek theory of humors.

ideas about a curse from Noah put upon Ham (and, presumably, his descendants). In the actual Biblical text, the curse was put upon one of Ham's sons, Canaan, who was said to have been the ancestor of several peoples, including the Canaanites that lived in the Palestine region. The commentaries, and their divergence from Biblical text, provided a justification for, and evidence of, racism directed at African peoples.

OTHER ANCIENT VIEWS OF HUMAN VARIATION. Romans, as their empire expanded, contacted many different populations of people, including northern Europeans, sub-Saharan Africans, and Asians from India and perhaps China. The Romans gave little attention to biological differences in these populations (Brues 1977). Later, Muslim merchants also became well acquainted with diverse human groups and, through slaving activities, brought individuals from these populations to their homelands. A developmental theory of human diversity arose in Muslim writings, in which it was believed that development of the fetus in the womb was analogous to a cooking process: people in the north had wombs that did not get hot enough, leaving infants pale and blond, while southern peoples had wombs that were too warm, scorching infants and causing their skin to turn black (Brues 1977; Lewis 1971).

WESTERN VIEWS OF RACE IN THE FIFTEENTH TO SEVENTEENTH CENTURIES. For Europeans, contact with peoples from distant lands was not common during much of medieval times, up to the time of the Crusades. It was not until the fifteenth century that distant travels became more common and reports of people who looked different became widespread. Written and oral descriptions of these other peoples, including those native to the New World, led to formulation of ideas about the causes of observed physical differences. Unfortunately, these ideas were confounded by garbled

FIGURE 6-2 Some of the more imaginative varieties of humans described by European travelers.

or patently false reports of "monsters": people with tails, dog-like faces, and so forth (see Figure 6-2). Some of these false reports may have been due to confusion with nonhuman primates, such as indris in Madagascar or baboons in East Africa. A dissection of the anatomy of a "Pygmy" was published by Edward Tyson in 1699 (McCown and Kennedy 1972) for instance. The so-called Pygmy was actually a chimpanzee. Linnaeus included these fallacious descriptions in his biological classification system, in which he divided humans into two species (*Homo sapiens* and *Homo monstrosus*, the latter containing the various nonexistent varieties of humankind). *Homo sapiens* in turn was subdivided by Linnaeus into five categories: American, European, African, Asian, and "wild men" (Hodgen 1964). The so-called wild men consisted of feral people, often abandoned as children and suffering from miscellaneous disabilities, either resulting in (or due to) their abandonment.

A Short History of European Race Concepts: Modern

MONOGENISTS VS. POLYGENISTS. A major debate that took place among European scholars in the eighteenth century was whether humans comprised one or several species. This issue was more than a scientific debate about the nature of human races. It also concerned the Christian theological idea that humans shared a spiritual unity based on a common descent from Adam (Greene 1959). The idea of the fixity of species was universal: differences in organisms were due to species differences inculcated during the Creation, or by natural processes that led to minor variability within species.

Polygenists (those who believed humans comprised several species) had an easy answer for population (race) differences: they were due to differences between species stemming from the Creation. **Monogenists** (those who believed humans were a single species), on the other hand, needed to develop a naturalistic explanation for how racial differences came about, since these were believed to have occurred after the Creation. This pursuit of naturalistic explanations led to the first scientific explorations of human population variation (Augstein 1997). Two of the leading monogenists of the time, Johann Friedrich Blumenbach and Georges-Louis Leclerc, the Comte de Buffon, both ascribed racial differences to degeneration from a more perfect type. The differences were said to be due to differential amounts of degeneration in the different races, with the rate and amount of degeneration due to the effects of "climate, diet, and mode of life" (Greene 1959, p. 224). These ideas included the belief that characteristics gained by an individual during his or her lifetime could be biologically transmitted to offspring. Blumenbach believed that the primordial type of human came from the Caspian Sea area because the people there were the most perfect in form. Thus, humans were originally white—with other varieties arising due to degradation. Blumenbach rejected Linnaeus' *Homo monstrosus* as being imaginary, and also rejected the "wild men" as constituting a racial category. However, all of these scientists were influenced by the highly ethnocentric and demeaning descriptions of non-Western people given by many of the same explorers who had described the human "monsters."

At least one individual, James Cowles Pritchard, disagreed with Buffon and Blumenbach, stating in 1813 that varieties *progressed* with time through environmental influence. He believed that a major process in this progression was self-domestication due to civilization, which permitted attainment of the European type. The mechanism for this process was, at least in part, mate selection based upon standards of beauty (this was termed "sexual selection" by Darwin).

Not all scholars accepted **environmental determinism** of traits, whether due to degeneration or progression. For instance, Pierre de Maupertuis, writing in 1745, presented a theory of particulate inheritance. In this view, when certain particles came together due to chance, individuals who were different from the rest of the population could arise. These individuals were forced out of society and made to live in less habitable climates of the earth. Other scholars, notably Immanuel Kant, combined ideas of environmental and internal causes leading to so-called racial varieties. For instance, Kant believed that skin color was inherited faithfully even when people migrated to a new environment; however, he also believed that the origins of skin color differences involved adaptation to environmental conditions where the race developed (see Greene 1959 for an extended discussion).

RACE AND RACISM. As can be seen, ideas about human races have been inextricably linked with notions of racism in Western thought. Most polygenists espoused clear racism: non-white races were seen as degenerate or undeveloped, falling lower than whites on the Great Chain of Being. Monogenists, on the other hand, were much more likely to make statements about racial equality (Harris 1968). Interestingly, scientists in the United States in the nineteenth century in general were more racist, and more likely to be polygenists, than their European colleagues; this was likely related to the institution of slavery that existed in the United States for the majority of that century. In fact, U.S. southerners were more likely to be polygenists than their Yankee countrymen. Ideas of race and racism were clearly related to justifications of slavery.

LAMARCK'S EVOLUTIONARY THEORY AND RACE. The nineteenth century brought with it ideas about change in living forms over time due to naturalistic processes. Early ideas about evolution presupposed a progression up the Great Chain of Being. Lamarck combined this idea with a notion of environmental forces leading to changes in biological form that would be transmitted to offspring, and it was applied to humans as well as other living organisms. Lamarck differentiated between the major evolutionary changes that occurred due to "the direct operations of nature" and accidental changes that occurred due to the "circumstances of habitation" (Greene 1959). The former were considered to be much more important than the latter in the evolution of species differences. However, it is the latter, accidental, changes that were seen to lead to variation *within* species, including human races.

By the early nineteenth century, belief in the Great Chain of Being began to ebb (Augstein 1997). Also, simplistic ideas about environmental determinism of racial variation were rejected, in part due to empirical data on the relatively unchanging characteristics of migrant communities resident in regions where other races were native. Race differences were seen as inherent and long standing.

DARWIN AND RACE. In *The Descent of Man*, Darwin's major work that focused on the evolution of humans, he stated that racial differences in our species were not primarily due to natural selection, but to sexual selection. Thus, human variability was not necessarily based on adaptations to different environments. The main features used to differentiate human races, such as skin color, hair texture, and facial features, indeed seem to have little adaptive import for survival, but Darwin, echoing Pritchard's earlier ideas, thought they had importance in mate attraction. The traits that determine desirability in a mate are at least partly determined by culture. These culturally based characteristics have biological consequences, however, as those individuals with more pleasing characteristics are more likely to find mates and therefore reproduce successfully.

SUCCESSORS TO DARWIN. Darwin's theory of evolution did not markedly change conceptions of race, at least not initially. After Darwin, scientists still fell into polygenist and monogenist camps. Scientific investigation of human race remained a matter of classification, and behavioral characteristics were included within the suite of characteristics used to distinguish racial groups.

Scientific methods were developed to study racial differences in people, including craniometry (the measurement of skulls) and phrenology (the study of the shape of the skull in order to understand the underlying brain structure, and also the mental characteristics of an individual). These methods were far from unbiased (Gould 1981), leading their practitioners to support racist theories that they purportedly tested. However, Boas, in the first decade of the twentieth century, used craniometry to demonstrate that the children of migrants to the United States had different skull shapes than their parents, with the cranial shapes, on average, being more like American averages than that of their parents (Gravlee et al. 2003). This suggested that head shape, long used as a racial characteristic, was subject to environmental influence and thus a poor trait to use in characterizing human races.

It was not until the 1920s and 1930s that scientists, largely anthropologists, began to reject racial explanations for cultural differences (Barkan 1992). The aftermath of the horrors of the Nazi holocaust ended much of what was left of scientific racism.

A major advance in anthropology came with the publication in 1950 of Coon, Garn, and Birdsell's (1950) book on human race that viewed races as variable populations whose genetic background and phenotypic traits could be viewed as having arisen due to adaptive processes (Leslie and Little 2003).

With the establishment of the United Nations after World War II, a mission given to UNESCO, the organization's scientific body, was to gather scientific information and from this present a statement on race. The organization stated that race is a classificatory device of humans based upon physical, but not cultural, traits; that humans have been classified into races in various ways, with the majority dividing the species into at least three major groups; that there is no evidence for "pure" races; and that behavioral differences among peoples are based primarily upon cultural, not racial, background (UNESCO 1952). An earlier statement by UNESCO made in 1950 also included the following: "The biological fact of race and the myth of 'race' should be distinguished. For all practical social purposes 'race' is not so much a biological phenomenon as a social myth . . ." (UNESCO 1969).

CARLETON COON AND THE ORIGIN OF RACES. In 1962, the physical anthropologist Carleton Coon published a book entitled *The Origin of Races* (Coon 1962). Coon's major thesis was that *Homo erectus* evolved into *Homo sapiens* five different times over a large geographical expanse in Europe, Asia, and Africa, and these different evolutionary events marked the origin of the five human races. Human races were thus seen to be very old, having been biologically separated even before our own species evolved. It was due to gene flow between races from human migrations that we remain a single species, but the gene flow was not sufficient to break down the major biological differences among these five groups. Genetic work has shown that Coon's scheme is highly unlikely. Moreover, Coon detracted from his own work's scientific value by stating that "each [race] had reached its own level on the evolutionary scale" (Coon 1962, p. vii). Thus, Coon not only had retreated to the long abandoned Great Chain of Being, but also contributed to racist predilections for ranking races in terms of "higher" or "lower" status (Montagu 1963).

THE "NEW" PHYSICAL ANTHROPOLOGY. Beginning in the 1950s, physical anthropologists with a specialty in human biology changed the focus of studies on human variation and race from classificatory issues to concern for the processes that led (and lead) to biological variability in our species.

For instance, Joseph Birdsell examined the spatial pattern of biological differences among Australian aboriginal populations as a function of genetics, marriage patterns, isolation, climate, and other factors (Birdsell 1953). Human biologists began to take a much more sophisticated approach to human biological diversity than simple environmental determinism. Also, the unit of study began to shift from a few racial groups to smaller groupings: human biological populations, often viewed as encompassing cultural groups, but not necessarily identical to them. For instance, Stanley Garn suggested that humans be grouped into three different classifications, namely geographical, local, and micro-races (Garn 1961). This suggestion was based on the increasing evidence that human population variation was not easily divisible into the large, continental-sized groupings that characterized earlier ideas of race (approximately coinciding with Garn's "geographical" races). Human biology now entailed the study of demography, population genetics, environmental physiology, and epidemiology, among other concerns, along with the more traditional studies of body composition and form (Little and Haas 1989), and this deeper understanding of human variability affected ideas about human races.

AMERICAN ANTHROPOLOGICAL ASSOCIATION STATEMENT ON RACE. The American Anthropological Association has also produced a formal statement about race. That statement makes clear that most contemporary anthropologists do not believe that biological race has utility for our species, as can be seen in the introductory paragraph:

> In the United States both scholars and the general public have been conditioned to viewing human races as natural and separate divisions within the human species based on visible physical differences. With the vast expansion of scientific knowledge in this century, however, it has become clear that human populations are not unambiguous, clearly demarcated, biologically distinct groups. Evidence from the analysis of genetics (e.g., DNA) indicates that most physical variation, about 94%, lies *within* so-called racial groups. Conventional geographic "racial" groupings differ from one another only in about 6% of their genes. This means that there is greater variation within "racial" groups than between them. In neighboring populations there is much overlapping of genes and their phenotypic (physical) expressions. Throughout history whenever different groups have come into contact, they have interbred. The continued sharing of genetic materials has maintained all of humankind as a single species. (American Anthropological Association, 1998; the full statement may be found at: http://www.aaanet.org/stmts/racepp.htm.)

To understand contemporary scientific views on human race, an overview of the extensive information about human biological variability is necessary. Human variability may be conveniently, and in some cases arbitrarily, divided into those complex phenotypic traits such as skin color that have commonly been used in characterizing races, and those traits for which the genetic basis is well known, although they have not traditionally been used in racial classifications, such as blood type. The rest of this chapter will examine some of the common phenotypic characteristics of complex inheritance used in studies of human variability, because these are often the traits used in constructing fictitious "racial" taxonomies of our species.

PHENOTYPIC CHARACTERISTICS OF HUMAN VARIABILITY

Nature Versus Nurture

Through much of the history of the scientific study of human variation, a dichotomy in approach has existed between those who emphasize human traits as having arisen due to *nature* (that is, genetics determining a trait's presence), versus those who have emphasized *nurture* (that is, environmental conditions determining a trait's presence). Debates have raged over whether specific traits such as intelligence, skin color, personality, and so forth are a part of our nature or due to our nurture. It has become clear that the complex traits that are of interest to human biologists, and to anthropologists in general, are not determined by only one or the other of these dichotomous factors. Complex traits have both genetic and environmental components, as we will see for the examples of phenotypic characteristics discussed below.

The rapid progress in understanding the molecular basis of inheritance, including the human genome project, has for a time tilted the discussion towards nature in the nature versus nurture dichotomy. However, other research has shown that environmental and epigenetic processes can have major effects on gene regulation and thus on the phenotype. Matt Ridley (2003) has contributed to this debate by introducing the notion of nature *via* nurture, stating that "genes are designed to take their cues from nurture" (p. 4). Thus, it is the interplay between the environment and our genes, sometimes in a very intimate way, that determines our biological traits.

HERITABILITY. Geneticists have developed an index for assessing the relative amount of genetic versus environmental influence on a variable trait in human populations, as noted in Chapter 4. This index is termed **heritability** and is defined as the proportion of a trait's variance in a population that can be explained strictly by genetics. If all the variability in a trait is determined by genetics, the trait would have a heritability of 1, while a trait whose variability is entirely due to environmental causes would have a heritability of 0. Thus, all traits of interest to human biologists have heritabilities between 0 and 1.

Actually, traits are not only affected by genetics and environment, but also by the **interaction** between genetics and environment. A given set of genes will yield different traits when in one environment instead of another, and environmental effects on a trait will differ depending upon the specific genome that is present. Thus, how a phenotypic trait manifests is a product of genetics, environment, and an interaction effect between genes and environment.

In practice, it is nearly impossible to determine heritability of traits in humans, as geneticists do not have the ability to perform mating experiments on people. In reality, heritability is estimated from studies within families: of twins—particularly by comparing relative similarities between identical (monozygotic) and fraternal (dizygotic) twins, of adopted versus biological children, and so forth.

Human Pigmentation: Skin Color

MELANIN. The most common characteristic used in racial characterizations is skin color. Scientific study of skin color has uncovered some of the complexities of this characteristic. The main contributor to variation in this trait is the amount and distribution of a dark pigment in the skin termed **melanin**. Actually, melanin comes in two varieties: eumelanin, the main component of skin color that has a dark color (and referred to hereafter simply as "melanin"), and phaeomelanin, which has a red hue. Cells called **melanocytes**, chiefly present in the germinative layer of the epidermis, or outer skin tissue, produce the melanin in the skin. Most melanin is present in vesicles termed **melanosomes** located within skin cells called "keratinocytes" (see Figure 6-3). The number of melanocytes in an individual is approximately the same for people of all skin colors (Brues 1977). What differs among people is the amount of melanin produced by each cell, the size of melanin granules, and how the melanin gets distributed in the skin. In general, people with dark skin color have melanocytes that produce melanin faster and distribute it more evenly (Szabo et al. 1969). Light-skinned people often have melanin granules clumped into groups; this sometimes leads to the formation of freckles upon exposure to the sun. Skin color is also affected by the depth of melanin below the skin surface.

BIOCHEMISTRY OF MELANIN PRODUCTION. Both eumelanin and phaeomelanin are derived from biochemical pathways that involve the common amino acids tyrosine and dihydroxyphenylalanine

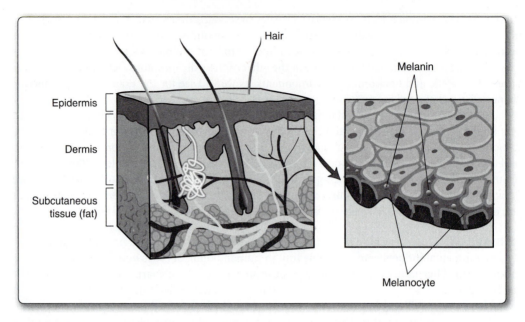

FIGURE 6-3 A cross-section of human skin, showing melanocytes and melanin distribution.

(DOPA). Figure 6-4 shows a simplified version of the biochemical pathways that lead to the two types of melanin. The actual pathways are more complex. Because of these complexities, several (at least six) genetic loci are known to make significant contributions to human variation in skin pigmentation (Parra 2007).

ENVIRONMENTAL EFFECTS ON MELANIN. Soon after exposure to ultraviolet light, melanin increases in the skin, possibly due to the photooxidation of preexisting melanin and its chemical precursors (Kollias and Bykowski 1999). This is followed by an increased rate of melanin production by melanocytes, with the increased amount of melanin lasting for several weeks (Brues 1977), producing a tan. The melanin is taken up by squamous epithelial cells which are eventually sloughed off, causing the tan to fade.

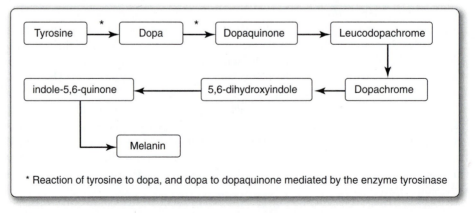

FIGURE 6-4 Simplified diagram of chemical pathways for melanin production.

GENETICS OF MELANIN PRODUCTION. Melanin production is affected by the action of several genetic loci and is incompletely understood (Barnicot 1957; Parra 2007). **Albinism** is a trait caused by the inability to produce melanin and can be caused by several different genetic conditions with variable degrees of melanin suppression. The trait is found in all human populations, but there is much diversity in the frequency at which the trait is found. Albinos possess melanocytes, but these cannot produce melanin. The absence of melanin not only affects skin color, but also has effects on some aspects of neurological development, particularly in the visual system. Albinos are at a very high risk for developing skin cancer, particularly in tropical environments (Robins 1991).

The genetics of variable melanin production in non-albinos is complex, involving several major genes in addition to a few modifier genes (Sturm et al. 2001). Some of the major alleles that have been implicated in normal human skin color variation include the melanocortin 1 receptor gene (MC1R), SLC24A5, membrane-associated transporter protein gene (MATP), OCA2, agouti signaling protein gene (ASIP) and the tyrosinase gene (TYR) (Parra 2007). In the mouse, which has been used as an animal model for the genetics of skin color, at least 150 alleles at over fifty loci have been identified in pigmentation regulation (Robins 1991). Thus, the genetics of human pigmentation is apparently quite complex and certainly imperfectly understood.

OTHER DETERMINANTS OF SKIN COLOR. Other factors that affect skin color stem from hemoglobin found in blood, carotene, and the thickness of the skin's stratum corneum (this is the outer layer of the epidermis that contains the chemical keratin, which has a slightly yellowish hue). The reddish hue from hemoglobin is determined principally by the amount of blood flow near the surface of the body. When there is dilation of superficial (that is, near the body surface) blood vessels, a reddish "blush" is visible. The reddish tint is in part obscured if the stratum corneum is thick (Brues 1977). Carotene is usually present in fairly small amounts and thus contributes little to skin color (Robins 1991). The amount of carotene is determined principally by diet.

THE MEASUREMENT OF SKIN COLOR. There is a problem in measuring skin color in studies of human biological variability: skin color is quite variable in individuals, so the circumstances of measurement have a great effect on what, in fact, is measured. Traditionally, human biologists used color charts to determine skin color. This method made it difficult to make quantitative assessments and involved much subjectivity. In 1926, the recording spectrophotometer was used, and it permitted more objective assessment of skin color. The device, also termed a reflectometer, allows measurement of the percentage of light reflected from the skin at selected wavelengths throughout the visible spectrum (Robins 1991).

Even with the use of reflectometers, the problem of individual variation in skin color over time remains. Exposure to UV radiation from sunlight leads to tanning due to an increase in melanin production and a resulting darkening of the skin. Thus, to obtain a baseline reading, one must measure "where the sun don't shine," a procedure that is often disconcerting to those being measured, and also variable in location depending upon cultural and environmental factors. Frequently the inside surface of the upper arm is used for measurements, but some sun exposure is likely in this location for many people, as evidenced by seasonal differences in values at this site that are presumably related to differential sun exposure.

INTRA-INDIVIDUAL VARIABILITY IN SKIN COLOR. There are several factors known to influence an individual's skin color. Tanning is obviously a critical factor, affected by exposure to sunlight. Age is a factor, as well: there is much less variation in skin color among newborn infants than in adults.

In some populations, studies have shown that skin color darkens around the time of puberty, possibly due to the effects of increased secretion of pituitary hormones (for example, Conway and Baker 1972), with skin color lightening again in adulthood. This change with age has not been seen in studies of some other populations (Robins 1991). With aging in adults, there tends to be a drop-off in melanin production in unexposed skin, and thus a lightening of skin color. However, the reverse is seen in exposed skin: older adults show darker skin color in exposed areas (Gilchrest et al. 1979). Elderly people also tend to have a more mottled skin color, with "age spots" and increased freckling common (Petit et al. 2003).

There are distinct sex differences seen in most populations for skin color: females tend to be lighter skinned than males (Jablonski and Chaplin 2000). This is particularly true at skin sites where there is sun exposure, as males tend to have more exposure than females in many populations. In most populations, females also have lighter skin color in unexposed areas, but there are exceptions (Robins 1991).

IS THERE SELECTIVE VALUE TO DIFFERENTIAL SKIN COLOR?   Given the variability in skin color among and within human populations, several explanations for why this occurs have been suggested. Most of the explanations are based on a general tendency for darker-skinned peoples to be found nearer to the equator than light-skinned populations. This trend is seen in many animals and has been termed **Gloger's Rule**. Gloger actually noted that darker populations of animals were found in warm, moist climates; those in cold, arid climates were pale; and those in deserts were yellow or reddish-brown (Robins 1991). Figure 6-5 shows the geographical distribution of human skin color in the Old World. The map is based on populations native to given geographic regions, not representing recent human migrations. Based on this map, there is a general trend to support Gloger's Rule in humans, but the relationship between latitude and skin color is not a strong one.

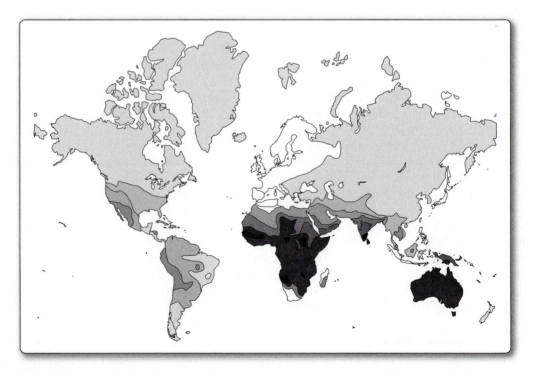

FIGURE 6-5 Map showing distribution of human skin color in aboriginal populations. Darker colors denote average darker population skin color.

Also, the map does not reflect the enormous amount of skin-color variation among individuals living within each region.

In fact, the distribution of human skin color is complex. The lightest colors are found among northern Europeans, with a **cline** in color such that populations further south in Europe have, on average, darker skin color. Skin color continues to darken in African populations as one moves south from Europe. People living in sub-Saharan Africa tend to have very dark skin, but there is quite a bit of variation. For instance, the San population of Southern Africa has considerably lighter skin color than most surrounding populations. In Asia, there is much less skin color variation based on latitude. There is a tendency for somewhat darker skin among populations in equatorial regions such as Indonesia. There are small populations, thought to be remnants of more widespread aboriginal groups, found in some areas of south and southeast Asia. These people have skin color that is as dark as many African populations, although they do not appear to be closely related to them genetically. Stretching east of this area, the populations of Melanesia are also dark skinned, as are aboriginal Australians, but Micronesian and Polynesian populations in the Pacific are much lighter skinned on average. There is, however, an enormous amount of diversity in skin color within Melanesia, with differences found between islands and also between neighborhoods on individual large islands (Norton et al. 2006). While there is no certainty, it is likely that the early inhabitants of tropical Asia and the Pacific were dark skinned, with later arrivals having lighter skin color.

The relationship between skin color and latitude among aboriginal groups in the New World is much less pronounced than is the case in the Old World. This is because all of these populations might be descended from northeast Asian populations within the last 15,000 years or so (there is much dispute over when the first Americans arrived in the New World) and therefore had less genetic variability in genes related to skin pigmentation than are found in other regions (Brues 1977).

UV RADIATION AND SKIN-COLOR VARIATION. Based on the trend for darker-skinned populations to be found at lower latitudes, a common hypothesis is that the darker skin color in the tropics is an adaptation to protect people from harmful ultraviolet radiation in sunlight. However, for this adaptation to have been naturally selected, some effect on reproduction would be necessary. Increased UV radiation exposure does lead to painful sunburn in previously unexposed, light-skinned people, and it does increase people's risk for skin cancer. Severe sunburn can damage sweat glands, increasing risk for infection and disrupting sweat production (Rees 2004). Except perhaps in albinos, in contemporary people skin cancer usually does not become a critical issue until late in life, when most people have already completed their reproductive lives. However, early hominid populations evolved in tropical areas and, before the adoption of clothing and shelter, were exposed to a much greater extent than contemporary humans (Jurmain et al. 2005). Thus, there may have been selection for dark skin color in early hominid populations.

SKIN COLOR VARIATION AND VITAMIN D SYNTHESIS. Another hypothesis for the origin of human skin color variability has to do with the ability to synthesize vitamin D in one's skin. Humans can synthesize vitamin D through a chemical reaction in which ultraviolet light helps transform 7-dehydrocholesterol (7-DHC), a compound related to cholesterol that is found in the epidermal and dermal skin layers, into vitamin D. Vitamin D is essential for proper bone development, and a deficiency during infancy or early childhood can lead to rickets, a disease characterized by the bowing of bones and improper tooth development. In particular, the disease can result in pelvic deformities, which can lead to severe difficulties for females in giving birth. While vitamin D is present in many foods, people with a diet deficient in vitamin D are at risk for rickets if their skins do not receive sufficient exposure to sunlight. In people who live at high latitudes where sunlight is seasonally limited and skin is often covered by clothing, dark-skinned people may well have been at higher risk for developing rickets, and hence lighter skin color may have been selected. People with dark skin require as much as ten times the sun exposure to produce the amount of vitamin D that light-skinned people can produce (Holick 2003). There is some evidence for this hypothesis in the fossil record: several Neanderthal specimens from northern areas of Europe show signs of rickets (Campbell 1985), suggesting that these early natives of high latitudes were imperfectly adapted to those conditions, possibly being dark skinned as well as having diets poor in vitamin D.

SKIN-COLOR VARIATION AND FOLATE PHOTOLYSIS.   Another vitamin-related theory for skin-color variation related to Gloger's Rule is the observation that high levels of solar radiation lead to the breakdown of folate, an important B vitamin, in the epidermis (Jablonski and Chaplin 2000). Folate is important in development of the nervous system in fetuses and also is necessary for successful sperm production, thus making protection of folate stores a potentially important selective force in humans. In fact, folate has become an important dietary supplement for young women, particularly those likely to become pregnant. Such neurological birth defects as anencephalus and spina bifida are more common in light-skinned populations than in darker-skinned peoples, giving empirical support to this theory.

SKIN-COLOR VARIATION AND CONCEALMENT.   Probably the most common reason given by evolutionary biologists for animal coloration is its ability to camouflage individuals from potential predators. This was discussed briefly in earlier chapters, where the example of industrial melanism in pepper moths showed that coloration clearly serves to enhance fitness. While the widespread use of clothing in contemporary people makes variation in skin color a poor candidate for camouflage, earlier hominids did not use clothing and may have needed concealment for protection from predators and possibly for sneaking up on prey (Cowles 1959). However, the details of human coloration do not support this idea very well. It is problematic as to whether dark skin may offer more concealment in a rainforest environment; most animals in this biome are brown or gray (Hamilton 1973). Better still for camouflage is the use of mottled colors or patterns. Also, humans in African savannas are perhaps darker skinned than their rainforest-living neighbors, and dark colors in the savanna make for greater visibility. Thus, it is unlikely that concealment has been a major factor in selection for population differences in skin color.

SKIN COLOR AS A RACIAL MARKER.   We are fairly ignorant of the genetic basis for skin color variability in humans. We do note geographic clines in mean skin color in many areas of the world, which has been related to Gloger's Rule. As noted, there are apparently selective reasons for this variation, related to protection of the skin against UV radiation, and also the relationship between solar radiation and vitamin anabolism (synthesis) or catabolism (breakdown) in the epidermis. This makes skin color a very poor attribute to use to define human races, as differences are not clearly clumped into large geographic regions, may have changed over time due to selective forces, and are hard to measure anyhow because of the short-term changes consequent upon exposure to the sun. Skin color variation, therefore, "reflect[s] *underlying environmental factors*, instead of population history" (Parra 2007, p. 101).

Understanding skin-color variability in human biology requires consideration of skin's function as a whole. Skin functions as a fluid barrier, temperature regulator, mechanical barrier to pathogens, UV shield, and a site for glandular secretions. Skin color needs to be viewed as one factor among many that allows skin to act as an adaptive barrier between an individual's interior and the outside world.

Human Pigmentation: Hair and Eye Color

HAIR COLOR.   There is considerably less variability in human hair color than in skin color. Essentially, with the exception of northern European populations, dark brown or black hair color is the norm in most people. European populations have expanded quite a bit in the past few centuries, however, and light-haired people have therefore become more common in other regions of the world.

Hair color is similar to skin pigmentation in that it varies principally due to the amount of melanin. Melanocytes are found in hair follicles and produce melanin that is transferred into the cells that make up hair (Brues 1977). The eumelanin makes up the hair shades that blend from straw color (very little melanin) to black. The red pigment phaeomelanin has an effect on hair color, with its hue very apparent in people with light-colored hair, but red tints also can be seen in people with darker shades of hair color. There is some tendency for dark hair to be associated with dark skin, but this is not always the case. Some very light skinned people have dark hair color. The reverse also sometimes occurs, but much more rarely; for example a phenomenon of "blondism" is fairly common among the fairly dark-skinned people of Melanesia (Robins 1991; Norton et al. 2006).

As with skin color, there has been much subjectivity in the measurement of hair color. Use of reflective spectrophotometers allows more objective measurement of variation in hair color (Vaughn et al. 2008).

AGE AND HAIR COLOR. With age, hair color may actually darken, as more melanin accumulates in hair. There are also color changes that coincide with puberty, with hair color sometimes darkening at this time, presumably due to hormonal effects. This usually is more striking in males than in females. As one gets older, some melanocytes die, leaving individual hairs with no melanin. As more of these essentially white hairs accumulate, a salt-and-pepper, or graying, tint is seen, with hair whitening as a greater percentage of hairs becomes depigmented.

GENETICS OF HAIR COLOR. As with skin pigmentation, the genetics of hair coloration is largely unknown. There is a high concordance of hair color in identical twins at all ages, considerably more so than in fraternal twins. Hair color certainly shows general familial patterns, but the actual genetics is complex. There are genetic effects on initial hair color, and independent genetic influences on color changes that occur due to aging. There are further complications due to different hair-color patterns between head hair and other body hair, including facial hair on men. Up to 20 percent of total hair color variance may be environmentally determined (Bräuer and Chopra 1980), further complicating analyses.

ADAPTIVE VALUE OF HEAD HAIR COLOR VARIATION. As with skin color, there may be an advantage to having dark hair in regions with high levels of UV radiation, as dark hair color is more protective against UV damage to underlying skin. Also, dark hair may serve to trap more heat, and since hair has insulating qualities, the heat may be transferred to the air rather than heating up skin (Brues 1977).

EYE COLOR. Iris pigmentation is also principally due to the amount of melanin present in melanocytes. Unlike in skin or hair, melanin in the iris of the eye remains in the melanocyte, and the melanocytes do not continuously produce new melanin throughout life. The blue color in eyes is not caused by a blue pigment. In irises with low levels of melanin, the iris is essentially translucent. This leads to what is termed "Tyndall scattering" of light, and, similar to what happens in the earth's sky, blue light is preferentially reflected (Robins 1991). While most eyes that are dark brown in color have a continuous layer of melanocytes, the layer is not continuous in the eyes of some people, particularly in those with lighter-colored eyes, and therefore the color is variable throughout the iris.

The iris is not the only portion of the eye that is pigmented, although it is most apparent. The interior portion of the eyeball, termed the fundus, is differentially colored from an orange tint in light-colored eyes to a chocolate brown in those with dark eyes. The retina also contains melanocytes, although they apparently produce melanin only during embryotic life, with no melanin produced after birth.

As with the genetics of other pigmentation, the genetics of eye color is complex and poorly understood. There is greater concordance among identical than fraternal twins, indicating that genetics is an important component of eye-color variation. As with hair color, environmental effects on eye color are also present.

Human biologists discern little adaptive benefit from differential eye color. Lighter-colored eyes are apparently somewhat more sensitive to red light. Albinos, with no melanin in their irises or retinas, have difficulty seeing in bright light. In general, neither eye nor hair color appear to be useful as traits for racial categorization: they have little geographic variability, have complex genetics, and their adaptive value is open to question.

Hair Form

Human hair form comes in several varieties, with characterization traditionally as "straight," "wavy," "curly," "woolly," and "peppercorn." These different forms actually represent points along a continuum. Hair form is principally determined by the shape of the hair shaft. Individuals whose hair shafts have a very round cross-section have straight hair, while those whose hair shafts have an ovoid cross-section end up with hair having a greater or lesser degree curl, depending upon how distended the ovoid is (see Figure 6-6). Use of objective measures of hair shape, based on amount of curl, waviness, number of twists in the hair shaft, and the radius of hair curvature, has shown that hair shape does not match up with continental races, but rather that there is variation within all populations and between populations within a given region of the world (De la Mettrie et al. 2007).

The genetics of hair form appears to be complex, as great variation is seen in the offspring of parents with different types of hair form. There is also little understanding about the adaptive value of different hair forms, although woolly or very curly hair provides more insulation, and may perhaps allow the underlying scalp to stay cooler under intense solar radiation exposure. It is in some

FIGURE 6-6 Hair-shaft cross-sections and hair form.

FIGURE 6-7 Eyelids. Top, no epicanthic eyefold; bottom, complete epicanthic eyefold.

tropical populations that highly curled hair varieties are most common, so there may be some selective value involving ultraviolet or heat protection to the head from these types of hair form.

Epicanthic Eyefolds

Another phenotypic characteristic that has been used in an attempt to identify racial differences in humans is the presence of the so-called Oriental eye. This structure is due to a fold in the eyelid termed the **epicanthic eyefold**, but its appearance is also due to differences in general facial structure such as size of the cheekbones and the amount and distribution of subcutaneous fat in the face.

There are five varieties of eyefold: no fold, internal epicanthus, external epicanthus, median fold, and complete; and one can have combinations of these present (see Figure 6-7). These eye-folds are not limited to East Asian populations; many individuals in other populations have one or more of these varieties (see Figure 6-8). It is the median fold that is so characteristic of East Asian populations—nearly all people in these populations have it. Some people in other populations also have it; in these people there seems to be a relationship with a low-lying nasal bridge. We do not understand this trait's genetics, and little is known about a possible adaptive value one way or the other, although the East Asian face in general may be adapted for cold climates with a non-prominent nose, broad face, and increased amounts of subcutaneous fat compared with other populations.

Body Size and Shape

HUMAN VARIABILITY IN STATURE. Body size represents yet another phenotypic feature of complex inheritance used to characterize human populations. For **stature**, environmental factors appear to be of great importance: many populations were thought to be genetically short, but people in these groups became much taller when nutrition and/or health status improved. Adult stature is based in part upon children's growth patterns; in general, taller populations show faster rates of growth in stature. A classic example of the environmental effects on stature has occurred among Japanese populations. Previous to World War II, heights of children in Japanese immigrant populations in California and Hawaii were compared with age-mates in Japan (Greulich 1976; Eveleth and Tanner 1990; Kano and Chung 1975). The children in California were tallest, followed by Hawaii,

FIGURE 6-8 Epicanthic eyefold in a non-East Asian and Asian. **A.** Jimmy Carter, **B.** Mao Zedung.

and then Japan. In the decades after the war the height differences among these three populations narrowed. This was due to a general increase in height among Japanese children compared with that from previous generations. The phenomenon of a general change over generations is referred to as a **secular trend**.

SECULAR TREND IN STATURE.   This change in height among Japanese children is part of a global phenomenon. People tend to be getting taller in successive generations throughout the world. The secular trend for increased stature, and faster growth in stature during childhood, has leveled off in developed countries (where it started several generations ago) but continues in developing countries. It is generally believed that the secular trend for increased height is due to improved nutrition and health care found in developed countries over the past century or two. Contrary to this, economic dislocation sometimes leads to a **negative** secular trend. This is a sign of serious concern for a region, as it may be accompanied by other indicators of childhood problems, such as increased infant and child mortality rates. Examples of this are present in children from several African populations (Tobias 1985) and also have been seen among Guatemalan children of high social class during a period of political instability (Bogin et al. 1996).

Because of the strong influence of environmental factors in determining a population's stature, whether during growth or at adulthood, stature is a very poor characteristic to use as a means of categorizing human races. Stature is clearly influenced by genetics as well as environment, however. Short-statured parents are probably well advised to counsel a child away from an intended career in professional basketball, given that he or she is also likely to become a short-statured adult.

SHORT STATURED POPULATIONS.   There may be cases where clear differences in genetics leads to population-based differences in stature. Two groups that have been particularly studied are the so-called pygmy groups of central Africa, and some aboriginal populations of southeast Asia and the Western Pacific. These two groups of short-statured peoples are not closely related genetically (Molnar 2002).

Research done among the Efe Pygmies of central Africa has indicated that these people are resistant to the growth-promoting effects of a protein termed insulin-like growth factor, or IGF_1, and that this resistance is probably due to a genetically based reduction in certain IGF_1 receptor sites on cells (Jain et al. 1998). Unfortunately, no research of this sort has been undertaken among southeast Asian populations, and therefore little is known of the mechanism causing the short stature in these people. The smaller stature among Pygmy and southeast Asian groups may be an evolutionary adaptation to cope with intermittent famine and the hot, humid climates in which they reside.

HUMAN VARIABILITY IN BODY WEIGHT. Tremendous variability in weight is observed within all human populations. Body weight is highly dependent upon environmental factors, namely diet and exercise. There is some variation among populations in tendencies to put on body fat when there is a steady and plentiful supply of food. For example, native American and Polynesian populations have high rates of obesity when they live under modernized conditions where food is plentiful and physical activity is often curtailed.

THE THRIFTY GENOTYPE. The higher rates of obesity in certain populations is hypothesized as being due to a **thrifty genotype.** A thrifty genotype is said to be caused by a combination of genes that leads to the rapid production of insulin when food is ingested. The insulin production permits the body to lay down fat efficiently and may be an adaptation to an environment characterized by cycles of feast and famine (Neel 1982). During feast periods, body fat is laid down, and during famine periods, these fat reserves are used as a calorie supply to allow survival until the famine ends. When these people reside in an environment where famine periods have become rare or absent, such as in modernized circumstances, the people continue to lay down fat, leading to high rates of obesity and high risk for developing diabetes mellitus. In fact, most human populations have thrifty genotypes, and the variability between populations is probably due to a complex mixture of environmental, social, and genetic factors, plus the interaction of these factors.

BODY SHAPE AND CLIMATE. General body form may be related to climatic factors. Two general rules have been established by environmental physiologists that pertain to climatic adaptations. **Bergmann's Rule** states that in a widely dispersed, warm-blooded species, the average body size is larger in populations that reside in areas where the temperature of the habitat is colder. **Allen's Rule** states that in a widely dispersed, warm-blooded species, extremities are reduced in size on average in populations residing in cold climates. Both rules relate to the connection between body volume and body surface area. As body volume increases, the amount of heat that can be generated by body mass also increases. As body surface area increases, however, the rate at which body heat is lost to the environment increases. Therefore, in cold climates, it is most adaptive to minimize surface area relative to volume. Large body size with short extremities helps maximize volume to surface area ratios. On the other hand, in hot climates people are better off transferring the heat their bodies generate to the outside, and this is best accomplished with the high ratio of surface area to volume provided by a linear body build with long extremities (see Figure 6-9).

TEMPORAL DIMENSION OF BODY SHAPE. Aspects of human body shape can also be determined in skeletal material, allowing investigation of this aspect of human diversity in ancient populations. It appears that a latitudinal cline in body shape is of long standing in the *Homo* genus and persists in modern human populations (Ruff 2002). This adds to the evidence for an evolutionary component to body-shape variability in our species.

The genetic basis for body-weight and shape differences among human populations is largely unknown. These differences surely involve many genetic alleles at multiple loci and involve complex molecular processes involving metabolism, digestion, growth, exercise physiology, and a host of other factors. Environmental factors are also important. For instance, mammals that develop at low temperatures have shorter appendages than siblings raised under warmer conditions.

FIGURE 6-9 Bergmann's and Allen's rules in human populations.

Head Form

Physical anthropologists have traditionally described population variation in many features of head and facial form, including overall facial shape, skull proportions, details of the shapes of the ears, lips, nose, and other facial features. For all these features, little is known about the genetic basis for variability, and there have been no credible explanations for how these differences may serve an adaptive purpose. Also, the heritability of these traits is not well understood. One feature, however, has had an impact on human biological studies in the early twentieth century, and again in the early years of the twenty-first century: overall head form.

In the nineteenth century, anthropologists commonly used head form as a racial feature, measuring skulls or living heads to derive an index of head breadth versus head length. This index of head shape, termed the **cephalic index**, differed on average among human populations. For example, East Europeans, including East-European-derived Jewish populations, have a higher cephalic index on average, and thus rounder head form, than Western European populations. However, in a study of the children of immigrants from Eastern Europe to the United States that was briefly mentioned earlier, Franz Boas (1910) showed that the children born in the United States had somewhat longer heads than their parents, and that the children whose mothers had been in the United States for over ten years before their birth had even longer heads on average. Since at the time the U.S. population mirrored Western Europe in having on average fairly long heads, the children of immigrants were becoming more like other U.S. children. Thus, head form was seen to be a plastic rather than a fixed trait. This undermined the considerable literature that until that time had considered head form to be an inherited trait that was an important component of racial categorization. It is hard to overestimate the impact of Boas's study on the history of human biology, as it called into question many of the suppositions about biological fixity of human types or races that fed the scientific racism of the time (Gravlee et al. 2003).

Boas worked at a time when the application of statistics to analyses of population data was still in its infancy, long before the invention of digital computers permitted the sophisticated analyses that are commonplace today. Two different groups of human biologists have reanalyzed Boas's data on head form in immigrants, and have reached different conclusions about the validity of Boas's conclusions. Gravlee and coworkers (2003) have suggested that, while new analyses add much detail to Boas's work, the basic conclusions that Boas reached were appropriate. On the other hand, analyses by Sparks and Jantz (2002) suggest that Boas may have underestimated the importance of genetic factors in head form. While these reinterpretations of this early data set have been debated in a lively fashion, the underlying notion that human phenotypic traits often have important environmental components has been demonstrated clearly for most characteristics that have been misused in racial categorization.

DERMATOGLYPHICS

A final example of a variable human physical characteristic that has a complex genetic basis is the pattern of ridges found on the fingers, palms, and soles. These ridges are found among nonhuman primates as well, and may have evolved as an adaptation in these arboreal animals for better gripping of tree branches. The study of these ridge patterns is formally termed **dermatoglyphics** (literally, "skin writings"). These skin patterns appear to be at least partially determined by genetics, but there are also important effects caused by developmental processes.

Skin ridges develop in humans between the 11th and 17th weeks of gestation and are affected by conditions in the uterus (Babler 1991). Once the ridges develop, the patterns remain stable for the rest of the individual's life. Thus, environmental influences on dermatoglyphics all occur before birth.

Identical twins have different fingerprints, due to differences in the environment for each individual while in the womb. However, there is greater similarity in identical than in fraternal twins in their dermatoglyphic patterns, suggesting genetic or shared intrauterine influences. Heritability of fingerprint patterns has been estimated at about 0.90 (Brues 1977), although this figure has been disputed (Borecki et al. 1985). The details of the genetic basis for dermatoglyphic variability in human populations are poorly understood and are likely to be highly complex (Chakraborty 1991). Individuals with certain genetic abnormalities display some specific ridge patterns, however. For example, people with Down's syndrome, a genetic abnormality in which an extra copy of chromosome 21 is present, tend to have an elongated ridge in their palm that is referred to as a "single palmar crease."

Brain and skin tissue derive from the same embryonic tissue, and it has therefore been suggested that developmental conditions that could lead to dermatoglyphic abnormalities may also be associated with neurological or psychiatric problems. For example, evidence has shown clear associations between reductions in palmar ridge counts and susceptibility to schizophrenia (van Oel et al. 2001; Markow and Wandler 1986).

Much work in dermatoglyphics has focused on ridge patterns on fingertips, in part because of the use of these patterns in identifying criminals. Fingertip patterns have been generally categorized into three basic types: arches, loops, and whorls (see Figure 6-10). Investigators have also examined ridge density in a given skin area, as well as the number of ridges between various landmarks in the ridge pattern. The ridges that make up these patterns appear at a glance to be continuous, but

Arch   **Loop**   **Whorl**

FIGURE 6-10 Major types of dermatoglyphic patterns on the fingertips: arch, loop and whorl.

actually have many branches, interruptions, and other irregularities. These irregularities give finger-prints their individuality.

Women generally have a higher ridge density than men (Acree 1999). Females also generally have a higher frequency of arches and a lower frequency of whorls compared to males (Fraser and Nora 1975).

There is some tendency for East Asian, Native American, and Australian aboriginal popula-tions to have a lower frequency of arches and a higher frequency of whorls than other populations (Brues 1977; Fraser and Nora 1975), but in general there are no clear worldwide trends in dermato-glyphic patterns. In fact, it has been estimated that 84 to 89 percent of the total human genetic diver-sity in dermatoglyphics is due to differences between individuals within major population groups (Chakraborty 1991). Varying frequencies of the patterns are useful in distinguishing closely related populations, however, and can help in understanding microevolutionary processes in human popu-lation biology (Meier 1991). For instance, differences in dermatoglyphic patterns have been found among different populations within Europe, with Lapp (Saami) and some other populations dis-tinct from other European groups (Jantz 1997). Differences have also been found within individuals on Easter Island (Rapa Nui) indicative of admixture between native Polynesians and Europeans (Meier 1975), and variation in dermatoglyphics patterns among people in Papua New Guinea has been shown to be closely related to linguistic differences among the New Guinea populations, with the linguistic differences associated with the distance of relationship between populations (Froehlich and Giles 1981).

Thus, dermatoglyphics, along with many other traits with a complex genetic basis, are of interest in studies of relationships among different human populations, but these traits are of little or no value in attempts to categorize human populations into larger groupings of races.

SKELETAL AND DENTAL VARIATION

Many anthropologists study skeletal and dental features of modern humans. Study of these human "hard parts" is useful in understanding human variation in the past, as these are the structures that may persist for long periods of time in fossil or archaeological contexts. The scientists who study human skeletal remains may also help in criminal investigations. These **forensic anthropologists** are involved in determining the identity of homicide victims through features found in the skeleton and teeth.

Age Differences in the Skeleton and Teeth

Age at death of a skeleton may be estimated by known changes that occur during growth and devel-opment and during aging. Baby teeth and adult teeth erupt at fairly predictable ages, and therefore the presence or absence of specific teeth helps in assigning an age estimate. Also, teeth tend to wear over time, allowing estimates of age, although one must account for the grittiness of food in the population's usual diet. Bone growth and development, and the eventual calcification of the bones, occur at a well understood rate for individual bones; again, this permits estimation of age. Finally, patterns of wear in the joints can also be used in estimating a skeleton's age.

Sex Differences in the Skeleton

There are some skeletal traits that show fairly clear differences between males and females, particu-larly in the pelvic area. The pelvic bones of women are adapted for childbirth, with females possessing a larger area in the region that forms the birth canal. This accommodation for childbirth is reflected in differences in pelvic-bone shape. In general, male skeletons tend to be larger and heavier than that of females, although there is much overlap between smaller men and larger women. A number of traits have been designated as "male" or "female" in skeletons, although most skeletons have some of each type. An estimate of the skeleton's sex is based on the preponderance of the evidence, with some features, such as in the pelvic area, rated more heavily than others.

PROFILE 6
María Eugenia Peña

María Eugenia Peña's main research interest is growth and skeletal maturation, though she is also interested in physical activity and health issues. Initially, her elementary-school teaching background drew her attention to the need for knowing more about children's growth. Consequently, she studied biological anthropology at the School of Anthropology in Mexico City and later pursued graduate studies at the University of Texas, where she began working with Dr. Robert Malina, a collaboration that has continued for many years. Her initial research involved applying the Fels method for assessing skeletal development, a method that involves examination of bone development in the hand and wrist area, to a comparative study of several populations. Her work led to the publication of a book, as well as various papers on skeletal maturation in children and youth in sports.

Her second major research theme derives from her background in kinesiology and her doctoral dissertation on the growth and physical fitness of schoolchildren in Oaxaca, Mexico, within the context of the project "Secular Trends in Size and Maturation." Research and teaching activities with colleagues from other countries have influenced her work. She has served as a guest professor teaching skeletal maturation at the University of Coimbra, in Portugal, as well as in a collaborative project as a member of the CAMBIO (Canada – Mexico Battling Childhood Obesity) group, promoted by Guadalajara University in Mexico and Canada's Queen's University. Dr. Peña has also participated in the research group on obesity and activity in Mexican children, focusing on the overweight and obesity problems that affect large groups in Mexico. At present, Dr. Peña is a professor of anthropology at the National School of Anthropology in Mexico City, where she conducts research on physical activity and health in schools as an aid in developing health promotion activities. Her research on growth and maturation is currently focused on developing references for skeletal maturation on cervical vertebrae and dental records for contemporary and skeletal Mexican populations.

Individual Variation in Skeletal and Dental Features

There are many features in the skeleton that result from medical conditions, whether from illness or trauma (for example, arthritis, dental cavities, healed fractures, and so forth) that can aid in identifying individuals. There are also some features that are related to known genetic polymorphisms. For instance, people differ in the number of cusps (the rounded bumps found on the chewing, or molar, teeth) that are found on their molar teeth, one example being Carabelli's cusp, a cusp that may be absent or present in various forms and whose presence is estimated to have a heritability of approximately 90 percent (Townsend and Martin 1992).

RACE AND INTELLIGENCE

A final complex trait that has been used in discussions of racial categorizations is intelligence. This is the most controversial issue in studies of human variability, and the one most enmeshed with ideas of racism. Accordingly, it is important that the issue is addressed, even though intelligence is a behavioral, rather than a biological, trait as traditionally defined. As with all complex human traits, there are aspects both of nature and nurture in producing intelligence.

What Is Intelligence?

One of the most important concerns in dealing with the race and intelligence issue is being clear about just what we mean by intelligence. A common definition of intelligence is "the ability to learn." Even if we accept this definition, it turns out that this does not really clarify what is meant by the term. The ability to learn what? There is no consensus as to what intelligence means, or even if there is only one entity or many different kinds of intelligence. For instance, we certainly like to think that humans are more intelligent than rats, as we can learn a lot more than they can. However, if we confine our subject matter to the ability to learn to run through mazes, rats clearly have more intelligence than humans.

IQ VERSUS INTELLIGENCE. The scientific study of general intelligence dates back to Francis Galton's work in the mid-eighteenth century. Modern attempts to measure intelligence stem from the work of French psychologist Alfred Binet, who developed the first intelligence test in 1905 (Molnar 2002). The test was based on typical questions used in school tests (Lewontin et al. 1984), and scores were based on the number of correct answers relative to the mean number of correct answers by children of the same age. Test scores were characterized as "mental age," with this score later divided by chronological age to derive an "intelligence quotient" or IQ (Gould 1981).

Binet himself differentiated between IQ scores and intelligence. He saw his test as a means for identifying children who needed special education, not for ranking all students in terms of general ability. It was others, particularly in the United States, who decided to use the test routinely to assess learning ability (Gould 1981). Ironically, when the test was first used in the United States, scores were relatively low, and the test was then "corrected" for Americans. This need for correction strongly suggested that the test was not deriving inherent ability, but rather measuring how well children had learned to deal with aspects of the culture of those people who created the test.

CHANGES IN IQ TESTS. Spearman (1904) also did early work on intelligence tests, with an assumption that scores on general intelligence tests could be divided into two components: an s component that described aspects of the score specific to the test, and a g component that accounted for aspects of the score that were general to scores on all intelligence tests (Brody 1992). The g component was what constituted a general intelligence measure, according to Spearman. Psychologists have debated the existence of g, and/or its utility, ever since (Carroll 1997).

IQ tests have been modified through the years to improve their ability to predict school performance, and questions that differentiated boys and girls were removed in early revisions, although this was not done for questions that differentiated by ethnicity or social class (Lewontin et al. 1984). Hence, IQ tests apparently became designed to be gender-free indicators of school performance. This is not the same as a measure of intelligence because school performance is based upon many factors besides a general learning ability, if such indeed exists.

Further attempts were made to improve IQ tests. The most commonly used IQ test in the United States in recent times is the Wechsler scales (Armour-Thomas and Gopaul-McNicol 1998). The Wechsler scales were first developed in 1939, but have gone through several revisions. Their popularity relates in part to ease of scoring, but they have been heavily criticized. For instance, there are concerns that the Wechsler scales do not accurately measure g, but rather are a composite of general and specific abilities (Colom et al. 2002).

IQ and Heredity

Great controversy has raged over the degree to which intelligence, however measured, is genetically determined. The controversy is scientific, but also reflects values of society's ability to educate its populace and improve learning performance, as well as one's ability for self-improvement. One thing is clear: IQ cannot be purely a genetic trait, as it is by definition age dependent, and there is some change in measured IQ over time in many people.

To estimate the heritability of intelligence, psychologists turned to twin studies. Sir Cyril Burt's work with identical twins who were separated soon after birth provided strong evidence for the importance of hereditary factors in IQ. Burt showed that the separated twins had very similar IQ scores, and that there was no relation between the environments of the separated twins and their similarity in IQ (Lewontin et al. 1984). There is one important problem with Burt's results: they were apparently based on fraudulent data. Other studies have been done with twins, and a range of computed heritabilities have been published, from near zero to near one, with most falling at or somewhat above the 0.50 level (Brody 1992). These types of studies have been criticized on methodological grounds, from improper standardization of IQ tests, to absence of corrections for age, to the unusual nature of twins, and also to the great similarity in environment of identical twins when raised together.

Other heritability estimates have been made based upon an overview of many family relationships, whether of twins, parent-child, sibling, and other relationships. The results fall in the range of 0.30 to 0.50, depending on whether heritability is defined in a narrow or broad sense (Daniels et al. 1997).

Studies have also examined the similarity in IQ scores among biological and adopted parents with children who had been adopted. These studies have shown effects both from genetics and environment, although the circumstances of the adoption process make accurate estimation of heritability impossible.

A note should be made about heritability estimates: they reflect the variability of the population being studied, both biologically and environmentally. Many IQ studies on heredity have focused on middle class European-American or European populations, usually urban, which surely have a much narrowed environment compared to that for all humanity throughout the world. This will tend to decrease the amount of variability due to environment and thus inflate the calculated heritability scores. At any rate, this is a complex and important subject that goes far beyond the bounds of this textbook.

Population Differences in IQ

The real crux of the concern with IQ is the reported differences in median IQ scores between human groups. There are two comparisons of North American populations that will be focused on here: comparisons between European-Americans and Asian-Americans, and between European-Americans and African-Americans.

ASIAN-AMERICANS VERSUS EUROPEAN-AMERICANS. Studies of Chinese-Americans and Japanese-Americans have shown that children in these ethnic groups average higher performance scores on IQ tests than other American children. There is variability in their performances, however. The Asian-American children get much higher scores on tests of nonverbal ability. They are somewhat above average in verbal ability at young ages, but their scores on these types of test decline as they get older, relative to other children. The less robust scores on verbal ability tests may be due to the higher proportion of Asian-American families in which English is not the primary language. Less difference has been seen in IQ scores between Asian children who reside in Asia and their American agemates, but this may be due to differences in how tests are administered. In fact, it is unclear whether the tests are measuring genetically based differences or culturally based emphases on education and testing.

AFRICAN-AMERICANS VS. EUROPEAN-AMERICANS. Comparisons of IQ scores between African-Americans and other groups have often been used as ammunition by racists to promulgate their view of inherent inferiority of some social groups, and therefore require careful scrutiny. Studies of African-American children have reported average IQ scores that are lower than European-American averages. This difference has been consistent over several decades of testing, and a difference persists when social class is taken into account (Herrnstein and Murray 1994).

There are essentially three explanations that have been given for the difference in average IQ score (principally on the Wechsler scales):

1. The scores are principally due to environmental differences, with African-Americans on average living in environments less conducive to scoring well on IQ tests;
2. The scores are due to genetic differences, with African-Americans on average having less innate ability to score well on these tests [the racist view]; and
3. The tests are culture-bound and simply reflective of cultural differences between African-Americans and European-Americans.

Some explanations have employed combinations of these three possibilities. For instance, one scholar has suggested that perhaps African-Americans on average have a much worse environmental circumstance than European-Americans but are actually genetically superior in IQ ability, reducing the otherwise greater environmentally caused difference (Block 1995). The environmental differences that can impact on IQ scores include nutrition, health, quality of education, influence of peers, and cultural values placed upon formal education.

What most social scientists agree on is that at least part of the difference in IQ scores is due to the nature of the tests themselves. A simple rule should prevail in the use of any tests or behavioral questionnaires: instruments designed for use in a single ethnic group are not valid for use in a multiethnic population unless specifically constructed for that purpose. The IQ test was originally designed to detect children with learning difficulties in Swiss classrooms and has somehow been transformed into a general measure of intelligence for people living throughout the world. It should be no surprise that children from populations that the test was originally designed for would perform better on average than children from different backgrounds.

There is an ethnic difference in average scores on the Wechsler scales between African-Americans and European-Americans. The important question is what this difference means. There has certainly been no demonstration that the difference represents an inherent difference in intelligence between these groups. The tests were also devised to predict school performance, and they may do that to some degree. African-Americans have often had more difficulties in school performance, mostly because the school environment has been designed by and for the European-American majority. Given that these tests have been shown to be sensitive to cultural differences in upbringing, the explanation of inherent intelligence differences between groups should be rejected.

THE BELL CURVE. The obvious racism that appears in the pages of Herrnstein and Bell's book *The Bell Curve* (1994), which purports to show that African-Americans are genetically inferior in intelligence to European-Americans, is abhorrent enough to have elicited vigorous rebuttal. Recitation of all the defects in intelligence testing have been included in these rebuttals: the difference between a score on an IQ test and intelligence, the poor understanding of genetic input on IQ scores, and the cultural bias in the IQ tests that are commonly used in the United States and elsewhere. Students are encouraged to read some of this literature. The citations included in this brief review provide a start.

PATTERNS OF HUMAN VARIABILITY

The trouble that quasi-scientific books about so-called racial differences in IQ scores have caused is symptomatic of the wider misunderstanding of the nature of human population differences. The complex features that have been used to characterize human races simply fail to distinguish large subdivisions of humanity. Most of the important physical traits in modern humans are clinal rather than clumped. That is, traits tend to change gradually on average over geographic ranges, rather than showing sharp borders between large groupings of people. Population differences certainly exist in physical features, at least based on averages (such as average skin-color reflectance values). These differences, however, vary enormously within populations, and there are great differences among populations that are often grouped into races.

In the next chapter, we will explore traits for which the genetics is much better understood than those characteristics described here. Examination of the genetic basis of human differences will allow much better understanding of the patterning of human biological differences throughout the world.

CHAPTER SUMMARY

People have divided themselves into categories for millennia, with these divisions reflecting cultural, environmental, and physical differences. The modern use of the term "race" implies that humans can be categorized into just a few large groupings, often of continental scale. The actual study of human physical traits shows that this categorization is false: human physical traits tend to vary more within populations than between them, and where there are population differences in trait averages, the geographic distribution of the differences usually changes gradually over large distances. This clinal distribution of human variation is not consistent with traditional racial groupings of our species. Therefore, race as used commonly in society has poor scientific support and no scientific utility.

The common traits that have been used to characterize race, such as skin color, hair form, eyelid folds, and body size are not simple genetic traits: they are complex traits that are influenced by many different genes, by environmental conditions, and by the interaction of genes and environment. Some of these traits may have selective value: for instance, darker skin color may protect against ultraviolet radiation in low latitudes where such radiation is high, and light skin color may enable the manufacture of needed vitamins in chemical reactions driven by sunlight. Other traits used in racial classifications have no known adaptive value.

The most insidious of the so-called racial differences are the pseudoscientific attempts by racists to assert that African-Americans are less intelligent than others. A closer look at the data shows that there is no credible evidence for this assertion. Human variation in IQ test scores has much to do with who creates the tests and how they administer it, and also on the effects of social environment. Children brought up in middle- or upper-class homes with well-educated parents and many learning resources perform much better on IQ tests than do children from less enriched environments.

CHAPTER 7

Genotypic Traits and the Tracing of Population Affiliations

Our examination of variable human phenotypic traits suggests that, for many of these complex traits, there is little understanding of their biological, particularly genetic, basis and also poor understanding of their adaptive value, if any. Humans also vary in traits that have a simpler genetic basis, such as the well known ABO blood types, although these traits have not been commonly used as a means for categorizing human "racial" or other population subdivisions. We will refer to these traits of simple genetic basis as **genotypic** traits, as opposed to the phenotypic traits of complex genetic and environmental origin that were considered in the previous chapter. Comparison of human groups for their degree of biological relatedness to each other is best done by evaluation of genetic differences. This type of evaluation can only be carried out when the actual genetic variability is known.

This chapter will therefore focus on common traits determined by fairly simple and well understood genetic mechanisms and how their distribution provides information on the relationship among human populations. How information from actual gene sequencing and genomic studies is used in understanding human population differences will also be described. Genetic information is not only useful in categorizing people, but also allows tracing of past human migrations, understanding the degree of genetic mixing of various ethnic groups with each other, and even reconstructing past changes in population size or structure that affected human groups.

GENOTYPIC TRAITS TRADITIONALLY USED IN HUMAN BIOLOGY

It was not until the early twentieth century that scientists discovered characteristics that varied among people for which they could make a simple genetic explanation. The discovery of the human ABO blood group by Karl Landsteiner (1900) is usually considered the first characterization of a now well understood human genotypic characteristic. Since then, many genotypic traits have been studied by human biologists, most characterized by biochemical variation and thus invisible to the naked eye. These traits often require special scientific procedures (sometimes involving chemical tests of blood samples) to become apparent.

The genotypic traits have been frequently observed through the action of the human immune system. An individual's immune system develops the capacity to distinguish chemicals that are "self" (that is, part of the normal biochemistry of that individual) from "non-self" (and therefore a "foreign" body). Immune system elements will attack non-self bodies in what is termed an antibody-antigen reaction. In simple terms, biochemical variation between individuals can be detected by the immune attack (usually by **antibodies**) of one individual upon the variant chemicals (**antigens**) of another individual. In recent times, specialized techniques in molecular biology have permitted fairly direct observations of genetic differences due to variability in the ordering of nucleotides in DNA or RNA or of amino acids in proteins.

There are exceptions to the need for special procedures to detect genotypic traits, as there are some easily observable variable traits, such as the attachment type of the lower portion of the ear-lobe to the head, that apparently have a simple genetic basis.

Anthropologists have been particularly interested in **polymorphic** (literally, "many forms") traits, referring to genetic loci that have two or more alleles present, with each appearing in at least 1 percent of the population. Polymorphic traits allow study of varying allele frequencies in different human populations. Other traits that show genetic diversity may include fairly rare mutations. These rare alleles may have important medical significance, or they may help us to understand the function of the more common alleles, but they have less utility for tracing population affinities.

Some common examples of polymorphic genotypic traits will be examined, with discussion not only of their genetic basis, but also of the geographic distribution of allele frequencies among human populations. This will allow population comparisons of genetic relatedness.

Blood Groups: The ABO System

The discovery of the ABO blood-group system resulted from the often catastrophic results of early attempts at transfusing blood into patients, where red blood cells would agglutinate, or clump together. The practice of blood transfusions was discontinued because of the immune responses it often generated. It was Landsteiner who demonstrated the different human blood types that led to many of the transfusion difficulties.

BASICS OF THE ABO SYSTEM. The basis of the transfusion problem is that some people carry substances in their blood that are capable of generating immune attacks when placed into the blood-streams of others. Substances that stimulate such an immune response are termed **antigens**. Landsteiner determined that there are actually two different kinds of antigen, termed A and B respectively, present in some people. Some people have only the A antigen (termed "type A"), others just the B (termed "type B"), others both the A and B ("type AB"), and still others have neither ("type O"). Blood transfused from an individual with the A antigen (the donor) into a person who also has the A antigen (the host) provokes no immune attack, as it is recognized as "self," part of the host's normal chemistry. However, blood transfused from the individual with A antigen into a host who has only B antigen will be recognized as foreign, and it will stimulate an immune response (see Figure 7-1).

Type O individuals have none of the antigens in their blood, so when they donate a blood transfusion they do not stimulate an immune response. This has led to the term "universal donor" for type O people. Unfortunately, they are not so lucky when they are in need of a transfusion them-selves; their immune systems will recognize blood from people with one or both antigens as foreign and reject the transfusion. Type AB individuals, on the other hand, are "universal recipients": since they have both types of antigen in their blood, the substances are recognized as normal components of the body. They therefore accept transfusions from other people without experiencing an adverse immune response.

THE ABO ANTIGENS. Much has been learned of the nature of the ABO antigens since the system's discovery. The antigens are comprised of glycoproteins (large molecules composed of chains of sugar molecules connected to a protein) attached to the red blood cell membrane. Although it had long been thought that type O individuals had no glycoprotein, it turns out that *all* individuals have a form of the glycoprotein; type A and B individuals have an added sugar at the end of the molecule,

PROFILE 7
Fatima L. C. Jackson

Fatimah Jackson's research in human biology spans the fields of nutrition, disease, ethnography, and genetics, and it has been carried out in the United States, Tanzania, Liberia, Cameroon, and Egypt. Her work focuses on the biocultural effects of choices people make, whether stemming from individual behavior or culturally based lifestyle alternatives. Her research has shown that the consequences of people's choices range from ecological effects to health outcomes to genetic changes in populations.

One area of her research has been the study of the coevolution of people, parasites, and plants in malaria-prone areas of Africa. One study showed that groups whose primary food is cassava had varying levels of the toxin cyanide in their diet, and populations in areas with high cyanide levels had lower allele frequencies of sickle-cell hemoglobin. This finding is due to the cyanide levels being too low to seriously poison the humans, but high enough to affect the malarial parasite. Hence, lower malaria rates are found in high-cyanide areas, resulting in lowered selection for sickle-cell heterozygotes and therefore lower frequencies for the sickle-cell allele.

Another area of research for Dr. Jackson is improving our understanding of the combination of ethnicity and genetics in complex populations. These populations, such as African-American groups in the United States, defy traditional racial categorization, but instead must be understood as amalgams of biology and culture, with intermixing from several populations both of genetics and of learned values and behaviors. Dr. Jackson has also helped establish the first human DNA bank in Africa as a means of better understanding the interaction of genetics and environmental factors to create phenotypic variation in people.

Dr. Jackson is Professor of Biological Anthropology at the University of Maryland, College Park. She combines her theoretical research with applied research that includes better understanding of the causes of health disparities in such illnesses as hypertension and cancer.

THALASSEMIA AND MALARIA.   Like sickle-cell alleles, thalassemia mutations are sometimes found in fairly high frequencies in human populations, and all the populations with these high frequencies are located in areas that are/were associated with high rates of malaria. The high rates are found in populations derived from several regions of Africa, the circum-Mediterranean region, India, and southern China.

HEMOGLOBIN E.   The beta globin gene has another fairly common variant besides HbS due to a point mutation, a variant termed hemoglobin E. Here, at position 26 of the beta chain, the amino acid lysine is substituted for glutamic acid. Populations with high frequencies of this variant allele are found in southern and southeast Asia and also in parts of Melanesia. Homozygotes are not selected against as severely as with sickle cell or thalassemia, but there is evidence for favored selection of heterozygotes (Hutagalung et al.1999). The high frequency populations are ones that also confront high risk for malaria.

OTHER VARIANT HEMOGLOBINS. There are several other hemoglobin variants that are found in polymorphic rates among certain populations, but these variants are more limited in areal distribution than the other variants discussed above. As with the others, populations having these polymorphisms are located in areas with high rates of malaria. It appears that several hemoglobin variants have independently evolved in the face of the heavy mortality caused by falciparum malaria across a large area of the Old World. There is no evidence for these variants having developed independently in New World populations, which were not subject to malaria until the disease was introduced to the region after European contact.

Glucose-6-Phosphate Dehydrogenase Deficiency

One other genetic polymorphism has been connected with malaria resistance: glucose-6-phosphate dehydrogenase deficiency (G6PD deficiency). G6PD is an enzyme common to all body cells, but it has a particularly important role in red blood cells, where it is involved in anti-oxidative processes that protect the cell from the harmful effects of its own metabolic products. Several variants of the allele for G6PD are known, and they all serve to lower the enzyme's activity. This condition has been referred to as G6PD-deficiency. When red blood cells are infected, such as with the malaria parasite, they tend to produce oxidative chemicals at a higher rate than usual. Thus, G6PD deficiency causes infected red blood cells to lyse (burst), which limits parasitic viability. There is, therefore, an advantage to having G6PD deficiency under the stress of high malarial prevalence.

Red blood cells with G6PD deficiency are also sensitive to many chemicals found naturally in plants, particularly one that is present in fava beans. Therefore, relative selective value of G6PD deficiency rests not only with malaria, but also with other environmental variables, including available plants, and cultural factors involved with food choices and taste sensitivity for the oxidative chemicals in potential foods (Greene 1993).

G6PD deficiency is somewhat different from the other genetic traits related to malaria in that it is an X-chromosome–linked trait. Thus, only females can be heterozygous for the trait. However, there is evidence that males (who have only the one allele for the deficiency condition) or homozygous females also have some resistance to falciparum malaria (Greene 1993).

GENETIC TRAITS FROM CONTEMPORARY MOLECULAR BIOLOGY USED IN HUMAN BIOLOGY

The revolution in molecular biology discussed in Chapter 4 has had an enormous impact on anthropological genetics. Traditionally, human biologists have examined phenotypic variation among humans and attempted to derive genetic variability that underlies the phenotypic differences. Via contemporary methods, human biologists can now directly examine genetic variability through detection of differences in the nucleotide sequences of human DNA. ABO blood tests are being supplanted in the field by searches for microsatellites and use of genetic chips. Much work has been done in particular on the *Alu* family of insertions (Perna et al. 1992). While these studies are interesting in their own right, they also have implications for our understanding of the total amount of human genetic diversity, on population differences and affinities, on estimates of diversion times of populations, and on migration patterns in human prehistory. Individual genotypic traits had been used for these kinds of studies previously, but the sheer amount of information available to us in recent years has made these studies much more robust.

The new methods in molecular genetics allow identification of specific mutations in a given allele, and they also aid in identifying sets of genetic markers present on the same chromosome, which are so closely linked that recombination almost never occurs. As noted earlier, these linked markers are termed **haplotypes**.

Major Types of Molecular Genetic Studies Used in Human Biology

MITOCHONDRIAL DNA. One of the first studies to employ contemporary molecular biology techniques for human genetics involved the study of the DNA present in mitochondria. Since mitochondrial DNA is primarily haploid (that is, does not come in paired alleles as is true for nuclear DNA), and therefore does not recombine during reproduction, and also is generally inherited maternally (passed down primarily through egg cells from mother to both sons and daughters), it is in some respects simpler to use in population comparisons than is nuclear DNA.

Early work with mitochondrial DNA used restriction endonucleases (restriction enzymes) to derive genetic variation among individuals and populations. These studies began in the late 1970s and early 1980s. They involved the use of only one or a few restriction enzymes (Brown 1980; Denaro et al. 1981), with greater numbers of enzymes used as techniques improved (Richards and Macaulay 2001). In general, the more restriction enzymes used, the higher the resolution of genetic variability one can deduce. These studies of humans became notable after publicity surrounding the high resolution studies of human mitochondrial DNA and its implications for understanding human evolution done by Rebecca Cann and her colleagues in Allan Wilson's laboratory at Berkeley in the mid-1980s (Cann et al. 1987).

Studies beginning in the early 1990s showed that human mitochondrial DNA, when studied in large regions such as continents, could be divided into just a few **haplogroups** (genetic markers that change slowly over time), a classification based upon basic differences in just one or a few restriction sites (Richards and Macaulay 2001). More recent studies have incorporated the use of a technique termed "denaturing high performance liquid chromatography," in which small conformational differences in short DNA chains can be detected by use of microsatellites as markers, or by use of DNA sequencing, to identify haplotypes within mitochondrial DNA. There is evidence that mitochondrial DNA has become incorporated into the nuclear genome, with this occurring throughout human evolution, including in recent times.

Y CHROMOSOME. While the Y chromosome is clearly part of nuclear DNA, it shares some characteristics with mitochondrial DNA. The Y chromosome is unpaired, and therefore large portions of it do not undergo recombination during reproduction. It is also passed down by only one sex, in this case from father to son. Thus, the Y chromosome also shares with mitochondrial DNA a greater simplicity for studies of population affinities. Also, as with mitochondrial DNA, human genetic studies have been done on the Y chromosome through use of restriction enzymes, denaturing high performance liquid chromatography, transposable elements, and actual sequencing of the nucleotide bases.

NUCLEAR DNA. Human population genetic studies have also utilized variations in the DNA on chromosomes other than the Y chromosome, or X chromosome when paired with the Y in males. These chromosomes are paired and undergo recombination during meiosis. Studies can be divided into those that examine the genes that code for proteins and those that study areas of the chromosomes where the DNA does not code for proteins. The latter regions of the chromosomes have been dubbed "junk DNA" because scientists once believed that they had no selective value. Evidence has accumulated that the non-protein coding regions may have selective import for individuals, and therefore these regions are not really junk.

USES FOR HUMAN MOLECULAR GENETICS STUDIES

Human biologists have used the information contained within the human genome in several ways. These uses include: deriving the genetic history of our species, tracing human population affinities and migrations, and examining the genetic background of health risk at both the population and individual level. The first two topics will be examined separately, although unfortunately not in great depth, given space limitations.

The Genetic History of Homo Sapiens

The evolutionary forces of selection, drift, and mutation lead to changes in the information contained in the human genome over time. These changes can be used to attempt a reconstruction of some of the major events that have occurred in the evolutionary history of our species.

One question that has intrigued human biologists for decades concerns how old our species is. This is actually a difficult, if not impossible, question to answer, because during the anagenesis process (speciation from one species to a new, single species over time) the time of separation between the species is usually arbitrary. It is, of course, impossible to perform breeding experiments on fossils to determine whether interbreeding is possible. Sometimes periods of rapid, "punctuated" change can be identified as a time for the origin of a given species during this process.

One method for estimating the time that a species has existed is to measure the amount of genetic diversity within individuals making up the species. Long-existing species have had more time to build up genetic diversity, and therefore should, on average, be older than less diverse species. There are difficulties with this, however. A species that has gone through a period of time when its population size has been small will tend to lose some of its diversity during this time, in what is termed a "genetic bottleneck," as noted in Chapter 3. Therefore, a relatively old species that has undergone a genetic bottleneck in relatively recent times will display only a small amount of genetic diversity. In general, genetic diversity is related to population size.

Also, genetic diversity may reflect the degree to which selective forces have been at work on a population, particularly if the species is widespread and thus faces different types of selective forces at different places in its range. Despite this, if a reasonable percentage of the genetic variants are due to drift (that is, non-selective forces), the amount of diversity is a mark of species longevity.

HUMAN GENETIC DIVERSITY. Molecular genetics techniques have been applied to samples of humans from throughout the world in order to determine the degree of genetic diversity present in our species. Early comprehensive studies examined mitochondrial DNA using restriction enzymes and discovered that humans have relatively little genetic diversity compared to other mammal, and in particular other primate, species (Ferris et al. 1981; Cann et al. 1987). Since then, many other studies have examined our species's genetic diversity. Other mitochondrial DNA studies using either higher resolution restriction enzyme analysis or sequencing have taken place since this early study, and they have confirmed the low level of genetic diversity in our species relative to other primates, particularly chimpanzees (Morin et al. 1994; Cann 2001), with chimpanzees having three or more times the amount of mitochondrial genetic variability. In fact, there is more mitochondrial DNA diversity in a single chimpanzee social group than in the entire human species (Gagneux et al. 1999; Cann 2001)!

Studies using Y chromosomes have also shown that humans possess considerably less genetic diversity than our closest living relatives, the chimpanzee and bonobo (Gagneux 2002). Some studies of DNA sequences of autosomal (non-sex chromosomes) and X-linked DNA have also shown chimpanzees and other apes to have much greater genetic diversity than humans (Kaessmann et al. 1999; Jensen-Seaman et al. 2001), again with three to four times the amount of diversity in the ape species compared with humans. Some conflicting reports suggest that for a wide range of nuclear DNA, there is actually less difference than thought, with chimpanzee genetic diversity equal to or at most 1.5 times the amount found in human DNA, and bonobo variability less than both chimpanzees and humans(Wise et al. 1997; Yu et al. 2003).

The possible different results in comparisons of mitochondrial DNA versus nuclear DNA diversity in apes and humans suggest an interesting evolutionary scenario. Yu et al. (2003) speculate that the difference reflects that effective population size has a greater effect on mitochondrial DNA diversity than it does on nuclear DNA, and that therefore the results suggest that the effective population size of the human lineage was reduced relative to the chimpanzee population size after the two groups speciated, perhaps due to a population bottleneck. "Effective population size" is a technical term used in population genetics. In essence, it refers to the size of the population that is actually involved in reproduction, excluding those who died before reproductive age or who were unable to find a mate (Freeman and Herron 2004). Another possible reason for the difference in genetic variability in mitochondrial versus nuclear DNA is that chimpanzee females may disperse further from their natal (birth) group on average than is true for female humans, and this would lead to greater effective population size for the more widely dispersed chimpanzee females.

In any event, these studies of genetic variability suggest that humans have a relatively low level of genetic variability, intimating that our species is a fairly young one, or at least that all modern humans are descended from a relatively small population of ancestors in the recent evolutionary past.

DATING DIVERGENCES AND ANCESTRY: THE MOLECULAR CLOCK. Human biologists have gone a step further and attempted to estimate the time of divergence of the human line from our closest living ape relatives. They have also tried to date the time of divergence of modern humans from the small ancestral population that gave rise to all contemporary humanity. The uncertainty level in assigning dates to species divergence is greater than simply ranking the relative degree of variability. Given the uncertainties we have seen with the latter, one must approach such dating with a healthy dose of skepticism.

The method for assigning dates of divergence in species through measurement of the quantity of genetic differences between them is often referred to as the **molecular clock**. The idea is that, over time, mutations are assimilated into a population's genome at approximately a constant rate. The rate will change somewhat due to changes in selective pressure, due to natural processes that might change the mutation rate, or due to changes in effective population size. The general notion is that these rate changes are, in the long run, small compared with the general rate of genetic change, as this is determined primarily from neutral (non-selected) mutations (Zuckerkandl and Pauling 1962). Thus, one can state that, if the percentage of difference between species X and species Y is half the percentage difference between both (X and Y) and species Z, then species X and Y speciated from species Z twice as long ago as X and Y speciated from each other. Thus, based upon the idea that genetic differences proceed at an approximately constant rate, one can calculate relative times of species divergence. If one knows an absolute date of species divergence (that is, an estimate of actual years since a given two species diverged), one can then calculate the date (that is, age) of divergence for all other species pairs for which one has relative divergence times. The initial absolute date is referred to as a "calibration point." For instance, if one assumes that the main mammalian families (specifically, primates and artiodactyls, such as cows and deer) diverged from each other 90 million years ago based upon data from the fossil record, then one can also calculate times of divergence of suborders of primates and other taxonomic groups within the Primate order. Using this calibration point and data on protein sequence differences, an estimated divergence between humans and chimpanzees is approximately 5.5 million years ago (Glazko and Nei 2003).

Although there are now some successes in obtaining DNA sequences from ancient DNA, for the most part the molecular clock works from comparisons of living organisms. An example of such a comparison using humans, several ape species and a monkey species is shown in Figure 7-8. For clarity, only the first 71 nucleotides are shown, although the original research report listed 898 nucleotides (Hayasaka et al. 1988). Table 7-1 replicates a portion of a table from the report, showing the percent of similarity among the species. Interestingly, chimpanzees are seen to be most similar to humans. In addition, chimpanzees are no closer in relation to gorillas than they are to humans; all the apes are more similar to each other than any of them are to the monkey (rhesus macaque); and

	1	10	20	30	40	50	60	70 ...
Human:	AAGCTTCACCGGCGCAGTCATTCTCATAATCGCCCACGGGCTTACATCCTCATTACTATTCTGCCTAGCAA ...
Chimp:	A		A T C		A		T	
Gorilla:	A		T G T	T		A	A	T
Orang:	A		A C C C	G T	T A C		C C G	
Gibbon:	A	T A T	A C G C		A A C T		C C G	T
Macaque:	A	T T T	A C C	G T T	A C C T	C A T A T		C

FIGURE 7-8 Comparison of a DNA sequence in a portion of the mitochondrial DNA of humans, chimpanzees, gorillas, orangutans, gibbons, and the Rhesus macaque. The entire sequence of humans is shown; for the other species, only differences are noted.

TABLE 7-1 Percent similarity of nucleotide sequences between selected primate species.

Species	Human	Chimpanzee	Gorilla	Orangutan	Gibbon	Macaque
Human	100	91.2	89.7	84.0	81.9	76.7
Chimpanzee		100	89.4	82.9	81.1	75.0
Gorilla			100	83.4	81.1	76.6
Orangutan				100	81.2	75.4
Gibbon					100	76.2
Macaque						100

the apes form a distinct group that are (approximately) equally different from the sole monkey species included in the example.

Geneticists usually use computer models to select the most parsimonious manner for the changes (that is, the order of changes in nucleotides that would require the fewest number of mutations). There is, of course, no assurance that the actual sequence of events in the evolution of nucleotide changes was in fact the most parsimonious sequence.

There are difficulties with use of the molecular clock. Some nucleotide similarities could be due to two (or more) mutational changes, as opposed to no changes (for example, a G could mutate to a C in one species, and then millions of years later the C could mutate to a G; in this case, we simply see a common G in two species). This sort of **homoplasy** (defined as a similarity in characteristics due to convergent evolution, rather than to common ancestry) will tend to lead to an underestimate of the actual age of divergence between two species. Similarly, a nucleotide could change twice (for example, from a G to a C and then from C to a T), but only the final change is noted in comparisons of living species, again leading to an underestimation of the amount of change. Intense selection will lead to greater rates of molecular change than predicted in a "neutral mutation" theory. Changes in mutation rate because of environmental influences (perhaps a temporary increase in cosmic-ray activity) will also lead to a nonconstant rate of change in DNA sequences.

Various studies that have estimated dates for the speciation of humans and chimpanzees from an ancestral species have been assigned dates ranging from 3.6 to 13.0 million years ago (Glazko and Nei 2003). This wide range of dates reflects differences in use of calibration points, types of DNA (mitochondrial, nuclear, or non-coding regions), and types of statistics for computations. Most estimates fall in the range of five to seven million years ago.

Another important date that has been estimated from molecular genetic data is the time since all contemporary humans shared a common ancestor, or at least a small ancestral population. This date is often considered to be fairly recent, given the relatively small amount of variability in the human genome. Estimates have tended to fall in the range of 50,000 to 200,000 years ago for the expansion of modern Homo sapiens, from an original population with an effective size of 10,000 (Cann 2001).

Genetics and Human Population Affinities

Just as species differences in nucleotide sequences can be used to understand evolutionary relations among the species and to date their divergence, human population differences in nucleotide sequences can be used to measure the historical affinities of the populations within our species. This provides us with a means to trace migrations, to explore relationships among populations, and to evaluate how much of human genetic variation coincides with traditional racial categorization of our species. Keep in mind this important point: although these studies focus on genetic differences between human populations, this actually represents a small proportion, perhaps 10 to 15 percent, of the total genetic variation in our species (Zegura 1985); the majority of genetic variation exists *within* populations.

THE HUMAN GENOME DIVERSITY PROJECT. The Human Genome Diversity Project (HGDP) developed as a means to broaden the scope of the Human Genome Project, which successfully sequenced the entire human genome (but actually of a single human), in order to encompass the range of human genetic diversity throughout the world. The HGDP's goal was to understand the range of human genetic variation, and also to provide genetic information that would be valuable to people from all populations, not just those in areas where gene-sequencing instruments are readily available. The creators of the HGDP also hoped that information from the project would "help combat the widespread popular fear and ignorance of human genetics and [would] make a significant contribution to the elimination of racism" (HGDP 1993, p. 4). Unfortunately, the HGDP met with suspicion in many communities, where concern about the misuse of genetic information and/or the use of the information for profit by developed countries at the expense of poorer communities led to criticism of the project. The project instituted policies such that each community that was involved in the study retained control of research access to the people in their population and to any commercial value from the research results, but concerns remained, leading to the project's discontinuation (Ilkilic and Paul 2008).

A similar venture, the Genographic Project, which is sponsored by the National Geographic Society, IBM, and private foundations, seeks to make use of mitochondrial DNA and Y chromosome sequencing studies in order to trace human migrations (Stix 2008). The project differs from the HGDP in that it is based upon voluntary participation by people from around the world without a clear bias towards indigenous communities (Behar et al. 2007), but it has still met with criticism (TallBear 2007).

Another human genetics effort, the International HapMap Project, which assembles the geographic variance in human haplotypes, involves scientists from a number of countries who provide data on genetic variation at both the individual and population levels. This project focuses primarily on human health issues and involves community members in the initiation and carrying out of project activities to a much greater degree than occurred in the Human Genome Diversity Project. Still, some individuals believe that more community involvement is warranted.

Genetics and Human Migrations

The use of genetics to trace human migrations is a broad topic. Here, we will simply note some examples of how this has been used, without attempting to cover the entire field.

OUT OF AFRICA. There is a contentious debate within the field of paleoanthropology on the origins of our species, *Homo sapiens*. Since there are no functioning time machines, we must rely on the fossil and archaeological record and on study of the biology of living humans to reconstruct our origins. It is well known from the fossil record that an ancestral species originally evolved in Africa, but populations migrated out of that continent to many places in Eurasia beginning over 1.5 million years ago. This ancestral species has been variously dubbed *Homo erectus*, *Homo ergaster*, Homo *heidelbergensis*, and *Homo antecessor*.

Within the debate on our origins, one school of thought suggests that, in many regions of the world, modern *Homo sapiens* evolved from the ancestral species at around the same time. This notion is commonly referred to as the "regional continuity" model, or the "multiregional evolution" model. The regional continuity group believes that the anagenesis of *Homo sapiens* occurred over a very broad geographic area, with gene flow assuring that cladogenesis (splitting into multiple species) would not occur because of insufficient isolation. Regional differences (according to the model) could persist during the process of overall species change. Thus, this model predicts that our species is fairly old and therefore genetically diverse.

Another model for modern human evolution is termed the "complete replacement model," or the "out of Africa" model. This idea is that all members of modern *Homo sapiens* stem from a single small population of ancestors that originally lived in Africa and then migrated out of that continent to fill the Old World and eventually all land areas. These modern humans would have completely replaced older populations of hominids (Homo erectus or the like) with no interbreeding. The model predicts that the human species is fairly young and therefore does not show great genetic diversity.

There are alternative explanations that are somewhat of a compromise between the regional continuity and complete replacement models, suggesting that humans evolved in Africa, migrated to other parts of the world, and some interbreeding took place with the older populations in those regions (Jurmain et al. 2005).

GENETIC DATA AND THE ORIGIN OF MODERN HUMANS. The models of human origins allow us to form hypotheses that can be tested with genetic data. As noted above, our species is not very diverse genetically compared with our fellow Hominoids, and this suggests that the complete replacement model fits the data better. There is more to the data, however. A consistent finding from many studies of contemporary humans is that there is a great deal more genetic diversity among African (or recently African-derived) peoples than in all other populations combined. Comparisons of the amount and placement of such mobile DNA elements as *Alu* and Line1 sequences also show that there is a greater variability within African populations than in other regional populations (Watkins et al. 2001; Xing et al. 2007). These results provide evidence that human ancestry is older in Africa than elsewhere, which is again what one would predict from the complete replacement model.

Studies on mitochondrial DNA extracted from the bones of Neanderthals show that these hominids diverged from the modern human lineage approximately 500,000 years ago, making them very distinct from any living human (Krings et al. 1997; Ovchinnikov et al. 2000). Nuclear DNA has also been derived from Neanderthals, with similar calculated divergence times from modern humans as found from the mitochondrial DNA studies (Green et al. 2006; Noonan et al. 2006). It appears that all modern humans are all very similar to each other, and, in reality, we are all Africans.

WHERE DID PACIFIC ISLANDERS COME FROM? One of the wonders to Westerners during the seventeenth and eighteenth centuries was the discovery of humans living on islands scattered throughout the Pacific Ocean, some of the islands thousands of miles from any other land (see map, Figure 7-9). We now know much about the navigational skills of the Pacific Islanders and their effective deployment of outrigger canoes to travel over great ocean distances. There have been conflicting theories about where these islanders originated from. The prevailing theory is that they stemmed from Southeast Asia, migrated through the western Pacific (in the region termed Melanesia), and then headed eastward through Polynesia and Micronesia. Another theory is that the Pacific Islanders moved westward from the Americas, a theory made popular through the writings of Thor Heyerdahl (1984). Again, genetic analyses can help in choosing between these theories.

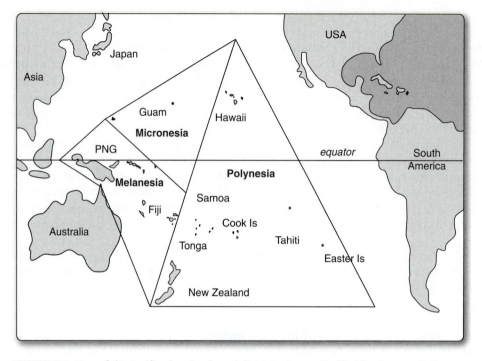

FIGURE 7-9 Map of the Pacific, showing broad divisions among Pacific-Islander populations.

Archaeological evidence shows that humans had entered western Melanesia by 40,000 years ago (Groube et al. 1986) and reached eastward to the Solomon Islands (located just above the word "Melanesia" on the map in Figure 7-9) by 29,000 years ago (Wickler and Spriggs 1988). Pacific islands become increasingly distant from each other as one moves eastward, making migration more difficult as one moves toward the east. Movement beyond the Solomon Islands, therefore, is not seen until a second wave of migration that took place within the past 4,000 years (Lum et al. 1998). Pacific islanders are split into two major linguistic groupings that appear to coincide with the two migration waves. These groupings are traditionally divided into Austronesian and non-Austronesian (sometimes termed Papuan) languages. Austronesian languages are found in Polynesia, Micronesia, and in some coastal areas of Melanesia. Papuan languages are found only in Melanesia, primarily in inland areas. Papuan languages are quite diverse, a sign of their great antiquity, while Austronesian languages are relatively less diverse due to their more recent common origin.

Initial genetic studies examined phenotypic traits. Pacific islanders are quite diverse in skin color, stature, and body composition (Howells 1973) suggesting that they either do not have a single population of origin, or that they started their migration a long time ago.

Study of genotypic traits such as blood groups provided additional information about the origins and affinities of Pacific Islanders. For example, there is a clinal distribution in frequencies of the MN blood group across the Pacific from west to east, with Polynesians in the east having higher frequencies of M than the Melanesians to the west. Indonesian populations are variable in frequency of the M allele, but are generally of low frequency as is found in eastern Melanesians. Native American populations generally have very high frequencies of the M allele (Molnar 2002). The Rh negative allele is virtually absent among Pacific peoples, but the CDe complex is in very high frequency among New Guinea populations and elsewhere in Melanesia, Micronesia, and also outside the Pacific island region in Indonesia. The values for this complex are somewhat lower in Polynesian populations (Kirk 1990).

The more detailed information that comes from molecular genetics has made Pacific affiliations more clear. For instance, analysis of mitochondrial DNA sequences have identified mostly

Asian haplotypes in Micronesians and Polynesians, giving very strong evidence for the Asian, as opposed to American, origins of these Pacific Islanders (Lum et al. 1998; Hertzberg et al. 1989; Sykes et al. 1995). Studies of nuclear DNA have shown Southeast Asian connections with Pacific Islanders, particularly with Austronesian speakers (Martinson 1996), and studies of the *Alu* family of transposable elements also point to a Southeast Asian origin for Polynesians (González-Pérez et al. 2006). Thus, it appears that Pacific Islanders moved eastward into the region, stemming from Asia, in two main waves of migration separated by tens of thousands of years.

There are differences of opinion about where in Asia the Austronesian-speaking Pacific peoples originated. Scientists espouse ideas involving various areas of Indonesia, the Philippines, Taiwan, or more generalized ideas of multiple origin sites in Southeast Asia (Solheim 1996; Meacham 1985; Melton et al. 1995). Continuing genetic studies may help us choose from among these theories.

THE EXPRESS TRAIN OR AN ENTANGLED BANK? Besides allowing us to identify where the Pacific Islanders came from, genetic analyses allow better understanding of the rate and pattern of movement. For movement of the Austronesian speakers into the Pacific, migrating beyond the large islands close to New Guinea, two different ideas have been promulgated. One, termed the "express train" hypothesis, states that the Austronesian speakers originated in island Southeast Asia and then migrated quickly through New Guinea and the rest of Melanesia, followed rapidly by expansion into Polynesia and Micronesia, with little genetic intermixing with the earlier, Papuan-speaking, populations of Melanesia (Diamond 1988). The other hypothesis, termed the "entangled bank," is that the Austronesian-speaking peoples spent long time periods in eastern Melanesia, interacting and exchanging genes with the Papuan-speaking populations, before these now-intermixed populations expanded into the western Pacific (Terrell 1988).

Genetic information from nuclear DNA shows that Micronesians and Polynesians share nearly 70 percent of their alleles with Asians and approximately 30 percent with Papuan-speaking populations from Melanesia (Lum et al. 1998; Serjeantson 1985; Martinson 1996). This suggests that at least some "entanglement" took place between Austronesian- and Papuan-speaking populations that later gave rise to Polynesians and Micronesians. Mitochondrial DNA data, however, show only about 5 percent input from Papuan-speaking populations, providing evidence for the express train hypothesis (Hertzberg et al. 1989; Lum and Cann 1998). These differences are probably due in part to the smaller effective population size with respect to mitochondrial DNA, since it is only passed through females, and in part due to smaller amount of female gene flow between populations from the two language families (Lum et al. 1998). Y-chromosome data, based on male-to-male inheritance, shows that Austronesian-speaking populations stem from both eastern Indonesian and Melanesian populations (Hurles et al. 2002). Thus, for the Pacific, some geneticists "see female settlement as an express train and male gene flow as an entangled bank" (Lum et al. 1998, p. 622; Cann and Lum 2004). While the story of human settlement in the Pacific is far from simple or clear, it is fascinating that evidence suggests different patterns for males versus females, giving us a hazy glimpse of the social circumstances surrounding this incredible feat of human migration.

THE PEOPLING OF AMERICA. As with the Pacific, the story of the migration of humans into the New World has long been of interest to anthropologists and other scientists. The long-accepted theory is that the original Americans migrated to the New World from northeast Asia, through a former land connection between Siberia and Alaska via what is termed the "Bering Land Bridge." Alternate theories have been presented, including some that have developed from the initial reports of so-called European-looking features found in the skeletal remains of Kennewick Man, which consist of a partial skeleton discovered in Washington state that are approximately 9,500 years old. Detailed scientific study of the specimens led to a report that the shape of the bones does not fit perfectly with any modern human population, but that the closest match is with northern Asian populations, such as the Ainu (McManamon 1999). However, some ideas of a migration (pre-Vikings) across the

Atlantic have persisted. Unfortunately, there has been no success in deriving DNA from the Kennewick bones due to degradation of the genetic material over time, and thus no definitive statement about the skeleton's origins can be made.

There is a plethora of evidence for the Asian origins of aboriginal Americans, derived from comparison of human populations throughout the world with phenotypic features of contemporary Native Americans, skeletal features of remains found in the Americas before European contact, and from genetic studies. However, some scientists do suggest that there may have been some input, particularly in South American populations, from Pacific island colonists (Salzano 1985), although this input may represent historical events in which Pacific Islanders were captured by Europeans and brought to South America to work as slaves. This brings up a concern with this type of research: one must allow for possible gene flow in historic times that will complicate interpretations of genetic comparisons in the reconstruction of ancient events.

There is a further refinement of the theory of the Siberian origins of Americans. Scientists have formulated a three-wave migration theory based primarily on a linguistic theory for the presence of three major language families in the New World. In this theory, it is believed that there were three main migration periods in the peopling of America, all stemming from Siberia. The first wave led to most present Amerindians, the second wave led to the present-day Na-Dene speakers (such as Athabaskans and Navaho), and the final wave led to the current populations that speak Eskimo and Aleut languages (Greenberg 1987). The linguistic theory is quite controversial (Bolnick et al. 2004), with many linguists parceling Native American languages into more than three groups (e.g., Campbell 1997).

Research on mitochondrial DNA has shown that contemporary Native American populations, when historical admixture is accounted for, are largely comprised of just five major haplogroups. Three of these five show clinal distributions from north to south, one is found almost entirely in North America, and the other does not show a distinct cline in its distribution, except that it is nearly absent from the most northern portions of North America (Schurr and Sherry 2004). These results suggest that migration occurred in a north-south vector in America, a finding that is in accord with the theory of a single migration path starting with the Bering Land Bridge. The Na-Dene and Eskimo/Aleut language groups largely lack one of the haplogroups, but a similar degree of diversity among the haplogroups suggests a single time of origin in the Americas.

Y chromosome data show connections between the haplogroups present in Native American populations and those present in contemporary Siberian populations (Schurr and Sherry 2004). One of the most common haplogroups shows a clear north-south distribution cline. Thus, genetic analyses strongly support the idea that Native Americans are of Siberian origin, and the evidence appears to best support a theory of a single migratory event (Mulligan et al. 2004; Zegura et al. 2004).

DATING AMERICAN ORIGINS. A final question to consider here is: when did the first people arrive in the Americas? Again, genetic information helps. Archaeological evidence has primarily supported an origin of about 11,000 to 12,000 years ago, based on the dating of early sites in North America associated with a particular tool tradition termed "Clovis," characterized by a unique type of fluted projectile point. There have been several sites discovered that have yielded pre-Clovis dates, although these remain controversial. Observations of variation in restriction length polymorphisms in mitochondrial DNA (more variation equals greater time depth) suggests a time depth of between 20,000 to 35,000 years for the haplogroups present in Native Americans, assuming a single migration. However, other factors could influence the amount of genetic diversity, including population bottlenecks or the influence of possible multiple migrations. These factors would change the amount of diversity in a given time period. Combining mitochondrial DNA and Y chromosome data for use in dating, a date of between 15,000 to 20,000 years ago is indicated (Schurr and Sherry 2004; Zegura et al. 2004), a date that pre-dates Clovis sites, but is not completely discordant with archaeological data. Clearly, further work in refining genetic analyses needs to be done.

TRACING THE ORIGINS OF SPECIFIC POPULATIONS THROUGH GENETICS. In a classic paper, William Boyd (1963) cited the use of genetics to trace population origins, helping to solve long-standing anthropological puzzles. Boyd cited studies on four populations: the Roma (a people commonly called "gypsies," but not a term appreciated by them), African-Americans, the Lapps (more properly termed the Saami), and Papuan pygmoid groups. Modern methods have improved our ability to answer questions about the origins of these populations.

The Roma. The Roma are a people found throughout Europe thought by some to derive from Egypt (from which the term "gypsy" originated), although they claimed an origin in India (see Figure 7-10). Linguistic studies suggested a connection with a modern Sanskrit dialect, and thus a connection with India. In a study of ABO allele frequencies of Hungarian Roma, it was noted that they were more closely related to Indian populations than they were to Hungarian populations, but there was also evidence for some intermixture with European populations, such as Hungarians (Boyd 1963). More recent studies, including use of Y chromosome and mitochondrial DNA analyses, show that Roma are indeed derived from Indian ancestors. The results also show that the many subpopulations of Roma share genetic haplotypes but differ given number of years of isolation and genetic drift (Gresham et al. 2001; Morar et al. 2004).

African-American Admixture. Genetic studies of African-American populations in the United States have emphasized not only the tracing of origins, but they have also described the degree of admixture that has occurred in historic times. These tasks are made more difficult by the complex nature of African-American origins: the slave trade drew from several populations in West Africa, and more recent immigrants from many areas of Africa have arrived in the United States. Adding to the African-American population's diversity has been the large degree of gene flow from other groups. Traditionally, in the United States, a child of mixed parentage with one parent being African-American has in turn been designated as African-American. Thus, it is possible for an individual with a small percentage of ancestry from African ancestors, at least in historic times, to be classified as an African-American.

FIGURE 7-10 A group of Roma in a photograph taken in the early twentieth century.

There are also geographic differences among African-Americans in the United States. For instance, some African-American communities have had more genetic admixture with Native Americans than was the case in other regions. There is evidence that the degree of admixture of African-Americans with European-derived peoples is lower in the Southeastern United States relative to other regions of the United States (Parra et al. 1998; 2001), with people among the Gullah Sea Islanders, a relatively isolated group in South Carolina (Pollitzer 1999) having particularly low amounts of admixture. Studies have used autosomal nuclear DNA data as well as mitochondrial and Y chromosomal markers and microsatellite loci. By comparing the mitochondrial and Y chromosome data, it is possible to discern a greater European contribution from males than from females in the African-American population (Parra et al. 1998; 2001).

Besides characterizing regional population differences in admixture, use of many genetic markers permits estimates of the degree of admixture in individuals. This is biologically important to understanding the origins of ethnic disparities in certain diseases. For instance, African-Americans have considerably higher rates of hypertension (high blood pressure) than do European-derived peoples in the United States, with this disease being an extremely important risk factor for the development of heart disease and strokes. This disparity has been variously hypothesized as being due to genetic differences or to environmental considerations (such as socioeconomic differences, stress caused by racism, and so forth). Genetic data show that African-Americans with lower levels of admixture with European populations do not have significantly higher rates of hypertension than more admixed African-Americans (Reiner et al. 2005). Also, people from African-derived populations living in Western countries (as is the case for African-Americans) have higher blood pressure on average than Africans, particularly those living in rural settings (Cruikshank et al. 2001). Thus, it appears social and environmental factors that predispose toward hypertension are more important determinants of the ethnic disparity in hypertension than are genetic factors; alternatively, it may be that genetics has importance in the disparity, but the genetic influence is only observed under certain environmental conditions.

How Do the Saami Relate to Other European Populations?   The Saami, who have long occupied high northern latitudes in Scandinavia, were said by anthropologists in the first half of the twentieth century to have ties with Asian populations (Boyd 1963), in part because they speak a non-Indo-European language (see Figure 7-11). Early genetic studies of blood groups showed that the Saami displayed distinctly different allele frequencies for these traits than other populations. While a distinct difference exists between the Saami and other European groups, there is a genetic cline in allele frequencies in nearby groups, demonstrating that gene flow has occurred between the Saami and their neighbors. The differences between Saami and other Europeans are not due to Asian ancestry, however: the Saami are quite distinct from Asian populations in the genetics of blood groups. The distinctiveness of the Saami from other groups has also been seen in studies of dermatoglyphic characteristics, which are determined in part by genetics (Jantz 1997).

More recent genetic studies of European populations using mitochondrial and nuclear DNA have shown that most populations are quite similar genetically, suggesting a recent common ancestry for these groups (Cavalli-Sforza et al. 1994; Bertranpetit et al. 1994; Chikhi et al. 1998). This has been hypothesized as due to an expansion of early farming populations into Europe from the Near East within the past 10,000 years (Ammerman and Cavalli-Sforza 1984). These studies have found exceptions to the genetic similarity of European populations, with the Saami population being singled out for its distinctiveness, thus confirming earlier research findings. It may be that the Saami represent a long-standing European population that was less affected by the recent Neolithic expansion, although some gene exchange has occurred with these relative newcomers.

The Ancestry of Papuan Pygmoid Populations.   The final puzzle posed by Boyd in 1963 was the relationship of the Oceanic pygmoid peoples to other populations (see Figure 7-12). These

FIGURE 7-11 Saami people in native dress.

A   B

FIGURE 7-12 Short-statured people. **A.** An African Pygmy man from the Central African Republic **B.** A Sakai man from Malaya.

populations featured people with small average stature, dark skin color, and frizzy hair, and they are chiefly found in the Philippines, southern Thailand, the Malay peninsula, the island of New Guinea, and the Andaman islands. The superficial similarities with sub-Saharan Africans led to early theories of direct, recent ancestry from Africa, particularly with the African Pygmies.

Early genetic studies of blood groups, in fact, showed very distant genetic relationships between African Pygmies and the Papuan pygmoid populations (Boyd 1963). The Papuan populations do show some similarity with contemporary Pacific peoples. Thus, genetic studies have falsified the initial hypothesis of African connections that were based on phenotypic similarities in some characteristics. More recent genetic studies have confirmed the great disparity between the genetics of the Asian pygmoid populations and African groups (Endicott et al. 2003).

While the genetic technology available has developed enormously since Boyd's 1963 article, it is interesting that newer studies have tended to confirm the findings he presented at that time.

Genetics and Disease Risk

As is the case for all complex human characteristics, susceptibility to disease is a characteristic that involves genetics, environment, and a complex interaction between the two factors. Here, it will suffice to note that extensive research has been done in using the methods derived from genomics studies to better understand why some individuals, and indeed some populations, have higher risk for certain diseases than do others. The topic is far too broad, and often too complex, to be covered in this textbook, although specific examples will be noted, such as the relation between hemoglobin variants and malaria susceptibility.

Genetics and the Notion of Race

The notion of human races has a long history, based on phenotypic differences, primarily in skin color, between large regional groupings of humanity (see previous chapter). Careful study of phenotypic and genotypic differences among human groups has shown that human differences are clinal, as opposed to clumped, in terms of geographical distribution. The much greater degree of genetic information available with recent advances in human genomics has provided support for this view. For instance, it has been noted that genetic studies have shown far more genetic variability among African peoples than among all other humans combined and that all modern humans stem from Africa within the past 100,000 years or so. Does it make sense to divide humanity into basic genetic groupings that are all based on subdivisions among African populations?

From a genetic perspective, humans do not clump into the categories commonly associated with human races. Thus, it is not at all useful to continue using race as a biological construct, anymore than it is scientifically valid to retain an earlier belief in phlogiston as the essence of fire rather than replacing it with the idea of oxidation.

However, it is important that we do not toss out the importance of human variability with the race bathwater, and it is also important to recognize that some important genetic variability is found between populations. In fact, health disparities between populations are present that may have, at least in part, a genetic basis. Focusing on high-risk populations may allow discernment of disease causation that would be otherwise more difficult to discover and therefore allow better health for people in at-risk populations, and indeed improve health for all humans. However, population-level differences simply do not translate into continent-wide genetic differences.

Jettisoning race as a biological classification device does not remove the reality of race as a social construct. A preference would be to make use of the term "ethnic group" instead of "race," to acknowledge the overweening importance of social as opposed to biological differences between such groups. What does it mean to be of "African-American race," when virtually all people classified as such have varying degrees of admixture with other so-called races? What does it mean to be a "native Hawaiian" when there are even greater admixture rates within this population? Yet these classifications have importance for people's self-identification with membership in a social group. These groups ought primarily to be defined socially, so as to allow better understanding of their similarities and differences from people in other social groups among whom they live. As this chapter has illustrated, understanding of biological differences between groups requires empirical research on the contributions of both genetic and non-genetic (that is, environmental) factors and how these factors interact.

CHAPTER SUMMARY

In addition to the traditional "phenotypic" traits that vary among people, simpler traits that have a known genetic basis have been used to study human diversity. Traits such as blood ABO, MNSs, and Rh factor have differing allele frequencies in different populations, and exhibit a clinal, as opposed to clumped, distribution. Some of these "genotypic" traits are related to selective factors, such as the connection between malaria and both sickle cell and thalassemia. New technologies allow more direct observation of genetic differences, including the actual sequencing of human DNA into the order of its nucleotide bases.

Studies of human genetics helps understanding of the evolutionary relationships between humans and non-human primates, aids in the dating of past speciations in our evolutionary history, and also allows reconstruction of genetic relationships among contemporary human populations. The latter studies of human population relationships have allowed anthropologists to trace the origins of populations, including the ancestors of modern Pacific Islanders and of Native Americans. These origins and relationships are often complex, mirroring the rich history of human groups over many millennia. One clear implication of the genetic studies is that humans are not easily characterized into continental races. In fact, modern humans appear to stem from African ancestors in the past 100,000 years or so, with major clades of humans deriving from distinctions among African peoples.

CHAPTER 8

Demography: Populations, Reproduction, and Mortality

Demography is the study of human population size, distribution, and structure, and how these change with time. Human demography deals with issues of profound importance to our world, such as global human population growth, the increase in elderly people as a proportion of the population in developed countries, and localized problems caused by population change in specific regions. An example of the latter would be the effect on rural villages of the migration of young men to urban areas to engage in wage labor.

Evolutionary biologists and ecologists often use population size and growth rate as crude measures of a species's relative success in adapting to its environment, with larger and/or more rapidly growing populations indicative of better success. Thus, the large, rapidly growing human population could be seen as a gauge of our species's remarkable evolutionary success. On the other hand, the rapid population growth of our species clearly has negative aspects, as well.

POPULATION ECOLOGY

Ecologists study population size and composition in various plant, animal, and microbial populations. The means by which they do this is applicable to the study of human populations, although traditionally there have been some methodological differences associated with human demographic studies. Population ecology considers general characteristics of population growth and its regulation.

Population Growth

Demographers define population growth as the change in numbers of individuals over time. Growth may impact populations, causing difficulties with finding resources or space for the increased numbers of individuals, or conversely causing difficulties in finding enough "warm bodies" if growth is negative. The impact of population growth can be due to factors other than absolute numbers, depending on circumstances. For instance (and very hypothetically), one may imagine how different a growth rate of one million people per year would be for the population of China versus that of a small city in the United States. In the case of China, that growth rate would represent a welcome respite from the normally much higher growth rates. However, for the small U.S. city, the increase of one million people in a single year would represent a catastrophic situation with which the society must cope, finding housing, food, space, and utilities for the burgeoning populace. The issue in this hypothetical situation is one of scale.

SPECIFIC GROWTH RATE. Population ecologists make use of a different measure of growth to deal with the problem of scale: the specific growth rate, defined as the change in numbers of individuals per year per initial population size. (Formally, $R = \Delta N / \Delta t N_o$), where R = specific growth rate, ΔN = change in number of individuals, Δt = time period under consideration, and N_o = initial population size.) The specific growth rate, by accounting for the population's size before the time period of growth commences, allows for the impact of scale; growth in China and a small U.S. city can be compared in this way.

BIOTIC POTENTIAL AND ENVIRONMENTAL RESISTANCE. The biological basis for population growth is reproduction. Each species has an inherent ability to reproduce at a given rate, referred to as its **biotic potential**. Some species reproduce slowly, such as orangutans, which tend to have single births spaced several years apart. If perturbations of the environment occur, such as extensive burning of habitat, it is very difficult for orangutan populations to spring back after the disruption because of their slow reproductive rate. Other species usually reproduce rapidly. For example, the prodigious reproductive rate of lemmings can lead to overpopulation and subsequent population "crashes" when environmental resources are overused. Their rapid reproductive rate generally allows lemming populations to quickly recover from these crashes.

Biotic potential is not enough to understand population growth rates, as the lemming example noted above suggests. Increases in population size from reproduction are opposed by a variety of forces, whether from other living organisms (biotic) or non-living (abiotic) characteristics of the environment, that inhibit growth. These forces, in totality, are referred to as **environmental resistance**. In habitats with extensive food resources, few predators, and otherwise ideal conditions, environmental resistance is low. Where food is limited, predators are abundant, and other harsh conditions are present, environmental resistance is high.

It is the interaction of biotic potential and environmental resistance that determines a given population's actual growth rate. To better understand population growth dynamics, these two forces must be considered in greater detail.

INTRINSIC RATE OF NATURAL INCREASE. When a species is in optimal conditions (that is, in a setting where the environmental resistance approaches zero), its reproductive rate reaches a maximum, termed the **intrinsic rate of natural increase**. This represents a population's maximum specific growth rate. The intrinsic rate of natural increase is species-specific, depending on such factors as generation time, litter size, length of developmental period, and degree of parental involvement in raising of young. Species with high intrinsic rates of natural increase have higher biotic potential under ideal environmental conditions than those species with lower rates.

POPULATION GROWTH CURVES. In conditions of low environmental resistance to population growth, species that have high intrinsic rates of natural increase can grow much faster than those with low biotic potential. Species may also differ in their degree of sensitivity to environmental resistance. For instance, resistance usually increases as population size increases because there is more competition for resources. The result of variability in biotic potential and sensitivity to environmental resistance leads to different patterns of population growth, reflected in different-shaped curves when population size is graphed versus time. The two basic shapes of these population growth curves are a **J-shaped** and an **S-shaped** (or **sigmoid**) **curve**.

Species with high intrinsic rates of natural increase and little sensitivity to environmental resistance show J-shaped curves of population growth when initially placed in conditions of low resistance. The population-growth curve shows a geometric increase with time, thus taking on a J-shape (Figure 8-1). These curves are seen, for example, during algal blooms, population cycles of lemmings, and the reproductive seasons of annual plants. Species with lower biotic potential and greater sensitivity to environmental resistance have a population growth curve under similar initial conditions that at first increases at a shallower angle, and the curve decreases in growth rate over time as population size, and thus environmental resistance, increases (Figure 8-2). This second type of growth curve approximates a "lazy S" shape (Kormondy and Brown 1998).

The population growth rate is partly determined by the **net reproductive rate**, which is defined by the average number of female offspring produced by each female in a population. If the net reproductive rate is one, each female is replaced by a single female in the next generation, and the population size will stay the same. With a net reproductive rate of two, each female produces two daughters, and the population size will double in a generation.

CARRYING CAPACITY. A given environment can only support a finite population size of a given species before the environment becomes degraded for that species. This maximum population size for a given species in a given environment is termed the **carrying capacity** (usually symbolized as "K") of that environment (and shown as a dashed horizontal line in Figures 8-1A and 8-2A). Populations that show S-shaped curves have population sizes that approach, but usually do not

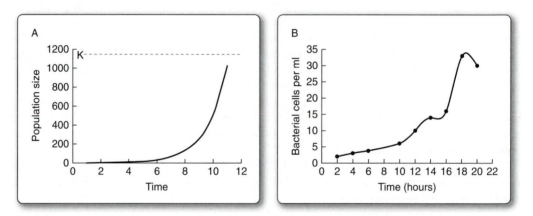

FIGURE 8-1 J-shaped curve of population growth. **A.** Theoretical curve. **B.** Actual growth data of bacteria in pond water.

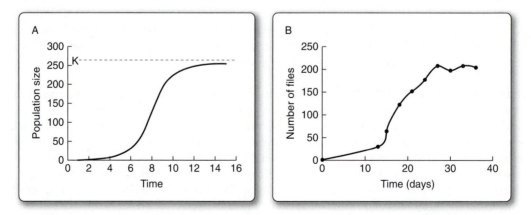

FIGURE 8-2 S-shaped curve of population growth. **A.** Theoretical curve. **B.** Actual growth data of a laboratory population of Drosophila menanogaster (fruit flies).

exceed, the carrying capacity because environmental resistance increases as population size approaches this capacity. Populations that show J-shaped curves rapidly approach the carrying capacity, and they often exceed it. This reaching or exceeding of the carrying capacity often is followed by a population "crash," where the population size rapidly diminishes.

SURVIVORSHIP. Population size is affected by **mortality rates** as well as by reproductive rates. It matters little how many offspring to which a female can theoretically give birth if she doesn't survive long enough to produce them. In fact, mortality rates are an important aspect of environmental resistance to population growth.

Different species tend to take on characteristic patterns of survivorship, although these patterns also depend greatly on specific environmental circumstances. For instance, many species tend to suffer very high mortality rates during early life stages. A large number of fish species show this pattern, for instance, with large egg production offsetting extremely high mortality of offspring before adulthood. Another less extreme example of this type of mortality pattern is found in humans living under poor socioeconomic conditions. Other species show the opposite pattern of low mortality early in life but higher mortality rates at older ages, a pattern shown by contemporary humans living in wealthy countries. Thus, it can be seen that a given species may show more than one pattern depending upon environmental conditions. Of course, many species will show survivorship patterns somewhere between the extremes of high or low early mortality, with chances of dying being fairly similar at different ages. These different patterns are illustrated in Figure 8-3.

POPULATION STRUCTURE. Populations are characterized not only by their rate of growth, but also by what types of individuals are included in them, particularly their age and sex. The proportions of individuals of given age and sex groups in a population—which defines the **population structure**—determine the population's potential growth rate. For instance, a population that is composed chiefly of elderly males is not likely to grow as fast as a population with a large proportion of females who have recently reached reproductive age.

AGE STRUCTURE OF POPULATIONS. It is common to break down populations into age groupings. The units used for this are dependent on the species's lifespan. For a short-lived species, the age groups might reflect months, or even days, while longer-lived species might be grouped into ten-year intervals. In general terms, the main distinctions are among three age classes: **prereproductive**, **reproductive**, and **postreproductive**. Species differ in the relative lengths of these periods; many insects, for instance, have very long prereproductive periods, short reproductive periods, and virtually no postreproductive period at all.

A population's age structure reflects reproductive rates and survivorship patterns. In populations with high reproductive rates and low survivorship at young ages, an age structure where a large proportion of the population is at prereproductive age will be present. In populations with long-lived individuals and slow reproductive rates, the prereproductive age group will be comparatively small.

Population age structure can be used to predict future population growth rates. Populations with a large ratio of individuals of prereproductive age are likely to grow rapidly when the large number of juveniles reaches reproductive age. On the other hand, populations with relatively large numbers of individuals that are of postreproductive age are likely to grow slowly or actually become smaller in size.

SEX RATIOS. Populations may also differ in the proportion of males versus females, expressed as **sex ratios**, often listed as the number of males per number of females. Thus, a population with a sex ratio of 1.0 has equal numbers of males and females, numbers above 1.0 show greater numbers of males than females, and numbers less than 1.0 denote just the reverse. The sex ratio is based in part on the proportions of sexes at conception or at birth (termed the **primary sex ratio**; often 1.0, but sometimes quite different), as well as differential mortality between the sexes at different ages. For instance, observed primary sex ratios among macaque and baboon troops ranged from 0.8 to 1.3,

time of stress. Thus, the temporary lowering of fecundity under stressful conditions makes evolutionary sense.

LACTATION AND FECUNDITY. In many populations, there is evidence for inhibition of fecundity due to nursing. A high intensity of breast feeding can lead to a phenomenon termed **lactation amenorrhea**. There is strong evidence that suckling by infants during breast feeding increases the levels of the hormone prolactin in mothers, with increased suckling leading to higher prolactin levels. This hormone stimulates the release of milk. High prolactin levels are also associated with amenorrhea. Thus, in populations where frequent breast feeding is common, women will display a greater inhibition of fecundity during the nursing period (Ellison 1995; Vitzthum 1995).

CULTURAL EFFECTS ON FERTILITY. Cultural factors are much more important than biological ones in the overall impact on fertility in most human populations. Social circumstances may influence people's perceptions of the benefits or costs of increasing their family sizes. In traditional/rural societies where agricultural activities are the primary occupation, having many children may be beneficial, as they can be put to work doing chores. In urban or modernized societies, large families may be costly, because children are generally non-productive for many years and thus are an economic cost. This perceived economic cost has led to a substantial drop in average family size in most modernized countries, as people have opted to use various means to reduce fertility. These means range from direct influences, such as abortion, contraception, and infanticide, to more indirect effects from attitudes about sex, marriage, divorce, and remarriage. This also may include postpartum (or other) sex taboos (that is, prescribed periods when people are to avoid sex, such as in a given period immediately after giving birth) and customary length for breast feeding (Moore et al. 1980). Culturally prescribed sex roles may also affect fertility because these roles may allocate certain types of work to women that lead to seasonal suppression of fecundity.

Mortality

The other side of the population growth equation from fertility is the death rate, or more formally the **mortality rate**, defined as the number of deaths per 1,000 population per year. It is not just the number of deaths that is important in population growth, but also who is dying and when. Deaths that occur at young ages are more significant for population growth than those that occur in the elderly, as the latter are past their reproductive ages. Thus, **infant mortality rates** (the number of deaths per 1,000 individuals between birth and one year of age in a given year) are of great importance for population growth.

MORTALITY FROM A GLOBAL PERSPECTIVE. There is great variability in overall mortality rates, and particularly in infant mortality rates, among world populations. Using 2005 figures for national rates, Iceland is lowest, with an infant mortality rate of two per 1,000 live births, while Afghanistan is highest, with a rate of 182 (UNICEF, 2006). Much of the difference in these rates stems from infectious disease: the countries that lead the world in mortality from infectious disease are precisely those that have the highest infant mortality rates. The high infectious disease rates partly stem from environmental causes, but they mainly stem from poverty. Poverty leads to poor nutrition, poor sanitation, and poor health care, and thus often catastrophic problems with infectious diseases. We'll deal more with these issues in Chapter 12.

LIFE TABLES. The delicately named **life tables** are actually death tables; they present a tabulation of mortality rates by age group for a given population. The life table can be used to derive some valuable mortality measures for a population. One of these is expectation of life, a measure of the mean number of years left in a given individual's lifespan. This measure is commonly used for individuals at birth, yielding the life expectancy at birth. However, life expectancies can be calculated at any age. Life expectancy at birth is very sensitive to infant mortality rates, as even just a few early deaths bring the population's average down considerably. In a hypothetical population where 30 percent of individuals die in early infancy but the other 70 percent all live to age 80, life expectancy at birth is 56, while life expectancy at age ten (or any age between one and 80!) is 80 (actually, it is 80 minus the individual's age, in order to derive the average numbers of years left in a lifespan).

Table 8-1 shows a classic example of a life table: that derived for the !Kung San people of southern Africa (Howell 2000). At the time these data were collected, most San maintained a traditional foraging lifestyle in the harsh environment of the Kalahari Desert. The table columns represent major measures of mortality: q_x represents the probability of dying while in a given age range; for young ages this is often a one-year period, but five-year periods are frequently used for older people. The symbol l_x refers to the number of people who survive to the beginning of a given age group. A standardized number of people, usually 100,000, are chosen at the starting point of birth, and l_x refers to how many are still alive at that age. Finally, e_x represents the life expectancy at the start of the given age range.

The San have a fairly high infant-mortality rate, with over 15 percent of infants dying in their first year of life, as seen in Table 8-1. Mortality rates drop rapidly after the first year. By age five, children can expect to live, on average, over 63 more years. At age 30, young adult San can expect to average 39 more years of life, or nearly the full three score and ten that people have come to expect in many parts of the world. A close look at the table also will allow observation of a problem: the San have a small population size, making it difficult to find a reasonable sample size at any given age group. This makes calculation of survival odds and other important mortality statistics problematic.

TABLE 8-1 Life Table of the !Kung San (modified from Howell 1979)

Age (years)	# Persons observed	Deaths at age x	q_x	l_x	e_x
0	164	25	0.152	100,000	49.44
1	151	3	0.020	84,800	57.25
2	135	4	0.030	83,104	57.41
3	115	3	0.026	80,611	58.17
4	97	1	0.010	78,515	58.71
5–9	78	5	0.064	71,468	63.45
10–14	64	0	0.000	71,468	58.45
15–19	71	0	0.000	71,468	53.45
20–24	66	0	0.000	71,468	48.45
25–29	66	1	0.015	71,468	43.45
30–34	78	1	0.013	70,539	38.99
35–39	67	2	0.030	69,551	34.51
40–44	69	2	0.029	67,480	30.49
45–49	64	1	0.016	64,939	26.59
50–54	44	4	0.091	63,575	22.10
55–59	39	1	0.026	59,135	18.58
60–64	37	3	0.081	55,754	14.55
65–69	27	5	0.148	50,885	10.70
70–74	17	5	0.294	41,270	7.61
75–79	12	5	0.417	26,875	5.35
80+	6	6	1.000	15,338	2.50

q_x = probability that an individual who survives to age x dies within the age interval; l_x = number (or proportion) of individuals who survive to age x, based on initial population size of 100,000; e_x = life expectancy at age x.

Table 8-2 shows life tables for the total population of the United States, broken down by sex (the table is slightly modified from Arias 2007). Here there is no problem with population size, and therefore we have the luxury of looking at subgroups, such as sexes, separately. A major difference between the U.S. population of 2004 and the San population from the 1970s can be seen when comparing statistics for young age groups. The U.S. population has a much lower infant-mortality rate. One can also pick out important sex differences rather easily. Women have lower mortality and higher life expectancy at every age compared with men. This is illustrated in Figure 8-4.

Life tables are very useful for human biologists, as well as for life insurance companies. The latter use mortality data to decide how much to charge for insurance policies. Human biologists use the data to pinpoint age and sex groups (or other subpopulations) with particularly high mortality risk. These times of high mortality risk are often clues to specific adaptive concerns of a given population. For instance, life tables from Colonial-era America would show a high mortality risk for women during childbearing ages; this was due to the high risk of dying in childbirth during those times.

CAUSES OF MORTALITY. If mortality risk is completely random, life tables would show the same probability of mortality (q_x) at every age. Mortality rates, however, are related to biological processes of growth and senescence. For instance, the immune systems of young infants are not fully developed,

TABLE 8-2 Life Table of the United States, 2004, total population (data from Arias 2007)

Age (years)	Males			Females		
	q_x	l_x	e_x	q_x	l_x	e_x
0	0.0075	100,000	75.2	0.0061	100,000	80.4
1	0.0003	99,253	74.7	0.0003	99,391	79.9
5	0.0003	99,124	70.8	0.0001	99,283	76.0
10	0.0002	99,043	65.9	0.0002	99,218	71.0
15	0.0009	98,936	61.0	0.0004	99,142	66.1
20	0.0014	98,486	56.2	0.0005	98,944	61.2
25	0.0014	97,809	51.6	0.0005	98,710	56.3
30	0.0014	97,148	46.9	0.0007	98,442	51.5
35	0.0019	96,455	42.2	0.0011	98,088	46.6
40	0.0029	95,527	37.6	0.0017	97,555	41.9
45	0.0044	94,154	33.1	0.0026	96,709	37.2
50	0.0065	92,078	28.8	0.0037	95,445	32.7
55	0.0090	89,089	24.7	0.0056	93,676	28.3
60	0.0138	85,067	20.8	0.0088	91,058	24.0
65	0.0203	79,213	17.1	0.0134	87,043	20.0
70	0.0304	71,168	13.7	0.0208	81,200	16.2
75	0.0460	60,336	10.7	0.0322	72,748	12.8
80	0.0682	46,461	8.2	0.0511	61,045	9.8
85	0.0958	30,619	6.1	0.0777	45,438	7.2
90	0.1272	15,948	4.4	0.1104	27,782	5.2
95	0.1566	5,808	3.2	0.1444	12,448	3.7
100	1.0000	1,261	2.3	1.0000	3,460	2.6

q_x = probability that an individual who survives to age x dies within the age interval; l_x = number (or proportion) of individuals who survive to age x, based on initial population size of 100,000; e_x = life expectancy at age x.

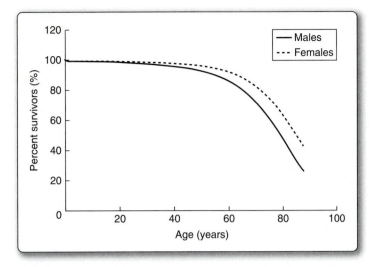

FIGURE 8-4 Survivorship of males and females, respectively, in the United States, 1998, based on life table data.

while senescence causes many changes including impaired immune function. Thus, the very young and very old are more susceptible to death from infectious diseases. Mortality is also related to less predictable circumstances related to age. For instance, in many populations adolescent and young adult males are more likely than other age-sex groups to be exposed to risky conditions for accidents at work and/or recreation. Obviously we are at risk for mortality from a host of circumstances and conditions. Several important mortality risks will be considered elsewhere in this text. We all must die sometime; it is the details and probabilities of death that are important determinants of population dynamics.

Migration

A third component to the demographic equation is movement of people from one population to another. **Migration** affects both populations, decreasing population size from the source population and increasing it in the host population. For instance, the majority of population increase in the United States in the early part of the twenty-first century is due to immigration, as opposed to drastic changes in fertility or mortality rates.

Migrants are usually far from a random sample of the source population. On the contrary, migrants often have special personality or demographic traits that influence their decision to move. In many cases, it is young adults who preferentially migrate, as they have fewer ties keeping them at home (such as family obligations) and are more likely to take risks. In a follow-up study of Samoans, for instance, those who later migrated to Hawaii were initially more likely to have reported relying on peers as opposed to family, had larger social networks, and more community involvement (Hanna et al. 1990).

Migration comes in many forms. It may be temporary, for instance, travel used for finding work with the intention of returning home when circumstances permit. It may involve multiple trips back and forth between source and host populations, sometimes on a seasonal basis. More permanent migration is also common. Previous migrants may act as intermediaries, helping newer migrants adapt to their new surroundings. When this occurs, ethnic enclaves of migrants may be formed as a distinct subgroup within the host population. Migration as used here refers to major changes of location, as opposed to commuting, tourism, moving households within a region, and so forth (Gage 2000). Migration may involve movement of major portions of populations or of a small number of individuals.

Many reasons for migration exist, and certainly not all are voluntary ones. These reasons are often characterized into two types: "pushes" and "pulls." Push factors, related to circumstances in the source population, include economic or ecological problems; religious, political or ethnic intolerance; and warfare. Pull factors, related to perceptions of circumstances in the host population, include perceptions of economic opportunity and better living conditions, but also include indentured servitude and kidnapping. It should be noted that both push and pull factors can be either voluntary or involuntary. In examining migration from Europe during the period 1913 to 1968, Davis (1974) estimated that about 58 percent of the total of 123.1 million migrants moved because of involuntary factors.

PROFILE 8

Peter T. Ellison

Peter Ellison's research has focused on the study of reproductive ecology, examining how environmental conditions such as malnutrition and high workloads affect a woman's ability to conceive and to carry a pregnancy to a healthy live birth. He has developed techniques that can be used in the field for studying levels of reproductive hormones without the requirement of collecting blood or refrigerating samples. This has enabled him and his collaborators to study details of how people manage to reproduce successfully in the face of environmental challenges. Dr. Ellison has shown how male reproductive hormones such as testosterone change during the life cycle in diverse populations. His work also examines the interactions of reproductive hormones with psychosocial stress and social relationships.

His work has ranged from studies in Boston's multiethnic population to research in arctic Norway among the Saami, from central and west Africa, where he has worked with Efe "pygmies," Lese, and Mandinka populations, to people living in the Chaco region of Argentina. In one study, Dr. Ellison and his collaborators discovered that Lese agriculturalists showed a distinct seasonal change in ability to conceive, while neighboring Efe foragers who had a more generalized diet displayed much less seasonality in their fecundability.

Dr. Ellison's research has allowed a much better understanding of human adaptation and reproduction under the enormous variety of settings in which our species resides. He is the John Cowles Professor of Anthropology at Harvard University and leads the Reproductive Ecology Laboratory at Harvard. He also serves as editor-in-chief of the *American Journal of Human Biology* and is the author of, among many other publications, *On Fertile Ground: A Natural History of Human Reproduction*.

HUMAN POPULATION GROWTH

Population Increase

GLOBAL POPULATION GROWTH. The basic components of demographic change, namely fertility, mortality, and migration, lead to changes in the total population size over time. In the long term, human population size has increased dramatically over time. As shown in Figure 8-5, human populations have increased at a geometric rate over the past 10,000 years, approximating a J-shaped curve. **Doubling time** is often used as a measure of the rate of population increase; it refers to the amount of time it would take for a population to increase its size by a factor of two if the then-present growth rate was to continue. Geometric increase in population size, if unchecked, can lead to outrageous results. The single-celled ameba, under ideal conditions, will divide into two amebas within about an hour. If these conditions prevail, within six days the offspring of a single ameba will outweigh the earth itself (Brown 1954). While human populations grow much more slowly, if our species's growth rate continues at its highest rate (reached in the 1960s), within a few thousand years the earth would be a mass of humanity expanding outwards in all directions at the speed of light (Ehrlich and Ehrlich 1970)! Obviously, these scenarios will not occur, because with population growth comes increased environmental resistance.

The human population's growth rate is estimated to have peaked in 1965 at an annual rate of approximately two percent, or a doubling time of about 35 years, but this rate had dropped by 1996 to about a 1.5 percent annual rate, or a doubling time of 47 years (Kormondy and Brown 1998), and further dropped to about 1.2 percent annually by 2005, or a doubling time of 58 years (Cohen 2005). The United Nations estimates that growth rates will continue to decline in the twenty-first century, with annual growth rates of about 0.93 percent in 2020, or a doubling rate of 75 years. As of 2005, the global human population increased by approximately 75 million people per year (Cohen 2005).

REGIONAL POPULATION GROWTH. The human population growth rate is not homogeneous. There are great disparities in growth rates in different parts of the world. In general, developed countries tend to have low, zero, or even negative growth due to fertility and mortality factors, while

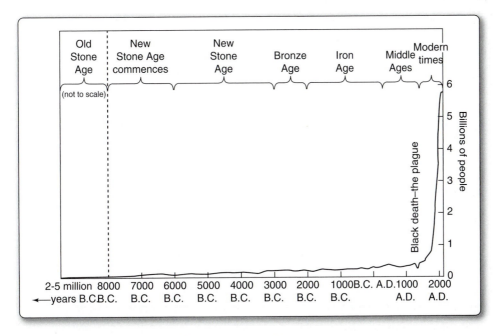

FIGURE 8-5 Population growth of humans (estimated).

many developing countries are experiencing very rapid increases. While there is a large amount of migration from developing to developed countries, this does not make up for the differences in population growth in the developing countries due to natural causes (that is, the relative disparity between fertility and mortality rates).

The world's population is estimated to increase by over two billion in the first quarter of the twenty-first century, with 94 percent of this projected increase occurring in developing countries (Kormondy and Brown 1998). The greatest population increase during this time period is expected to occur in India, which is expected to have a doubling time of only 36 years. It is particularly troubling that the projected increase in population will fall so heavily in poor areas where the greater needs that are associated with this increase will be very difficult to cope with.

Human Population Structure

Predictions of future population growth are based in part on the population structure. Percentages of the population that are found in specific age-sex categories provide information about likely changes in growth rates. For instance, populations that have a high percentage of postreproductive age people will likely grow at a slow or negative rate in the future, while populations with a large percentage of prereproductive age children, especially girls, are likely to experience rapidly rising numbers in the future.

Figure 8-6 shows the age structure of human populations in selected countries. The figure shows five-year age groups separately for males and females. The linear, somewhat urn-shaped structure of the Japanese and Italian populations suggest slow or even negative future growth, while the large bases of the age structures for India and Zambia suggest rapid population growth in the near future. The U.S. population structure is somewhat urn-shaped, but less so than that for Italy and Japan. A close look at the Chinese population's age structure shows a greater number of males than females for many age groups from infancy to young adulthood, a result of the one-child per family policy and a cultural bias for having male children. Many Chinese families opt to abort female fetuses in order to have a son as their only child.

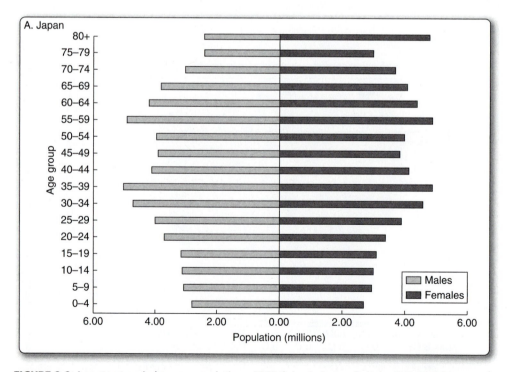

FIGURE 8-6 Age structure in human populations: 2008 data. **A.** Japan; **B.** Italy; **C.** United States; **D.** India; **E.** Zambia; **F.** China.

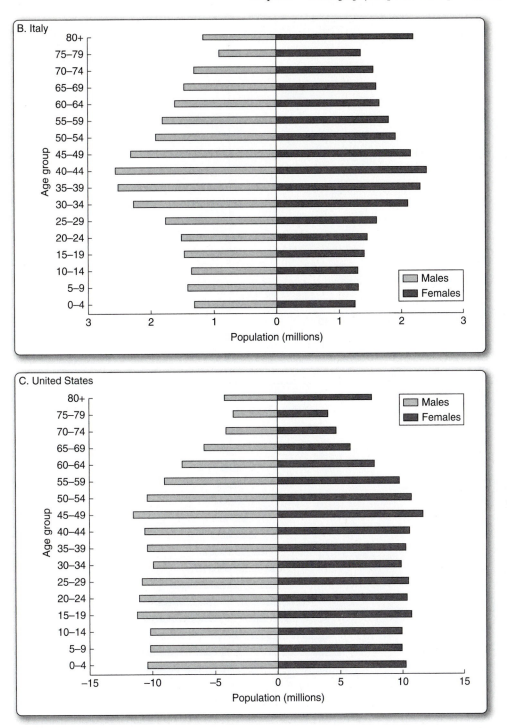

FIGURE 8-6 Continued.

Implications of Growth

There are implications to the expected prodigious increase in human populations. More people require more resources. Two centuries ago, the economist Thomas Malthus pointed to the disparity between the tendencies for a geometric increase in population but only an arithmetic increase in

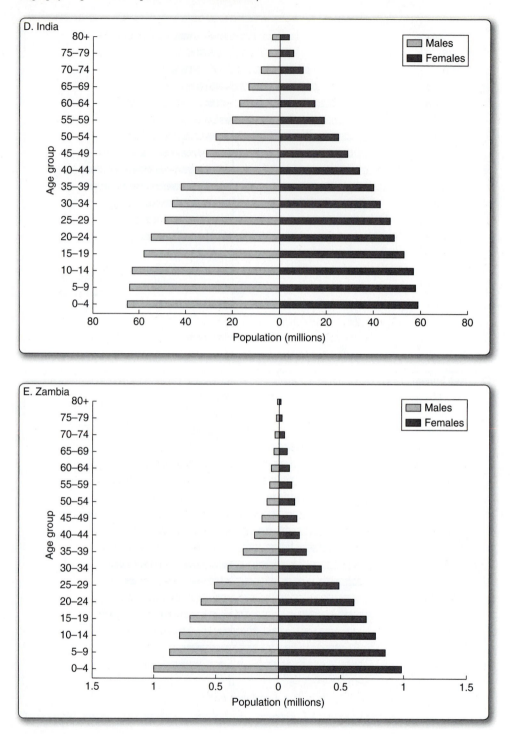

FIGURE 8-6 Continued.

subsistence. The increased human numbers would be constrained by famine, disease, or war in the absence of "moral restraint" (namely, delayed marriage and forms of sexual abstinence).

Many of the direst predictions of impending calamity have not occurred. This has been due in part to the "moral restraint" noted by Malthus: birth rates have declined in many countries, particularly

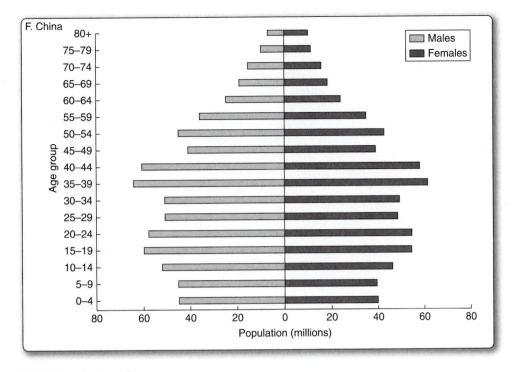

FIGURE 8-6 Continued.

those in the developed world. Also, expansion of agricultural lands and the "green revolution" in agricultural techniques have allowed enough food to be produced to feed the expanding world population, although local regions have experienced food shortages due to conditions that inhibit transport of food from more productive areas. Estimates of current food shortages do suggest that there is cause for concern. For example, about 20 percent of the world population is believed to be chronically malnourished (McAfee 1990): approximately 146 million children under age 5 are underweight (UNICEF 2006), a sign of malnutrition.

The question becomes whether the global increases are sustainable. Agriculture has already expanded into land areas that are ill suited for it, with the potential for long-term land degradation. Certainly, expansion of agricultural lands is limited in the future. This impends further adaptive challenges to individuals in dealing with the rigors of malnutrition and disease while retaining reproductive success. Natural selection, since it works on the individual level, leads to a notion of "success" defined as increased numbers of offspring, even though one can suggest that the greater good of the population would emerge from less so-called success at the individual level.

Human biologists often work on a local scale, observing population growth's effect on resources. One example where this growth has led to problems has occurred on the small islands that make up Micronesia. Population density on the atolls of Micronesia have long been very high, with the population supported both from agriculture on the small land area, but also from ocean resources, particularly those found on coral reefs that surround these islands. Rapid population increase (the Federated States of Micronesia have had population growth of approximately 29 percent in the years from 1980 to 2000), and the loss of agricultural productivity from saltwater intrusion into groundwater that is an omen of sea-level rises stemming from global warming, has led to migration of atoll dwellers to the volcanic "high" islands of Micronesia, where local resources are greatly supplemented through global trade, or on to Pacific Rim countries such as the United States.

Clearly, population dynamics present important challenges to human populations, and these challenges have both global commonalities and local, idiosyncratic elements.

CHAPTER SUMMARY

Populations have a tendency to increase at a geometric rate, with this ability termed the "biotic potential" and yielding a J-shaped growth curve. Various factors usually act to slow the growth rate, with these factors comprising environmental resistance. Actual growth rates of populations are based on the interaction of biotic potential and environmental resistance, with resistance usually greater at higher population densities, yielding an S-, or sigmoid-, shaped growth curve. Some populations have high mortality rates at early ages but slower rates later in life, other populations have relatively constant mortality rates throughout the life span, while still other populations have low mortality among the young and higher rates of death in older individuals.

Human populations, despite having generally low birth rates because of long gestational periods and a tendency to give birth to only one offspring at a time, have increased at a rate approximating a J curve over the past few centuries. The growth rate is slowing but continues, and the future population increase will primarily occur in poor, developing countries. The growth rate of human populations is based largely on fertility rates that are, in turn, primarily based upon cultural factors but also are related to fecundability, the biological ability to reproduce. Fecundability is related to nutrition, physical activity levels, and disease, among other factors. Growth is also based on mortality rates, with modernization leading to sharp drops in infant mortality and resulting in increased life expectancy.

CHAPTER 9

Life Span: Growth and Development

Much of the discussion about human biology and evolution thus far has focused on the adult organism. Biological individuals do not arise full grown from the womb, however, nor do they remain young adults forever. A full understanding of human biology requires an examination of ourselves throughout the life span. This life span approach to humans views the individual as undergoing change throughout his or her life, and these changes have repercussions for individual adaptation, as well as for population-level concerns such as those related to demography. It is not sufficient to possess a genetic background that enables one to be a successful adult; one must adapt and cope as an infant, child, adolescent, and also when one reaches elderly status.

In this chapter, we will explore the portion of the life span that precedes adulthood. Humans show general patterns of physical growth and development that occur during this period of life, but, as with all biological traits, they also show variability. The prereproductive period is a critical time of life, as difficulties that occur in this period may become magnified as time passes. Also, selective forces may have greater effect in this time period, since adaptive problems can completely preclude any reproductive success for the individual.

THE GENERAL PATTERN OF HUMAN GROWTH

Anyone who has analyzed mathematical relationships knows that it is much easier to understand linear connections than nonlinear ones. In this sense, it is bad news that the human growth curve is decidedly nonlinear, with spurts of rapid growth followed by slower growth. This nonlinearity of developmental patterns is found for studies of whole body growth, but also when one focuses on the development of specific body parts.

Prenatal Growth

Growth begins at conception, with most development of the major physiological systems taking place long before birth. Until recent times, much of the prenatal growth period was hidden from our examination, except for observation of aborted human fetuses or of the fetuses of other species. Common use of fairly noninvasive observation techniques, such as ultrasound, has allowed much more detailed study of this developmental period (see Figure 9-1). Incredible photographic images have also been taken of fetal growth using an endoscope (a medical instrument inserted into the body that allows images of internal organs or other features); an example of such a photograph is shown in Figure 9-2.

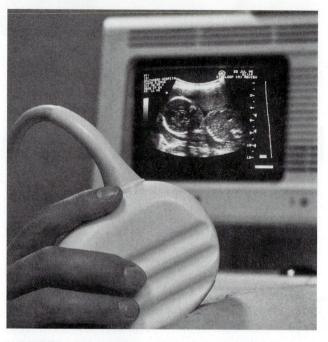

FIGURE 9-1 Ultrasound photograph of a human fetus.

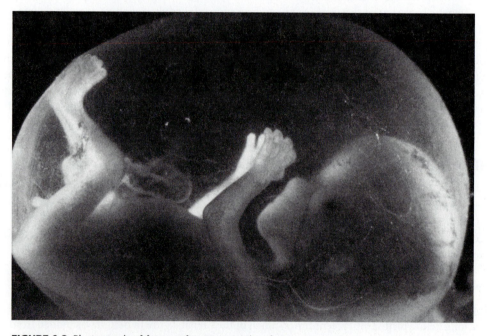

FIGURE 9-2 Photograph of fetus at fourteen weeks of age.

Fetal age is usually measured in terms of the time since the onset of the mother's last menstrual period, which usually occurs about two weeks before fertilization. While imprecise, this most recent menstrual period is often the only temporal landmark that is observed (Tanner 1988).

EARLY DEVELOPMENT. The ovum's fertilization by sperm occurs in the oviduct. Soon after fertilization occurs, the **zygote** (fertilized egg) begins to divide by mitosis while floating in the oviduct toward the uterine cavity. The dividing zygote forms a hollow mass of cells, termed a "blastula," within a few days, and this mass continues to grow and divide. At this time, the blastula implants in the uterine endometrium. By the beginning of the third week of development, invagination of the blastula occurs in a process termed "gastrulation." This leads to the creation of three distinct embryonic layers: an outer layer termed the **ectoderm**, an inner **endoderm** that forms a tube, and a middle layer termed the **mesoderm**.

Ensuing stages of development have been defined very specifically in what is termed the **Carnegie stages of development**. These stages are illustrated in Figure 9-3. Any glitch in the early developmental process can have enormous implications for later stages, since much of growth and development builds upon earlier stages. Because of this, growth, and particularly early growth, is highly **canalized**, meaning it occurs in narrowly circumscribed "channels" of allowable development (Waddington 1966). In other words, natural selection usually acts very strongly against variable growth patterns in early development. Minor variation from developmental patterns is usually met with compensatory growth that brings the fetus back into the normal growth channel. This is evidence that, to a great extent, growth is a target-seeking process that is self-stabilizing.

THE EMBRYONIC PERIOD. The embryonic period of development begins near the end of week three after fertilization, and lasts through week seven (England 1996). The period begins at the point where it is first possible to distinguish head from tail (more formally: cephalic versus caudal) and right from left in the developing embryo. By the end of the embryonic period, limbs have clearly formed, eyes and ears are visible, and reproductive organs are well developed (corresponding with the final stage, number 23, shown in Figure 9-3). Thus, by the embryonic stage's end, most major structures have appeared in the developing human, though total body mass remains quite small.

THE FETAL PERIOD. Beginning with the eighth week after fertilization, development enters the fetal stage. The fetus undergoes major growth in size, and many organ systems further develop. The fastest growth in general body height (or length, as it is termed for infants and fetuses) occurs at about

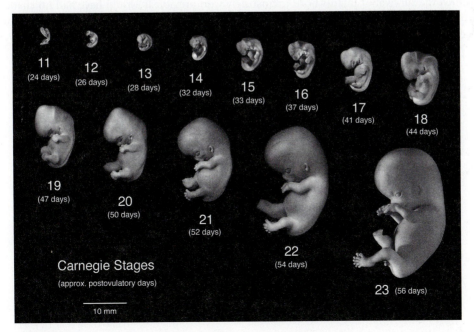

FIGURE 9-3 Carnegie stages of embryonic development in the human.

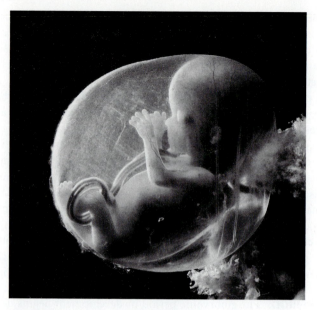

FIGURE 9-4 Fetus at age four months.

18 weeks of fetal age (see Figure 9-4), slowing somewhat thereafter. The fetus is still quite small relative to birth size at this stage however, with an average crown-rump (head to "tail," or crown-rump) length of approximately 160 mm, or about 6.3 inches (England 1996). By week 23, the crown-rump length averages about 225 mm (8.8 inches). Figure 9-5 shows the growth in length and weight during the prenatal period. Neither length nor weight changes in a linear fashion with time, but weight is more exaggerated in its nonlinear pattern, with most weight gained in the final weeks of pregnancy.

EFFECTS OF PREMATURE BIRTH OR DISRUPTED FETAL DEVELOPMENT. Medical advances have permitted the survival of infants born prematurely who previously would have had no chance for survival. Infants smaller than 400 grams and with shorter gestation than 23 weeks rarely survive (Lucey et al. 2004), and those at these limits of survivability often have serious neurological,

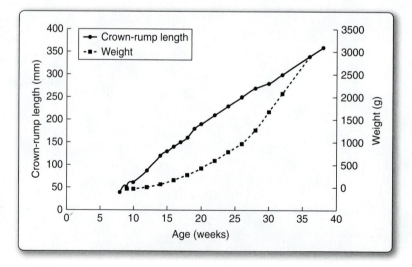

FIGURE 9-5 Growth in length and weight during the prenatal period.

pulmonary, or retinal impairments in later life (Vanhaesebrouck et al. 2004). The major limiting factor for survival of the extremely premature appears to be lung development.

Disruptions of fetal development can have major effects in later life. An early indication of these long-term effects was seen in the Dutch Hunger Winter Study, which was a follow-up study of people whose gestational period or early infancy coincided with the severe famine in the Netherlands during the Nazi occupation in the winter and spring of 1944 to 1945, near the conclusion of World War II (Ravelli et al. 1976). The people born or *in utero* during the famine period had significantly elevated rates of obesity in later life, along with higher rates of the chronic diseases associated with obesity.

Evidence for the delayed effect of early growth disruption became much stronger with the studies of Barker and colleagues that showed an association between low birth weight and elevated risk for developing cardiovascular disease and diabetes in adulthood (Barker et al. 1989; Barker 1994). For instance, by 50 years of age, the risk for development of insulin resistance, a condition that often leads to diabetes mellitus, was ten times higher in people with a birth weight of less than 2,500 grams (about 5.5 pounds), compared with people who had a birth weight of 4,500 grams or more (Barker et al. 1993). Barker and colleagues hypothesized that the increased disease risk in adults who had been born small was due to impaired function of insulin-producing cells caused by intrauterine undernutrition (Hales et al. 1991). Further research has shown that both genetic and environmental factors affect the reduced fetal growth seen in these at-risk individuals (Levy-Marchal and Jaquet 2004).

The above example of the effects of low birth weight on illness risk among adults underlines the importance of a life-span approach to many human biology concerns. Understanding of critical medical issues requires a long-term study of the individual, from conception until old age.

Growth after Birth: General Patterns

WHOLE-BODY GROWTH PATTERN. Much more is known about the general pattern of growth after birth than prenatally, mainly because it is easier to observe. Figure 9-6 shows a general, whole-body growth curve for humans. It can be seen that growth starts out at a very rapid pace for the first few years, slows somewhat in childhood, and then accelerates again in adolescence during the **adolescent growth spurt**. The growth graph shown in Figure 9-6 is based on **cross-sectional** data of the U.S. population (circa 2000). That is, the data are based on population medians for a given age. A given individual may be taller than the median at one age, and below the median at

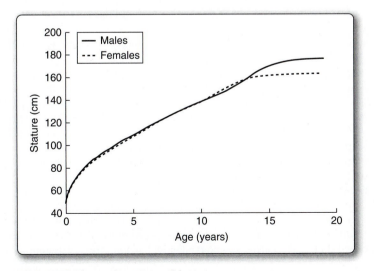

FIGURE 9-6 Change in stature with age.

another age. Thus, the pattern of growth, as well as the overall size at a given age, differs to a degree between individuals. To understand individual variability in growth patterns, we would need to follow individuals over time, in what is termed a **longitudinal** design. Because of the difficulty in following children over the many years of growth, not to mention the expense that such a study would entail, only a few large longitudinal studies have been carried out. One of the best known is the Fels study, with over 1,000 participants living in southwestern Ohio studied over a 60-year period (Roche 1992). In the Fels study, pregnant women were contacted and asked to allow their child to participate, and measurements began very soon after birth. The study has lasted long enough that children and even grandchildren of participants have also been enrolled in the study.

Because of the long time span and great effort required to obtain repeated consent from children and their parents in longitudinal studies, the research is not only difficult to carry out, it is expensive. The studies also must deal with the problem of attrition (subjects dropping out of the study before it is completed). **Auxologists** (a formal word for those who study human growth) sometimes use what are variously termed semi-longitudinal, cohort, or mixed designs. In these studies, a few different age groups (that is, cohorts) of children are studied over several years, with the ages of the cohorts at the end of the study overlapping the age of the next-oldest cohort at the start of the project. For instance, Brown et al. (1991) studied a group of schoolchildren in Hawaii over a four-year period, with cohorts starting in grades one (approximately age six), four (age nine), seven (age 12) and ten (age 15). At the end of the study, the youngest cohort had been measured at age nine, the next-oldest at age 12, and so forth. The mixed design permits observation of individual growth patterns, including growth velocity and acceleration, without the need for a study to last 18 years or more. A possible drawback is that the cohorts may differ from each other, particularly if they stem from a population that is going through rapid ecological or social change. For instance, today's 12-year-olds may have faced different challenges when they were infants than today's four-year-olds.

A Brief Aside on Sampling Issues.

Human biologists face difficulties in carrying out their research due to sampling constraints. Ideally, all population members would be included in any human biology study. The ideal situation almost never occurs, because it is usually impossible to measure each individual, given finite resources of time and money. Therefore, the human biologist recruits a **sample** of individuals from the population, and then relies upon statistical analysis to determine to what degree the sample is likely to represent the population as a whole.

Usually, the best type of sample to use is a completely random one, as there are well known statistical techniques for this type of sample for estimating population parameters. However, it is virtually impossible to obtain a random sample of a human population. For one thing, participation in a research project must be completely voluntary, with informed consent from all who participate (or, for the young, consent from their parents). Therefore, samples are always biased by the interest level of the potential participants. Also, picking individuals randomly from a large population is very difficult. Choosing names from a phone book, for example, will exclude those with no phones or unlisted numbers. Choosing from voter registration rolls or property-ownership records also will exclude people who either do not register to vote or are not rich enough to own land. For this reason, most samples used in human biology studies are at best *randomized*, without being truly random.

Some research in human biology is concerned with variable traits that are present in only a small proportion of the population. A completely random sample is likely to contain too few people with the rare trait or require an impractically large sample. In these cases, the sample needs to be weighted toward sampling people with the rare trait. This leads to choosing what is termed a **stratified sample,** in which populations are subdivided into subpopulations, and randomized samples are chosen from within each of the subpopulations.

Life-span studies that attempt to use longitudinal designs have the extra complication of attrition (that is, people dropping out of the study before it is completed). In the end, only the people who were motivated enough to put up with the research activities over a period of time are in the final sample, and people who will do this may be quite different in many ways from people who decline to participate. One example can be seen in studies of obesity and risk for diabetes: it may be that people who are obese are less likely to put up with being measured by researchers in certain social settings. On the other hand, it may be people who worry about being at risk for an illness who will participate in a study designed to examine risk factors for that illness.

While it may be impossible to obtain a perfect sample in a human biology study, high-quality research examines potential bias caused by sampling problems and attempts to account for it in analyzing study results. Human biology students generally learn quite a bit about research design and statistical analysis as part of their training—skills that are essential in any field of population biology.

DISTANCE, VELOCITY, AND ACCELERATION OF GROWTH. As in Newtonian physics, we can speak about distance (that is, a given measurement), velocity (rate of change of distance with time), and acceleration (rate of change of velocity with time) when discussing growth. Growth velocity and acceleration for individuals can only be measured in longitudinal studies. Individuals differ not only in their growth velocity at any given age, but also in when they reach growth-velocity maxima. Figure 9-7 shows individual differences in growth-velocity curves for stature.

THE HUMAN GROWTH PATTERN. Studies of many species of mammals have revealed that the human growth pattern appears to be unique in many ways. The main difference in human growth is that it is prolonged, stretching the growth period for many years after birth. Humans also experience their peak rate of growth before birth, whereas other mammals have peak growth rates in the time period soon after birth. This high-growth velocity *in utero* is made possible by the small number of offspring born at one time (termed "litter size"; for humans, usually singletons; twins and other multiple human births usually average smaller birth weight) and greater efficiency of the human placenta in carrying nutrients to the fetus (Bogin 1999).

Most non-human mammalian species show similar growth curves to each other, with a peak in growth velocity soon after birth, and a steady decline in growth until adulthood (Brody 1945;

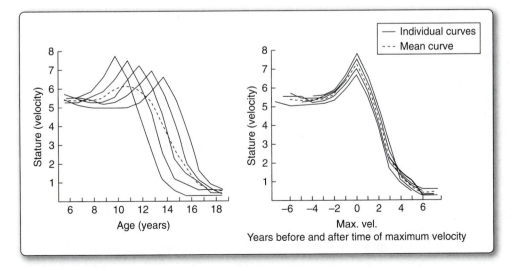

FIGURE 9-7 Examples of velocity curves of stature with age. Individual versus mean velocities.

Tanner 1962). Humans, to the contrary, have a long period of slow growth after initial high rates soon after birth, followed by an accelerated growth rate at adolescence. There is also a mid-growth spurt in humans at approximately the age of seven (Gasser et al. 1991).

THE THREE GROWTH STAGES. Human growth after birth is usually characterized as falling into three basic stages. The first is **infancy**, which is characterized by initial high velocities of growth that diminish over time. The second stage is **childhood**, in which growth proceeds at a slow but fairly steady rate. This usually coincides with what has been termed the **juvenile** growth stage, which is defined as the period of growth after weaning from the mother, but before **puberty**, the time of reproductive maturity. Finally, the stage of **adolescence** is reached, in which growth velocity increases considerably for a short period, approximately coinciding with puberty.

Humans differ from the majority of mammals in having an extended juvenile stage of growth, but this stage has also been noted in other social mammals, such as whales, elephants, and most primates (Bogin 1999). Juveniles are in many ways "betwixt-and-between." They generally must find their own food and safety from predators, although the social groups in which they live provide some support.

SALTATIONAL NATURE OF GROWTH. Although growth curves shown in the figures in this chapter appear to be smooth, this is actually an artifact of the length of time between measurements and the technical aspects of the smoothing techniques used in the graphing process. Detailed studies of infants over short intervals, for instance, daily measurements over a four-month time period, have shown that growth actually consists of a series of spurts interspersed with periods of little or no growth, leading to saltations ("leaps") in growth (Lampl et al. 1992). Saltational growth has also been observed in human children between six and eight years old (Lampl et al. 1998).

The growth spurts that do occur appear to be of variable intensity, both within and between individuals. That is, for a given individual, some growth spurts are greater than others, and differences in both size and timing of spurts occur in comparing different individuals with each other (Lampl et al. 1995).

SEX DIFFERENCES. People are clearly very interested in the differences in body form between the sexes. The origins of these differences are found in genetic differences, with females possessing two X chromosomes and males possessing one X and one Y chromosome. However, during fetal development and through much of childhood, overall body form is not much different between the sexes. It is variable growth patterns during adolescence that lead to most of the body-form changes between the sexes.

The initial determination of sex is the result of the action of a gene carried on the Y chromosome, with the gene's effects occurring during fetal development. The gene is located on a particular section of the Y chromosome termed the SRY (**S**ex-determining **R**egion of the **Y** chromosome). People without this gene develop female genitalia, while those with the allele develop male genitalia. The gene's precise effects are not fully understood, but they probably involve initiation of a cascade of gene effects that initiate male sexual development (Knower et al. 2003). Much of the later sex differences in growth are due to the effects of the sexual organs, particularly the testes and ovaries, which secrete hormones that in turn affect all parts of the developing body.

Because of the sex differences that become marked during adolescence, it is usual to represent growth patterns of males and females separately. In general, girls mature faster than boys, going through the adolescent growth spurt at an earlier age and completing their growth earlier, as well. At adolescence, girls develop secondary sexual characteristics, including breast development and increased hip size. For boys, adolescence brings a relative increase in muscle mass and decline in body fat, so that they complete adolescence being on average larger, more muscular, and generally

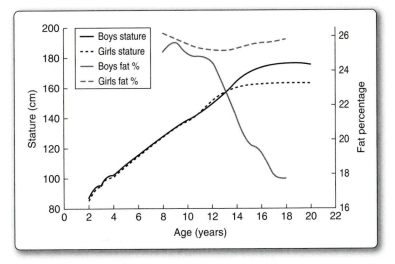

FIGURE 9-8 Sex differences in stature and percentage of body fat by age. Stature data from CDC; fat percentage data from Dai et al. (2002).

leaner than girls. This can be seen in Figure 9-8, which superimposes stature and percentage of body fat data from two different samples of the U.S. population.

GROWTH OF SPECIFIC BODY PARTS

While whole body growth has a pattern of initial rapid growth that slows during childhood and accelerates in adolescence, different biological systems may show quite different growth patterns. One illustration of this is seen in the change in body proportions at different ages (see Figure 9-9).

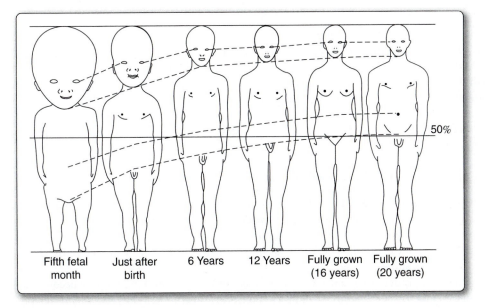

FIGURE 9-9 Changing body proportions with age.

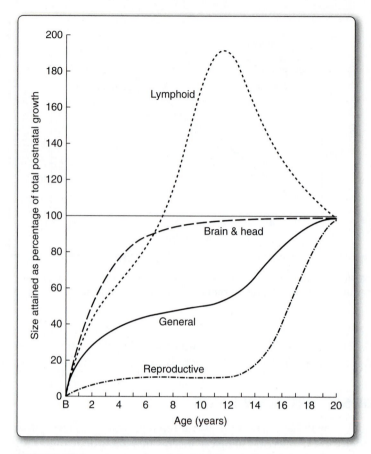

FIGURE 9-10 Scammon curves of postnatal growth of major body-part types.

It is also illustrated in Figure 9-10, which is a rendering of the classic Scammon curves. These curves show four major body systems: lymphoid, representing the immune system; neural, representing the neurological system; genital, representing the reproductive system; and general. The general growth curve outlines what has been discussed: rapid early growth, deceleration of growth in childhood, and an adolescent growth spurt. The neurological system develops quite early: at birth, the brain is 25 percent of its adult weight and reaches 90 percent of adult size by age five (Tanner 1988). The immune system also develops early but has a decidedly different trajectory: it actually peaks in function during childhood and then declines through adolescence until reaching adult levels. The reproductive system is very slow developing, with most growth occurring rapidly during adolescence.

Development of Differential Systems

NEUROLOGICAL DEVELOPMENT. The growth pattern of the different biological systems noted in Figure 9-10 can be seen as reflecting an adaptive developmental process. Humans are a large-brained species reliant upon learned behaviors, and it is the young child who must do the learning. Therefore, a rapidly developing nervous system, although constrained by the size of the birth canal, is a critical adaptation.

In very early development, within three weeks of fertilization, a neural plate becomes discernable in the embryo, subsequently forming a neural groove and neural tube, the latter developing into the brain and spinal cord. A neural crest also forms at this early stage of development, and the cells in the crest eventually migrate along the developing spinal column, forming portions of the spinal nerves (Corliss 1976). Early in its development, the neural tube becomes enlarged in the cephalic (head) region, and this area differentiates into three areas: primary forebrain, midbrain, and hindbrain. Forebrains and hindbrains each differentiate into two different regions, resulting in five differentiated regions of brain formation by the seventh week of fetal development. Subsequent brain and spinal cord development is quite complex, both in the formation of structures within the brain, and the growth of individual nerve cells, whose axons may stretch large distances, connecting with other neurons and/or with other cells. Many more nerve cells are present in the fetus than are found in adults, with a selective process occurring in which many neurons are lost during development. The density of cells per unit area of brain also decreases, by a factor of greater than ten, between six months fetal age and birth (Rabinowicz 1986).

Neurotransmitters, chemicals that are released at nerve endings to permit communication between neurons, are produced during fetal development. The neurotransmitters are not produced at a constant rate, but instead seem to be expressed intermittently, with the idea that this production occurs during specific, critical periods of development (Herlenius and Lagercrantz 2004). The neurotransmitters may influence how neurons form synapses with other nerve cells during the formation of nerve connections. At birth, a large amount of neurotransmitters is produced, and this production may have important behavioral effects, such as helping establish the mother-infant bond (Sullivan et al. 1994).

IMMUNOLOGICAL DEVELOPMENT. Infants are exposed to a whole world of new pathogens after birth. *In utero*, the fetus is protected by the mother, and this maternal protection persists for the first months after birth, mainly in the form of immunoglobulin G (IgG). The infant's immunity stems both from immune factors passed to the fetus before birth, and from immune factors passed to the infant in breast milk, particularly in colostrum, which is produced by the mother's breasts in the first few days surrounding birth. The young child must develop immunities to the pathogens in her environment, and this form of learning takes place at a rapid rate after weaning. The continuous runny nose of toddlers is the outward sign of this process. Thus, the immune system must do its hardest work in early childhood.

Early development of the immune system does start in the fetus, where lymphocytes (both B and T cells) and other white blood cells are produced. The lymph system develops in the sixth to ninth weeks of fetal development (Corliss 1976). The main development of the immune system comes after birth (Hayward 1986), however, when the individual is exposed to environmental antigens; these are usually proteins that are foreign to the individual's body.

REPRODUCTIVE SYSTEM DEVELOPMENT. The reproductive system's late development also makes adaptive sense due to what would be the inefficiency of supporting a system that does not function until adolescence. There is an energetic cost to the rapid growth that comes at adolescence, and part of this energetic cost is incurred to support the reproductive system's development.

There is some development of the reproductive organs during the prenatal period, and, in fact, these organs have an important role in the development of sexual differentiation (Sizonenko and Aubert 1986). Initially, there is no sex difference in the gonads, but by the seventh week of fetal development the gonads of XY individuals begin to exhibit male characteristics. Apparently, the gonad develops into an ovary unless there is specific, genetically induced stimulation to develop into a testis (Jost et al. 1973), principally by testosterone and its metabolic products (Wilson et al. 2002). In girls, the ovary does not differentiate until after ten weeks of gestation, and this is a more passive process than the development of the testes in boys (Sizonenko and Aubert 1986).

The development of the reproductive system at adolescence involves a sequence of events that obviously differs between boys and girls. This sequence of events is fairly similar among all children, but the actual ages at which the various events occur is quite variable. For girls, the stages include: initial breast development, completed development of reproductive structures (vagina and uterus), peak in rate of growth in stature, and first menses (termed menarche). For boys, the sequence is usually: accelerated growth of reproductive organs (testes and scrotum), penis, facial hair, peak in rate of growth in stature, and peak in rate of increase in muscular strength. For both sexes, the adolescent development events are spread over time. Figure 9-11 illustrates the sequence and range of ages at which these events occur.

Development of Selected Other Systems

While a study of the details of human development is far beyond what can be covered in this introduction, the development of certain biological systems are of particular interest to human biologists. A few will be briefly discussed here.

DENTAL DEVELOPMENT. Because teeth are the hardest part of the body, they are preserved longest after death, and they often comprise the major portion of fossil material. Tooth form reflects dietary habits of organisms, and so the study of ancient teeth allows reconstruction of the dietary ecology of hominid populations. Also, teeth develop in a regular fashion, and the presence or absence of specific teeth is an important means of determining individual age at death based on remains. Like all other primate species, humans have two sets of teeth during their life: deciduous (baby or milk) teeth, followed by permanent teeth. The deciduous teeth are fewer in number (usually 20, instead of

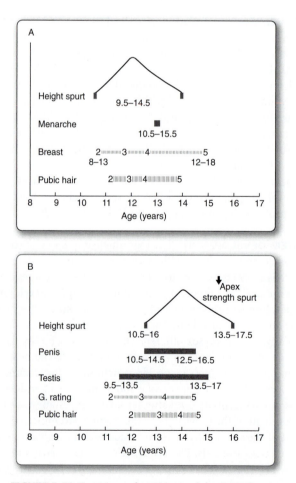

FIGURE 9-11 Sequence of events at adolescence for girls (A) and boys (B) respectively.

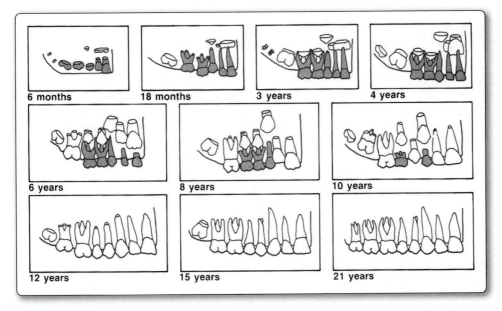

FIGURE 9-12 Pattern of tooth eruption with age in humans. Deciduous (milk or baby) teeth are shaded.

the 32 permanent teeth found in most adults) and smaller in size, to fit in the small jaws of infants and young children. As shown in Figure 9-12, specific teeth erupt at certain age intervals during development, and deciduous teeth are also shed at specific ages. While there is a range of ages for the eruption or shedding of teeth, for the majority of individuals this is a fairly narrow range. Therefore, if a skull is discovered with teeth still in the jaw, inferences about age at death can be made, often with great accuracy when the remains are of children.

SKELETAL GROWTH. The skeleton also often survives for many years after death, and it provides a record from which age at death can be ascertained based on the skeletal growth pattern. Both bones and cartilage develop from **mesenchyme** (cells derived from the mesoderm). Cartilage formation begins about the fifth week of embryonic life. A connective-tissue sheath, termed "perichondrium," develops around the cartilage. Specialized mesenchymal cells, termed "osteoblasts," form bone (Roche 1986; Shipman et al. 1985).

Intramembrous bones (also termed "dermal bones") begin to ossify at areas of primitive connective tissue membrane where there is a large amount of blood vessels (usually near the center of the future bone). Osteoblasts appear there first and calcification begins, with spicules of bony material spreading by broadening and thickening of the spicules. This forms the trabeculae, or strands of bone. Also, as this occurs, a periosteum forms around the growing bone's outer margins. Periosteum, like perichondrium, is a connective-tissue sheath, but it contains osteoblasts. At birth, ossification is incomplete, with much membrane left between bones. These areas are called fontanels.

The rest of our bones are formed by the replacement of hyaline cartilage. The cartilage grows first, taking the shape of the future bone. Ossification occurs by the destruction of a small volume of cartilage and its replacement by bone, in a manner similar to that in intramembranous bones. In long bones, this usually occurs at three ossification centers: a primary one in the center of cartilage (of the diaphysis, or shaft) and secondary ones in the epiphyses (ends). Diaphysis bone formation begins shortly after the second fetal month, but epiphyses bone formation doesn't begin until after birth. Bone growth, which parallels general body growth, is not complete until after adulthood.

Long bones retain a cartilaginous band between the diaphysis and epiphyses (the epiphyseal line) until growth is complete; this band is later seen as a slight band or not at all.

There are individual, population, and sex differences in skeletal features related to age, and this can lead to errors in the process of identifying age at death in skeletal remains, especially since European-derived populations have been the most studied, and males have generally been better studied than females. It is known that females, in general, show a more advanced stage of bone growth relative to chronological age than males. Also, the better the diet and health care, the more advanced bone growth is relative to chronological age, at least until early adulthood. Age estimation is more accurate for younger age groups—in general, the younger the individual, the more accurately the age at death can be determined.

Prolonged malnutrition slows bone development (Dreizen et al. 1964; Massé and Hunt 1963), with this retardation greater in young childhood than in adolescence (Frisancho et al. 1970). Skeletal maturation in living children is assessed through study of x-rays, particularly those taken of the hand and wrist region, as this area contains several bones, with variable times of ossification, that can be used in the assessment (Garn and Rohmann 1960).

DEVELOPMENT OF ADIPOSE TISSUE. Fat cells, or adipocytes, first appear at, approximately, the 15th week of gestation. Growth of this tissue is very rapid for the next eight weeks and then slows. There are two types of adipose tissue: brown and white. Brown adipose tissue contains many mitochondria and is highly active metabolically. White adipose tissue is less metabolically active, serving as an energy-storage depot for the body. Brown adipose tissue is present in infants, and may be involved in heat production. In adult humans, virtually all fat is white adipose tissue (Faust 1986).

Human infants have a much higher percentage of fat at birth compared with other mammals, a possible adaptation to the dietary disruption at birth that lasts until lactation starts (Kuzawa 1998). Fat is then laid down rapidly by infants, and this may be an adaptation to food disruptions that often accompany the transition from breast milk to supplemental foods at weaning (Kuzawa 1998). As a result, young human children show much higher levels of adiposity than other species display.

Given the obesity epidemic in modern human populations—and concomitant epidemics of obesity-related diseases such as diabetes, heart disease, and hypertension—it is of great importance to understand how adiposity develops in humans. The obesity epidemic increasingly includes children, and physicians of the early twenty-first century are confronted with more and more cases of children who have type 2 diabetes (once termed "adult onset" diabetes).

Adiposity, like most human traits, is a consequence of both genetic and environmental factors, as well as the interaction of these factors. The geneticist J. V. Neel has suggested that some individuals develop a genetic susceptibility to obesity when living in an environment that contains large amounts of calorie-rich foods (Neel 1962; 1999). This idea has been expanded to suggest that certain populations have higher rates of the genes that increase susceptibility to obesity; it is termed the "**thrifty genotype**" hypothesis. People in these populations adapted to "feast and famine" conditions by selection for biological mechanisms allowing the rapid storage of food energy as fat during "feast" times, with this fat allowing survival through "famine" periods.

Another hypothesis, discussed earlier in this chapter, states that the origins of obesity and the diseases that are associated with excess adiposity occur during fetal development. Specifically, the work of Barker and coworkers shows that infants born at very low birth weight are at great risk in later life for obesity and its associated diseases: diabetes, heart disease, and other chronic diseases (Barker 1994; Hales and Barker 1992; Stern et al. 2000; Lackland et al. 2000). It is believed that these low-weight infants were exposed to severe stress *in utero* and this led to life-long alteration of metabolic processes that have been termed a "**thrifty phenotype**." The two theories of the origins of obesity are not mutually contradictory: it is likely that both genetic and environmental factors and their interaction are involved in causing this complex trait. It is interesting that early development may play such an important role in a process that has its major effects much later in life.

GROWTH AFTER BIRTH: POPULATION DIFFERENCES

Marked differences exist in body size per age between populations as a result of both genetic and environmental differences, although the latter accounts for most of the population variability in growth rate. The growth curve's general shape is less variable among populations than the size-per-age of the growth parameter. That is, populations tend to differ in the median age at which a given size is attained, but they maintain similar growth patterns.

Environmental Effects on Growth

Growth is very sensitive to environmental conditions: stressful environments, particularly those that are deficient in food, lead to disruptions in growth. Reduction in linear growth rate is referred to as **stunting**. In fact, many times the most prominent indicator of a population under stress is growth stunting. Figure 9-13 contrasts the U.S. population figures (the same as shown in Figure 9-8) with growth figures for a highland New Guinea population (the community in the Lufa region, studied in 1984) that had been faced with nutritional deficiencies (Norgan 1995).

Bones and teeth develop characteristic markings in individuals who have gone through stressful periods, particularly due to nutritional problems. In bones, lines found near the ends of shafts, termed **Harris lines** (also termed Park-Harris growth arrest lines), denote periods of stress during bone development (Harris 1933; Nowak and Piontek 2002). These lines are used in individual variability studies, as well as in identifying populations that have gone through periods of stress. Similarly, **hypoplasias** on teeth, which are areas of thinned enamel that are exhibited as irregular grooves or pits in the enamel surface, also demark periods of developmental interruptions due to stress (Goodman et al. 1980). In a study of Guatemalan children, it was found that dietary supplementation led to a decreased number of hypoplasias in young children (May et al. 1993). Hence, dietary stress may be the critical factor in dental hypoplasia formation.

SECULAR TRENDS IN GENERAL GROWTH. An important kind of evidence for the significance of environmental factors on growth is the observed change over generations in attained body size per age in a single population. Since the same population is observed, there is unlikely to be a major difference in genetic backgrounds over a generation or two. What *has* changed in the intervening time period is

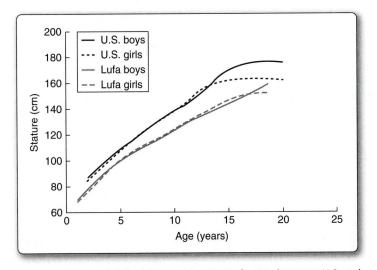

FIGURE 9-13 Population difference in stature for age between U.S. and Lufa (Papua New Guinea) children.

environmental circumstances. A population change in a biological characteristic that occurs over a period of time, often over generations, is termed a **secular trend**, and includes the example of increased body size of Japanese children in those born after World War II compared to earlier generations.

The secular trend in growth has been observed in developed nations for over a century, with succeeding generations growing faster. This trend was seen first in children of high socioeconomic status. The trend has slowed, and the slowing was also observed earliest in children of higher status. Secular trends are now small in the richest countries, but these trends are marked in many developing countries.

WHY THE SECULAR TREND IN GROWTH? It is unclear precisely what has caused the secular trend in growth, but the circumstances that change in populations when the trend becomes evident are associated with conditions of **modernization**. Modernization is a complex process that involves many specific environmental alterations, including improved nutrition, decreased incidence and severity of infectious and parasitic diseases, smaller family sizes, and urbanization (Eveleth and Tanner 1990).

NEGATIVE SECULAR TRENDS IN GROWTH. It is also possible to have a negative secular trend in growth, in which succeeding generations actually grow more slowly than previous ones. As noted in an earlier chapter, negative secular trends have been observed in some African populations and among children of high socioeconomic status in Honduras (Tobias 1985; Bogin et al. 1996). In these cases, environmental or political disruptions have led to poor nutrition, sometimes accompanied by decreased access to medical care.

EFFECTS OF UNDERNUTRITION ON GROWTH. The maintenance of life requires a fairly constant intake of nutrients, particularly energy and protein. Sustaining growth processes requires additional nutrients beyond those necessary for general maintenance activities. The evidence for growth retardation in undernourished populations is clear (Gracey 1991), but these populations usually suffer from other stresses as well, including relatively high infectious and parasitic disease rates. However, growth reduction in children with either anorexia nervosa or with untreated celiac disease (a condition in which food is poorly absorbed from the intestines) provides strong evidence that undernutrition is an independent cause of slowed growth in individuals (Prader et al. 1963; Gracey 1991).

Undernutrition is much more severe for children than for adults, in part because children have smaller reserves (fat and lean tissue that can be used for essential nutrients), faster metabolism, and greater protein requirements to allow biological development. When faced with protein shortages, or with total undernutrition, two diseases of malnutrition become evident: **kwashiorkor** and **marasmus**. Children with kwashiorkor have lost much of their muscle tone due to their bodies' use of muscle-tissue protein for other essential tasks. These children often, ironically, have pot bellies—not from overeating, but due to the loss of strength of their abdominal muscles. Marasmus manifests as a loss of fat stores, as well as muscle depletion, and the child also often has diarrhea, leading to dehydration. Both diseases can be fatal.

The importance of undernutrition for growth is clear, but it brings up another question: Do all kinds of stress lead to growth disruptions?

EFFECTS OF OVERNUTRITION ON GROWTH. Another form of malnutrition, the intake of too much food, leads to the acceleration of some aspects of growth. Children who overeat are more likely to become obese and to become at high risk for developing diabetes later in life. In fact, the rate of obesity is skyrocketing in children living in developed countries, and, as noted earlier, this is lowering the age at which obesity-related diseases, such as type 2 diabetes, appear. Pediatricians now must be concerned with a disease that was once considered to be solely found in adults.

Children who are over-nourished also may develop at different rates than their agemates, at least at young ages. Overweight girls tend to start their menstrual periods at an earlier age than normal-weight girls (Garn 1980; Brown et al. 1996). However, there is some evidence that obese children lag behind leaner children in skeletal development (Lascano-Ponce et al. 2003), perhaps due to the reduced physical activity levels associated with obesity. A study in Japan noted that obese children had lower bone density after puberty than non-obese agemates (Nagasaki et al. 2004).

EFFECTS OF DISEASE ON GROWTH.   The interconnectedness of poor nutrition and parasitic disease in children makes it difficult to ascertain specific causes for stunting in many populations. Some data suggest that parasitic diseases are an independent cause of slowed growth in children. Stunting is present in several populations that have high parasite loads without the presence of **wasting** (low weight-for-height), suggesting that there are sufficient calories in the diet. Studies have suggested that such parasitic diseases as schistosomiasis, filariasis, giardiasis, various round worm infections, hookworm, and whipworm all can cause growth retardation (Stoltzfus et al. 1997; Steketee 2003). Parasitic infections may stunt growth by impairing the body's efficiency at using nutrients, and therefore these infections may be seen as an indirect form of nutritional inadequacy.

The evidence for population differences in growth rates is clear for differences in socioeconomic status: poor children grow more slowly than rich children. Poverty is associated with poorer nutrition, greater disease rates, and less access to medical care (Stinson 2000), making it difficult to understand the independent effects of these factors in growth disruption.

EFFECTS OF HIGH-ALTITUDE HYPOXIA ON GROWTH.   The lowered oxygen pressures at high altitudes leads to hypoxic conditions for fetuses, children, and adults who live in mountain regions. Placentas are relatively heavier in high-altitude populations, suggesting that adaptations to the low oxygen conditions have occurred. Despite this, birth weights are lower in high altitude than in sea-level populations. Many high-altitude populations, such as those in the Andes region of South America, also have lower nutritional intake levels than many sea-level populations, making interpretation of the birth weight data problematic. Studies of the Leadville, Colorado, high-altitude community—a well nourished community—show significantly lower birth weights than other U.S. communities, supporting the direct effect of hypoxia on lowering birth weight (Frisancho 1993; Lichty et al. 1957). Also, studies of various socioeconomic classes in Bolivian lowland and high-altitude cities have shown that high altitude appears to affect birth weight independently of economic status (Giussani et al. 2001).

Postnatal growth rates for children in several high-altitude populations were also observed to lag behind that of sea-level populations. This was posited to be caused by the lowered oxygen availability present in high altitude environments (Frisancho and Baker 1970). Since these populations also tended to be undernourished, the growth retardation could have been solely due to nutritional stress (Greksa et al. 1984). Some studies have attempted to compare high-altitude populations with those of similar nutritional intake, and they have concluded that the high-altitude populations grow more slowly (Haas 1976; Hoff 1974; Beall et al. 1977). Nutritional-intake comparisons are very difficult to make in a precise manner, however. Where high-altitude populations are better nourished than nearby sea-level populations, growth rates are actually higher despite the hypoxia (Clegg et al. 1972; Frisancho et al. 1975). Also, increases in postnatal growth rates have been seen in high-altitude populations (Leonard 1989), coincident with improved health and nutrition. It appears that hypoxia does cause slowed postnatal growth independently of nutrition, but this reduction is relatively small.

CATCH-UP GROWTH.   When an individual has undergone a temporary cessation or slowing of growth due to environmental conditions (nutritional, health, or hypoxic disorders, for instance), there is a tendency for growth to increase above normal rates after the disruption has ended. The individual thus begins to "catch up" with the body size that he or she would have had at a given age had the disruptive forces not been present. This phenomenon of speeded-up growth after a disruption is termed **catch-up growth**.

PROFILE 9
Noel Cameron

Dr. Noel Cameron was born and raised in the United Kingdom, but after obtaining his doctoral degree at the University of London's Institute of Child Health, he spent many years teaching and doing research in South Africa. Much of his research has been devoted to studying the normal and abnormal growth of children in developing countries. His work in Soweto-Johannesburg, South Africa, illustrated the poor conditions for children during the time when the racist apartheid system of government ruled that country, with clear evidence for growth stunting in many children. His work has also shown that improvement in growth characteristics of poor children after apartheid in South Africa has been slow.

Dr. Cameron has also undertaken important research on growth in developed countries, producing growth standards for children in the United Kingdom and exploring the causes and consequences of childhood obesity, including the reasons for sedentary behavior in adolescents. Many of his studies have focused on skeletal growth using measures of bone mass in addition to anthropometric assessments of body size. He also has contributed to ideas about critical periods of development that have effects for the rest of an individual's life, and he has advocated the use of a life-span approach to the understanding of human biology and human health, including a focus on basic genetic mechanisms that link early growth with later chronic disease risk.

Besides publishing many groundbreaking papers in scholarly journals, Dr. Cameron has edited the books *Human Growth and Development,* published by Academic Press, and *Methods in Human Growth Research,* published by Cambridge University Press. He serves on the editorial boards of several human biology and anthropology journals and is co-editor of the *Annals of Human Biology*. He is currently Professor of Human Biology and Director of the Centre for Human Development and Ageing at Loughborough University in the United Kingdom.

There are many variables related to how rapidly individuals grow during the catch-up period, including the amount of the previous growth disruption, the child's age and gender, and the conditions during the catch-up period. In a classic study on catch-up growth, Stini (1969; 1971) examined the effect of long-term protein malnourishment on a population in Colombia. When nutritional intake improved, girls showed catch-up growth in the preadolescent period, while boys did not.

Genetics and Population Growth Differences

Clearly, some of the population variation in growth rates is due to genetic factors. For instance, there is evidence that the slow growth of African Pygmy populations is not solely due to nutritional deficiencies. A study of Efe Pygmies showed that the children display a normal growth curve, including an adolescent growth spurt, and their weight-for-height was actually above the median for U.S. children, who are among the heaviest for age in the world (Dietz et al. 1989; Eveleth and Tanner 1990), but the height-for-age of Efe children was below other population averages at all ages. Thus, the data show stunting but not wasting in the Efe children.

AFRICAN SHORT-STATURED POPULATIONS. Pygmy populations have lowered blood levels of IGF-1 (insulin-like growth factor-1, a protein that plays an important part in growth processes) and lowered sensitivity to IGF-1 by cellular receptors, possibly due to a variant in IGF-1 gene regulation; there is apparently no difference in the DNA sequence of this allele between Pygmies and non-Pygmy African populations (Merimée et al. 1987; Bowcock and Sartorelli 1990; Diamond 1991; Geffner et al. 1995; Hattori et al. 1996). It has been speculated that there may be a mutation in the regulatory gene(s) that control the IGF-1 locus (Merimée et al. 1990; Shea and Bailey 1996).

SHORT-STATURED POPULATIONS IN SOUTHEAST ASIA. Studies of some short-statured populations in Southeast Asia, such as the Aeta and Mamanwa in the Philippines, have also shown decreased levels of IGF-1 (Clavano-Harding et al. 1999; Davila et al. 2002), although measurements among Bundi and Mountain Ok populations of Papua New Guinea, among the shortest in the world, found IGF-1 levels to be in the normal range (Schwartz et al. 1987; Eveleth and Tanner 1990). These populations do tend to share lowered levels of growth hormone binding protein (Clavano-Harding et al. 1999). It is unclear, however, if there is a genetic basis to the small stature in these populations. But it is clear that these Asian short-statured populations are not related closely to African Pygmy populations (Thangaraj et al. 2003) and may be genetically dissimilar to each other. More detailed studies are necessary to understand the complex interaction of genetics, nutrition, and disease that leads to short-statured populations.

GROWTH AND DEVELOPMENT: A FINAL CONSIDERATION

The events involved in growth and development are best viewed as one part of the continuing process that characterizes the entire life span of human beings. The life-span approach to human biology sees the individual as constantly changing, and the events that take place at one point in time may have effects that carry over into later life. This view of the human condition complicates matters, but it also deepens our understanding of the multifaceted nature of our species. The adult is the product of the child, and the child is the product of the infant and fetus. In the next chapter, we will extend this view to the later stages of life.

All life stages are the product of the complex interaction of one's genes and the environment. Genetics includes the epigenetic phenomena associated with the genome; and the environment includes physical, biological, and cultural components that all interact and affect the individual. We are indeed a complicated bunch.

The study of growth and development *per se* is a fascinating and important topic, but for human biologists it holds perhaps its greatest import as the time in life when selective evolutionary forces are at their greatest. Mortality at an early age yields no reproductive success, and thus selection against deleterious genes is strongest when it occurs before adulthood. In some respects, fetuses, infants, and children are more vulnerable than adults. Their immune systems have not developed specific resistance to common antigens to which all adults have become accommodated. Their knowledge of behavioral means of adapting to the environment is incomplete, a particular concern given the emphasis humans as a species have given to learning about and understanding their environment in order to devise coping strategies. The growth process itself is a fragile enterprise: environmental assaults can easily derail the process, at least temporarily. When human biologists wish to assess a population's relative success in its environmental adaptation, they often first look to the growth process: growth disruption is usually the first sign of a population in crisis. And the effects of these disruptions can be felt by members of these populations many decades into the future.

CHAPTER SUMMARY

Human growth and development, both before and after birth, play a major role in determining the human adult phenotype. The embryonic period, from week three through seven after fertilization, is a time when major organs develop. Striking growth in size occurs during the subsequent fetal period. The general whole-body growth pattern after birth is characterized by rapid growth in infancy, slower growth during childhood, and a spurt in growth at adolescence. Individual biological systems have different patterns of growth. The neurological system is highly developed at birth and rapidly approaches adult size in the early years after birth. The immunological system develops very quickly after birth, peaking in childhood and actually becoming reduced in function after the childhood peak. The reproductive system is very poorly developed until adolescence, at which time rapid development to adult levels occurs.

There is variability in the growth rates seen in people, with some population differences present. Females generally develop faster than males, and well-nourished people also have faster developmental rates than those raised under poorer conditions. Much individual variation in growth is related to environmental factors, although genetic factors also contribute to variation. The presence of secular changes in growth rates within populations provides evidence for the importance of changing environmental conditions in variability of growth rates. The conditions that affect growth include nutrition, disease, and environmental stressors such as high-altitude hypoxia. If the stress is temporary, growth rates tend to accelerate after the stress is removed, a phenomenon termed "catch-up" growth.

Some populations tend to have short stature, such as the Pygmy populations of central Africa. This may be due in part to genetic factors. However, most population differences in growth are a result of exposure to environmental stress, and therefore growth rates are often an indicator of how well a population is adapting to its environment.

CHAPTER 10

Life Span: Aging and Senescence

We now turn to the final stages of the life span, a period that is often defined by a gradual decrease in body function eventually ending with death. Why do we age? It is an ancient lament; the question of aging has no easy answer, and in fact it may mark our ignorance of the process. Does aging differ in our later years from in our youth? That is, is aging a cumulative, gradual process, or is it, like growth, marked by varying rates or critical periods of special import? Can the aging process be stopped, or at least slowed? Is aging a natural characteristic that accompanies life, or is it a process that has undergone natural selection, evolving in some (most? all?) populations?

The human life cycle can be divided into several stages: embryo, fetus, infancy, childhood, adolescence, adult, elder. The age borders of these categories are uncertain, as are the number of categories. In fact, some of these divisions are arbitrary, particularly that between adult and elder. There is much variation in how people age, with some people remaining active well into their nineties, such as the famed evolutionary biologist Ernst Mayr (Figure 10-1). It is not terribly important to find a neat dividing line between the later life stages, and the focus of this chapter will therefore be on the *processes* that occur in this portion of our life cycle.

We often hear the credo: "Age is just a number!" In simple terms, **aging** denotes increasing age; as in the expression, age *is* a number denoting the passage of time. **Senescence**, by contrast, is the *process* of growing old, including a decline in function with age; senescence need not correspond to a given number. Understanding both aging and senescence requires a look beyond humans at the general biology of senescence.

THE BIOLOGY OF SENESCENCE

The process of aging takes somewhat different forms in different species, but there are general characteristics shared by all multicellular organisms, both at the cellular and organismal levels. These can be summed up as a loss of function in biological systems.

Aging at the Cellular Level

Old cells function differently than young cells. They stop dividing, lose contact with other cells but become more attached to the extracellular matrix, display marked changes in chromatin structure, and alter the manner in which genes are expressed. In cell culture, senescent cells enlarge and become flattened (Ben-Porath and Weinberg 2005). The similarity of the process across a wide variety of cells, and across species, suggests that there is a "program" of cellular

FIGURE 10-1 The evolutionary biologist Ernst Mayr as a young man and when he was in his late 90s.

senescence as opposed to simply a random decline in certain processes. Evidence shows that prokaryotic cells display evidence for aging as well (Nystrom 2003). We will focus our discussion on eukaryotes, however.

HAYFLICK AND LIMITS TO MITOSIS. The classic research of Leonard Hayflick and coworkers first published in 1961 showed that there was a limit to the number of times cells could undergo mitosis in cell cultures (Hayflick and Moorhead 1961; Hayflick 1965) and that this limit was fairly consistent for given cell types taken from individuals of a given age. Furthermore, cells derived from older individuals had a lower limit of mitotic divisions in the cell cultures than those taken from younger individuals (Hayflick 1987). Clearly, there is a decline in cellular reproductive function with age. Hayflick's research has been replicated by many researchers studying diverse eukaryotic cells. The ubiquity of the loss of ability to undergo mitosis in senescent cells can be viewed as a means to control tissue growth, a critical ability in multicellular organisms.

THE CELL MEMBRANE AND CYTOSKELETON IN SENESCENCE. Chemical changes occur in the cell membrane and cytoskeleton (the cell's skeleton) during cellular senescence that lead to functional changes for the cell as a whole. The actin cytoskeleton is the means by which the cell allocates functions and reacts to signals stemming both from internal and external sources (Gourlay and Ayscough 2005). During senescence, the cytoskeleton becomes less flexible, due to changes in the actin protein that is its chief constituent, and the cell loses its ability to make changes in cytoskeletal structure. In some cells, there is also a reduction in the number of microtubules (the structure of which the cytoskeleton is composed) with senescence.

There are also characteristic changes to the cell membrane's function during aging. The amount of phospholipids that make up the membrane declines with age, while the amount of cholesterol increases. Accompanying these changes, but likely not caused by them, is increasing membrane rigidity (Yu 2005). Due to the critical nature of membrane functions for the cell's integrity, some researchers have hypothesized that membrane changes are the root cause of senescence of the organism as a whole (Zs-Nagy 1994; Spiteller 2001). It should be noted that reduction in function of membranes refers not only to the external membrane, but also those membranes enclosing such cellular organelles as mitochondria and the nucleus.

AGING AND THE MITOCHONDRION. Mitochondria, the organelles within which aerobic metabolism takes place, are particularly susceptible to damage over time, and this damage contributes to senescence. The main effect is that the mitochondria become less efficient, producing less energy for the cell. With age, mitochondrial membranes have lowered electrical potential, and more highly oxidizing molecules leak out of the mitochondria and damage cellular proteins (Ames et al. 2005).

AGING AND LYSOSOMES. Lysosomes are cellular organelles that function in the destruction of cellular molecules or organelles through enzymatic means. Lysosomes are critical to the cell's function: they remove damaged material through a process termed "autophagy" (literally, self-eating). With age, lysosomes function less efficiently, allowing damaged and/or poorly functioning molecules to build up in the cell and making the cell less able to defend itself against damaging agents (Cuervo 2004). For some forms of autophagy, age-related decreases in the receptors on lysosome membranes lead to reduced uptake of materials that are to be degraded.

AGING AT THE ORGANISMAL LEVEL. There are characteristic changes that occur with advanced age that are obvious when we observe our own species, but there are also general changes common to all animal species. These changes are pervasive, going well beyond the superficial level of "looking old." Senescence affects tissues, organs, and systems, and it also influences behavior. Of particular importance is the effect of aging on musculoskeletal, immune, cardiovascular, neurological, and reproductive systems. Of course, we are all interested in the more superficial changes that occur with age, as attested to by the multibillion dollar industry involved with making us look younger.

AGING OF THE MUSCULOSKELETAL SYSTEM. Aging is normally associated with a decrease in muscle mass, strength, and velocity of contraction, a condition termed **sarcopenia**. There is a decrease in specific muscle fibers, including type 2 fibers and certain myocin heavy chains (Karakelides and Nair 2005; Deschenes 2004). People usually lose over 30 percent of their muscle fibers by age 80 (see Figure 10-2). This condition creates issues of ability for aged individuals in all

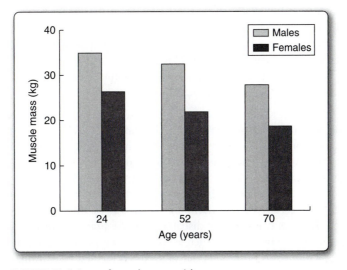

FIGURE 10-2 Loss of muscle mass with age.

animal species to move about and therefore to obtain resources without help, but also makes elderly humans frail and susceptible to injury from falls (Nikolic et al. 2005).

Senescence also affects the skeletal system, with decreases in bone mass associated with osteoporosis the most common problem, particularly in post-menopausal women. Bone aging is also associated with higher risk for development of bone cancer. During adulthood, bone is constantly remodeled in the body, with cells termed **osteoclasts** breaking down bone and **osteoblasts** building up new bone. Through most of adulthood, resorption (destruction) and creation of new bone occurs at equal rates, but during senescence resorption outpaces rebuilding of bone (Chien and Karsenty 2005).

Associated with skeletal aging is the erosion of joints that is linked with osteoarthritis. These changes lead to the disease arthritis, which is a general term for many disorders of the joints. In osteoarthritis, which is very common in the elderly, both the cartilage covering the ends of bones as well as membranes in the joint area undergo change, and inflammation occurs within the joint. This is often accompanied by joint swelling, causing pain during movement (Spence 1989).

AGING AND THE IMMUNE SYSTEM. The immune system becomes impaired during senescence, leading to increased susceptibility to infectious disease and to increased rates of immune diseases and cancer (Effros 2001; Sabastián et al. 2005). Senescence leads to diminished functioning of both **innate** and **adaptive immunity**. Innate immunity, the so-called first line of defense, consists of nonspecific defenses against pathogens that are activated immediately after contact with an antigen. Adaptive immunity refers to antigen-specific defenses, such as antibodies, that are usually activated after the innate immune system has responded. Immune cells such as T-cells, B-cells, and macrophages are altered during aging, with the changes leading to functional impairments. Not only do the impaired immune cells perform poorly in attacking pathogens, but they are also more likely to assault healthy tissues, actually causing illness.

AGING AND THE CARDIOVASCULAR SYSTEM. There is a sharp increase in cardiovascular diseases, and mortality from those diseases, in the elderly. There are many reasons for this elevation in vulnerability, including the lowered activity levels in people of advanced age due to sarcopenia. However, much of the increased risk for these diseases is related to senescence of the cardiovascular system itself. The heart muscle cells undergo senescence, leading to lowered rates of growth and increased rates of **apoptosis** (a process of programmed cell death), which, in turn, leave the heart with lowered performance and diminished contractility (Sussman and Anversa 2004).

Senescence of the endothelial cells that line blood-vessel walls is also a factor in increased cardiovascular disease among the elderly. Atherosclerosis, the process of blood vessel plaque growth, proceeds steadily, and over time these plaques may block blood vessels, causing heart attacks or strokes depending on where they are located. This condition is made worse by the blood vessels' progressive loss of ability to dilate, due to senescence of endothelial cells (Brandes et al. 2005) and to an increase in inflammatory processes with age (Finch 2005).

AGING AND THE NEUROLOGICAL SYSTEM. The rates of such neurological disorders as Alzheimer's and Parkinson's diseases increase sharply with age. Both the gray and white matter of the brain decrease in size with advanced age. This has led to the idea that neurological diseases and a decline in mental function in general are a byproduct of the brain's natural aging process (Keller 2005; Hof and Morrison 2004). The decline in cognitive function includes reduction in memory, spatial ability, and cognition speed. This decline is believed to be due in part to loss of nerve cells (neurons) with age. The loss is not evenly distributed in the brain, however. There appears to be greater neuron loss in certain brain areas, such as the hippocampus and deep layers of the cerebral cortex. There is also a reduction in the number of synapses formed by neurons in the elderly, and this may account for some of the cognitive decrement that accompanies aging.

There is now evidence that the brain compensates for the aging process, undergoing functional reorganization to mitigate the effects of senescence (Reuter-Lorenz and Lustig 2005). Also, neurons can be replicated and then used to replace some of the lost cells. The brain can reestablish synapses; for example, studies that provided supplemented estrogen in animals led to synapse reformation and improvement in cognitive ability.

The process of neurological senescence is quite complex, in part due to the brain's complex nature, but also because the consequences of aging in other biological systems in turn affect the brain. For example, aging blood vessels increase the risk of stroke. On a more subtle level, aging of the small blood vessels in the brain leads to lowered blood supply to some brain areas. Brain function has been shown to be closely related to blood supply, and therefore the lowering of blood supply to certain brain areas may account for much of the cognitive decrement associated with aging (Riddle et al. 2003; Finch 2005).

AGING AND THE REPRODUCTIVE SYSTEM. Changes in reproductive function are much more apparent in females than in males. As noted, women begin their reproductive lives at the time their first menstruation occurs, termed **menarche**. They cease their reproductive lives after they have their last menstrual period, termed **menopause**. In human females, all primordial egg follicles are formed in the fetus between six and nine months of gestation. During this period, there occurs a marked loss of egg cells due to apoptosis. The number of primordial follicles decreases progressively, until very few — if any — are present after the menopause at about 50 years of age. Some of this loss of egg cells is due to monthly ovulation (a few hundred follicles), but most loss (about seven million follicles) is due to the process of **atresia**, in which the egg follicles degenerate (Leidy 1994; te Velde et al. 1998). Figure 10-3 illustrates the change in number of egg follicles with age in a typical woman.

In general, in the months before menopause there is a decline in estrogen output and a variable increase in the hormones FSH (follicle-stimulating hormone) and LH (leuteinizing hormone). These hormones play important roles in the female reproductive system, and they are major controls of a woman's monthly cycle (Reame et al. 1996; Santoro et al. 1996). Following menopause,

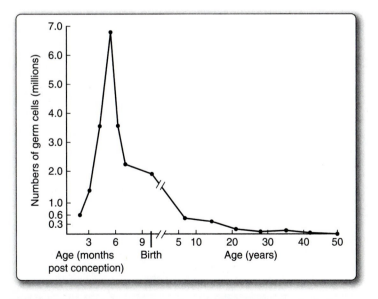

FIGURE 10-3 Estimated number of egg follicles by age in a typical woman.

there is a significant decline in estrogen concentration and LH as time from menopause increases (Jiroutek et al. 1998). These hormonal changes are associated with variation in age at menopause and some of the symptoms attributed to menopause (for example, hot flashes). Hormone replacement therapy, whether with estrogen or combinations of estrogen and progesterone, ameliorates the symptoms associated with menopause, but it has also been implicated as elevating risk for heart disease and some cancers.

For men, beginnings and ends of reproductive life are not well marked, although fecundity increases rapidly during puberty and gradually declines in later years. Sperm production declines in elderly men, along with the motility of the sperm that are produced (Spence 1989). Figure 10-4 shows the decline in fecundity with age for males and females, respectively. Part of the loss in male fecundity is due to a decline in older men of testosterone production. The **andropause** has been defined as a condition analogous to menopause, but occurring in men over age 50 who show a cluster of symptoms associated with testosterone deficiency (Tariq et al. 2005). These symptoms include impotence and some characteristics associated with aging in general, such as frailty, sarcopenia, memory loss, and depression. Testosterone replacement therapy has been successful in ameliorating these symptoms.

Superficial Changes During Senescence

Humans are usually very good at appraising the ages of their fellows, simply from a glance. There are subtle and not-so-subtle changes that occur to the hair, skin, and other superficial structures as we age. Hair lightens with senescence due to the loss of melanocytes and reduced melanin content in hair follicles (Commo et al. 2004). Gray hair has some structural differences from pigmented hair, being coarser and less manageable (Van Neste and Tobin 2004). Head hair thins, particularly in men, even in those without male pattern baldness or other genetically based conditions that lead to premature hair loss. Hair thinning with age involves both a slightly decreased number of hair follicles and a miniaturization of some follicles (Sinclair et al. 2005).

THE HAIR CYCLE. Scalp hair follicles undergo a cycle of growth and decline, followed by a new growth cycle. The hair-growth phase of the cycle is termed **anagen**, and during this phase there is not only active hair growth, but a large number of active melanocytes in the follicle. When the anagen phase nears its end, melanocytes reduce production of melanin, and the follicle shortly after enters

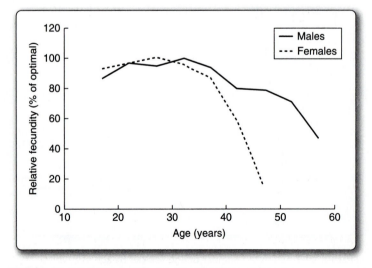

FIGURE 10-4 Relative fertility by age of males and females.

PROFILE 10
Lynnette Leidy Sievert

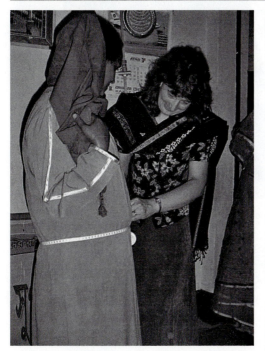

Lynnette Leidy Sievert's research has focused on menopause as an aspect of human variation. Her interest in menopause began when she was a hospital nurse in her early twenties. She watched some of the older nurses open the windows in winter and fan themselves, and she wondered why some women had hot flashes at menopause while others never felt any changes with age. For her doctoral dissertation, she interviewed women in upstate New York in an attempt to find out why some women experienced their last menstruation at 45 while others menstruated until almost 60. From there she became interested in untangling the underlying biological changes of midlife from the influence of particular cultures. During the last 20 years, she has studied menopause among women residing in western Massachusetts; Hilo, Hawaii; Puebla, Mexico; the Selska Valley, Slovenia; Asuncion, Paraguay; Sylhet, Bangladesh; and London.

Dr. Sievert is a professor of Anthropology at the University of Massachusetts at Amherst. In addition to symptom experience and age at menopause, she has written about the evolution of menopause and the uniqueness of the length of the human post-reproductive life. She has studied how married women have later ages at menopause compared with unmarried women, how women at midlife are more likely to complain of musculo-skeletal-joint pain and stiffness than hot flashes, and how attitudes toward menopause are more strongly related to depression and mood changes at midlife than hot-flash experience. With British colleagues, she found that Muslim women in Bangladesh demonstrated more hot flashes than Hindu women, perhaps in relation to differences in dress and religious ritual. With colleagues in Hawaii, she found ethnic differences in the number of reports of hot flashes, a finding that replicated results from previous studies, but when hot flashes were measured objectively through electrodes placed on the chest, no clear ethnic differences were present. The ethnic differences in hot flashes may be more a cultural difference in how people report their conditions than it is a biological difference between populations. Dr. Sievert is the author of numerous articles, chapters, and the book *Menopause: A Biocultural Approach*.

the regression phase of the cycle, termed **catagen**. Melanocytes largely disappear from the follicle during this phase, although there may be a process of de-differentiation (that is, a loss of specialization) of these cells, followed by re-differentiation in the new cell cycle. Apoptosis may also be involved with the loss of many follicular cells during catagen. Catagen is followed by **telogen**, a resting phase where the follicle is much smaller than it was in the growth phase (Tobin and Paus 2001). A new cycle beginning with anagen follows, with the hair follicle enlarging and melanocytes reappearing.

AGING AND THE HAIR CYCLE. Aging is associated with a 10 to 20 percent decrease in active melanocytes in the skin for every ten years of age after 30 (Quevedo et al. 1969). Active melanocytes decline from all parts of the body, including the hair follicle, beginning around age 50. Individuals can

FIGURE 10-5 Comparison of the face in men at different ages.

sustain melanin production through approximately seven to 15 hair cycles; afterward, graying of hair due to loss of melanin production is seen. This may reflect a genetically based decline in the hair follicle's ability to regenerate active melanocytes in succeeding hair cycles (Tobin and Paus 2001). Graying is also due to the greater length of the telogen phase of the hair cycle in older people.

SKIN AGING. Skin becomes less elastic with increasing age, leading to wrinkles and a looser fit with the underlying bony structure. Skin aging is accelerated by sun exposure, as first demonstrated by comparison of the necks of sailors with those of nuns, perhaps through the mechanism of induced inflammatory responses (Giacomoni and Rein 2004). It appears that darker-skinned people show a slower skin-aging process, presumably because of the greater amount and more even distribution of melanin that helps ameliorate sun damage (Taylor 2002).

Superficial changes with aging also include changes in facial features. These changes are in part due to the continual slow growth of cartilage in the ears and nose. Earlobe size increases with age, particularly in height (Brucker et al. 2003). Nasal cartilage, like cartilage in general throughout the body, becomes more fibrous and more compliant to compression forces in older people as well (Rotter et al. 2002). Figure 10-5 shows a general conception of how the face changes with time.

THEORIES OF SENESCENCE

The effects of senescence are well studied, but the question arises: why does this occur? Causal theories of senescence fall into two types: mechanistic theories that ascribe senescence to natural phenomena in the environment, and evolutionary theories that suggest that there has been natural selection for genomes that cause, or at least permit, senescence to occur. These theories attempt to deal with the evidence for the universality of senescence in multicellular organisms, and for the evidence that not only organisms senesce, but their cells do, as well.

Mechanistic Theories of Senescence

There are many theories of senescence that can be classified as mechanistic, meaning that the theories look for proximate causes of the aging process, as opposed to positing natural selection as an ultimate cause. A common theme for many of these theories is that senescence is due to the *cumulative* effects of a natural process, a process that builds with time. The theories also need to account for the greatly varying rates of senescence: from decades in humans and elephants to days in fruit flies.

OXIDATIVE DAMAGE. One of the earliest and most commonly cited theories of senescence is that reactive oxygen molecules (termed "reactive oxygen species," or ROS) cause cellular damage that accumulates over time (Harman 1956; 1962). Since most oxidative metabolism in eukaryotes occurs in mitochondria, most of the ROS are also produced in these organelles. The oxygen radicals cause the production of hydroxyl radicals (OH·) that can damage many kinds of biological molecules, including proteins and DNA (Hughes and Reynolds 2005). Oxidative damage in the cell is widespread, affecting membranes and thus reducing cell permeability, thereby damaging DNA. This leads to production of altered proteins that function improperly, causing damage that stimulates apoptosis (Crews 2003). Mitochondrial DNA sustains more oxidative injury than nuclear DNA, due not only to its proximity to where most of the ROS are produced, but also because mitochondrial DNA is more fragile than nuclear DNA. Furthermore, DNA repair systems are more poorly developed in the mitochondria than in the nucleus (Crews 2003).

Senescence has been shown to be related to the increase in types of proteins and nucleic acids that result from oxidative damage (Sohal et al. 1995). Furthermore, increased longevity has been seen in organisms with greater oxidative stress resistance, including increased expression of genes known to code for antioxidants (Arking et al. 2000; Dudas and Arking 1995). Treatment of organisms with antioxidants not normally found in their bodies also has been shown to slow senescence (Melov et al. 2000). A final type of evidence for this theory is the slowed senescence found in organisms where reactive oxygen molecule generation is slowed (Hughes and Reynolds 2005).

NONENZYMATIC GLYCATION. Glucose and other simple sugars can chemically combine with proteins to form glycoproteins, in a process termed glycation. This process may be directed by enzymes, but it also occurs without enzymes when proteins are exposed to high levels of sugar. The products of the reactions are termed "advanced glycation end products (AGEs)," and these can accumulate over time. The glycated proteins function abnormally and can lead to reduced functioning of the cells in which they are found. Thus, the accumulation of AGEs is seen as a mechanism for aging (Suji and Sivakami 2004). Also, ROS are released during the glycation process, further causing deleterious changes associated with senescence.

Nonenzymatic glycation has been linked to several diseases associated with accelerated senescence, particularly diabetes. Individuals with the disease diabetes mellitus develop high concentrations of blood sugar because their cells do not take in sugar as quickly as do the cells of nondiabetic individuals. One of the severe consequences of diabetes is that the high blood-sugar levels lead to increased nonenzymatic glycation and the accumulation of AGEs. Proteins in blood-vessel walls—such as collagen—become glycated, and this leads to an increased rate of inflammation and in growth of atherosclerotic plaques that narrow arteries (Basta et al. 2004). Glycation also increases arterial stiffness and thickness (Yoshida et al. 2005), which increases risk for cardiovascular diseases. Collagen glycation occurs in all individuals, not just diabetics, and these changes in collagen normally occur at a predictable rate, such that one can determine an individual's age fairly accurately simply by examining their collagen (Hamlin and Kohn 1972). Since diabetics have an increased rate of glycation, their collagen ages at a faster rate than that of nondiabetics.

As with the oxidative damage theory, the theory of nonenzymatic glycation is based on the notion that problems accumulate over time, leading to the loss of function that characterizes senescence.

CROSS-LINKAGE. The cross-linkage theory states that proteins become denatured over time by the formation of chemical bonds between segments of the proteins that are termed "peptides." These so-called cross-linkages change both the structure and the function of proteins, and therefore lead to a loss of body function over time (Spence 1989). It is cross-linkage that causes the changes in the cytoskeleton that lead to loss of flexibility and resulting inability of the aging cell to react to its environment as well as young cells do.

MITOCHONDRIAL CHANGES. The theory concerning mitochondrial changes is related to the oxidative damage theory, in that both posit that effects of senescence are due to alterations in mitochondria. In the oxidative damage theory, ROS damage cellular structures, including mitochondria. In the mitochondrial change theory, senescence is caused by mitochondrial changes that may be due to several factors, with ROS damage only one of them (Crews 2003). Because mitochondrial DNA is not repaired adequately, cumulative changes lead to loss of cell function, particularly in aerobic metabolism.

TELOMERE SHORTENING. The theory of telomere shortening refers to cells that are undergoing mitosis. As noted in Chapter 4, when chromosomes are duplicated during mitosis, the mechanics of the process leads to a shortening of the very tip of the chromosome, which is referred to as the telomere. The telomere consists of a large number of repeated sequences of nucleotides, and therefore the number of repeated sequences is reduced each time that mitosis occurs. When the telomere becomes considerably shortened, duplication of the chromosome cannot proceed properly, causing the cell to reach its "Hayflick limit" of the number of times that mitosis can occur. This acts as a timekeeper for how long cells can be functional in a reproductive sense.

An enzyme, termed "telomerase," permits telomere lengthening, thus essentially reversing this process of senescence and allowing mitosis to occur (Gilley et al. 2005). There is a possible down side to this, however, as cells tend to accumulate mutations with successive cell divisions, and these mutations can build up, leading to increased cancer risk. Thus, telomere shortening and eventual cessation of mitosis may be an important means of preventing cancer (Campisi 2001). In fact, many malignant cells can divide indefinitely, in part, because they activate telomerase activity (Gilley et al. 2005). On the other hand, it appears that senescent cells are more likely to become cancerous than non-senescent ones. Thus, senescence cannot simply be viewed as an adaptation to prevent cancer. It may be that cell senescence early in the organism's life is preventative of cancer, but at older ages senescence takes on a maladaptive role.

Evolutionary Theories of Senescence

Several theories about senescence suggest that causes beyond simple wear and tear exist. These theories suggest that senescence, in evolutionary terms, has been positively selected for. For this to be the case, there must be a genetic component to senescence.

A general consideration for all evolutionary theories is that natural selection works with less force on older individuals. This can be understood if one considers that in a hypothetical population which has no senescence, the probability of dying remains constant at all ages (at least, all ages after adulthood is reached). This could refer to a population of well-made ceramic dishes. There is no appreciable change in a dish's chances for death (that is, breaking) over time, assuming a constant rate of use. However, as time goes by, more and more of the dishes do get broken, and the population of dishes shrinks. Figure 10-6 shows the rate of dish "mortality" (this rate can also apply to any other non-senescing population) over time; in this example, the population loses ten percent of its members each year, presumably due to butter-fingered dish washers. Since the number of individuals (dishes) in the population diminishes over time, there are simply fewer individuals on which natural selection forces can act as time goes by, and therefore selective processes are weaker on older individuals.

THEORY OF MUTATION ACCUMULATION. In a biological population, the meaning of the change in selection's force over time becomes clearer: any mutation that would cause a negative effect later in life would not be selected against as much as deleterious mutations that act at earlier ages.

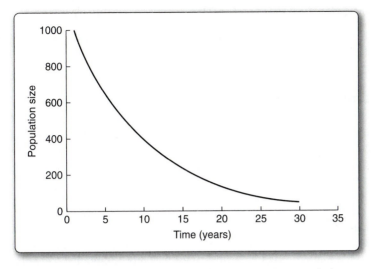

FIGURE 10-6 Change in size over time of a non-senescing population.

Conversely, favorable mutations that act early in life are selected much more strongly than favorable mutations that take effect in later life. In many generations, the population would tend to build up favorable mutations that act in early life. Fewer favorable mutations, and more deleterious mutations, that have their actions later in life would accumulate. The result of this process is the evolution of senescence in the population (Hamilton 1966). This has been termed the "theory of mutation accumulation."

The theory suggests that many mutations will accumulate, and that therefore senescence is the result of the actions of many genes, not just one or two genes that have striking effects. While it is possible to have single genes with large detrimental effects, in this theory it is expected that the cumulative effect of many deleterious genes would be the major factor causing senescence.

THEORY OF ANTAGONISTIC PLEIOTROPY. Another evolutionary theory considers mutations that cause different effects on the individual at different times in the life span. A gene with multiple effects is said to be **pleiotropic**. For instance, some mutations might be favorable at young ages but detrimental at older ages. Because of the differential force of selection at different ages, these types of mutations would be favored in evolution. There is evidence in many biological populations that individuals with more reproductive success at young ages (a very favorable characteristic for natural selection) often have greater mortality rates as they age (Sgrò and Partridge 1999; Arantes-Oliveira et al. 2002). Thus, in this theory, senescence is seen as being due to selection for mutations that improve early-life performance to the detriment of function later in life.

DISPOSABLE SOMA THEORY. The disposable soma theory is somewhat similar to the antagonistic pleiotropy theory, but here the main idea is that maintaining and repairing the body (the "soma") are intrinsically costly, and that resources used for reproduction take away from what can be used for maintenance. Thus, individuals that devote more resources to reproduction will break down faster from the various suggested mechanical causes of aging because they have fewer resources available for repair and maintenance. Due to the importance of reproduction to evolutionary success, selection would favor individuals that allocated resources primarily to reproduction, with maintenance costs kept as low as possible to allow survival over a fixed time period (Kirkwood and Holliday 1979; Hughes and Reynolds 2005).

Selected System-Specific Senescence Theories

Some theories deal with senescence of specific body parts or specific conditions associated with old age, as opposed to the general process of senescence. Two examples specific to human biology will be presented here.

MENOPAUSE AND THE GRANDMOTHER HYPOTHESIS. Why do women run out of egg follicles while they still have many years of life ahead of them? It would seem that the loss of follicles that leads to menopause would be selected against, since women with a longer reproductive period would have greater reproductive success. And no other species has a menopause (there is some evidence for a cessation of ovulation in aged gorillas in captivity). A possible answer to this conundrum is that older women might improve their reproductive success more by increasing their *daughter's* fertility than by increasing their own (Hawkes 2003).

Humans are born helpless, and they rely on their parents, particularly their mothers, for many years. A woman encumbered by an infant has both greater nutritional requirements, since she must feed the infant as well as herself, and less ability to forage for food due to the need to carry and care for the child. If her own mother assists her at this stage, her probability of successful child rearing increases markedly.

If the grandmother has her own young children to care for, she cannot assist her adult daughter very much. Also, an older woman's offspring may have a lowered probability of survival due to the lowered functional ability of their aged mother, and perhaps due to their mother's death before they can care for themselves. Thus, foregoing her own reproduction and assisting her grown daughter would benefit the grandmother, as long as the chances for survival of the infant, who shares a quarter of the grandmother's genes, are improved sufficiently to offset a smaller probability of success with the grandmother's own infant, who inherited half of her genes. In this scenario, selection would occur to eliminate reproductive activity in older women, leading to the evolution of menopause. It is only in humans, with the combination of extremely long life spans and much reliance on social behavior, that the conditions favorable for selection of menopause occur.

THE COGNITIVE RESERVE HYPOTHESIS. Because of the extreme reliance on social behavior and learning in humans, there may have been selection for long life spans, allowing the wisdom of elders to be utilized by human groups, particularly within families. For most of human evolution, no historic record was available, and therefore knowledge of events that were spaced far apart in time, such as long droughts or flooding, would reside in the memories of living people or in oral traditions handed down in populations. Hence, a family that shared a genome permitting long life would have greater reproductive success than families who had no elders who could pass on information that improved success in avoiding hazards or gaining resources under rare but critical conditions. For elders to be valuable as knowledge repositories, they would need to maintain both good cognitive function and the ability to communicate (Allen et al. 2005). Given that there is a decrement in cognitive ability with advancing age, there would be a need for a "cognitive reserve," such that sufficient cognitive ability would be retained into old age. The hypothesis suggests that this cognitive reserve is found in the large brains that characterize our species. Thus, the need for elders of both genders would lead to the evolution of both greater longevity and larger brains in the hominid ancestors of humans.

Conclusion: Theories of Senescence

There are an enormous number of theories concerning senescence, from ideas about ultimate causation, to ideas about the mechanics of aging, to ideas about why certain characteristics related to senescence have evolved. These theories also vary considerably in the amount of data that supports or refutes them. The number of theories reflects the importance we humans place on the subject. We will all grow old someday, unless a worse alternative occurs, and while in many cultures there is great value placed on the elderly, in others, including Western culture, it is youth who are revered.

There are seemingly no ends to which people will not go to undo the effects of senescence, from masking them with makeup to treating them with plastic surgery. There are untold numbers of seekers of the philosopher's stone or fountain of youth. It appears that many of these pilgrims today are scientists, and they believe that an ability to turn back the effects of aging requires knowledge of how, and perhaps even why, senescence occurs.

THE HUMAN POPULATION BIOLOGY OF SENESCENCE

If one or more evolutionary theories of senescence are correct, population-genetics differences among human groups could very well lead to variability in senescence. Mechanistic theories of senescence could also lead to human population variability in senescence, in this case due to general environmental differences. Individual differences in aging are present among humans: to a degree, some people seem to look younger than others of the same age. The question is: do these individual differences also exist at the population level?

Population Differences in Life Span

LIFE EXPECTANCY. Human populations differ considerably in life expectancy. This demographic statistic reveals the number of years of life an individual of a given age can expect to live based upon averages in his or her population. A given human population also changes life expectancy over time. For instance, the life expectancy at birth in the United States has risen markedly in the past two centuries, mostly as a result of better nutrition and medical care.

A closer look shows that this does not reflect on maximal life span: life expectancy at birth has risen greatly over this time period. However, what changes have occurred in life expectancy at age 80? Figure 10-7 shows the life expectancy at various ages for the U.S. population over a hundred year period, beginning with data from 1900 to 1902, and ending with data from 2004 (data from Arias, 2007). As can be seen, the life expectancy at birth has increased markedly: from 49.2 years in 1900 to 1902, to 77.8 in 2004, a difference of 28.6 years. However, the differences between the curves narrow as the age at which the life expectancy is computed goes up. At age 80, people in 1900 to 1902 had a life expectancy of 5.3 more years; in 2004, the life expectancy at age 80 was 9.1 years, a difference of only 3.8 years. The main difference in the two curves is a much greater mortality during infancy

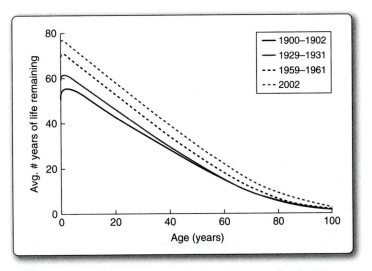

FIGURE 10-7 Change in life expectancy at various ages for the U.S. population over a 100-year period.

and childhood in the 1900 to 1902 population; after survival to adulthood, life expectancy is much more consistent.

The U.S. population has changed in several ways in the last century. The ethnic composition has changed, with European Americans representing a smaller percentage of the population than previously. The population has also become older on average, in part due to increased life expectancy, but also due to a reduced fertility rate. This fertility reduction occurs because, on average, people marry later in life and have fewer children. However, genetic changes in the population have probably not been large: migration and selective reproduction have surely led to some changes, but perhaps not sufficient to lead to major changes in the genetic background of life span. Great environmental changes have occurred in technology, medicine, agriculture, and many other areas. These environmental changes have affected survival at young ages much more than they have affected survival of the elderly.

MAXIMUM LIFE SPAN. People, even health professionals, often confuse maximum life span with life expectancy. Life expectancy represents population *averages*, but the *maximum* age of any individual in a population might be a better indicator of differences in senescence, or at least in the *rate* of senescence. Here there is virtually no difference: in any human population the maximum life span is approximately 120 years. As seen in Figure 10-7, what has changed in the past century is not the maximum life span but the proportion of people who approach it (Hayflick 1994).

SPECIES DIFFERENCES IN MAXIMUM LIFE SPAN. Anyone who has had pets is aware of the great differences in life span between different species. One's pet gerbil will probably only live a couple of years, while one's dog becomes elderly at about age 15. Early researchers such as Weismann (1889) and Pearl (1928) noted a relationship between "rate of life" (basal metabolic rate) and longevity across many species of mammals, with extended longevity associated with slower metabolism (Cutler 1978; Hayflick 1994). Across many species, there appears to be an equal number of heartbeats in a lifetime, or of breaths. While this seems enough to keep one awake at night counting one's heartbeats or breaths, longevity is also related to body size, brain weight, the ratio of brain size to body weight, and total lifetime metabolism (Crews 2003). Because of this, humans have a greater maximum life span than would be predicted from our metabolic rate alone. This is illustrated in Figure 10-8. Figure 10-9 shows that the association between maximum life span and body size (which in turn is related to metabolism) differs somewhat for different kinds of animals. Primates (as shown in Figure 10-9), birds and bats, and aquatic mammals live longer than other mammals of similar size (Prothero and Jurgens 1987).

SHANGRI-LA OR BUST. There have been reports in the popular press of exceedingly long-lived human populations, often from isolated, mountain environments such as the Andes, Caucasus, and remote areas of western China. In fact, it has seemed that the lesser the knowledge of these populations, the more likely it was that they reportedly possessed prodigious life spans. With more scrutiny, these claims for extended life span have been debunked.

SARDINIA. One population does show unusual longevity, at least for men. Many studies of individual **centenarians** (people who live to age 100 or older) show that women have better odds of reaching this age group than males, by a five-to-one margin. On the Mediterranean island of Sardinia, there are an unusual number of male centenarians, nearly equal to the number of female centenarians (Poulain et al. 2004). The mortality rate for females over age 80 on the island is approximately the same as it is for other populations in developed countries, but the mortality rate for men over age 80 is much lower than other populations (Koenig 2001; Deiana et al. 1999). Ongoing research in the population seeks to determine whether genetics, lifestyle (including drinking the local red wine), other environmental conditions, or combinations of these, are responsible for the lowered mortality rates of elderly men in Sardinia.

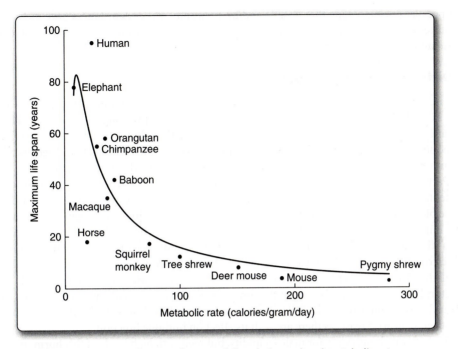

FIGURE 10-8 Maximum life span of mammals in relation to basal metabolic rate.

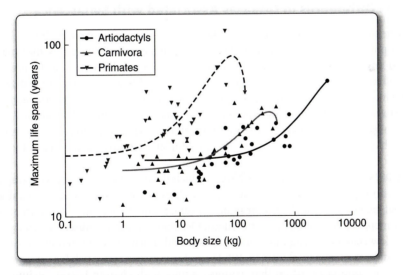

FIGURE 10-9 Relation between maximum life span and body weight in different groups of animals.

For the island of Sardinia, the prevalence of living centenarians is 16.6 per 100,000 residents, a figure considerably higher than the rate of ten per 100,000 seen in Europe as a whole. In one province of Sardinia, Nuoro, the prevalence of centenarians is 17.9 per 100,000. Careful validation of the ages of centenarians has increased confidence that this is an actual long-lived population. The upper limit of approximately age 120 for maximum life span in humans is not breached in this

POPULATION DIFFERENCES: CONCLUSION. There are clear population differences in the rates of diseases that have been associated with aging. However, these differences appear to be due more to environmental or social conditions than they are to genetic differences among the groups. It is clear that there are genetic differences among individuals that influence life span, and some of these genetic differences may actually influence the rate at which senescence occurs. However, there is no evidence for population differences in genetics that make one population longer-lived on average than another. While it is possible that these population genetic differences exist, their effects are masked by the more important influence of environmental conditions.

Conclusion

Aging is a topic that interests all of us, since we are all destined to cope with its effects, that is, if we are fortunate enough to live long enough to face it. The common observation that "aging is not for sissies" is both a recognition of the aches and infirmities that come with age, and a sign of our determination to persevere in the face of these problems. The rapid increase in our knowledge of human genetics and the molecular basis for its actions brings hope that we may find the philosopher's stone that allows us to conquer the detrimental effects of aging and its ever-present sibling, mortality. One must balance this hope with the reality of the universality of senescence in living organisms. Life extension, not immortality, is a more realistic goal. However, we must also realize that the peculiarities of Western culture, where youth is admired and aging is dreaded, exaggerate our fear of this natural part of our life span.

CHAPTER SUMMARY

Senescence, the biological process associated with aging, appears to be universal among eukaryotic organisms. Senescent changes occur at the molecular, cellular, tissue, and organ levels of organization of individuals. Normal cells appear to be programmed to be able to undergo mitosis only a limited number of times, and apoptosis, or programmed cell death, puts a final limit on a cell's existence. On the organismal level, skin becomes less elastic, muscles become weaker, bones more brittle, and other organs, in general, work less effectively as we age.

There are many theories for how senescence occurs, and these theories can be divided into those that address the mechanics of how senescence occurs, and those that address the broader question of why the changes occur, through consideration of evolutionary forces that may foster senescence. Many of the mechanistic theories of senescence focus on general wear and tear that builds up in individuals over time, with this deterioration caused by the effects of oxygenation, glycation, cross-linkage of proteins, or other chemical processes that accumulate over time. The deterioration particularly affects mitochondria, and it also can lead to mutations in nuclear or mitochondrial DNA, with the build up of mutations leading to the characteristics associated with senescence.

Human populations vary considerably in life expectancy, which is based on the average age at death for the group. However, there is very little variation between populations in the maximum age that individuals live, with this age being approximately 120 years. It is likely that there are complex genetic effects that impose a limit on life span, as suggested by the species differences in maximum life span. Wear and tear may also play a role, since species' maximum life spans lengthen as their metabolic rates are reduced, suggesting that the effects of metabolism have a role in setting age limits on organisms. Ultimately, the limits to life occur when disease or deterioration of necessary biological systems reach a fatal threshold. Cardiovascular disease and cancer are the two biggest killers in the developed world, and these diseases are closely connected with the aging process.

CHAPTER 11

Human Adaptability to Physical Stressors

Humans are found throughout the world, from the sub-zero temperatures of the Arctic to the sweltering jungles of the tropics. Such a widespread distribution is unusual in a single species, and would usually be accompanied by a great deal of regional biological diversity to allow for adaptation to such disparate environments. As we have seen, humans are not very genetically diverse. It is likely that the complex behavioral and cultural adjustments that humans use in adapting to the environment have permitted their wide distribution without the need for major genetic differences. Still, humans do show some genetic diversity, and a portion of that variation is related to environmental conditions. To understand the way that humans have succeeded in colonizing most of the earth, we will need to consider both biology and culture.

LIMITING FACTORS, TOLERANCE, AND ENVIRONMENTAL PHYSIOLOGY

Populations are not made up of identical individuals, but rather contain diversity, a major theme of this text. The variation among individuals results in differences in ability to adapt to a given environmental condition. However, the individuals that make up a species or population within a species share a basic means of adapting: for example, individual cacti may differ in ability to withstand hot and dry conditions, but no cactus can survive well in a rain-forest environment. This chapter will focus on the population level of analysis, but will also examine individual differences in adaptation where appropriate.

In examining how populations adapt to stressful environmental conditions (stressors), it can be seen that ability to cope with most stressors is not sufficient; *all* stressors must be accommodated to assure survival. Adaptation to all but one stressor will not allow survival and reproduction. Thus, a population's ability to survive in a given environment is based upon the idea of a least common denominator, whether it be temperature extremes, acidity, salinity (saltiness), or some other factor, and this is termed a **limiting factor**, because it places limits either on a species's population size or on its range.

Law of Tolerance

In fact, limiting factors can have an effect on populations whether they are present in a deficient or excess amount. For instance, temperatures can either be too low or too high for an organism to survive, or pH can be too acidic or too alkaline. The **law of tolerance** states that either an excess or a deficiency of some factor may limit an organism or a population. Given species tend to have characteristic ranges for any factor that they can tolerate, although there is often some diversity in

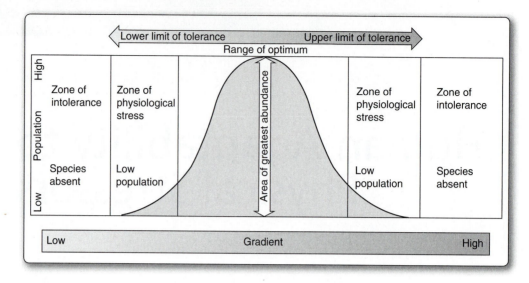

FIGURE 11-1 Tolerance to a gradient of environmental conditions.

tolerance range among the individuals making up the species. Usually, species thrive when conditions are near their tolerance range's midpoint. As the limits of tolerance are reached, the stress level increases, until a point is reached where survival is impossible. This is illustrated in Figure 11-1. An environmental condition that is near the tolerance limit serves as a (**stressor**) for an organism, and acts as a limiting factor for the population.

Limiting factors can be either density dependent or density independent. Density-dependent factors are influenced by the number of individuals in the population that are present in a given area; that is, they are related to the population density of the species in a given ecosystem. These factors include such things as nutrients in the food supply or infectious diseases that are passed from individual to individual. Density-independent factors limit populations no matter what the population size is. For instance, if temperatures in a given environment are too low for individuals in a species to withstand, this will usually prevent the species from being present in that environment without regard to population size. In other words, both density-dependent and density-independent limiting factors may place boundaries on a species' range, but density-dependent limiting factors also can affect the population density of the species in areas where it is present.

Environmental Physiology

The study of the adaptation of individual organisms to environmental change and stress is termed **environmental physiology**. The central concept used in the field, derived from physiology (the study of body function), is the notion of **homeostasis**, which refers to the relatively constant conditions within the body. Environmental physiologists study the active processes used by the body to maintain these constant internal conditions.

The processes used to cope with stressors can be viewed at either the individual level or the population level. At the individual level, adaptations can occur due to behavioral, physiological, or developmental accommodations. At the population level, adaptation can occur through cultural, demographic, or genetic (and thus evolutionary) means.

INDIVIDUAL LEVEL CHANGES: BEHAVIORAL ADAPTATIONS. Behavioral adjustments are found in all organisms. They range from light-seeking movement ("tropism") of plants, to bacteria following chemical gradients either toward resources or away from danger, to complex learned behaviors of chimpanzees in using simple tools for extracting termites from mounds. Humans have the most complex behavioral repertoire, and many of these behaviors can be viewed as being adaptive, although some of our species's behaviors may also create more problems for us than they solve. One characteristic of all behavioral adaptations is that they are relatively quickly employed and can be stopped relatively quickly as well. Another important characteristic of this mode of adaptation is that it is reversible. For example, an animal can sun itself in cold conditions to build up body heat, but then seek shade if climbing temperatures during the day make conditions too hot to tolerate. Thus, behavioral adaptations are well suited for dealing with rapidly changing conditions.

INDIVIDUAL LEVEL CHANGES: PHYSIOLOGICAL ADAPTATIONS. Organisms can cope with stressors through autonomically controlled changes in body function. These accommodations occur through **phenotypic plasticity**, or observable biological changes that are induced by the environment. For instance, upon exposure to bright light, our irises expand, causing contraction of our pupils and thus lowering the amount of light entering our eyes. Should we move into dimmer light, our pupils will rapidly dilate, allowing more light into our eyes. Similarly, when exposed to cold we will begin to shiver, with this forced muscle movement generating metabolic heat that warms our body. When the temperature rises, shivering will stop, preventing creation of too much heat metabolically when we are also exposed to hot environmental conditions. These examples show that physiological adaptations are also reversible and relatively quickly employed, much like behavioral adaptations.

Some physiological adaptations take some time to take effect, however. For instance, when first exposed to the low-oxygen conditions of high altitude, humans hyperventilate to bring more oxygen into their lungs, but this over-breathing also eliminates too much carbon dioxide from their bodies, causing a condition known as respiratory alkalosis due to an increased pH (pH is a measure of the relative acidity or alkalinity of substances). After a few days, the renal system excretes excess alkaline compounds from the body, thus bringing the body's pH back to normal, homeostatic conditions. Therefore, it takes several days for an initial physiological accommodation to high altitude to occur. Another adaptation to low-oxygen conditions is to increase the amount of hemoglobin, an oxygen-carrying molecule, in the blood. This process starts almost immediately upon exposure, but it takes several weeks until enough hemoglobin is produced to make an appreciable difference in the blood's oxygen-carrying capability.

INDIVIDUAL LEVEL CHANGES: ACCLIMATIZATION. **Acclimatization** is a form of phenotypic plasticity that enables an individual organism to accommodate to a complex of environmental factors. Acclimatization involves a set of physiological changes that permit adaptation to a myriad of factors in a given environment. For instance, a mammal may acclimatize to a seasonal change (for example, to winter) by increasing the amount of fur on its body surface, elevating basal metabolic rate (BMR), and reducing blood flow to superficial regions of the body. Humans acclimatize to high-altitude environments by excreting alkaline urine, breathing fast and deep, thickening blood with extra hemoglobin, and so forth. An important feature of acclimatization is that, like the individual physiological changes comprising it, it is reversible.

INDIVIDUAL LEVEL CHANGES: DEVELOPMENTAL ADAPTATIONS. Another form of phenotypic plasticity is change that can occur to an organism during its developmental period. Developmental period in this instance refers to any point in the life span before adulthood. For humans, this includes *in utero* development, infancy, childhood, and adolescence. A hallmark of this form of adaptation is that it is usually not reversible. One type of developmental adaptation, termed "developmental conversion," refers to a process whereby exposure in early life determines which genetic programs are activated in the organism (Hoffman and Parsons 1991). The ability of high-altitude natives of the Andes to perform vigorous activity while exposed to the low-oxygen conditions of high altitude may be due to developmental adaptation. Andean natives who are born and raised at low altitude but move to high altitude as adults are not able to perform as well as those individuals who grew up at high altitude (Frisancho et al. 1994).

POPULATION LEVEL CHANGES: CULTURAL ADAPTATIONS. Culture consists of the shared understandings and behaviors of a group of people, with these understandings and behaviors passed down through generations by learning. Many components of culture may be viewed as adaptive, including learned techniques for finding food and water, making clothing and shelter, and organizing labor to produce what a single person could not do on his or her own. Humans create a microenvironment (literally, small environment) through their culture that is distinct from the surrounding, natural environment (or macroenvironment). The microenvironment is, in many cases, less stressful for people than the macroenvironment. For instance, in a cold macroenvironment people may build a well-insulated structure heated by a fireplace that creates tropical-like conditions for people when indoors.

It must be noted that not all human behaviors, and certainly not all cultural phenomena, are necessarily adaptive. The recent history of terrorism, warfare, environmental degradation, and crime found in many human societies surely suggests that some elements of culture may prove to be extremely maladaptive, either in the short term or in the long run.

POPULATION LEVEL CHANGES: DEMOGRAPHIC ADJUSTMENTS. When organisms do not easily adapt to environmental stress, it can lead to changes in a population's size or composition. As shown in Figure 11-1, density-dependent factors can limit population size, and limiting factors in general can place boundaries on a population's distribution. There may simply be no organisms of a given species in a given place.

Specific environmental stressors may also have particularly potent affects on certain sex or age groups in a population and thus cause changes in the population structure of a human group. For instance, young children are more susceptible to some forms of protein malnutrition than are either infants (who, if breastfed, usually receive sufficient high-quality protein), or older children and adults (who have greater stores of protein to rely on during periods of poor nutrition).

POPULATION LEVEL CHANGES: GENETIC ADAPTATIONS. All biological adaptations in the long term of "evolutionary time" are based upon genetic adaptations that result from natural selection and are passed down to succeeding generations. Many organisms show plasticity in their ability to change in adjusting to stress, but this ability itself is based upon a genetic background that permits these changes to occur.

Human Adaptability

There is **plasticity** in human biological responses. People are capable of changing their behavior and biology in order to adapt to environmental conditions. The field of **human adaptability** studies the environmental physiology of our species, examining the flexibility of responses that permits humans to live successfully in disparate environments throughout the world. One of the major attributes of humans is our ability to modify the environment, creating habitable microenvironments within the larger, and less hospitable, macroenvironment.

THE "SINGLE-STRESSOR" MODEL. A "single-stressor" model has been developed within human adaptability to permit understanding of the two-faceted—behavioral and biological—response to environmental stress (Thomas 1975; Thomas et al. 1989). The model, shown in Figure 11-2, focuses on a specific stressor present in the macroenvironment. People respond to the stressor behaviorally and culturally, creating a microenvironment in which the stressor is either eliminated or ameliorated. For instance, people living in the northern plains of North America may spend much of their time during the winter in centrally heated homes, in which temperatures are semi-tropical. If the microenvironment is still stressful, people will then respond biologically in order to

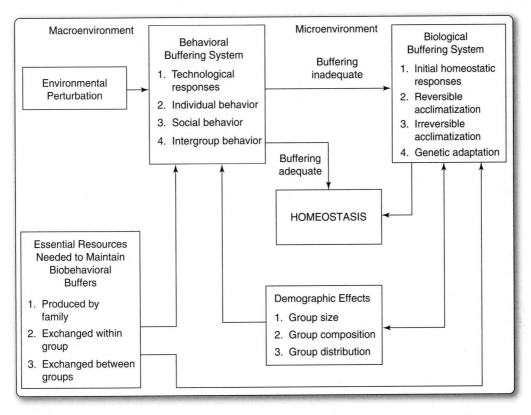

FIGURE 11-2 Single-stressor model of human adaptability.

cope. For instance, should the heating system fail for the northern plains person, or if an individual should leave his or her heated home wearing inadequate clothing, shivering and constriction (narrowing) of blood vessels in the skin may ensue. Should the biological responses be inadequate, the stress may lead to functional impairment or even death, thus leading to demographic changes in the population. In the plains example, people caught outside in a winter storm could suffer permanent impairment, such as frost bite, or even freeze to death.

In understanding human biology, it must be recognized that a given macroenvironment does not always lead to evolutionary selection for biological adjustments to those general conditions. Humans respond biologically to the microenvironment next to their skin, not to theoretical problems that may be present nearby. On the other hand, one must also consider rare breakdowns in the behavioral and cultural buffer that creates microenvironments, as these can lead to rapid evolutionary selection for those individuals with characteristics that allow them to survive, and reproduce, despite the breakdowns.

ESSENTIAL AND KEY RESOURCES. Finally, the model in Figure 11-2 addresses the resources that are needed to combat the stress; these are termed **essential resources**. Should these resources be missing, such as fuel for central heating, people will not be able to cope with the stress, or at least will have to find a different means for adapting. Also, while resources may be available, they may be difficult or expensive to acquire. Essential resources that are rare, expensive, or hard to obtain are termed **key resources**, because they are often a key factor in understanding how human groups can adapt to a given environmental stressor.

PROPERTIES OF STRESSORS AND RESPONSES. A stressor's general characteristics establish how people respond to it. For instance, the intensity, frequency, duration, and predictability of the stressor combine to determine what kind of response is required. Factors such as time to engage, duration, strength, frequency, and reversibility are important characteristics of the stress response. One must also consider whether **effectiveness**, **efficiency**, or minimization of **risk** is the critical factor in responses. For instance, people living in Los Angeles are faced with a few cool days in the winter, but may not opt for highly insulated houses with heavy-duty central heating systems to cope with this mild stress. Their response may emphasize efficiency rather than effectiveness. However, people living in Minneapolis in the northern plains would probably invest resources on the most effective heating systems that are feasible, given the much more intense cold stress they face during long winters. In addition, people exposed to severe stress that could be life threatening would be advised to employ responses that have less risk of failure. Thus, Minneapolis residents would be advised to avoid the risk accompanying installation of heating systems that often fail to work, as this could lead to catastrophic problems. Of course, assessment of risk is hardly foolproof, and often the resources needed to reduce risk are beyond the capabilities of individuals or of groups.

LIMITATIONS OF THE SINGLE-STRESSOR MODEL. The single-stressor model is quite valuable in allowing understanding of the parameters involved with how humans cope with specific stressors that are present in their macroenvironment. However, the model is designed to examine only one stressor at a time, when in fact many people live in an environment that contains multiple stressors. Confusion can occur when ideal responses to one stressor interfere with appropriate responses to a second stressor. For instance, people exposed to cold may generate heat by engaging in physical activity, but this may be a poor response when the cold is experienced at high altitude where increased physical activity may lead to acute altitude sickness because of a lack of sufficient oxygen. Also, the model assumes that people are only exposed to stressors that are present in the macroenvironment, and that the behaviors reduce the stress. In fact, our behaviors may actually create or exacerbate stress, making our microenvironment more stressful than the general macroenvironment, for instance, in high-crime inner-city neighborhoods.

We will examine how humans cope with specific stressors, and these examples will also illustrate both benefits and limitations to the single-stressor model. Also, much of this chapter's focus will be on population differences in adaptability. In fact, it must be understood that all populations contain much individual biological variability, both in genetics and phenotype, that has bearing on adaptability. Beyond this, there is much variability in individual exposure to environmental stresses, based on differences in gender, age, occupation, socioeconomic status, access to technology, and even in politics within the group.

ADAPTATION TO COLD AND HEAT

Thermoregulation

Thermoregulation refers to the ability to adjust to extremes of temperature, whether external conditions are too cold or too hot. Humans evolved in the tropics, and this has led to a biology better suited to handling heat than cold. However, for any type of thermoregulation, humans rely a great deal on behavioral and cultural adaptations. An understanding of basic factors involved in temperature regulation is required to make sense of human adaptations to extreme temperature conditions. In general, organisms generate heat as a side effect of metabolism, and they may either gain or lose heat to the environment through heat exchange at their body surfaces.

For adaptive purposes, it is common to divide the body into two zones: the **core**, or internal area of the head and trunk, and the **shell**, which includes the rest of the body. The core can tolerate a very narrow temperature range: approximately 35 to 41°C (95 to 106°F) (Sawka and Wenger 1988). Beyond this range, body function is compromised, and death may ensue. The shell has a much broader allowance for temperatures, from about 0°C (32°F) for short periods, to temperatures hot enough to cause burning of body tissues.

METABOLISM. Metabolic heat gain may be due to either basal metabolism (heat generated when the body is at rest) or active metabolism (heat generated during muscular activity). Heat exchange occurs through four processes: radiation, conduction, convection, and evaporation.

RADIATION. Radiation can lead to either a gain or loss of energy due to the exchange of electromagnetic energy between objects within line of sight of each other. Since light is a form of electromagnetic energy, an object's visibility generally means that one can exchange electromagnetic energy with it. The body radiates heat in all directions and obtains radiative heat from all directions. In general, there is a net gain of energy from objects that are hotter than the body (such as the sun) and a net loss of energy to objects that are cooler than the body, such as the night sky. The rate of radiative heat exchange depends upon the temperature difference between the object and the various elements in its surroundings, the object's reflectance and surface area, and the relative surface area of objects visible to it (Kerslake 1972).

CONDUCTION. Conduction refers to the exchange of energy through direct contact between two solid objects, with the heat transferred from the kinetic energy imparted to the collision of molecules at the area of contact. Again, a hotter body loses heat to a cooler body, so sitting on a cool floor will result in a loss of body heat, while leaning on the door of a warm oven will cause the body to gain heat. The conduction rate depends on the objects' temperature difference, the contact area, and the objects' thermal conductivity (Gates 1980).

CONVECTION. Convection refers to heat exchange between an object and a fluid (gas or liquid), with the exchange based on molecular collisions where contact is made. This differs from conduction in that the fluid moves, in part due to the heat exchange, but also possibly from other factors. For instance, when the body is in contact with cool air, the air is heated by the energy exchange, and this warm air rises. Cooler air moves into the space vacated by the warming air. If this natural convection did not take place, the body would soon heat the air surrounding it, and thus there would be a reduced heat loss to the air. Instead, constant replenishment of cool air to the area near the body causes a faster heat exchange from the body surface. Movement of a fluid can also be caused by an outside force (such as wind), which speeds the replenishment of fluid that has not been heated (or cooled) by contact with the body. This is the basis of the "wind chill factor." In the cold, wind increases convection and leads to a much more rapid loss of body heat. Thus, the convection rate depends upon the temperature difference between the object and the fluid, the area of contact, the thermal conductivity of the object and fluid, and the speed of movement of the fluid.

EVAPORATION. Unlike the other forms of heat exchange, **evaporation**, usually of perspiration, leads only to a loss of body heat. In this case, energy, and thus heat, is lost when a fluid on the body surface evaporates. This is because it takes energy, referred to as the latent heat of vaporization, to convert the liquid to a gas. The rate of heat loss due to evaporation depends on surface area, vapor pressure of the environment (which partly determines the rate of evaporation), the object's surface temperature, and the amount of liquid present on the surface (Hanna and Brown 1983).

HEAT BALANCE EQUATION. The combination of metabolic heat gain and heat exchange determines an individual's heat gain or loss over time. To maintain homeostasis over the long term, individuals need to balance heat gain and loss, maintaining a fairly constant body temperature. This is summarized in the heat balance equation:

$$\Delta S = M_b + M_a \pm K \pm C \pm R - E$$

where ΔS is the change in the amount of heat contained by the body, M_b is the basal metabolic rate, M_a is the metabolic rate due to activity, K is conduction, C is convection, R is radiation, and E is evaporation. As seen in the equation, metabolic activities lead to heat gain, evaporation leads to heat loss, and the other three factors (conduction, convection, and radiation) may lead either to heat gain or loss, depending on the circumstances. ΔS must equal 0 over the long run.

This equation sets the requirements for adaptation to cold or heat. In a cold environment, people need to increase metabolic activity, avoid evaporation by staying dry, and reduce heat loss due to radiation, conduction, and convection. In a hot environment, people need to minimize heat gain from metabolism, maximize evaporative heat loss, and allow heat loss from radiation, conduction, and convection. Specific circumstances dictate how these adaptations take place.

Cold Adaptation

Hominids first entered cold macroenvironments between 1.6 and 1.8 million years ago, when they first migrated out of Africa. Modern humans migrated out of Africa in the past 100,000 to 200,000 years, and these ancestors were exposed to cold conditions in the ensuing millennia. In the time since, people have thrived in various types of cold macroenvironments, primarily by reliance on excellent behavioral and cultural adaptations. The kinds of cold environments that people encounter include arctic regions that entail intense seasonal cold, temperate zones that have fairly intense seasonal cold (Hanna et al. 1989), and mountainous areas, which typically have large temperature swings during each day (from 25 to 30 C° [45 to 54 F°] in the Himalayas and Andes, for instance) (Ekvall 1968, Little and Hanna 1978).

BEHAVIORAL AND CULTURAL ADAPTATIONS TO COLD. Humans are adept at constructing warm microenvironments even when outside temperatures are quite low. They do this through elevated physical activity levels and scheduling of activities, clothing, shelter, bedding, and use of fuel to generate heat. Humans attempt to stay sheltered during very cold times, and they tend to stay physically active when away from shelter during cold times. Shelter includes fairly permanent structures that have a great deal of insulation, and it also may involve temporary or emergency shelter when the situation dictates. For instance, the Athabaskan people take shelter in temporary snow houses called Quin-zhee that are constructed very quickly when an individual cannot return to a more permanent shelter due to a storm or other circumstance. A more permanent snow house is the well-known Central Inuit igloo (Figure 11-3), which cuts down on convective heat loss through the insulative nature of snow, use of a small entryway and a snow wall to reduce drafts (thus minimizing convective heat loss), and also employment of a raised floor to further reduce drafts and to take advantage of rising warm air (Rapoport 1969).

FIGURE 11-3 Central Inuit igloo.

FIGURE 11-4 Quechua people of the Andes wearing traditional clothing.

Cold-weather clothing is designed to trap air, which then acts as insulation. This can be accomplished through use of loose weaves, and/or through the wearing of several layers of clothing. The latter is a particularly useful practice of high-altitude peoples: layers can be removed or added as the temperature changes diurnally (Figure 11-4). Where getting wet is a possible concern, the outer layer of clothing is often waterproofed to some degree. Similar to clothing, bedding employs trapped air as an insulator. In some societies, people sleep in family groups, sharing body heat during the night.

The most direct means to cope with cold behaviorally is the use of fire. Burning of various fuels heats up a space, and, when combined with insulative shelters, can provide a semi-tropical microenvironment within an arctic setting. Another important use of fire is in cooking. Here, warm food and drink are brought directly into the center of the body, the area most vulnerable to cold.

Finally, people have used miscellaneous other means to cope with cold, from ingestion of alcohol, which has a beneficial short-term effect of increasing metabolic heat but a poor long-term effect of causing faster heat loss from the body, to use of other drugs. An example is the chewing of coca leaves in the Andes region, where the coca causes superficial blood vessels to constrict, thus keeping blood deeper in the body where it is more insulated from the outside cold.

BIOLOGICAL RESPONSES TO COLD EXPOSURE. There are two main ways that humans adapt to cold biologically: through insulative and metabolic adjustments. Insulative adjustments include an even distribution of subcutaneous fat, a redirection of blood away from superficial blood vessels, and body size and shape considerations. Fat is a good insulator, and having a thick layer of subcutaneous fat distributed all over the body will slow heat loss from the body's core. Similarly, when people are exposed to cold they turn pale, a sign of the constriction of superficial blood vessels. This redirects blood to deeper areas of the body, and, since blood is usually at body core temperature, this greater distance from the surface provides more insulation and thus slower loss of core heat. Blood vessels into the arms and legs that are located deep beneath the body's surface are aligned such that arteries, which carry blood outward from the heart, are located close to veins, which carry the blood back towards the heart. The outgoing blood in arteries warms the returning blood in veins before it reenters the body, and this **counter-current heat exchange** lowers heat loss in the peripheries. Superficial arteries and veins tend to be located further apart from one another, so that during heat exposure, when blood is distributed more towards superficial blood vessels, there is less of this countercurrent heat exchange, and thus more heat loss in the peripheries.

Body size and shape also lead to variation in insulation from the cold. Body heat is generated in the body's cells, and the amount of heat generated is proportional to the body's mass, and also to its volume. Heat is lost through the body's surface area. Thus, heat gain is related to volume, and heat loss is related to area. In a cold climate, low surface area to volume is beneficial, as it leads to a slower loss of the heat that is generated metabolically. Since volume increases by the cube as body size increases, and area only increases by the square, the surface area to volume ratio is lower in large people. As stated previously, **Bergmann's Rule**, proposed in 1847, states that for widely distributed homeotherm species ("warm-blooded" animals), organisms in colder environments will tend to have larger body size (Roberts 1978). Similarly, **Allen's Rule**, proposed in 1877, states that in widely distributed homeotherm species, organisms in colder climates will tend to have shorter extremities (Hanna et al. 1989). The short extremities reduce surface area, and thus slow heat loss. Worldwide surveys of human populations have shown a slight positive relationship between environmental temperature and both body size and limb length (Roberts 1978), suggesting that these rules apply to some degree in humans. Experiments in cool conditions suggest that individuals with shorter limbs lose less heat than those with long limbs (Tilkens et al. 2007). Figure 6-9 in Chapter 6 shows the contrast between a person well adapted to cold (relatively low surface-area-to-volume ratio) and a person adapted to deal with a hot environment (high surface-area-to-volume ratio).

METABOLIC ADJUSTMENTS TO COLD EXPOSURE. The most common metabolic adjustment made in response to cold exposure is an increase in active metabolism. This involves either voluntary exercise or involuntary muscle movement that is termed **shivering**. In each case, muscular movement generates metabolic heat. Shivering can cause metabolism to increase up to three times the basal rate. Some mammals, when exposed to cold, exhibit an elevation in basal metabolic rate through **non-shivering thermogenesis**. This non-shivering metabolic response appears to be stimulated by both the sympathetic nervous system through release of norepinephrine that stimulates brown adipose tissue (Klingenspor 2003), and the thyroid gland through enhanced secretion of thyroxin (Leppäluoto et al. 2005). There have been some studies on humans that suggest the presence of non-shivering thermogenesis as a seasonal adaptation in traditional women divers in Korea and Japan (Hong 1973), as well as in other winter swimmers (Lesná et al. 1999). People indigenous to Arctic regions have increased basal metabolic rates (BMR) relative to other populations (Rode and Shephard 1995; Leonard et al. 2002; Snodgrass et al. 2007), with these differences in part due to seasonal variation in thyroid function. There is much individual variation in all populations, based on both genetic and environmental factors. For instance, people who are physically fit show a higher BMR due to their increased muscle mass and also greater metabolic heat production during cold exposure than less fit individuals (Maeda et al. 2007; Andersen 1966).

HABITUATION RESPONSES TO MODERATE COLD. The non-shivering metabolic adaptations in humans apparently only occur among those exposed to very severe cold conditions. Human groups exposed to more moderate cold stress tend to habituate to it; that is, they simply react less to it, as measured by a reduction in the temperature at which shivering is normally induced (Young 1988), as well as in a lowered sympathetic nervous system response to exposure (LeBlanc 1978). A benefit of the habituation is that it enables people to sleep during cold exposure; those who are not habituated will be kept awake at night by shivering. The habituation response has been seen in Australian aborigines and San people of southern Africa who live in desert environments in which nighttime temperatures occasionally drop to near-freezing levels (Scholander et al. 1958; Wyndham and Morrison 1958).

PERIPHERAL COLD EXPOSURE. Often, people are not exposed to cold over their whole body, but rather have only a part of the body exposed. For instance, clothing may cover almost the whole body but not the face. It is common for just the peripheries—hands and/or feet—to be exposed, and the stress is greater when the exposure is to cold water rather than to cold air, because water draws heat much more quickly than does air. This may occur when people wade in cold streams while fishing or submerge their hands in cold water while doing laundry. During cold exposure, some people show a cold-induced vasodilatation (CIVD) response, in which periphery temperature drops during the exposure period, but after a few minutes actually rises again. When the hand or foot, but more commonly the hand (Reynolds et al. 2007), is exposed to cold, there is an immediate vasoconstriction in which blood flow is slowed, and thus body heat in the core is conserved. During a CIVD response, there is a temporary vasodilation of blood vessels, blood—and thus warmth—flows into the periphery, and then vasoconstriction reoccurs, with temperatures again dropping. People acclimatized to cold exposure show a CIVD response over a greater range of temperatures than do people who are not acclimatized (Frisancho 1994; Nelms and Soper 1962; Krog et al. 1960), and the presence of a CIVD leads to an increase in the average temperature of the periphery during the cold exposure.

ADAPTIVE CONSEQUENCES OF COLD STRESS. Human biological adaptability to cold stress is distinctly underwhelming compared with many other mammals. The main way in which people adapt to cold is through their behavior and culture. Our species is so adept at handling cold through our behavior that cold does not really play a major role in natural selection for our species. People rarely freeze to death, and when they do it is usually because of some sort of accident, such as falling from a boat, crashing through thin ice, or getting caught in a storm. Infants and children are somewhat more at risk, due in part to their small body size, but also because they suffer greater exposure to conductive heat loss when they crawl on the ground. People must allocate resources, such as fuel, clothing and shelter, to cold adaptation, and therefore there is a cost to our adaptation to cold climates.

Figure 11-5 summarizes the single-stressor model of cold for a human population. Specifics of the model will change for specific groups, but the figure shows general cold adaptation considerations.

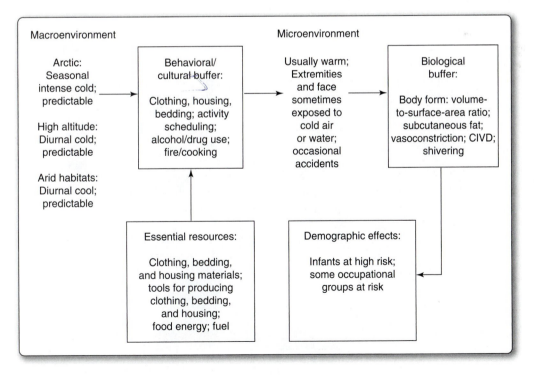

FIGURE 11-5 Single-stressor model of human adaptation to cold.

Heat Adaptation

There are two types of hot macroenvironments, with each having different implications for adaptation: hot-dry and warm-humid. Humans adapt in such different ways to these two types of macroenvironments that they will be considered separately.

Hot-Dry Macroenvironments

Hot-dry macroenvironments, epitomized by hot deserts, are usually characterized by cloudless skies, high solar radiation and thus high daytime temperatures, and cool nights due to heat radiation through the cloudless sky and out to the universe (Fitzpatrick 1979). The dry air permits very fast evaporation, which can be used for cooling, but the arid environment also often means that water is scarce (Hanna and Brown 1983). The aridity of hot-dry environments may also limit tree growth, and thus shade may be difficult to find.

BEHAVIORAL AND CULTURAL ADAPTATIONS TO DRY HEAT. Humans make use of effective evaporative cooling and diurnal temperature change to help in coping with dry heat. Activity scheduling is important, with active metabolism confined as much as possible to cooler parts of the day. Siestas or other types of mid-day rest periods reduce metabolic heat gain at the hottest part of the day. Housing in hot-dry conditions is actually much like that in the cold: insulation is stressed. In this case, insulation allows retention during the day of cool night air inside the shelter, and it also allows the warmth that gradually increases during the day to ameliorate the nighttime coolness (see Figure 11-6). Related to housing, shading is an important means of reducing solar heat gain. Shading may come from roof overhangs, awnings, or umbrellas (coming from the Latin *umbra*, meaning "shade"). If water can be obtained, tree planting in strategic places can provide shade.

Clothing in hot-dry conditions serves to slow solar radiative heat gain and reduce convective heat gain (Adolph 1949), while preventing sunburn from solar UV radiation. There is a trade-off between use of light-colored clothing to minimize heat gain, and use of darker-colored clothing to deter sunburn (Hanna and Brown 1979).

A major behavioral means of coping with hot-dry conditions is employment of evaporative cooling wherever water resources permit this. Use of fountains, pools, irrigated gardens, or the

FIGURE 11-6 Pueblo housing showing an emphasis on insulation, including thick walls, small windows, and minimized surface area.

wetting of millet-plant screens in windows such as used in northern India (Planalp 1971) are all methods found in desert regions where water can be spared. In an example from Iran, wind towers on houses enhance convective cooling (Bahadori 1978). In Arabia, a complex cooling method is found where houses are situated next to two courtyards. One courtyard is made of stones, while the other is an irrigated garden. The stone courtyard heats up, air rises, and cooler air from the garden courtyard is drawn through the house to replace the rising air (Rapoport 1969).

BIOLOGICAL RESPONSES TO DRY-HEAT EXPOSURE. When the behavioral and cultural adaptations to dry heat break down or are otherwise inadequate, humans can rely on a very effective biological buffer to cope with the stress. The need for biological adaptations principally occurs when muscular activity must be undertaken during hot conditions. The biological adaptations speed the transfer of heat to the body surface and allow evaporative cooling by sweat production.

HEAT TRANSFER. In some ways, adaptations to heat are the opposite of those to cold. For heat adaptation, subcutaneous fat is best minimized, or at least distributed unevenly to permit areas with less insulation to quickly transfer heat. Also, body-surface area to volume is optimally increased, with small size and long limbs contributing to swift heat dissipation.

VASCULAR RESPONSES. Superficial and extremity blood vessels dilate under hot conditions, routing blood toward the body's surface so that the blood can act as a carrier of heat from the core to the shell, and countercurrent heat exchange is minimized. The pooling of blood in the peripheral circulation can lead to faster and harder heartbeats, however, and this increased cardiovascular strain can be fatal when people are subjected to extreme heat (Sawka and Wenger 1988).

SWEATING. Humans adapt to dry heat primarily through the production, and evaporation, of sweat. Perspiration is stimulated when skin temperature reaches a threshold, with this threshold being somewhat variable between individuals. Sweating starts on the trunk and then spreads to extremities in unacclimatized people, but the order is reversed in acclimatized people (Hofler 1968). The greater surface area to volume ratio of extremities makes heat loss in this region more efficient than on the trunk. This is an advantage to acclimatized people, who also begin sweating sooner than unacclimatized individuals, and thus heat loss is accelerated after acclimatization to heat.

Humans can sweat prodigiously compared to other mammals. Most sweat during heat is produced by **eccrine sweat glands** (see Figure 11-7), which produce a saltwater mixture that is similar to the content of body water in general (Hanna and Brown 1983). We also produce sweat through **sebaceous sweat glands**, which are associated with hair follicles and produce a fluid that is rich in lipids and proteins. Humans average over a million active eccrine sweat glands and can produce a natural sweat rate of 500 gm/m^2/hour, a rate which is approximately five times the maximal rate for a horse (Folk 1974; Baker 1988). Actually, our sweating ability exceeds the maximal evaporation rate except in the very driest of conditions, leading to the loss of water through dripping sweat (Newman 1975) that provides no direct cooling to the body surface. This exceedingly rapid production of sweat suggests that human ancestors were exposed to very arid environments where such sweat rates would be advantageous, at least if water sources were available to replenish body water. The rapid sweat rate can lead to dehydration. In fact, humans sweat faster than our brain registers thirst, leading to "voluntary dehydration" (Newman 1970). Elite endurance athletes must learn to hydrate at a faster rate than their bodies seem to tell them to.

A possible disadvantage to our copious sweat rate during heat exposure is a loss of salt from the body, since perspiration is made up of salty water. People who are acclimatized to hot environments are able to reabsorb more salt in their eccrine glands, thus producing less salty sweat and conserving salt (Buono et al. 2007). For athletes who have suffered severe cramping due in part to salt loss during exercise in the heat, the importance of salt conservation is painfully apparent.

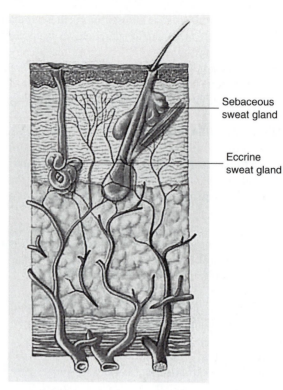

FIGURE 11-7 A cross-section of skin showing an eccrine sweat gland and a sebaceous sweat gland.

ACCLIMATIZATION AND INDIVIDUAL DIFFERENCES IN HEAT ADAPTATION. All healthy humans can acclimatize to dry heat stress, including those from populations with long histories in cold climates (Edholm and Weiner 1981), allowing sweat to begin at lower skin and core temperatures and increasing maximal sweat rates (Wenger 1988). Acclimatization accounts for most of human variability in heat adaptation, with body size, shape, and composition accounting for much of the rest. There is little evidence for population genetic differences in the ability to adapt to heat (Hanna et al. 1989). Figure 11-8 summarizes human adaptability to dry heat stress.

Warm-Humid Environments

Warm-humid environments, such as those found in rain forests, present humans with a special problem: the high humidity of these regions slow or stop evaporation, and thus a major means of cooling is negated. Also, the usual cloud cover in humid areas reduces the amount of diurnal variation in heat: it never gets as hot in daytime as it does in dry areas due to reduced solar radiation, but it also never cools as much at night due to reduced radiative heat loss.

BEHAVIORAL AND CULTURAL ADAPTATIONS TO HUMID HEAT. Because of the lack of extreme diurnal temperature changes, insulative adaptations in shelters are not useful, and people therefore opt for structures that maximize ventilation, thus increasing convective cooling. Structures are usually also designed to protect from frequent rainfall, with roofs and eaves emphasized and walls minimized in favor of windows or other openings, and houses are often raised on stilts to increase ventilation and protect from flooding (see Figure 11-9). Fans are commonly used to increase ventilation. In modernized environments, air conditioners and dehumidifiers can successfully ameliorate warm-humid conditions, but at a great cost in energy use. Clothing is not needed to reduce sun burning in humid heat, thus it is usually minimized to allow radiative and convective heat loss. While environmental temperatures rarely are as extreme as those found in dry environments, our behavioral and traditional cultural

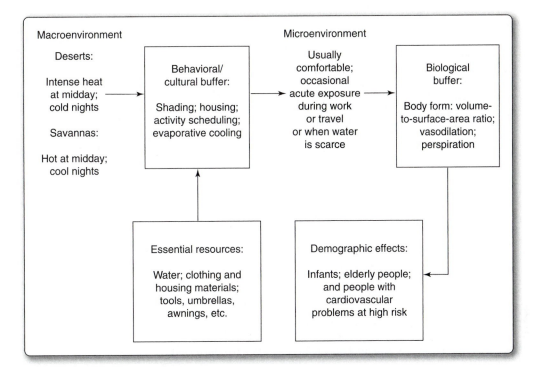

FIGURE 11-8 Single-stressor model of human adaptation to dry heat.

FIGURE 11-9 Thatched, raised house in a warm-humid climate.

adaptations are less effective in dealing with this stress. The real problem comes when people must be active in these conditions, generating heat that must be quickly removed from the body.

BIOLOGICAL RESPONSES TO HUMID HEAT EXPOSURE. Our biological response to humid heat is identical to our reaction to dry heat. The difference is that perspiration mostly drips off the skin without evaporating, and thus it fails to cool the body. Therefore, humans must rely on rapid transfer

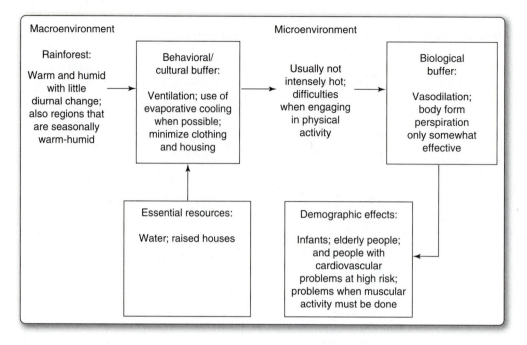

FIGURE 11-10 Single-stressor model of human adaptation to humid heat.

of heat from core to shell through high surface-area-to-volume ratios, absence of even distributions of subcutaneous fat, and redirection of blood flow to superficial areas and extremities as the critical means to adapt. It may be that the presence of so-called Pygmy populations, mostly in rain forest biomes, is in part a result of a reliance on Bergmann's rule for heat adaptation in these regions, since small body size maximizes surface area (where excess body heat is released) per volume (where metabolic heat is generated), and thus increases effectiveness of heat loss.

Figure 11-10 summarizes the main adaptive issues of coping with warm-humid environments.

Conclusion to Thermoregulation

All humans share an exquisite biological ability to adapt to dry heat, but are somewhat less adaptable biologically to cold and warm-humid conditions, reflecting our evolutionary origins in the hot, dry African savanna. In the modern world, people rarely die from freezing to death or from heat-related stresses, but this does happen. For instance, in a 1995 heat wave that hit the Chicago area, an estimated 700 people died from heat-related causes. The selective forces from these stresses probably were greater in prehistory, when our cultural defenses were not as well developed.

While there do not appear to be population genetic differences in the physiology of heat adaptation, Bergmann's and Allen's Rules do appear to operate among human populations. Groups who live in hot environments are more likely to be of short stature, such as the Pygmy groups of central Africa, or to have linear body shapes with long extremities.

ADAPTATION TO HIGH ALTITUDE

When humans ascend to high altitudes, they are confronted with many environmental challenges, such as large diurnal swings in temperature that lead to cold nights virtually all year long, aridity, high levels of ultraviolet radiation, dustiness, poor soils and other difficulties with farming, lack of

FIGURE 11-11 The summit area of Mauna Kea, Hawaii, at 4,200 m altitude.

fuel sources for cooking and heating, isolation, and rough terrain (making it seem to the pessimist that one must always walk uphill). One environmental stress is unique to high altitude however: the low oxygen pressure present in the air, termed **hypoxia**. Hypoxia is a particularly difficult stress for humans to cope with, because there is little in the way of effective behavioral adaptations that are possible, beyond carrying oxygen tanks or pressurizing living areas. People therefore must rely on biological adaptations for their survival in high mountain ecosystems (see Figure 11-11). The neurological system is particularly vulnerable to hypoxic conditions, and there is evidence that acute exposure to high altitudes degrades cognitive and psychological function (West 2006).

The stress of hypoxia is related to the altitude at which one is exposed. There is a rapid decrease in the barometric pressure of air as one ascends, because air pressure is based in large part on the weight of air in the atmosphere pressing down from above on the surrounding air. As one gets higher in elevation, there is less air above oneself, and therefore less air pressure. The percentage of oxygen in the air (approximately 21 percent) is the same at high elevations as at sea level. It is the overall air pressure, and the part of that pressure that is due to oxygen, that decreases at altitude.

Altitude stress also is related to the rate at which one ascends. Rapid ascents provide less time for acclimatization, and therefore they create greater stress.

Behavioral and Cultural Adjustments to Hypoxia

As noted, there is little that people can do behaviorally or culturally to adapt to high-altitude hypoxia. One possibility is to avoid high altitudes completely, but this is impossible for a resident of Tibet, or of much of the Andes region. An important behavior is to reduce physical-activity levels as much as possible. Activity requires muscular action, which in turn requires additional oxygen. In a low-oxygen environment, reducing oxygen needs is a simple way of avoiding overburdening one's adaptive ability.

In some circumstances, such as at the astronomical observatories on the summit area of Mauna Kea in Hawaii, people have considered pressurizing working areas or adding oxygen to the air. For many years, these alternatives have been rejected, in large part because of concerns about the effects of an instantaneous change to hypoxic conditions when workers would leave the oxygen-enriched environment. New astronomical observatories in Chile at even higher elevations (for example, the Millimeter Array at 5,000 meters elevation) have caused a rethinking of this idea, with oxygen-enriched air part of the basic plans for the facilities (Napier and West 1998).

Biological Adaptations to Hypoxia

By becoming more efficient at the transfer and use of oxygen within the body, people can adapt to hypoxic environments. This adaptation process can be broken down into four major steps: transfer of air into and out of the lungs (termed **ventilation**), movement of oxygen from the lungs into the blood (through the processes of **perfusion** and **diffusion**), **circulation** of the blood throughout the body, and transfer of oxygen from the blood to tissues (**diffusion**).

VENTILATION. The most evident adaptation to hypoxia involves a sharp increase in ventilation of air through both faster and deeper breathing (Heath and Williams 1977). This has the salutary effect of bringing oxygen into the lungs at a faster rate. The hyperventilation comes at a cost, though: a rapid loss of carbon dioxide in exhaled breath. Carbon dioxide plays a major role in the acid-base balance of body fluids, through its chemical reaction with water to form carbonic acid:

$$H_2O + CO_2 \leftrightarrow H_2CO_3$$

The chemical equilibrium moves in both directions, and therefore when CO_2 is lost from the body, the equation shifts to the left, leaving less carbonic acid in the body fluids (Lenfant and Sullivan 1971). The result is a condition termed **respiratory alkalosis** (an excess of alkaline due to over-breathing). The excess alkaline stimulates the brain's respiratory center to slow ventilation, but this leads to lowered oxygen intake. It is only after approximately two days that the body acclimatizes, with the kidney beginning to excrete excess alkaline in the urine. This lowers the body's alkaline level, and ventilation increases (see Figure 11-12).

OXYGEN MOVEMENT FROM LUNGS TO BLOOD. The diffusion of oxygen from the lung to the blood occurs in the **alveoli**, which are tiny air sacs at the ends of the lung's bronchial tree, the network of tubes through which air enters the lungs. The blood is distributed through small vessels

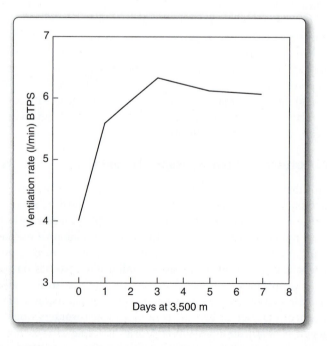

FIGURE 11-12 Changes in ventilation rate over time during acute exposure to high altitude (3,500 m).

termed "capillaries," and oxygen diffuses through the alveolar wall and into the blood. The distribution of blood in the lung, termed perfusion, allows a great deal of surface area for rapid oxygen diffusion. There is an increase in the number of active capillaries in the lung upon exposure to high-altitude hypoxia (West 1979). The lung is adapted to route blood away from damaged areas through a constriction of blood vessels located in regions of low oxygen. At high altitude, however, all areas of the lung have low oxygen levels, and therefore a widespread vasoconstriction occurs, causing the blood pressure in the lungs to rise. This response is actually somewhat maladaptive because it reduces surface area and causes diffusion to occur against a high-pressure gradient, thus slowing oxygen movement into the blood.

CIRCULATION. Oxygen is transported by blood circulation to all body tissues. Upon exposure to high altitude, there is a temporary increase in blood pressure and heart rate, but this only occurs for a few minutes. The vast majority of the blood's oxygen is carried by the protein **hemoglobin**. Upon initial exposure to high altitude, the hormone erythropoietin is secreted, and this stimulates an increase in production of red blood cells and hemoglobin (Albrecht and Littell 1972). Over several weeks, the amount of red blood cells and hemoglobin increases, causing a condition termed **polycythemia** ("many cells"). Polycythemia increases the oxygen-carrying capacity of the blood, but it also makes the blood thicker, and this puts more strain on the heart. Furthermore, through constriction of blood vessels in certain tissues such as skin, and dilation of vessels in other tissues including the brain, blood flow is redirected to critical areas of the body during hypoxic exposure.

TISSUE AND CELLULAR ADAPTATIONS. The most complex portion of the adaptation to high-altitude hypoxia occurs at the tissue level. The number of active capillaries increases throughout the body, increasing the oxygen diffusion rate between blood and tissues. Myoglobin, a molecule that assists with oxygen transfer to tissues, is elevated in muscles that are habitually used, thus increasing oxygen availability to these muscles (Frisancho 1994). Another molecule that appears to have important effects at the tissue level during hypoxic exposure is termed hypoxia inducible factor 1 (HIF1). HIF1 has many effects, acting as a regulator of the expression of several genes. One important effect of HIF1 is to act as a switch, changing metabolism from usual aerobic pathways to anaerobic, or oxygen-free, metabolic pathways and increasing use of the simple sugar glucose as an energy source through regulation of the genes for many enzymes involved in metabolic activities (Semenza 2001). Another effect of HIF1 is to induce production of the enzyme that in turn produces nitric oxide, a molecule that causes blood-vessel dilation. Thus, HIF1 may be involved in the redistribution of blood flow that is seen during acute exposure to high-altitude hypoxia.

Population Differences in Adaptability to High-Altitude Hypoxia

There are a few populations that have been resident at high altitudes for millennia, long enough to have evolved genetic adaptations to these conditions. Primary areas where these populations reside are in the Andes of South America, and the Himalayas and Tibetan plateau of Asia. These populations have adapted to high-altitude hypoxia in markedly different ways (Beall 2006).

ANDEAN POPULATION ADAPTATIONS. Studies of Andean populations have shown that native highlanders have, on average, larger hearts and lungs (so-called barrel chests), higher concentrations of red blood cells, and a reduced reaction of their ventilation to hypoxic exposure than sea-level dwellers (Frisancho 1994). As a result, the highlanders are well adapted to living at high elevations, and have even been seen to play soccer at elevations of over 15,000 feet. Their adaptations occur as a result of a lifetime of acclimatization. Individuals of these populations who grow up at sea level do not become as well adapted if they move to high altitudes later in

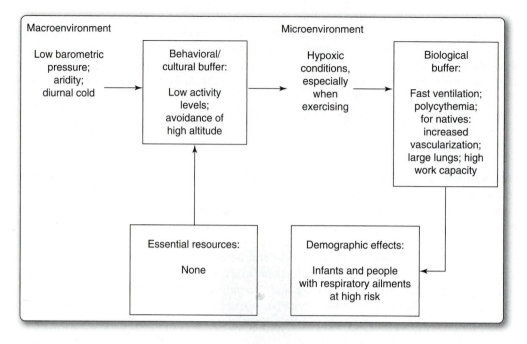

FIGURE 11-13 Single-stressor model of human adaptation to high altitude hypoxia.

life. Thus, they show a developmental adaptation to hypoxia. The development of their adaptations requires more than simply living at altitude: they also must be physically active during their childhood (Frisancho et al. 1994; Frisancho and Greksa 1989) and adolescence (Greksa et al. 1985). Adaptations are far from perfect, with occasional cases of chronic mountain sickness, a disease in which individuals lose their acclimatization to hypoxic conditions, and low average birth weight which leads to increased infant-mortality rates. While population differences exist in the average ability to adapt to altitude, all populations exhibit a great deal of variability in adaptive ability among individuals.

TIBETAN POPULATION ADAPTATIONS. Tibetan populations have also been resident at high elevations for thousands of years, perhaps for a longer period than Andeans (Gao et al. 2005), and they have evolved a different means of adapting to hypoxic environments. Tibetans tend to have lower red blood cell concentrations than Andeans, but do not show a blunted ventilatory response; in fact, Tibetans maintain a very high ventilation rate at high altitude (Beall 2000). Thus, Andeans seem to emphasize a blood-based physiological adjustment, while Tibetans emphasize a ventilatory one.

A special problem with adaptation to high-altitude hypoxia is providing sufficient oxygen *in utero* and immediately after birth. A condition termed subacute infantile mountain sickness is commonly found in nonnative peoples who give birth at high altitudes, and avoidance of this illness often requires a move to lower altitudes. Tibetans on average are better adapted to provide a sufficient blood supply to the placenta during pregnancy to allow larger birth weights and healthier babies than are found in other populations (Moore et al. 2001). This in turn improves reproductive success, and thus has important evolutionary implications.

It is interesting that evolutionary adaptations to high-altitude hypoxia that occurred independently in at least two different areas of the world have led to different kinds of human adaptations to this severe stress. Figure 11-13 shows a general outline of human adaptation to high-altitude hypoxia.

HIGH ACTIVITY LEVELS

Another physical stress that humans must withstand is that caused by performing at high levels of physical activity. In developed countries, this stress is primarily encountered during sports or other recreational activities, but, throughout most of human history, high activity levels have been associated with work, from digging tubers to hunting large game to clearing fields for agriculture. Work is usually measured by the expenditure of energy in the carrying out of some task (Ulijaszek 2000). This stress differs from others discussed in this chapter in that it is self-administered.

The Requirements of Work

People engage in many kinds of work that require high levels of physical activity, with the kinds of work depending in part on the type of subsistence relied upon by the population, the specialization in occupation by the individual, or even by individual preferences in leisure activities. There are general characteristics of muscles to consider for people doing high levels of work no matter what the specific activity; these include strength, power, speed, and endurance. **Muscular strength** is defined as the maximum amount of force a muscle can exert and depends on the cross-sectional area of the muscle. **Power** refers to the amount of work completed in a certain time period, and hence powerful activities entail rapid movements that also involve much force. **Speed** is measured by distance per time, and can involve the entire body or of parts of it. **Endurance** refers to the ability to perform a given amount of work for a long duration, and involves the time it takes for fatigue to set in. Different activities require different amounts of these four muscular characteristics, and people are quite variable in their individual abilities to perform given activities.

Behavioral and Cultural Adjustments to High Workloads

In the sense that physical activity is self-imposed, one can avoid the stress of activity by simply not doing it. There are times, however, when activity is required in order to get resources needed for survival. There are other behavioral and cultural adjustments that can be made, such as distributing workloads within a group and assigning high workloads to those who can withstand them. Thus, healthy adults are usually assigned intensive work, while children, the sick, and the aged are given lighter tasks. In all too many societies, work is not voluntary, but rather coerced by people in power, with slavery the most extreme form of forced labor.

Training in how to perform strenuous tasks is also critical. This may involve practicing a task at a lower workload, developing techniques to reduce stress on body parts (for instance, learning how to balance a jug on one's head when fetching water), or learning how to use technological aids in carrying out tasks. Much of human technology has been devised to assist with work and presumably is intended to reduce necessary physical workloads.

Biological Adaptations to High Workloads

There are two challenges posed on the body by high workloads: generation of heat and a high rate of aerobic metabolism. People who are frequently exposed to high workloads become acclimatized to heat stress, showing fast and copious sweat responses, initiation of sweating on the limbs, and lowered salt content of perspiration.

PHYSICAL FITNESS. Physical fitness, which is the ability to maintain physiological homeostasis during high workloads (Åstrand 1956), involves both heat acclimatization and efficient use of oxygen in metabolic activities. Some of the oxygen-efficiency adaptations are similar to that seen in high-altitude adaptation: faster diffusion of oxygen from lungs to blood and an increase in the number of active capillaries in muscles (Morehouse and Miller 1967). Physically fit people are more metabolically efficient than non-fit people, and also display higher work capacities, being able to perform tasks that non-fit people would find impossible.

AEROBIC CAPACITY.   Over the long term, our metabolism is based on the burning, or oxidation, of food. Therefore, our rate of oxygen consumption is a measure of our metabolic level, which in turn is a measure of our ability to do work. The highest rate at which one can use oxygen to drive metabolism is referred to as **aerobic capacity**, and this differs considerably among individuals, depending upon such factors as age, sex, physical fitness, and health (Bouchard et al. 1993). There is also a genetic element to aerobic capacity (Henderson et al. 2005; Myburgh 2003).

Much more controversial is the idea that there may be genetically based population differences in average aerobic capacity, or in frequency of individuals with unusually high aerobic capacities. As one example, the large number of elite endurance runners from East Africa that has become evident in the latter stages of the twentieth and early part of the twenty-first century has led to investigations of whether these runners represent populations with genetic predispositions for high aerobic capacity. Importantly, these discussions usually deal with extraordinary athletes, those who represent a small fraction of one percent of a population, and are not about the ordinary people that make up the vast majority of populations (Marks 1995). There is also great difficulty in apportioning general population differences into those that are due to genetics and those that are due to the myriad of nongenetic factors, particularly levels of physical fitness due to differences in habitual activity and general health. With these caveats in mind, studies of Kenyan endurance runners have begun to uncover why these athletes have met with such spectacular success. Interestingly, the vast majority of Kenyan elite runners come from just a few tribal groups that are a small minority of the country's population (Larsen 2003). When these athletes were compared with Scandinavian runners, an important difference noted was that the Kenyans were better able to resist fatigue (Holdin 2004). Specifically, lactate, a product of anaerobic metabolism that accumulates in muscles and leads to fatigue, increased more slowly in the Kenyans than in the Scandinavian runners, and this may be due to the average longer, thinner legs of the Kenyans (Larsen 2003). Aerobic capacity of the Kenyan athletes tends to be no different from that of elite runners from other ethnic groups.

TYPES OF MUSCLE FIBERS.   Physiologists have distinguished two main types of muscle fibers in humans: slow twitch (type I) and fast twitch (type II), with the latter having two subtypes, intermediate (IIa) and very fast twitch (IIb). The fibers get their names from the speed at which the muscles can contract; fast-twitch fibers can contract more quickly than slow-twitch fibers. There is much diversity among people in their percentage of muscle-fiber types. Slow-twitch fibers have greater concentrations of mitochondria and can keep high activity levels with little generation of lactate, while fast-twitch fibers can contract more rapidly. Unsurprisingly, elite endurance runners have high percentages of type I fibers, on the order of 80 percent, while sprinters have a high percentage of type II fibers, again nearly 80 percent. There is evidence that endurance training can lead to type IIb fibers transforming into type IIa fibers. It is possible that type II fibers can be transformed into type I fibers under severe endurance-training regimens (Thayer et al. 2000); however, there is no evidence that slow-twitch fibers can change to the fast-twitch variety. Much of the variability in percentages of muscle-fiber type appears to be genetically determined.

Again, studies of genetically based population differences are controversial, and such studies principally involve the small minority of elite athletes that are found in any given population. Population differences in percentage of muscle-fiber types deal with frequencies of the fiber types in given groups; performance differences in elite athletes deal with unusual individuals who perform at levels vastly beyond population norms, and these individuals achieve their abilities through a mixture of genetics, training, intense motivation, and perhaps even characteristics that stem from early development. Some studies have focused on differences among athletes who derive from West Africa versus East Africa, with the former tending to have a higher percentage of fast-twitch fibers and be sprinters, while the East Africans, as noted, include many elite distance runners who possess high

PROFILE 11
William R. Leonard

William Leonard's research examines how modern and prehistoric human populations adapt to both ecological and social stresses. He has conducted research among native populations living in the arctic regions of Siberia (Russia), the high altitudes of the Andes mountains, and the humid jungles of the Amazon region of South America. He is interested in people's acclimatization to these stressful environments, and how these stressors influence physical growth and development and nutritional health.

Dr. Leonard's work has shown how socioeconomic and environmental stressors interact to shape variation in health and biological function in human societies around the world. His research among traditional farming populations of highland and lowland South America has shown that the poor growth and small adult body size are the consequence of both seasonal fluctuations in food availability and conditions of poverty limiting the availability of high-quality market foods.

In his work in Russia, Dr. Leonard has documented the important roles that both cold stress and economic upheaval have had on the biology of native Siberian groups. He and his colleagues have shown that native Siberians have adapted to their arctic climes through increased metabolic heat production (elevated basal metabolic rates). These elevated BMRs are promoted through both short-term acclimatization and genetic adaptations, operating through the action of thyroid hormones. In addition, Leonard and colleagues have demonstrated that the economic stress caused by the fall of the Soviet Union resulted in dramatic increases in child undernutrition and growth stunting among the indigenous Siberians.

Dr. Leonard has also drawn on research from both human and primate ecology to develop models for better understanding the evolution of our hominid ancestors. He and his collaborators have shown that compared to our primate kin, humans spend a larger share of our metabolic rates to feed our large brains (20 percent versus 8 percent of BMR). To support the increased metabolic demands of our large brains, humans consume diets that are more dense in calories and nutrients than other primates of similar size. In looking at the fossil record, it appears that dietary and foraging changes were critical for supporting major brain expansion in the hominid lineage at approximately two million years ago.

William Leonard is currently Professor and Chair of the Department of Anthropology at Northwestern University, and co-director of the university's Laboratory for Human Biology Research. He has authored over 120 publications and co-edited (with MH Crawford) the volume *Human Biology of Pastoral Populations*.

percentages of slow-twitch fibers (Holden 2004). It is conceivable that habitual work requirements may have led to differential selection for muscle-fiber type in different populations, but as of now this is simply supposition. Being from a given population does not assure success in any athletic endeavor, nor does origin from another population preclude such success.

Adaptive Consequences of Work Capacity

From an ecological perspective, human populations must gather resources necessary for survival, and this requires specific forms of work to be done. There are types of work that require great effort, whether of strength, speed, or endurance. There conceivably could be selection for individuals capable of performing these tasks, but also there is much variation within a population in the ability to perform certain forms of work.

FACTORS AFFECTING WORK REQUIREMENTS. Variation in work abilities includes age and sex differences, but also differences within given sex-age groups. Humans are technological creatures, and often the biological performance of work is greatly changed by the types of tools available in a culture to handle given tasks. Also, humans are social animals, and work is often performed cooperatively. This, too, impacts the requirements of a given individual in terms of work capacity. Beyond these factors, work is often involuntary, forced upon individuals by powerful people in oppressive societies. This coercion may be direct and forced, as in slavery, or more subtle, in imposing limits on the choice of how one makes a living.

IMPACT OF MODERNIZATION. Modern life includes modern conveniences: automobiles, remote controls, comfortable recliners, and many occupations that involve very little physical activity. The result of this is a greater prevalence of people who have poor physical fitness. The primary concern of this decline in fitness is an increased risk for developing such ailments as heart disease and diabetes. Beyond this, there is also a decline in the physical work capacity of many people. So long as our work requirements do not require physical fitness, work productivity may not be appreciably affected. Should work requirements be changed, or rare requirements to perform physical activity be a part of one's necessary chores, productivity may decline.

CONCLUSION

The physical stressors of temperature extremes, high altitude, and intense physical activity are probably not a major force driving human biological evolution in the present day. Most of these stresses are avoidable or ameliorated by behavioral and technological adaptations. This is not always the case, however, and people do die in heat waves and from freezing, or from high-altitude pulmonary edema or cerebral edema, or from heart attacks brought on by unusual strain caused by physical activity. These tend to be rare cases compared to the more common causes of human mortality in the present day. Certain populations, or individuals with given occupational exposures, do have to cope with these problems. In the past, however, many of these stressors probably played a more important role in human evolution. For instance, the excellent biological adaptability of our species to dry heat likely derives from our origins in the open woodlands and savannas of Africa. The current human variability in coping ability for these stresses, stemming both from genetic and acclimatizational differences, gives insight into our past and helps explain the human diversity we see today.

CHAPTER SUMMARY

Humans adapt to physical stressors such as cold, heat, and high-altitude hypoxia through a combination of behavioral/cultural and biological adjustments. Biological adaptations may be temporary and reversible such as acclimatization responses, or more permanent, due to developmental or genetic processes. In exposure to extremes of temperature, it is useful to divide the body into two parts: core and shell, with the core having a much narrower range of temperature than can be tolerated. Heat is generated by metabolism within the body approximately in proportion to the body's weight or volume. Heat is gained or lost from the body through its surface area, and this heat transfer can be due to radiation, conduction, convection, or (loss only) evaporation.

Humans adapt to cold primarily through their behavior or culture, with shelter, clothing, physical activity, or use of fire or other heat source the main ways to combat cold. Biologically, humans respond to cold by diverting blood away from the surface vessels of the circulatory system or by shivering. People with more subcutaneous fat are better insulated from cold environments, and large people with short extremities retain body heat better than individuals with greater surface-area-to-volume ratios. Our species adapts to heat behaviorally through the use of shade, ventilation (in humid heat), insulation (in dry heat), scheduling of activities, and use of water, fans, or air conditioning to cool the environment. Biologically, humans adapt to heat through diversion of blood preferentially to superficial blood vessels and through the evaporation of sweat, and people with less subcutaneous fat and greater surface area to volume ratios are more efficient at ridding their bodies of excess heat.

Humans can do little behaviorally to adapt to high-altitude hypoxia. Instead, biological adaptations are relied upon, including an increase in ventilation, perfusion of the lungs with blood, increase in hemoglobin concentration of the blood, and biochemical changes that make oxygenation of tissues more efficient. Humans can also be exposed to the stress of intense physical exertion, although this is a self-induced condition. Humans adjust to exertion through the cultural means of making work more efficient, or through the development of physical fitness, in which muscular activity becomes stronger and more efficient, endurance increases, and heat acclimatization occurs.

CHAPTER 12

Human Adaptability to Biological Stressors

Besides adjusting to physical stressors, our species has had to cope with the vicissitudes of life on the food chain: finding food while avoiding being eaten. Finding sufficient food continues to be, at least in certain circumstances, a serious problem for many human populations. Predation by lions, tigers, bears, and other carnivorous mammals is much less of an issue for our species in recent millennia, but we still face the challenge of being the preferred food for a large variety of microbial organisms. Thus, this chapter will explore in general terms how humans adapt to the biological stresses caused by malnutrition and infectious disease. As will become evident, these two stresses are interrelated.

MALNUTRITION

Malnutrition, defined as poor nutrition, whether from too little food, too much food, or a poorly balanced diet, may be seen as evidence for a failure in adaptation. This failure may be at the level of the individual, of a family, or of an entire population. In the terms of the single-stressor model used in the previous chapter, the behavioral/cultural buffer against malnutrition consists of all the food-getting activities that people use, from foraging for wild plants and animals, to managing vast agricultural systems, to trading for or buying food items in markets. It is only when these various activities are unsuccessful that human bodies are placed in a microenvironment that leads to malnutrition. The lack of success could be due to many factors, including environmental changes, such as persistent droughts; poor methods of production, such as overexploitation of garden plots that leads to long term degradation of soils; and/or influences from external human forces, such as tenantship of land with wealthy landowners skimming much of a farmer's food production. In fact, much of the problem with malnutrition in the world is due to social inequalities that leave many individuals without the resources to produce sufficient food for themselves and their families.

Food Versus Nutrients

We must distinguish between **food** and **nutrients**. The latter refers to substances that provide nourishment required by our bodies for reproduction, function, and survival. Food, on the other hand, is a culturally based concept that refers to what people recognize as acceptable forms of nutrients. For example, in the United States, cockroaches are a source of nutrients, but they are not considered an acceptable food. These conceptions about food differ considerably among human populations (Farb and Armelagos 1980). For instance, cows are a common food source in the United States, whereas in many parts of India cows are not acceptable food sources. There are populations where dogs are a common food source, but most Americans would be appalled at the idea of eating dog meat. It should be noted that ideas about nutrients as elements of food are also culturally mediated.

Since all populations distinguish between food and nutrients, the options for individuals in obtaining the nutrients they require are always limited to some degree. Many people also include a category of "starvation foods," items that are not considered to be palatable normally, but are recognized as an emergency source of nutrients during hard times. Examples of starvation, or famine, foods are baobab tree bark among the Mbeere of Kenya and bark, roots, and seeds of various kinds among some Native American groups (Riley and Brokensha 1998; Kuhnlein and Turner 1991). An interesting hypothesis has been made that the high rates of neurological diseases found in the population of Guam, peaking in the years immediately after World War II, was due to ingestion of cycad seeds as a starvation food during the war (Garruto 2006). The cycad seeds are known to contain the chemical beta-methylamino-L-alanine, which is neurotoxic when ingested in large amounts.

Types of Nutrients

There are two basic needs that humans take care of by ingesting foods: the need for energy and the need for materials. Energy is released by "burning" nutrients, while other nutrients are used in assembling the structural elements of the body needed for growth and maintenance activities. When we eat, we break down food into its constituent biochemicals, and our bodies then assemble these biochemicals into the structures necessary for human life. Nutrients are also categorized by how much of them are needed: macronutrients (needed in large quantities) versus micronutrients (needed in small amounts).

MACRONUTRIENTS. The three types of macronutrients are carbohydrates, proteins, and lipids. All of these macronutrients can be used as fuel for producing energy, and all of them, but particularly protein, are used in constructing necessary structures within the body. Carbohydrates, either sugars or starches, are primarily used as fuel for quick-energy needs. Carbohydrates are stored in the body in the form of glycogen, a starch found in the liver, but this storage depot only provides energy for a short period, perhaps a day or so.

Lipids are more energy-dense than carbohydrates, and they provide long-term energy storage in the body. These include fats, oils, waxes, and triglycerides. Proteins are essentially strings of amino acids and are principal components of body structures. Proteins are sometimes chemically combined with carbohydrates to form glycoproteins or with lipids to form lipoproteins.

MICRONUTRIENTS. Micronutrients come in many forms, but they are usually categorized into two main types: vitamins and minerals. Electrolytes, such as sodium, potassium, and calcium, are present in fairly large amounts in humans, and they are therefore sometimes classified as macronutrients. Many micronutrients play key roles in enzymatic activity, and therefore they can have major effects on the body, belying their small quantity.

The lack of any essential nutrient can have dire effects on an organism, and many diseases of malnutrition have been identified that are associated with the lack of a specific nutrient.

PROTEIN-CALORIE MALNUTRITION

When people lack food, the major deficiencies are in protein and in energy as measured in kilocalories. Thus, protein-calorie malnutrition (PCM, also sometimes termed protein-energy malnutrition) is associated with periods of starvation, whether from a total lack of food or from an insufficient quantity of it. Long-term PCM has catastrophic effects, both biological and behavioral, as the body actually burns itself for fuel. This becomes evident in the depletion of muscle and fat stores in the body that provide the protein and calories, respectively, that are missing from the diet. Protein can be used as an energy source, and therefore it is not possible to have a diet that is deficient in energy but sufficient in protein. The reverse does occur however: some diets have adequate energy sources but are inadequate in the amount of protein.

Protein Deficiency

As noted previously, protein is made up of amino acids, with the type and order of the amino acids determining the structure and function of the protein. There are 20 different amino acids commonly found in the body. When an individual eats protein, digestive processes break down the protein into constituent amino acids, which in turn are used to construct proteins using instructions carried in the genome. We have the ability to convert one type of amino acid into another for most of these molecules. However, there are eight amino acids that cannot be formed from other ones by humans; they must be present in the diet. These eight are termed **essential amino acids** for this reason. Protein deficiency can actually be conceived of as a general form of amino acid deficiency, and thus one could conceivably list each of the eight essential amino acids as a separate dietary deficiency under given circumstances.

PROTEIN QUALITY OF FOODS. When we synthesize proteins in our cells, we need to assemble the correct amino acid in the correct position on a growing protein chain. If we do not have a sufficient amount of any given amino acid, the protein synthesis will not be successful. This occurs even if we have boatloads of all other amino acids. Thus, a deficiency in any of the essential amino acids causes a general protein deficiency in the body. Ideally, our diet would consist of proteins that have amino acids in the precise ratios that we use in our own bodies; this would be considered the highest possible quality of protein. One might suppose that cannibalism would be the way to go here, but, as noted earlier, humans distinguish between what is considered food from what contains nutrients; cannibalism is frequently forbidden. In general, however, organisms that are more closely related to us evolutionarily are more likely to have a great number of similar proteins, and thus higher-quality protein. Thus, animal sources of protein are usually of higher quality than plant sources.

Populations whose diets rely predominantly on a single plant source are more likely to experience poor protein quality (Stini 1975). If several plant sources are used, there is usually sufficient variation among the plants in amino acid frequency that adequate amounts of all the essential amino acids are present. An example of mixing plant foods to yield a high-quality protein diet is found in the traditional Mesoamerican diet (from the Maya and Aztecs of the past to many people living in Mexico and Central America today) where beans and maize (corn) are the staples. Maize has a high proportion of sulfur-containing amino acids (methionine and cystine) but is low in the essential amino acids isoleucine and lysine. Beans are relatively high in isoleucine and lysine but low in the sulfur-containing amino acids (Kormondy and Brown 1998). The combination of beans and corn provides a good balance of essential amino acids (see Figure 12-1).

GLOBAL VIEW OF PROTEIN DEFICIENCY. In the modern world, protein deficiency is an all too common affliction. It is found most commonly in developing countries, particularly those in tropical regions, where people rely on a single plant item for the majority of their diet. The problem is acute in populations that eat a diet consisting almost entirely of maize (some poor areas of Mesoamerica, South America, and Africa), sweet potatoes (highlands of New Guinea), manioc (Amazon region of South America), or millet (Africa) (Heywood and Jenkins 1992; Dettwyler 1994; Sullivan et al. 2006).

Protein deficiency is often associated with weaning. Children fed with breast milk consume an excellent quality protein source. However, when they are weaned onto solid foods, in some populations they are fed thin gruels or starchy vegetable foods that contain low amounts of protein or protein of poor quality. A nutritional deficiency disease associated with protein malnutrition is termed **kwashiorkor**, which is a word derived from the African Ga language meaning "disease that occurs when displaced from the breast by another child" (Jelliffe 1968).

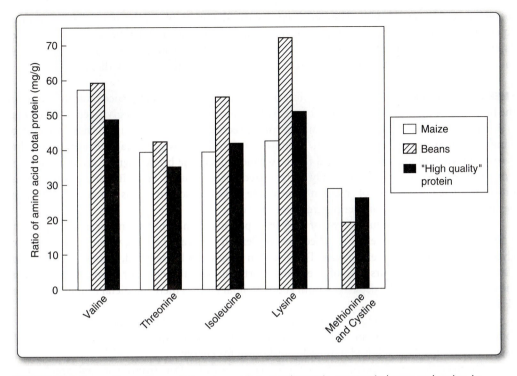

FIGURE 12-1 Proportions of essential amino acids to total protein content in beans and maize, in relation to high-quality protein.

THE BIOLOGY OF PROTEIN DEFICIENCY. In simple terms, protein deficiency causes the body to break down some of its own protein to allow synthesis of critically needed proteins. If protein deficiency is mild or moderate, plasma proteins such as albumin are secreted into the intestine, where they are digested into constituent amino acids. This process of secreting plasma proteins into the intestine increases the efficiency with which dietary protein is digested and utilized (Stini 1975). If protein deficiency is severe, or moderate but long term in nature, skeletal muscle is broken down and used as a source of amino acids. If prolonged, severe effects can ensue.

One of the most threatening effects of protein deficiency is a breakdown of immune-system proteins, leaving the individual more susceptible to infectious diseases. In fact, people rarely die because of the direct effects of protein malnutrition: they succumb to an infection before using up their protein reserves. Children are at greatest risk, in part because they have a smaller protein reserve. Growth requires a steady supply of dietary protein because much protein synthesis is involved in growth. Growth slows or even stops during protein malnutrition. This slowed growth is particularly evident for measures of stature, with children showing **stunting** (low stature-for-age). If the period of malnutrition is not too prolonged, growth will temporarily speed up once the diet improves, and this **catch-up growth**, as noted earlier, may allow the child to reach normal levels of stature-for-age. Girls seem more resilient than boys in catch-up growth levels following a period of protein deficiency (Stini 1972). Periods of growth disruption are often permanently stamped on an individual in the form of Harris lines that appear on long bones as a result of malnutrition during bone development.

Protein-Calorie Malnutrition: Total Undernutrition

When the total amount of dietary intake is reduced below acceptable levels, individuals are faced with both protein shortages and a deficient amount of dietary energy. Humans are large animals with high energy requirements, and these requirements are particularly high because our large brains

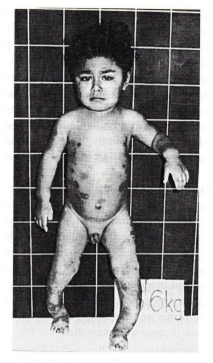

FIGURE 12-6 A child with rickets.

termed **rickets**, which is associated with bowing of bones, delayed tooth eruption, and defective tooth enamel (see Figure 12-6). In adults, the deficiency manifests as **osteomalacia**. It is a particular problem in pregnant or lactating women where calcium needs are high. Vitamin D requirements may have figured in skin-color variation in people, as the lighter skin found among northern peoples may be an adaptation to enhance vitamin D synthesis. Vitamin D insufficiency, a milder form of malnutrition than vitamin D deficiency, is fairly common, even in developed countries such as the United States. Vitamin D insufficiency has been implicated as a risk for chronic illnesses including cardiovascular disease, cancer, and osteoporosis.

Electrolyte and Mineral Deficiencies

ELECTROLYTES. Electrolytes are elements that are the constituents of salts and form electrically charged ions in solution. Certain of these elements are critical for survival, including sodium and chloride (the components of ordinary table salt), as well as potassium, calcium, and magnesium. For most human populations, these elements are abundantly available, particularly for those living near the ocean or having access to ocean resources. While rare, salt deficiency can be a serious adaptive problem, and there is some evidence that human populations that deal with salt scarcity have adjusted to withstand a low dietary salt intake (McArthur 1977).

Acute problems with salt scarcity may occur with certain pathologies, as well as during periods of long-lasting physical work in which much salt is lost in perspiration. Some diets may lead to salt deficiency. For example, a rice soup diet commonly used to combat diarrhea in Korea may lead to generally low electrolyte concentrations if used over a long period (Park et al. 2006). **Hyponatremia** is a term that refers to sodium depletion, while **hypoelectrolytemia** refers to low concentrations of sodium, potassium, and chloride. During endurance exercise, chances of developing hyponatremia increase if a great deal of water or other liquids are consumed (Upadhyay et al. 2006). There is an increase in risk for sodium deficiency with age. An interesting hypothesis has been advanced

(Grim et al. 1995) that individuals sold into the slave trade were exposed to harsh conditions that would have led to salt depletion, and that this led to selection of people who could withstand low levels of sodium. This hypothesis is controversial, however.

IRON. Iron deficiency was termed "the most prevalent nutritional problem in the world today" (Scrimshaw 1991, p. 46) in the early 1990s, and that statement remained true over a decade and a half later (Zimmermann and Hurrell 2007), with 67 percent of children in developing countries, and 33 percent of women in childbearing years estimated to suffer from iron deficiency to some degree. Iron is an important component of hemoglobin, and a deficiency therefore leads to **anemia**. Anemia in turn has bad consequences, lowering work capacity and reducing cognitive performance. Infants are at greatest risk, in part because of high growth rates, but also because milk, including human breast milk, is low in iron (Jelliffe 1968). Under severe shortages, all people will develop anemia, but there is biological variability in ability to cope with mild to moderate degrees of dietary iron shortages (Haas and Pelletier 1989).

IODINE. Iodine is a necessary component of thyroid hormones, which function as a major physiological control for metabolic level. When our diets are insufficient in iodine, the thyroid gland swells in a futile attempt to increase hormone levels, resulting in a **goiter** (see Figure 12-7). When goiters become large, they not only are disfiguring, but they also can impinge on the windpipe. Long-term iodine deficiency causes reduced thyroid function, and this leads to lowered general metabolic rates, resulting in sleepiness, sluggishness, reduced heart rate, heightened risk for obesity, decreased growth, skin problems, and increased levels of blood lipids, which can lead to cardiovascular disease. Severe loss of thyroid function is termed **myxedema** and involves edema throughout the body. If very low thyroid function is present in infants or young children, cretinism can develop, a disease that causes serious physical stunting and impedes mental development; if prolonged, cretinism can cause permanent neurological damage. Iodine deficiency is most common in populations far from the ocean, and mountain populations appear to be at greatest risk.

FIGURE 12-7 A woman with a large goiter.

CALCIUM. Calcium deficiency problems mirror those found with vitamin D insufficiency, since vitamin D allows calcium to be employed by the body. Calcium is crucial for the development and maintenance of bones and teeth, and it is also necessary for proper nervous-system functioning. Deficiencies lead to slowed bone growth, or, in adults, loss of bone mass. This can lead to **osteoporosis**, a condition especially prevalent in postmenopausal women, in which bones become brittle and can easily fracture. Very low calcium levels can cause neuromuscular problems. It is thought that low calcium levels may contribute to arctic hysterias (*pibloktok*), behavioral disturbances that have been described in Arctic populations (Foulks 1972; McElroy and Townsend 1989). Attacks of *pibloktok* last for a few minutes to a few hours, and include such behaviors as removing clothes, running outside even in extremely cold conditions, rolling in the snow, speaking incoherently, and throwing things.

Overnutrition

The form of malnutrition that is most common in the developed world today is the problem of too much food, not too little. While one can be concerned about the superficial effects of obesity, there are actually serious conditions, such as diabetes and cardiovascular disease, that are increased in prevalence by the excess body weight that comes with overeating. Of greatest concern is a major epidemic of childhood obesity that has come at the end of the twentieth and early part of the twenty-first centuries. So-called adult-onset diabetes has become all too common among children, even in preadolescents, and this disease may lead to a shortening of life expectancy in coming generations.

CONCLUSION: MALNUTRITION

Malnutrition can be viewed as a sign of a population's failure to adapt to its environment. This failure may be due to poor food-production choices, environmental crises, or socio-political events that are beyond the population's control. Biological adaptations to undernutrition represent a stalling for time until sufficient food can be obtained, in particular when confronted by insufficient amounts of macronutrients. The ability to withstand periods of food scarcity has probably evolved over millions of years, as scarcity was probably present at least occasionally throughout our evolutionary history. However, much of the response to malnutrition is not adaptive at all, but simply a manifestation of the ill effects of nutritional deficiencies. Deficiencies of specific micronutrients without general food scarcity may be a more recent challenge for our species, as this is mostly found among agricultural communities that rely on a single food crop as the major part of their diet. It must be emphasized that nutritional problems do not exist independently of other environmental stressors, and this complication can make it difficult to disentangle the effects of the multiple stresses.

The relationship between nutrition and infectious disease is a particularly important one. Infectious disease may exacerbate nutritional problems, for instance by inhibiting digestion, causing internal bleeding that leads to nutrient loss or reducing work capacity that could have assisted with obtaining food. Malnutrition also can inhibit the body's immune system, making people more likely to become infected with a given pathogen. Infectious disease can be viewed as a second form of biological stressor to which humans must adapt, but one must bear in mind the links between nutrition and infectious diseases. These two stressors remain common challenges for humankind.

INFECTIOUS DISEASE

Life on both sides of the food chain can be difficult. Food can be scarce, and attacks by parasites may be all too common. Infectious agents come in a variety of sizes, from the molecular-sized viruses that can be barely imaged by our most powerful electron microscopes, to the feet-long worms that invade our intestinal tracts. Infectious agents also come in many types, including viruses, bacteria, yeast and fungal cells, and a host of multicellular organisms that include the aforementioned worms. Infectious diseases have represented a major cause of human mortality for thousands of years, and they thus act as an evolutionary selective force on humans. In fact, individuals differ in their degree of susceptibility to specific diseases, with the difference in part due to genetic factors.

Infectious agents may be somewhat rare, but when present in the environment are frequent causes of disease. Other agents are common in the environment, and even frequently found in humans, but only occasionally cause disease (Dubos 1965). The modern germ theory of disease is not a simple idea that if one "gets" a germ (that is, an infectious agent) one becomes ill. Rather, the cause of disease involves the interaction of the germ, the condition of the germ's host (which we have seen may involve nutritional status), and environmental conditions that may increase or decrease the germ's infectivity.

Host-Parasite Relationships

There is a wide range of conditions associated with parasitism. Tiny germs may multiply quickly and almost always cause the death of their host, or the germs may hide within the host for long periods, living off the host's resources but otherwise doing little harm.

EVOLUTION AND VIRULENCE. In many cases, there may be selection among both hosts and parasites for a reduction in **virulence** (in simple terms, the amount of damage an infectious agent does to its host). For the parasite, killing its host is like killing the golden goose—what does one do now? And for the host, selection surely favors those best able to survive a parasite attack. The selection of less virulent parasites and more resistant hosts over time may be why relatively new diseases, such as HIV-AIDS and Ebola, are very virulent, while ancient diseases such as the many viral diseases that comprise the common cold tend to be mild. The selective process may be much more complex than this. Among parasites living within a host, there may well be selection for individuals who multiply more quickly and thus have more reproductive success. This type of selection actually favors increased virulence. On the other hand, virulent germs may kill their host, and thus ultimately die with the host. The critical factor is apparently the relative difficulty of moving to a new host. If transmission is easily accomplished, the parasite does not suffer for killing its host, and virulence will increase or stay at a high level (Ewald 1993; 1994).

In the host population, genetic variability in the immune system may be of critical importance in adapting to new diseases (Black 1992). Viruses, in particular, are able to evolve quickly to deal with host immune systems, given their rapid reproductive rates. And if they move to a new host with a very similar immune system, they will be preadapted to deal with the new host's defenses. As will become evident, viral diseases have become much more common in the past 10,000 years or so of human history, and much of human evolution in this time period may well have taken place within the immune system to deal with this challenge. Ethical considerations preclude human experimentation to determine genetic variation in susceptibility. However, "natural experiments," in which observations are made on differences in susceptibility among people in high-risk conditions, have permitted some understanding of the genetic basis of varying degrees of infection resistance.

Infectious agents have a natural environment, termed their **reservoir**, which may be biological or nonbiological. Biological reservoirs can consist of either other humans or nonhuman animals. For instance, smallpox had only a human reservoir. In the greatest achievement of twentieth-century public health, the disease was eliminated through extensive vaccination campaigns throughout the world. Once the human reservoir was eliminated, there was no more disease left in the world, save in certain biological laboratories. Nonbiological reservoirs for diseases can include water in hotel air conditioners or cruise-ship spas, as is implicated in cases of Legionnaire's disease (Rota et al. 2007; Kura et al. 2006).

CONSIDERATIONS IN DISEASE TRANSMISSION. Germs can be transmitted in many ways. We will consider these modes in some detail. Once the germ has entered the host's body through some portal (for example, mouth, breaks in skin, etc.), disease does not occur immediately, if at all. Infection

human livestock and then be transmitted to humans, spurring global pandemics. The 1918 to 1920 strain may have developed from pigs (hence, "swine flu"), and in the early years of the twenty-first century, a bird flu strain has appeared, although it has not caused a pandemic at the time of this writing.

VIRGIN SOIL EPIDEMICS. When populations first meet, whether due to exploration, migrations, aggressive raids, or other reasons, one unintended consequence of the meeting may be the passing of germs to a population that had never encountered the pathogen previously. The newly exposed population represents "virgin soil" in which the germ may grow, since the population has developed no immunological resistance. The result may be catastrophic, with nearly every population member being infected with the pathogen simultaneously, and the virulence level is often extremely high. These events are termed **virgin soil epidemics**, and they have been the cause of such high mortality that they have led to the demographic collapse of some societies (Dobyns 1983; Verano and Ubelaker 1992; Stannard 1989).

Virgin soil epidemics have had a major role in history, as well (McNeill 1976). For instance, it is hard to believe that the Spanish conquistadors would have had much success in their attacks on the huge empires of the Aztecs and Incas, respectively, had these empires not been beset at the same time by the infectious diseases that had arrived from Europe. Since the ancestors of the native populations in the Americas migrated from Eurasia thousands of years ago, they were never exposed to the diseases that developed in Eurasia and Africa after the invention of agriculture. Imagine what the history of the Americas would have been like had the Aztecs defeated Cortez and the Incas prevailed over Pizzaro.

Diseases Due to Intimate Contact

Diseases that are passed through intimate contact, such as sexually transmitted diseases (STDs), are transmitted by direct contact between people, whether from exchange of body fluids (such as semen, saliva, or blood) or by skin-to-skin contact. The major difference here is the degree of contact necessary for disease transmission to occur. The major factor in passing along these intimate-contact diseases is sexual behavior, but such activities as needle sharing by drug users, inadequate sterilization of medical equipment, and even breast feeding of infants can be important means of transmission.

TREPONEMAL DISEASES. There is a set of diseases caused by a single pathogen: spirochetes (a type of bacteria) in the genus *Treponema*. There are four major Treponemal diseases, the best known of which is venereal syphilis, but also including yaws, pinta, and nonvenereal (or endemic) syphilis. **Venereal syphilis** is, as the name implies, a sexually transmitted disease caused by *Treponema pallidum*; the disease may also be transmitted *in utero* from mother to fetus. The disease is characterized by multiple stages, with lesions (termed "chancres") developing, a period of remission, and later stages involving neurological and/or cardiovascular damage.

Yaws is an ancient disease caused by *Treponema pertenue* that causes lesions that are somewhat different from the chancres of syphilis. Yaws is transmitted by direct contact with a lesion. It may even be passed by flies acting as mechanical vectors. The yaws lesions may become very painful, causing debilitation, and in late stages serious bone and skin damage may occur (Brown et al. 1970). **Pinta** is a mild skin disease caused by *Treponema carateum* that causes areas of depigmentation, but it is not otherwise associated with severe symptoms. Finally, **nonvenereal syphilis** is caused by *Treponema pallidum* and is spread by contaminated water or food, or by skin contact. Lesions of nonvenereal syphilis often form around the mouth. This makes oral routes of transmission, from kissing to sharing drinking water, significant ways of spreading the disease.

All the Treponemal diseases are caused by the same—or closely related—species of pathogen, and people who have had one of the diseases are resistant to the others. These diseases are, in a sense, simply different manifestations of a single disease, in which the pathogen has adapted somewhat to different environmental circumstances to optimize transmission. Since the major disease manifestation is venereal syphilis, control measures must focus on education in safe sex, abstinence, decreased sexual promiscuity, and control of prostitution. These are difficult behaviors to alter or even, in some circumstances, to discuss, as they involve religious beliefs, stigma associated with commercial sex workers, and deep-seated cultural conceptions of propriety.

HIV/AIDS. Another sexually transmitted disease that has great importance in contemporary times is HIV/AIDS (Human Immunodeficiency Virus/Acquired Immune Deficiency Syndrome). The disease is caused by a **retrovirus**, a type of virus that contains RNA rather than DNA. Two major viral strains have been identified, HIV-1 and HIV-2, and there are many variants of these major strains; for our purposes these will be grouped into the single designation of HIV. The virus is transmitted through exchanged body fluids. It enters cells, and its RNA is used as a template for the construction of DNA molecules that in turn are transcribed into messenger RNA molecules that direct protein synthesis (see Figure 12-9). The virus preferentially infects immune cells, and thus the disease directly attacks our own defense system.

HIV/AIDS is a relatively new disease on the global scene, having first been observed as a distinct disease in the United States in 1981, although it may have existed at low levels for many years previously in Africa, and the strains evolved from simian immunodeficiency viruses that infected chimpanzees and mangabeys, respectively. Africa remains the area hit hardest by the disease, with over 70 percent of the world's 40 million cases (as of 2001) found in sub-Saharan Africa (Buvé et al. 2002).

The disease is passed through sexual contact, both heterosexual and homosexual, and also through other contact with body fluids, whether through shared needles, blood transfusions, or other means of contacting a carrier's body fluids. Because of this, behaviors associated with sexuality, including promiscuity, contact with commercial sex workers, and use of "safe sex" practices have a major effect, be it negative or positive, on disease transmission. Moreover, drug users are at high risk due to the repeated use of hypodermic needles without proper sterilization, often involving reuse of shared needles.

There is great variability in the relative degree of resistance to the HIV virus among individuals, and also between populations (Arenzana-Seisdedos and Parmentier 2006; Heeney et al. 2006). Studies have shown that relative degrees of resistance are affected by many genes, and these genes act at the level of viral entry as well as in the replication of the virus within cells. The genetic differences allow some people to live with the virus for twenty years or more, while others die within just a year or so after infection (O'Brien and Nelson 2004). Also, the genetic differences affect how people respond to anti-HIV drug treatment and the types and severity of their symptoms.

One specific genetic polymorphism related to HIV resistance occurs in a chemical receptor found on certain immune-system cells. This is the chemokine receptor 5 (CCR5), which has two major alleles at its genetic locus, the "normal" allele and one that has a deletion mutation that eliminates 32 nucleotide pairs and actually prevents the receptor protein from being manufactured. People who are homozygous for the allele with the deletion mutation are highly resistant to HIV-1 infection, and heterozygotes have some resistance (Galvani and Novembre 2005). This resistance allele is of particularly high frequency in certain European populations, and it has been hypothesized that its presence is the result of previous selection from a different disease that also was less virulent in people with the mutated allele. One hypothesis is that the previous disease was bubonic plague, which struck several times in Europe between the 1300s and 1600s (Stephens et al. 1998). However, it is unlikely that bubonic plague, which is caused by a bacterium, is the actual selecting agent, since the mutation deals with a receptor involved with viral infections. The hypothesis was modified to posit a hemorrhagic viral disease that accompanied bubonic plague (Scott and Duncan 2004). An alternative hypothesis is that the previous disease that led to selection for this mutation was smallpox, a viral disease that caused millions of deaths in Europe over the past few thousands of years (Galvani and Slatkin 2003) before its eradication in 1979.

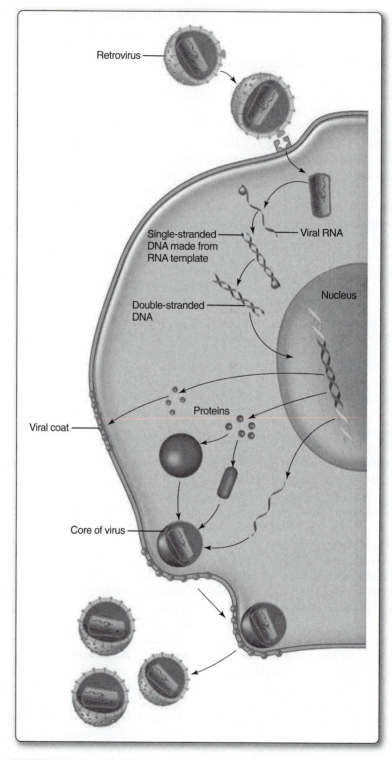

FIGURE 12-9 How the HIV virus replicates in a cell.

There are some similarities between measles and HIV infections, including the types of cells infected and a resulting suppression of the immune system. One study found that people who had just recovered from a measles infection had antibodies to HIV in their blood serum, thus showing cross-reactivity between the diseases (Baskar et al. 1998).

Poor-Sanitation Diseases

The final type of infectious diseases to be considered here are those passed due to unsanitary conditions, in which germs from human wastes get into water or food supplies. This is the "fecal-oral" route of disease transmission, and the diseases probably became of importance to human populations when sedentary life arose. Nomadic foragers live in fairly small groups, usually moving on before sanitation issues become a concern. Archaeologically, the absence of parasitic worm eggs associated with human remains in ancient sites suggests that these diseases only became important with the introduction of agriculture and settled life in the past 12,000 years or so (Dunn 1968).

ASCARIS. Parasitic infections with the nematode *Ascaris lumbricoides* are very common throughout the world, with nearly 25 percent of the world's population infected in any given year. The worm lives in the small intestine, and female worms can lay up to two million eggs per day! The eggs are eliminated from the body in feces, and they can stay viable for long periods, even years, in soil. The infection is usually transmitted by eating raw fruit or vegetables that have been contaminated by the worm eggs (Sarinas and Chitkara 1997). Individuals with a heavy worm load lose nutrients to the parasites, and this load results in slowed growth rates in infected children. There is evidence for cognitive decrements due to infection, and about 20,000 deaths occur each year from the disease (Khuroo 1996).

In areas of heavy *Ascaris* infestation, nearly all humans are open to infection. However, there is a great deal of individual variability in both the distribution of infection and the level of worm burden in these regions. These differences are thought to be due to two major factors: behavioral differences that place some individuals at more risk and genetic variability in susceptibility. The behavioral differences are related to exposure to poor sanitation and are usually associated with poverty. Two genes have been identified as being related to human susceptibility to *Ascaris*, with one localized to chromosome 1 and the other on chromosome 13, although the actual alleles have not been identified (Williams-Blangero et al. 2002)

CHOLERA. Cholera is an acute diarrheal disease caused by bacteria in the genus *Vibrio*. In 2006, there were a total of 236,896 cases and 6,311 deaths officially reported to the World Health Organization. The disease mostly exacts its toll by causing dehydration through diarrhea and vomiting. It is a waterborne disease, and it tends to occur in outbreaks where one or a few individuals are exposed at first, and these individuals then produce millions of bacteria that get into the water supply through poor sanitation practices that are exaggerated by the volume of wastes produced by the victims. The infection quickly spreads to other people in the population, and an epidemic results. Humans appear to be the only carriers, and they only transmit the bacteria for a short period of time. It is unclear how the disease takes on an endemic form in some areas, particularly south Asia, which then serve as reservoirs for epidemics that occur sporadically throughout many areas of the world. It is a question that has no answer as of now.

As with other diseases, there is individual variation in cholera susceptibility, based in part on acquired immunity from past infections, but also based upon genetic differences. Humans who are blood type O in the ABO blood system are more likely to be infected and/or hospitalized during cholera epidemics. It is believed that the low genotype frequencies for OO blood types in areas within India that traditionally experience endemic forms of cholera are due to selection against the O allele (Harris et al. 2005).

PROFILE 12

Stephen T. McGarvey

tephen McGarvey is a biological anthropologist with additional training in epidemiology who has studied international health in the Pacific and Asia. His research is concerned with understanding the broad range of causal factors for disease, examining environmental, genetic, behavioral, psychological, and cultural phenomena that place individuals at risk. His research focuses on populations that have high incidence rates for specific illnesses, studying the factors that make the population as a whole, as well as some individuals within the population, more susceptible. His research goals are to increase understanding of the health problems in these populations as a means to inform public health action.

Dr. McGarvey has devoted much of his career to the study of modernization's effects on the health of Samoans, both in the U.S. territory American Samoa and the nearby independent country of Samoa. These Polynesians have experienced a sharp increase in obesity rates and a concomitant increase in the diseases associated with the metabolic syndrome: hypertension, heart disease, and type 2 diabetes. Dr. McGarvey's research has shown a steady increase in these problems over time, although obesity rates are beginning to plateau in American Samoa. His research also examines means for preventing or ameliorating obesity in Samoan children.

Parasitic diseases are also of concern in Asia and the Pacific, and Dr. McGarvey has studied the causes and effects of these diseases, particularly examining schistosomiasis, a parasitic disease passed by a snail vector in infested water sources, in the Philippines and China. His research has focused in particular on the affects of schistosomiasis on children.

Dr. McGarvey also is undertaking research in South Africa on nutrition transition in a large rural community with high HIV prevalence and initial utilization of anti-retroviral therapy.

Stephen McGarvey is Professor of Community Health and Anthropology and Director of the International Health Institute at Brown University Medical School. He serves as a co-editor of the *Annals of Human Biology*, is on the editorial boards of the *American Journal of Human Biology* and *Anthropological Science*, and is an elected fellow of the American Association for the Advancement of Science.

BALANCING IMMUNE PROTECTION AND IMMUNE DAMAGE. While the immune system is vital in protecting us from the depredations of various germs, there are sometimes negative side effects of a too strong or flawed immune response. These side effects involve allergic reactions and include serious respiratory ailments, such as asthma and COPD (chronic obstructive pulmonary disease). Of interest is the immune response involving T-helper 2 (Th2) immune responses, which are thought to have evolved in mammals as a defense against parasitic infection (Le Souëf et al. 2000; 2006). These infections are more common in tropical areas, and there is some evidence that allele frequencies in genes related to the TH2 response differ between tropically derived populations and those in more temperate zones, with tropical populations having higher frequencies of alleles that favor strong inflammatory responses. However, these alleles are also associated with greater risk for asthma and COPD in people living in modernized environments. There may be selection for a reduced Th2 response in people living outside the tropics and in modernized circumstances.

CONCLUSION: INFECTIOUS DISEASES

Infectious diseases remain a major source of misery and death for humans throughout the world. Triumphant statements about the imminent eradication of infectious diseases were common in the 1960s and 1970s, at least in regard to developed countries. The advent of antibiotic-resistant strains of many common infectious diseases, in part due to the overuse of antibiotics, has put a damper on the hopes of eliminating this scourge. The biological stress of infectious disease remains, as it has for the past several millennia, a major source of mortality, and perhaps of selective pressure, for human populations.

GENERAL CONCLUSION: THE IMPACT OF BIOLOGICAL STRESSORS ON HUMAN BIOLOGY

Both disease and malnutrition have been major sources of human mortality, and this suggests that these misfortunes have had evolutionary implications as well. Humans in general are able to draw on food reserves from their bodies, stalling for time during times of undernutrition to survive until nutrients become available, likely because of millions of years of natural selection for individuals who could survive temporary food shortages. There is good evidence that human genetic variation exists in the ability to handle infectious diseases, and that the genetic mutations, as with sickle-cell

FIGURE 12-10 The four horsemen of the apocalypse: famine, pestilence, and associated horsemen representing war and death. Woodcut by Albrecht Durer.

anemia, can have multiple affects, both good and bad. Again, there is evidence that selective forces have led to the differential susceptibility of people to disease. As noted before, there is a strong positive feedback connection between malnutrition and infectious disease, with the presence of one increasing the likelihood of the development of the other (see Figure 12-10).

Exposure to biological stressors can also affect one's ability to withstand other stressors. People with influenza are less able to handle heat stress, for example. Also, people with an iron deficiency are much less able to withstand high-altitude hypoxia, since the malnutrition-induced anemia reduces the ability to transport oxygen to body tissues.

Biological stressors have a particularly negative effect on young children. Malnutrition in children can have horrendous consequences, including death, but it can also have more subtle results, such as inhibiting mental development, that can cause cognitive disabilities that last for the rest of the individual's life (Brown and Pollitt 1996). Disease, too, has dire consequences in children, who have not had the chance to develop resistance to the many pathogens they confront in their early years. People have adapted to these two major stressors both behaviorally and biologically. It is likely that they will continue to act as selective forces on humanity for untold years to come.

CHAPTER SUMMARY

Two of the greatest selective forces on modern humans have been, and continue to be, malnutrition and infectious diseases. Malnutrition may be due to an overall reduction in the *quantity* of dietary intake, leading to protein-calorie malnutrition, or it can be due to a poor *quality* of diet, causing either protein malnutrition or a deficiency in one or more micronutrients, such as vitamins or minerals. People adapt to nutritional problems through a complex web of ecological and economic behaviors that allow them to obtain food for themselves and their families. When people cannot obtain an adequate diet, their bodies adapt by stalling for time, making use of the body's own resources to burn for calories or to obtain other needed resources, until adequate nutrition can be obtained. When the body's resources have been used up, serious nutritional diseases manifest, and these can lead to permanent disability or death. When protein intake is inadequate, people lose some of their immune system's function, and they therefore become highly susceptible to infectious diseases. Children are particularly vulnerable to the bad effects of malnutrition, in part due to their greater need for nutritional resources to sustain their own growth, and in part because they have smaller bodily reserves to draw upon during periods of dietary stress.

Infectious diseases remain a leading cause of mortality for humans around the world, with greater problems in poor regions. These diseases are spread by germs, usually microscopic organisms that parasitize humans, sapping resources from the body and sometimes causing direct damage to body structures. The chances of obtaining a disease are related to contact with the germ; the condition of the host, particularly the host's immune system; and environmental factors. Infectious diseases can be divided into four major types based upon the means by which they spread: vector borne, direct contact, intimate contact, and sanitation related diseases. Risk for vector-borne diseases depends a great deal upon human interaction with disease vectors, whether mechanical or biological, and on the vector's characteristics. Direct-contact diseases are spread from person to person, usually by the droplet route, and are largely dependent upon demographic and cultural factors related to human interaction. Intimate-contact disease risk is primarily related to sexual behaviors, but such diseases also may be spread by shared drinking vessels or other contact with body fluids, including use of poorly sterilized hypodermic needles, as is all too common among drug users. Diseases of poor sanitation are largely transferred by the fecal-oral route, in which unsanitary conditions lead to contaminated food or water. Many infectious diseases are related to poverty, thriving in conditions where people do not have the resources to prevent disease spread. Infectious diseases may lead to nutritional problems because of the damage caused by germs or the germs' depletion of their human victims' resources; on the other hand, nutritional deficits often cause a deficit in immune function, thus permitting germs to establish themselves in their victims.

CHAPTER 13

Human Biology in the Modern World

Humans live in a very different world today than their ancestors experienced. Human evolution over millions of years probably involved circumstances where small groups of foragers hunted animal prey, gathered edible plants, and scavenged whatever foods could be found. These ancestors also needed to avoid predators and cope with parasites. In more recent times, the invention of agriculture led to settled life for a majority of people, with greater availability of food. An expanding population, however, required more food to sustain the group, as well as, at times, a reliance on a very small variety of food sources compared to earlier years. These conditions led to changes in evolutionary pressures. For instance, the higher population density led to an increase in infectious diseases, and this in turn resulted in selection for those with immune systems that could fight the now common germs.

In the past century or two, the human condition has changed radically. Instead of hunting antelope or hoeing gardens, many people sit at desks to earn their livings, and then drive automobiles through snarled traffic to their homes, where they sit on couches with TV remotes in hand. Food is overabundant in developed countries, and people are apt to eat more than they require for their basic needs. Modern conditions have also led to changes in other aspects of the environment, with pollution in our air and water, strange chemicals in our food, and extensive travel leading to the rapid transport of pathogens throughout the world. It should not be surprising that these new conditions have created new selective forces that act on our species. Human evolution has often been viewed as an historical event as opposed to a continuing process, but the latter is the case, as can be seen by the changes occurring now.

The modern world is a complex one, and therefore this chapter can only give a broad overview of contemporary human adaptation. Four topics will serve as foci, illustrating major factors that our species confronts in current times. These topics are: possible reduced natural selection, general stress, adiposity (body fat), and pollution. They are related to three major selective forces that have become common in the modern world: heart disease, diabetes, and cancer.

POSSIBLE REDUCED SELECTIVE FORCES

In what some believe is sky-is-falling hyperbole, but others believe is a major long-term issue for the human species, some researchers have suggested that the complex technology of modern life has reduced evolutionary selective forces. This has permitted people who would never have survived to adulthood in past circumstances, let alone reproduce, to succeed in passing on their genes to a new generation. It must be noted that humans have changed their microenvironments since the species first evolved in order to handle challenges from the outside (environmental stressors) as well as for intra-population challenges (for example, communication systems, marriage and reproductive controls, care of the sick or disabled). Human biological adaptation, and thus selection pressures on our species, is based upon the conditions of the microenvironment. Modern life brings with it an increased ability to create microenvironments that differ from the external macroenvironment. It therefore appears that modern conditions have increased our ability to handle our environment through behavioral means, but this is not a qualitative change from the way that humans have handled their world throughout our existence. Thus, effects on human genetics from reliance upon our technology are not specific to the modernized world of the twenty-first century. However, concern about these possible genetic effects has led to some reactions that raise ethical concerns.

The **eugenics** movement was started in large part due to fears about genetic changes in the population because of lowered selection. Eugenicists believed that the solution to the problem was to stop the reproduction of individuals thought to have detrimental genes (negative eugenics), and encourage the reproduction of those thought to have superior genes (positive eugenics). The highly subjective nature of determining what is a detrimental or a superior trait, and lack of certainty about what gene determines the trait, leads to the question: who decides? During the time when the eugenics movement was most popular, the early to mid twentieth century, the answer was that those in power decided. In some cases, authorities aimed their efforts against specific ethnic or "racial" groups. Nazi attempts to eliminate entire ethnic groups, such as the Jews and Romany, marked the eugenics movement's lowest point. Ethical issues, thankfully, ended popular support for eugenics, although there are still those who would seek to determine who should be allowed to reproduce and who should not.

Genetic counseling has become an accepted component of our health care system. This service provides couples with information about the risk for having children with genetic abnormalities. Genetic counseling is somewhat controversial: there have been allegations of racism when counseling involves genetic traits that are most common in certain populations, such as sickle-cell trait in some African populations, and Tay-Sachs disease in European Jewish (Ashkenazi) populations (Fost 1992; Charrow 2004). Also, we are still left with the overarching questions: what is "normal," and who decides?

Since all important human traits have both genetic and environmental components, one can also create changes (or "improvements," although this is a subjective term whose applicability could be debated in individual cases) through a different movement: that of **euphenics**, in which attempts are made to improve the *phenotype* of humans through environmental changes (Cavalli-Sforza and Bodmer 1971). One hypothetical approach to euphenics would be to intervene in the biologically based developmental process of individuals to produce a desired adult phenotype (Lederberg 1963). This approach comes with its own ethical concerns about our interventions in other individuals' lives. It is worthwhile to give a measured look at some of the concerns that ignited the eugenics movement, but, in doing so, to place them in the context of what efforts can be used to improve the environmental conditions in which we live. We will also examine the idea that a longer-range view may find a positive side to the perceived relaxed selection in modern times, and also question if selective forces have indeed been lowered in recent times.

The Accumulation of Minor Genetic Problems

One concern about reduced selection is that it might lead to an increase in suboptimal alleles at many loci. The idea is that our technology allows us to accommodate the symptoms of these genetic weaknesses, but that the technology does not actually cure the problem (Boyden 1970). While any one of these conditions is not a serious problem, some have suggested that the accumulation of many of these difficulties will spell serious trouble for our species in the future.

MYOPIA. One classic example of such a minor problem is myopia. Myopia is the inability to focus one's vision properly on distant objects due to refractive errors in the eyes. We have developed antidotes to this condition: eyeglasses, contact lenses, and laser surgery to improve the focus problem. Very near-sighted people would have had difficulty surviving without these technological aids in non-modern conditions. The rate of myopia is increasing rapidly throughout the world, but it is particularly common in urban areas of Asia (Hosaka 1988; Saw et al. 2002). One question is whether the increase in myopia that is evident in the modern world is due primarily to genetic changes, or whether it is mostly a result of environmental changes that are part of modern circumstances, such as spending a great deal of time focusing on close-up objects, for instance, during reading.

Myopia is actually a symptom that may have multiple causes. Mild-to-moderate cases ("low myopia") have both environmental and genetic causes, and the genetics is likely due to the multiple effects of many alleles. Some more severe cases of myopia ("high myopia") may have a strong influence from a single major allele (Goss et al. 1988; Jacobi et al. 2005), and these cases can lead to marked disabilities in some people. Children of myopic parents are more likely to develop myopia than children of parents without the disorder. The higher rates of myopia in developed Asian countries suggests population genetic differences in susceptibility, but also may be due to the cultural environment, for example an emphasis on children spending a large amount of time reading.

It is unclear whether the increase in myopia is of great concern for our species, given the fairly simple means we have developed for ameliorating its effects. Certainly taking away people's eyeglasses and placing them in circumstances where hunting antelope is necessary for survival will lead to selection against any genes that might code for myopia, but there is little likelihood of this scenario occurring. In fact, one can posit the removal of any cultural adaptation, and worry about whether humans could adapt without it. The loss of eyeglasses is perhaps no more likely than the loss of our ability to make fire and therefore to adapt to cold climates.

DENTAL CARIES. The frequency of dental caries ("cavities"), or, more broadly, periodontal disease in general, has increased markedly in human populations since the development of agriculture. It is thought that the high caloric density of agricultural foods increases the risk of bacterial infections of periodontal tissues, leading to tooth decay (see Figure 13-1). The rise of modern dentistry and the spread of preventative practices such as tooth brushing and flossing have led to reductions in the prevalence of severe effects of periodontal disease. However, there are a minority of individuals, approximately 10 to 15 percent of the population, who are at high risk for these severe effects (Johnson et al. 1988).

While the major concern for periodontal disease risk is environmental, there is also evidence for genetic contributions to risk based on family studies, including research using linkage analyses and twin concordance (Kinane and Hart 2003). There are many possible mechanisms for genetic variability in resistance to dental disease, from immune system function to tooth morphology.

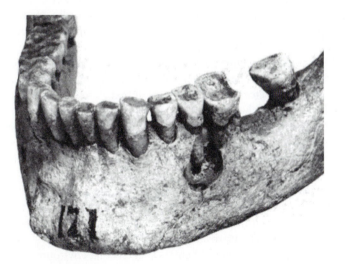

FIGURE 13-1 Dental decay in a specimen from an archaeological site.

Modern dentistry allows intervention in dental disease from both preventative and treatment modalities. These interventions reduce selection against the genotypes that lead to increased risk for periodontal disease, and therefore they may increase the ratio of people who are at high risk. If these treatments are unavailable or unused, serious effects of periodontal disease can ensue, including potentially fatal systemic infections. There is also evidence that poor dental health increases risk for cardiovascular disease (Beck and Offenbacher 2005). However, one can again wonder why anyone would think the loss of dentistry is a likely scenario for the human future.

CAN CUMULATIVE MINOR EFFECTS LEAD TO BIGGER PROBLEMS? The two examples given here, of myopia and dental disease, seem like minor irritations given our ability to handle them. Wearing glasses and taking a few minutes a day to brush and floss seem easy enough. However, the concern is that an accumulation of these irritations can add up to serious issues for our species. Or is this much ado about nothing much?

Reduced Selection Due to Medical Interventions

Other instances of reduced selection against certain genetic variants may have greater apparent risk for humanity. A few examples will be given here, with a brief analysis of the effect of reduced selective pressure.

TYPE 1 DIABETES MELLITUS. Type 1 diabetes, also known as "juvenile" diabetes, is a disease caused by the loss of the cells that normally secrete insulin. The disease is usually observed in young children, and it is believed to be due to an autoimmune attack on one's own insulin-secreting beta-cells in the pancreas. There is a strong genetic component to the risk of developing type 1 diabetes, and the disease is much more prevalent in European populations than in other human groups (Karvonen et al. 1993; Onkamo et al. 1999). The disease is increasing in frequency at a rate of 3 percent per year, suggesting that environmental as well as genetic changes are fueling this rapid increase (Patterson et al. 2001; Gillespie 2006). Alleles have been identified that are associated with increased risk for the disease, and the genome areas related to the immune system and to insulin, respectively, are sites where such alleles have been localized (Davies et al. 2002). It is generally understood that having genes that make one susceptible to type 1 diabetes is insufficient to cause the disease; there must also be an environmental trigger to initiate disease symptoms. There is strong evidence that exposure to the Coxsackie B virus provides one such trigger (Haverkos et al. 2003), because a protein on the virus is structurally similar to a protein on the surface of insulin-producing cells. When the immune system fights back against a Coxsackie B virus infection, it may then be primed for an attack on the insulin-producing cells.

It is likely that a change in environment is increasing the **penetrance** of genes (that is, there is an increase in the degree to which the genes' effects are expressed in the individual's phenotype) that predispose towards type 1 diabetes. Twin studies suggest that 70 to 75 percent of risk for the disease is due to genetic effects, while such environmental factors as use of cow's milk in the diet, shortened period of breast feeding, nitrites and nitrosamines in the diet, and, as noted, exposure to viral infections have all been implicated in type 1 diabetes risk (Pitkäniemi et al. 2004).

In earlier times, victims of this disease did not survive long, and therefore strong selective pressure was exerted on alleles that increased risk for developing this form of diabetes. The introduction of injectable insulin provided a means of living with the disease, and although this does not represent a cure, it has led to a reduction in selection against genes that might predispose people to type 1 diabetes. Thus, people with type 1 diabetes can now lead normal lives, although they must monitor their blood-sugar levels regularly and regulate their insulin use.

The rapid rise in incidence of type 1 diabetes suggests that environmental factors are important, but there is a key genetic component to the disease risk as well. This has led some researchers to hypothesize that different combinations of environmental and genetic risk factors interact to produce type 1 diabetes, and that these combinations vary from individual to individual (Dahlquist 1998, Åkerblom et al. 2002). Thus, it is not genes that cause this disease; a combination of certain genes in certain environments appears to be the cause. Thus, rather than worry about reduced selection leading to greater susceptibility, it would make more sense to discover more details about the gene-environment interactions so that we can intervene and reduce the incidence of the disease through changing the environmental circumstances that put individuals at risk.

PHENYLKETONURIA. Phenylketonuria (or PKU) is a genetically determined condition in which individuals cannot metabolize the amino acid phenylalanine, since they cannot manufacture the enzyme phenylalanine hydroxylase (PAH). There are many different alleles at the locus for PAH, and several of these result in PKU (Kidd et al. 2000). As a result of the absence of the enzyme's activity, phenylalanine levels in blood are considerably elevated, and this high concentration of the amino acid is toxic to the developing nervous system in infants. If untreated, children with PKU become severely mentally retarded. Beginning in the 1960s, widespread testing of newborns for PKU was undertaken. When PKU is discovered, placing those people on special diets that minimize phenylalanine levels effectively prevents the neurotoxicity and concomitant cognitive effects of the disease.

PKU is most common in northern European populations; the presence of several different alleles at the PAH locus that cause the disorder among Europeans suggests that the trait has multiple origins from separate mutation events. Our ability to identify PKU in newborns and to intervene through dietary restriction prevents the ill effects of the allele from manifesting. This, therefore, is an example of euphenics, a change in an individual's phenotype through a change in development (due to dietary restriction) that has negated the need for genetic change, whether from negative eugenics or natural selection.

CYSTIC FIBROSIS. Cystic fibrosis is a devastating disease in which a recessive genetic defect leads to an impaired ability to transport chloride and other ions across the cell membrane. The major symptom is thickened mucus, which leads to much greater vulnerability to respiratory infections, and the disease is more common among European populations than in other groups. Until late in the twentieth century, it was rare for a victim of cystic fibrosis to live to adulthood. The median life expectancy at birth for those with cystic fibrosis has risen, and expectancy is expected to continue to increase to about 40 to 50 years on average for infants born in the early twenty-first century (Doull, 2001). Could the incidence rate of cystic fibrosis increase because the recessive gene that causes the disease may increase in the general population now that homozygotes usually live to reproductive age? If any increase in disease incidence occurred at all, it would do so at a very slow rate because the odds of recessive alleles combining in a single individual remain quite low unless allele frequencies rise markedly.

An interesting theory suggests that the allele for cystic fibrosis actually arose as an adaptation, because heterozygotes may be more resistant to such bacterial-caused infectious diseases as cholera and/or salmonella (Dean et al. 2002). Thus, cystic fibrosis may be the unfortunate outcome of a balanced polymorphism, similar to the explanation for high rates of sickle-cell disease in some populations. If this is the case, selection for the cystic fibrosis recessive allele may actually be decreasing because of the availability of antibiotics to combat bacterial diseases and thus reduce the relative fitness of heterozygotes.

MAGNITUDE OF THE PROBLEM. Does the hypothesized reduced selection against these diseases with some genetic base lead to marked increases in the allele frequencies of the defective genes? Does the allele frequency change lead to significant increases in disease prevalence? The answers to these questions depend on the heritability of the diseases, the degree to which modern medicine reduces their effects, whether the alleles have dominant or recessive effects, and the allele frequencies of the defective genes. However, in general the increase in frequency over time would be quite slow, particularly for recessive alleles (Cavalli-Sforza and Bodmer 1971).

Does it matter? This depends upon our ability to handle the symptoms of the problem in those with defective genes. For minor annoyances, such as low myopia, it matters little, if at all. For diseases such as cystic fibrosis, where individuals face lowered life expectancy and a life made difficult by sometimes invasive treatments and anxiety over susceptibility to respiratory infections, increased disease frequency does have significance. We can only hope that advances in medical care will lead to cystic fibrosis becoming much more like PKU, where a relatively simple intervention can eliminate the disease's ill effects.

One can take an even longer view and find a positive effect of reduced selection. The ability of a species to adapt evolutionarily to future conditions is based in part on the degree of genetic variability present in the species. Species with very little genetic variability may not have the ability to respond evolutionarily to a rapid environmental change. This is seen in the vulnerability to extinction for species that have lost genetic variability due to small population size, either presently or in the past (a genetic bottleneck). Reduced selection *increases* the amount of genetic variability. Perhaps these variants, which yield suboptimal phenotypes in today's circumstances, would actually be the individuals who could survive in a changed future environment. A current example that provides perspective is the previously discussed sickle-cell trait. This genetic trait is a negative condition for those living in many parts of the world because homozygotes develop a serious anemia that can be fatal. In an environment where malaria is a major source of misery and death, those heterozygous for the sickle-cell trait are resistant to malaria, and thus much more likely to survive and reproduce. A genetic "defect" must be seen as a conditional entity: the perceived defect lies in the nature of the "fit" between the gene and the environment. More diverse genomes may allow survival in more variable or rapidly changing environments, and hence reduced selection may actually benefit the evolutionary health of our species.

One can also argue whether there actually is reduced selection acting upon modern humans. Species adapt to their environments, and selection usually increases when environmental change occurs. Since the human environment is primarily a cultural one, and culture change is occurring faster now than ever before in human history, one can argue that selective forces on our species are actually *increasing*. Whether selection is increasing or decreasing, it is certain that these selective forces are *changing*, and this will lead to biological changes over the long term.

GENETIC ENGINEERING. Perhaps the ultimate behavioral intervention in our evolutionary process is the ability to actually change our genes or those of our offspring. This, like eugenics, is a controversial subject. Do humans have the ethical right to intervene in the natural process of reproduction, creating Frankenstein-like monsters to fit our whims? Is there a brave new world in the future where we create humans geared to certain jobs, from a servant class to a supercharged athletic breed, that are designed in laboratories? If this scenario seems outrageous, how about circumstances where gene therapy changes a fetus's allele from one that will lead to cystic fibrosis to one where the phenotype will be "normal"? What is the dividing line in determining what is ethical? For that matter, what is the dividing line for determining what is normal? Like much in life, no simple answers present themselves. Clearly, having those in power decide who can reproduce, no matter how noble their intent may be, is abominable.

GENERAL STRESS

Humans confront specific environmental stresses in many ways, from mounting immune responses to infection, shivering in the cold, sweating in the heat, and hyperventilating in response to hypoxic conditions. Along with these specific responses to stress, we also exhibit general responses that occur no matter what the specific circumstances are. These general responses often occur before the actual stress is felt; that is, they are anticipatory, allowing the individual to prepare for the coming challenge.

The Nature of General Stress

STRESS DEFINED. Stress has been variously defined as a condition of the environment that challenges the individual to adapt (a "stimulus," in psychological parlance) or as the condition of the person in reaction to the environment (a "response"). Actually, general stress is best conceived as neither stimulus nor response, but as a "mediating variable" that connects given environmental stimuli with behavioral and biological responses. Hans Selye, who did much of the pioneering research on stress, has defined general stress as the nonspecific demand on the body for adaptive activity (Selye 1973). This adaptive activity may be behavioral, biological, or both. General stress is a cognitive process in which the brain interprets circumstances as either potentially stressful (adaptive activity required) or not. It is the cognitive process that recognizes a need for adaptation that constitutes general stress.

STRESS THEORIES. A number of theories have been formulated to explain how the brain recognizes circumstances as requiring adaptive activity. Many theories highlight perceived threat as the main component of general stress, with the threat being something that can potentially disrupt the body's **homeostasis** (the constancy of the body's internal conditions). For instance, Lazarus (1966; 1993) states that stress is defined by circumstances where there is a perceived threat that cannot be coped with routinely. This involves two types of cognition: recognition of threat and understanding of the normal coping response repertoires. For instance, if one steps into a crosswalk on a city street and then sees a truck coming, one simultaneously evaluates whether the truck is a threat (definitely) and whether it can be coped with routinely (depends on the truck's distance and speed, and the individual's walking speed, among other variables). A stress is present if the truck is close by and moving so quickly that the individual perceives that he or she cannot easily get out of its way.

People react to circumstances as if they are stressful even though they are unlikely to cause a direct problem for physiological homeostasis. For example, a reprimand from one's boss may be deemed stressful, as it could lead to a loss of job and hence needed resources (and thus indirectly lead to homeostatic challenges). A student taking a standardized test or an oral examination similarly is in what is only indirectly a biological threat, if one imagines that flunking will lead to a loss of opportunities for a high-paying job that will secure necessary resources. Clearly, humans have developed the ability to make complex computations of risk, and this permits assessment of a wide assortment of situations as having possible bad consequences. Using Lazarus's stress theory, one can see that both the perception of the threat and of one's coping ability are largely culturally determined. Therefore, different individuals react quite variably to the same circumstances.

THE SYSTEMIC GENERAL STRESS RESPONSE. While any number of stimuli can trigger a general stress determination, all people share a similar response to that determination. The biological response consists of increased activity in two major physiological systems, or axes: the hypothalamus-pituitary-adrenal–cortex (HPA) axis and the sympathetic nervous system-adrenal medullary (SAM) axis. Both systems are triggered by cognitive areas of the cerebral cortex that stimulate areas of the brain stem, including the rostral ventrolateral medulla (RVLM), the locus coerulus, the hypothalamus, and the amygdala. These areas in the brain stem release neurotransmitters such as norepinephrine, corticotropin-releasing factor, and arginine vasopressin. Interestingly, the neurons that release these different neurochemicals stimulate each other, leading to a physiological response that is generally common to all stress determinations (Chrousos and Gold 1992; Calogero et al. 1988; Charmandari et al. 2003). These responses are sometimes termed the "alarm reaction," and they take place soon after stress is appraised by the brain. In sum, a host of different circumstances may trigger a stress response, but the initial biological response is virtually (but not entirely) the same, no matter what the stimulating circumstances might be.

THE HYPOTHALAMUS PITUITARY ADRENAL (HPA) AXIS. In a stress response, the brain's hypothalamus releases corticotropin-releasing factor, which stimulates the pituitary gland to release adrenocorticotropic hormone (ACTH). This hormone stimulates the cortex of the adrenal gland to

POLLUTION: THE FOULING OF THE ENVIRONMENT

A final factor associated with modern environments to be discussed here is the increase in pollution: of the air, water, and land. Our concern here is not so much the eyesores and loss of habitat for wildlife that ensue from pollution, but its potential biological effect on humans. Pollution can be defined as a resource that is out of place in the environment (Kormondy and Brown 1998); it is a relative concept in that one organism's resource can be pollution to another. For instance, oxygen is a by-product of photosynthesis. This represents a life-giving resource to humans, but a dangerous pollutant to obligate anaerobic bacteria.

Air Pollution

While modernized environments are noted for air pollution, this is also found in many traditional settings. In fact, both natural and human-generated air pollution were present before modern *Homo sapiens* evolved.

SMOKE. One of the most prevalent forms of air pollution is smoke. This pollutant is concentrated in human homes due to heating or cooking activities. There is considerable evidence that exposure to wood smoke in traditional societies increases respiratory disease rates in children (Anderson 1978; Pandey et al. 1989; Morris et al. 1990; Collings et al. 1990; Naeher et al. 2007). Increased lung cancer rates have been associated with use of coal-burning stoves in Shenyang, China (Xu et al. 1989).

SMOG. Smog (a combination of smoke and fog) is a more recent form of pollution, and is associated with the burning of fossil fuels such as coal (Figure 13-7). A newer form of smog is the photochemical fog that results from reactions caused by sunlight acting on air pollutants that are usually associated with automobile exhaust. Smog is primarily an urban affliction, with London and Los Angeles particularly noted for high levels. There have been acute instances of smog that have led to

FIGURE 13-7 Urban smog.

widespread mortality, such as the approximately 5,000 deaths that occurred during the smog disaster of December 1952 in England (Greenwood and Edwards 1973). In the United States, 20 people died during a two-day period in Donora, Pennsylvania, during an acute smog episode in late October 1948 (Owen and Chiras 1995).

CHEMICALS IN AIR POLLUTION. Many potentially harmful chemicals have been identified as being common in air pollution. These include carbon monoxide, sulfur oxides, nitrogen oxides, ozone, and hydrocarbons. Carbon monoxide is a particularly toxic chemical, as it combines strongly with hemoglobin, preventing oxygen molecules from binding. Sulfur and nitrogen oxides can have serious respiratory effects, including causing or exacerbating asthma and emphysema (Schwela 2000). Ozone also has serious respiratory effects (Menzel 1984) and also negatively affects the immune system.

PARTICULATES IN AIR POLLUTION. Another major cause for concern in air pollution is the presence of particles, whether of solids or liquid droplets (aerosols). These particles may be ash, tiny pieces of metal, or other materials. Particulates are usually characterized by size, such as PM-10, which refers to particles less than 10 microns (thousandths of a millimeter) in diameter, or PM-2.5, which refers to particles smaller than 2.5 microns. Smaller particles may have greater health effects (Stolzel et al. 2006), perhaps in part because they are more easily inhaled deeper into respiratory passages.

THE HEALTH EFFECTS OF AIR POLLUTION. As noted, many forms of air pollution have been linked to respiratory illness. Asthma frequency has risen significantly in both children and adults. Part of this rise may be due to chronic exposure to air pollution. Other explanations for the increased incidence of asthma exist, including the "hygiene hypothesis" that states that reduced exposure to parasites, as is the case in many modernized settings, leads to heightened immune responses from T-helper 2 (Th2) cells, and this in turn leads to increased rates of allergies, which can trigger asthma (Pollard 2008).

There is also concern that air pollution can cause lung cancer. For example, one study examined mortality rates in six U.S. cities and found that those cities with high air-pollution levels had higher mortality rates from respiratory diseases, including lung cancer (Dockery et al. 1993). There are many forms of air pollution that often occur simultaneously, and this makes it difficult to single out specific causes of the high mortality. There is one form of air pollution whose health effects are indisputably negative: cigarette smoke. Cigarette smoking is considered the single most important cause of preventable mortality in the United States (Bloom 1988). This is a danger not only to smokers, but to those around them, as the effects of secondhand smoke have become recognized (Yuan et al. 2007; Hackshaw et al. 1997).

While populations as a whole are often exposed to air pollution in a given region, there is often an uneven exposure for individuals. The poor often cannot avoid exposure to various forms of air pollution, either in their residences or in their workplaces. Wealthier people, in contrast, can choose less polluted areas in which to reside and work.

Water Pollution

Like air pollution, water pollution can cause health problems for humans. As discussed earlier, infectious diseases can be spread through water-borne pathogens due to poor sanitation. Illnesses can also be caused by chemicals found in modernized settings (Figure 13-8). Industrial wastes can seep into both freshwater and marine environments, including gasoline that leaks out of corroded storage tanks (Owen and Chiras 1995).

AGRICULTURAL SOURCES OF WATER POLLUTION. Besides industrial wastes, agricultural pollutants can degrade the water supply. Fertilizers, pesticides, and herbicides—all derived from fossil fuels—can seep into reservoirs that supply humans with drinking water. Exposure to pesticides and

The genetic basis of susceptibility to ill health from exposure to pollutants, including cancer risk, is not a simple one. There have been specific alleles linked to diseases associated with specific chemicals, but the list of chemicals, and possible alleles, is a long one (Nebert 2005). Many of the traits are likely to involve many genes that have variable penetrance. What is of interest to human biologists is that when the pollution-based diseases affect reproductive rate (for instance, as in childhood cancers), natural selection for individuals who can better handle pollutants may ensue. While we may conjure up future humans who can handle foul air and water, one can also propose that a better solution to the issue would be to clean up the environment.

CONCLUSION

The challenges facing humans today from "diseases of modernization" such as cancer, heart disease, and diabetes suggest that our complex technology has not ended our need to cope with our environment. What we have done is to change the environment to which we must adapt. This conceivably places new selective pressures on our species, with people who are genetically more sensitive to pollution, stress, physical inactivity, or overnutrition potentially less able to have reproductive success than others. However, we are adapting to a moving target. Our environment changes at an ever-accelerating rate, and thus the selective forces acting upon *Homo sapiens* are also changing rapidly.

CHAPTER SUMMARY

Humans are confronted with a new set of challenges in the modern environment, and these challenges affect health, mortality, and reproductive success. The genetic and behavioral adaptations that served humanity for thousands of years are often ill-suited to today's world. It has been suggested that modernization has reduced selective pressure on our species, and this has resulted in an increase in the frequencies of alleles that previously would have been eliminated by natural selection. Several conditions, from minor conditions such as myopia to more serious illnesses such as type 1 diabetes and cystic fibrosis, may have increased as a result of this relaxed selection. However, it is unclear if selection has been reduced, or whether the form of selection has simply changed, due to living in modern environments. The increase in disease rates may actually be due more to a changed environment than to changes in genetic susceptibility.

People in modern environments may be exposed to greater levels of general stress, stemming from the varied stimuli with which they are confronted daily. Exposure to novel circumstances causes general stress reactions, and therefore people who are frequently exposed to novelty, such as those who are experiencing rapid culture change, often undergo high stress levels. Stress has been implicated as a factor in increasing rates of several serious diseases, including hypertension and heart disease.

Modern environments are also notable for promoting high rates of obesity and the diseases related to the metabolic syndrome, such as type 2 diabetes and heart disease. People in modern settings enjoy a greater availability of calorie-rich food and the ability to avoid doing much physical activity, and this combination has led to ever-increasing obesity rates. While environmental, including cultural, factors are the major cause of increased obesity, there are also genetic contributions to obesity risk in individuals, and perhaps also in populations. The complexity of obesity causation makes it unclear whether, or to what degree, population differences in rates of obesity and its harmful effects are due to a thrifty genotype or other genetic causes.

Another challenge of modern environments is increased pollution levels. This increase is caused both by higher population density and by technological changes associated with modernity. Air pollution from smoke, smog, or other sources of chemicals and particulates are distributed unevenly in the environment, often affecting poor people more than others, and this can have deleterious effects on health, particularly increasing the amount and severity of lung diseases. Water pollution is also unevenly distributed, often affects those in poverty more than others, and has adverse health effects. Solid-waste pollution is also implicated in disease causation. Besides differences in amount of exposure to pollution, individuals differ in their genetically based sensitivity to its effects.

Studying the problems of human adaptation to modern environments, including scrutiny of the causes and effects of these modern ills, will enable better strategies for ameliorating these problems. While genetics affects people's susceptibility or sensitivity to the modern environment, it is the human ability to change the microenvironment that will allow solutions to these problems. The sheer rapidity of environmental change in current times presents an adaptive challenge, because the corrections we make may be obsolete before they can be accomplished.

with funders, colleagues, persons studied or providing information, and with relevant parties affected by the research. Researchers must expect to utilize the results of their work in an appropriate fashion and disseminate the results through appropriate and timely activities. (Code of Ethics of the American Anthropological Association, 1998, http://www.aaanet.org/committees/ethics/ethcode.htm)

The AAA's Code of Ethics further states that an anthropologist's obligations to the people they study and work with may supersede the goal of gaining new knowledge. Anthropologists are responsible for communicating well with the people they study, for enhancing mutual understanding of possible research effects and of the wishes of the community, and for honoring their wishes to either be kept anonymous or to receive recognition. At the same time, anthropologists must also uphold high ethical standards in the scientific work that they present. It is understood that the competing obligations of the anthropologist will lead to "ethical dilemmas at every stage of their work, and [they] must make good-faith efforts to identify potential ethical claims and conflicts in advance when preparing proposals and as projects proceed" (Code of Ethics of the American Anthropological Association, 1998, http://www.aaanet.org/committees/ethics/ethcode.htm). This code of ethics applies to human biologists as well, whether their home academic discipline is anthropology or another field such as epidemiology, biology, or medicine.

HETEROGENEITY OF CULTURE AND OF COMMUNITIES. In making ethical decisions, human biologists must recognize that communities are not a single, monolithic entity. People within a given community differ considerably in their behavior, beliefs, values, and biology. This makes ethical decisions even more complicated, because it will be difficult in many cases to get unanimity from a group in their attitudes towards research activities. For a newcomer to a community, such as a human biology researcher, it will be very hard to understand the community's diversity of opinions, but it would be paternalistic to attempt to make the "right" decisions for that community. Therefore, what is critical for ethical research is to attempt to do no harm, to practice "full disclosure and informed consent, warnings of possible outcomes (good and bad) of the research for the people involved, and a careful weighing of the risks and benefits of the study for the people being studied" (American Anthropological Association Commission, 1995).

WHAT IS NORMAL?

The idea of normality is odd in some ways, as it simultaneously involves what philosophers term a normative judgement, that is, a judgement of correctness or rightness such as a moral judgement, and a statistical judgement, which involves judging frequency within a population. A "normal" trait is therefore both *common* (frequent or average) and *correct* (adaptive or healthy). In common usage, the term "normal" assumes that what is frequent is also good. There are many examples where this is not the case, including the existence of dental caries, which are very common in modern populations but not considered to be a good thing to possess.

Anthropology is the study of human variability in biology, behavior, and language, in the present and over time. Anthropologists have often focused their study on normality, focusing on accepted norms of behavior and biology. Anthropologists have examined how various societies have defined what is normal in different ways from other cultural groups. These conflicting definitions result in a given behavior being regarded as normal in one culture, and abnormal in another (Benedict 1934). All cultures contain, and accept, differing degrees of behavioral and biological diversity within the group, but they all also set bounds on what they accept as normal.

Similarly, human biologists have often focused their attention on the normal range of biological characteristics in our species, as opposed to pathological or other abnormal conditions. Human biologists are more likely to seek objective ("scientific") boundaries for normality than do cultural anthropologists, who typically assume that there are no objective standards for normality and therefore rely on subjective evaluations by people who make up the communities in which they work. Do such objective criteria exist? One area of interest where such objective criteria are often assumed to exist is in the distinction between health (or normality) and disease (or abnormality).

HEALTH AS NORMALITY. An example of the challenge of defining normality in some objective manner comes in attempts to define health-related conditions, with disease seen as abnormality. The term "illness" is typically used to define conditions that are subjectively defined by members of a community as deviating from a healthy state. The states of health and disease are commonly seen as being defined by objective criteria, but definitions for the two, as found in many dictionaries, are often tautological: health is defined as the absence of disease, and disease is defined as the absence of health. These definitions provide no means to make the distinction.

Another way to define disease is as an abnormal condition that is not present in the majority of a population. Here, the definition hinges on commonality. A clear counterexample of the commonality definition for health occurs in Egypt. After the building of the Aswan Dam, standing water led to a proliferation of snail vectors of the parasitic disease schistosomiasis. By the mid-1960s, over 50 percent of the population in some regions of Egypt was infected with the parasite. Does this mean that in these communities people with *no* parasites were "diseased" while those *with* parasites were "healthy"? Are people with the parasite "normal" and those lacking it "abnormal"?

There are instances when determination of health versus disease is clearly arbitrary. For example, there is a range between individuals of average resting blood pressure values, and it has become common to define systolic blood pressure values consistently over 140 mm Hg, or diastolic blood pressure values over 90 mm Hg, as constituting hypertension. Thus, an individual with a blood pressure of 140/90 is hypertensive (or "abnormal"), while someone with a blood pressure of 139/89 is healthy (or "normal"). In the 1950s, normal blood pressure was defined as within two standard deviations of the average blood pressure for one's age; this meant that for a 70-year-old person, normal blood pressure could include a value of 170/110, a value that would be seen today as indicative of hypertension, and therefore abnormal. Also, a new condition, termed "pre-hypertension," has been defined, including individuals with blood pressures above 120/80 but below 140/90 (Chobanian et al. 2003). Are pre-hypertensives abnormal?

BIOLOGICAL CHARACTERISTICS AND NORMALITY. Other characteristics besides health versus disease challenge our idea of normality. Is myopia (near-sightedness) outside the range of biological normality? How about having one hemoglobin allele for sickle cell, and thus being heterozygous for an abnormal gene? There are individuals with hydrocephaly (a condition where pressure from excess fluid in the brain often leads to destruction of much of the brain's tissue) who are functionally and intellectually normal despite brain-tissue loss (Lewin 1980), apparently thanks to developmental plasticity. As technology changes, attitudes about what constitutes normality may change as well. Changing definitions of normality apparently reflect what characteristics are fashionable at a given time (Amundson 2000).

ETHICS AND NOTIONS OF NORMALITY. A real concern is that definitions of normality can have negative effects on those defined as "abnormal." While individuals confined to wheelchairs for mobility are not necessarily blamed for their condition, characterizing them as "abnormal" may stigmatize them. Thus, the human biologist must carefully consider the value of some arbitrary distinction about normality and the possible ethical implications of this categorization.

The labeling of disabilities as "abnormal" has had negative consequences. The Disability Rights movement began during the 1970s and resulted in the 1990 passage in the United States of the Americans with Disabilities Act. The viewpoint of this movement challenged entrenched judgements of normality. It was argued that labels of "normal" and "abnormal" had been used to justify discrimination against certain groups of citizens. The labeling of wheelchair use as "abnormal" justified the construction of sidewalks and public buildings that were inaccessible to wheelchair users. The labeling of deaf people as "abnormal" justified television broadcasts without captioning, which made them inaccessible to the deaf. Even though most people believe that wheelchair use and deafness are maladaptive, the disability rights advocates claim that the "badness" of those and other disabilities comes more from social discrimination than from physical impairments themselves. Confinement to wheelchairs and deafness can generally be coped with when the environment is accessible to the disabled person. Disability-rights advocates therefore claim that the label "normal" has been used to segregate people with varying abilities and should be abandoned. Discrimination on the basis of normality should be no more justified than discrimination on the basis of sex or ethnicity.

VARIATION IS NATURAL. Evolutionary theory views biological diversity as a resource for natural selection, and thus variability in many cases is an evolutionary boon. This provides a reasonable justification for an ethic that values the wonderful diversity of our species.

CHAPTER SUMMARY

What will people look like in the future? It is impossible to be sure, but consideration of evolutionary principles and examination of current trends allow reasonable conjectures. Common conceptions of what individuals will look like in the distant future are often based upon projections of the evolutionary trends that have occurred in the past few hundred thousand years, with the major trend that of pedomorphism, including an enlarged brain. Other possible changes could include increased genetic variability both from natural means and from artificial manipulation of our genome. On the population level, improved transportation increases the amount of contact between people born in distant places, and this leads to greater genetic admixture. This greater admixture will lead to greater genetic variability within populations but less variation between populations.

Human population biology is an exciting field that allows us to understand ourselves as humans from a broad perspective. Human biologists have a responsibility to undertake their research in an ethical manner that does not harm the people they study, either directly or indirectly. Research participants must be fully informed about the research in which they will be involved and about any research implications that may affect them. Concern must be given not only to individuals, but to communities as a whole, to insure that research results do not provide fodder for misuse or prejudice. Human biologists often team with community members in the formulation and carrying out of research projects that have value to the participants.

Anthropologists and human biologists often focus their research on the study of normal variation present in our species as a whole and in the groups of people that make up our species. However, determination of what is "normal" is not an objective undertaking. Normality is a culturally constructed concept that differs in varying settings and changes over time. Human biologists should therefore concern themselves with the entire range of human biological variation.

GLOSSARY

Acclimatization – A form of phenotypic plasticity that enables an individual organism to accommodate to a complex of environmental factors.

Adaptation – A structure, function, or behavior of an organism that helps it survive and reproduce.

Adaptive immunity – The part of the body's immune system that is directed toward specific antigens.

Adaptive radiation – The rapid cladogenesis of a species into many descendent species.

Adiposity – The amount of body fat an individual possesses.

Adolescent growth spurt – A period of rapid growth that occurs around the time of puberty.

Aerobic capacity – The highest rate by which an organism can use oxygen to drive metabolism.

Aging – Increasing age; time passage from birth or conception.

Albinism – A characteristic of many mammals, including humans, in which a genetic mutation results in the inability to produce melanin pigment, thus resulting in individuals with very light skin and hair color.

Allele – The specific gene type, defined by a particular sequence of DNA nucleotides, found at a genetic locus; one of a pair of genes found at a specific genetic locus.

Allele frequency – Within a biological population, the proportion of alleles of a specific type at a given genetic locus.

Allen's rule – The idea that, within a warm-blooded species that is spread over a large geographic area, populations in colder climates tend to have shorter limbs, hence having a lower surface-area-to-volume ratio.

Allopatric speciation – A type of speciation in which new species are formed in a process where populations are geographically isolated from each other.

Alveoli – Tiny sacs in the lung where air diffuses from the lung to the blood.

Amenorrhea – The cessation of menses in women during the reproductive stage of life.

Amino Acid – A type of organic molecule that contains both an amine and an acid chemical group; amino acids form the basic structural unit of proteins.

Anagen – Growth phase of the hair cycle.

Anagenesis – A form of speciation in which a single ancestral species is transformed into one new species over time.

Analogous structures – Anatomical traits that are similar in different species due to functional necessity as opposed to shared evolutionary ancestry.

Andropause – Time in a man's life cycle when a reduction in testosterone production may lead to development of a host of symptoms, including sexual dysfunction and depression.

Anemia – A deficiency of hemoglobin.

Anorexia nervosa – A psychiatric eating disorder characterized by very low body weight and a distorted body image.

Anthropoids – The taxonomic grouping of primates that includes monkeys, apes, and humans.

Anthropological linguistics – The subfield of anthropology that studies language and its relation to other aspects of culture.

Anthropology – The study of human variation in behavior and biology, both in the present and through time.

Anthropometry – The measurement of human body size and proportions.

Antibody – A class of proteins that neutralizes potentially harmful molecules in the body.

Antigen – A molecule that triggers the body's immune response, particularly an antibody response.

Antigenic drift – Minor year-to-year changes over time in the influenza virus's DNA through mutation and selection.

Antigenic shift – A major, rapid change in the influenza virus's DNA that make it resistant to human immune defenses.

Antiserum – A liquid fraction of blood that contains antibodies obtained from exposure to antigens.

Apoptosis – The process of programmed cell death found in multicellular organisms.

Archaeology – The subfield of anthropology that studies past societies through examination of the material culture left behind.

Ardipithecus – A genus of early hominids that dates back earlier than five million years ago.

Arteriosclerosis – Condition in which arterial blood vessel walls "harden" and become brittle.

Ascaris – A genus of parasitic worm that causes disease in humans throughout the world.

Assortative mating – Non-random patterns of mating within a population, such that individuals with a given allele are either more or less likely to mate with an individual with the same allele.

Atherosclerosis – Plaque growth in arterial blood vessels that can lead to a disruption in blood flow.

Atresia – The process by which egg follicles degenerate.

Australopithecus – A genus of early hominids that contains diverse species, dating from about 1.5 to four million years ago.

Austronesian languages – A large group of related languages spoken in many Pacific island populations; the languages are thought to be descended from that spoken by a group of people who entered the Pacific region within the past 4,000 years.

Autophagy – Literally, "self-feeding"; refers to the degradation of a portion of the cell's contents, usually by enzymatic processes in the lysosome.

Auxology – The multidisciplinary study of human –physical growth.

Balanced polymorphism – A set of alleles at a locus for which the heterozygote is selected, thus establishing an equilibrium in allele frequency.

Basal metabolic rate – The amount of energy expended in a given time period by an individual while at rest.

Bergmann's rule – The idea that, within a warm-blooded species that is spread over a large geographic area, populations in colder climates tend to have larger body size.

Beriberi – A vitamin-deficiency disease caused by low levels of thiamine that involves an inability to properly metabolize carbohydrates.

Biogeography – The study of the spatial distribution of living organisms around the world.

Biological anthropology – The subfield of anthropology that studies human biological variation, both in space and time.

Biome – A major type of ecosystem with a characteristic set of environmental conditions to which the community of species that dwells in it must adapt. Examples of biomes are: deserts, rain forests, grasslands, arctic tundra, and so forth.

Biotic potential – A species's maximum reproductive capacity, expressed as a rate.

Bipedalism – Form of locomotion involving walking with a striding gait on only the hind limbs; a characteristic of hominids.

Body-mass index – The ratio of weight in kilograms to stature in meters; it is used as an estimate of adiposity in population studies.

Canalization (of growth) – Process of growth that is highly structured, with changes occurring in narrowly circumscribed "channels" of allowable development.

Cancer – A term that encompasses diseases due to the uncontrolled growth of body cells in a multicellular organism.

Carbohydrates – A form of nutrient made up of carbon, oxygen, and hydrogen and consisting of sugars and starches, forming the basic source of food energy for organisms.

Cardiovascular disease – Disorders of the heart and circulatory system, including heart disease, hypertension, and stroke.

Carrying capacity – The maximum population size of a species that a particular environment can support.

Case-fatality rate – The measurement of the rate at which patients die from a particular disease.

Catagen – Regression phase of the hair cycle.

Catch-up growth – A period of accelerated growth that ensues after a growth disruption.

Centenarians – Individuals who are aged 100 years or older.

Centromere – A portion of a chromosome, usually in or near the center, where mitotic or meiotic spindles attach.

Cephalic index – The ratio of head breadth to head length; this was once thought to be a relatively stable, genetically based trait, but the ratio has been shown to change in the children of migrants.

Chiasmata – The site where homologous chromosomes intersect during meiosis, allowing crossing over of alleles from one chromosome to the other.

Chloroplasts – Organelles found in plant cells that carry chlorophyll and where photosynthesis occurs.

Cholera – An acute bacterial disease that is passed through polluted water and causes diarrhea and dehydration in its host.

Chondrichthyes – Class of cartilaginous fish that includes sharks and rays.

Chromatin – A dispersed form of chromosome, composed of a strand of DNA and associated proteins, found in the nucleus of eukaryotic cells.

Chromosome – A long thread of DNA and associated proteins that is found in the nucleus of eukaryotic organisms.

Cladism – A type of biological taxonomy that strictly reflects biological ancestry.

Cladogenesis – A type of speciation in which one ancestral species splits into two new species.

Class – In taxonomy, a group of related orders that share a common ancestor.

Cline – A distribution of some characteristic that varies in a continuous gradient over a geographic area.

Coevolution – A process in which evolutionary changes in one species affect the evolutionary forces acting on one or more other species.

Cold-induced vasodilatation (CIVD) – Dilation of peripheral blood vessels during exposure to cold.

Core – In thermoregulation, the internal area of the head and trunk that has a narrow tolerance for temperature fluctuation.

Cori cycle – A chemical process in which energy from fat is used to synthesize sugars from lactate in the liver, and the sugars are then used as an energy source in muscles through their breakdown into lactate.

Cortisol – A steroid hormone produced by the cortex of the adrenal gland; it is secreted during a general stress response.

Counter-current heat exchange – Transfer of heat between arteries and veins that warms venous blood that has cooled in peripheral areas.

Countershading – A trait found in many fish, whereby the top portion of the animal is dark colored and the bottom portion is light colored; this is an adaptation that makes it more difficult for potential predators to see the fish.

Creationism – The belief that living organisms were created by a deity in their present form, and that evolutionary processes, if present at all, act only below the species level.

Crossing over – The process in which there is physical switching of parts of DNA strands between homologous chromosomes during meiosis.

Cross-sectional study – Study carried out during a single time period, as opposed to a longitudinal study, which follows changes over time.

Cultural anthropology – The subfield of anthropology that studies variation in culture throughout the world, both in the present and in the recent past.

Culture – An organized set of learned behaviors and conventional understandings that characterize human societies.

Cystic fibrosis – A disease in which a recessive genetic defect leads to an impaired ability to transport chloride and other ions across the cell membrane.

Cytoskeleton – A structure within cells that provides scaffolding for the cell and its processes.

Darwin's theory of evolution – A scientific theory for how evolution occurs, with competition between varieties leading to natural selection of those individuals best able to survive and reproduce, passing their adaptive traits to descendants.

Decline, Idea of – The notion that circumstances invariably get worse as time passes; refers both to the human condition and to the world in general.

Deep time – The idea that time stretches far back into the past for billions of years.

Demography – The study of human population size, distribution, and structure, and how these change over time.

Dental caries – A disease in which dental structure is damaged, commonly referred to as tooth decay or cavities.

Dermatoglyphics – The study of variations in the skin ridges that form finger, palm, and sole prints.

Diaphysis – The shaft portion of a long bone.

Diffusion – Movement of fluid (liquid or gas) from an area of high to low concentration.

Directional selection – A form of natural selection in which organisms at one end of a phenotypic distribution have less reproductive success, leading to a change in the phenotypic distribution over time; or a change in allele frequencies such that the proportion of one allele increases in comparison with another allele at the same locus.

Diversifying selection – A form of natural selection in which organisms at the middle portion of a phenotypic distribution have less reproductive success, leading to an increase in the proportion of individuals at either end of the distribution.

DNA – Deoxyribonucleic acid; the chemical that makes up the genetic information contained in living organisms. DNA is composed of a linked chain of sugars, phosphate groups, and nucleotide bases.

DNA chips – A matrix composed of many specific oligonucleotides attached to a square of silicon to form a matrix that can be used to identify specific variant sequences of DNA.

Dominance, Principle of – One of the principles of Mendelian genetics: for a pair of alleles at a single locus, the biological effect of only one of the pair is dominant over the other, and thus appears in the organism's phenotype.

Doubling time – The amount of time a population takes to increase its size by a factor of two.

Eccrine sweat gland – Structure found in the skin that produces a salty water solution that constitutes perspiration.

Ectoderm – The outermost of the three embryonic germ layers.

Embryo – An individual organism soon after conception, once development allows distinguishing head from tail; in humans, the embryonic period is from approximately three to eight weeks after conception.

Endoderm – The innermost of the three embryonic germ layers.

Endosymbiotic theory – An explanation for the origin of many of the organelles, such as mitochondria, found in eukaryotic cells, involving a past parasitic entry into the cell by a bacterium, and the bacterium's eventual transformation into a cell subunit.

Endurance – The ability to perform a given amount of work for long duration before fatigue sets in.

Energy balance – The balance between energy intake and energy expenditure, often measured in kilocalories; a positive energy balance means more energy is consumed than expended, and a negative energy balance means more energy is expended than consumed.

Environmental determinism – The belief that certain biological or behavioral traits are solely a result of the effects of an individual's environment.

Environmental physiology – The study of the adaptation of individual organisms to environmental change and stress.

Environmental resistance – The totality of environmental forces that limit a population's reproductive rate.

Enzyme – A protein that acts as a biochemical catalyst for reactions inside living organisms.

Epicanthic eyefolds – A fold in the eyelid found in individuals in many human populations that often covers corners of the eye.

Epidemiology – The study of the causes and distribution of disease in populations.

Epigenetics – The study of hereditable changes in gene function that occur without alteration of nucleotide sequences.

Epinephrine – A hormone produced by the medulla of the adrenal gland; it is secreted during general stress responses.

Epiphyses – The proximal and distal end segments of long bones.

Essential amino acids – The eight amino acids that humans cannot form from other amino acids: they must be present in the diet.

Essential resources – Materials that are required to support a group.

Estrogen – Reproductive hormone found particularly in females, responsible for the development and maintenance of female secondary sexual characteristics.

Ethnic group – a collection of people who share a common history, culture, or ancestry.

Ethnicity – Of or relating to ethnic-group affiliation.

Eugenics – The idea that human evolution can and should be directed by manipulation of reproduction, thereby changing the human genotype. Negative eugenics advocates limiting reproduction by some individuals, while positive eugenics advocates increasing reproduction by other individuals.

Eukaryotes – A major grouping of kinds of organisms whose cells contain nuclei and other organelles.

Euphenics – The idea that the human biological phenotype can be improved by changing the environment, particularly during development.

Evolution – The process by which populations of living organisms change over time.

Exon – The portion of messenger RNA that is used in coding for the sequence of amino acids during protein synthesis.

Extinction – The loss of a species in evolution. This usually refers to the loss of a species without issue; that is, the species has not left descendant species.

Family – In taxonomy, a group of related genera that share a common ancestor.

Fat – A form of nutrient that is insoluble in water, contains glycerol and fatty acids, and provides large amounts of metabolic energy for living organisms.

Fecundability – The likelihood that a fecund couple will conceive during a month during which unprotected intercourse takes place.

Fecundity – The biological capacity to reproduce.

Fertility – The number of offspring produced over a given period of time; the fertility rate of a human population is the number of live births per 1,000 women between the ages of 15 and 49.

Fetus – A period of development before birth; in the human organism the period from eight weeks after conception until birth.

Fontanels – Soft spots on an infant's cranium where ossification is incomplete that permit flexibility in the skull in order for the newborn to pass through the birth canal.

Food – What people, through their culture, recognize as acceptable sources of nutrients.

Forensic anthropologists – Scientists who study the dental and skeletal anatomy of humans and assist in identifying remains in criminal investigations.

Fossil – A physical vestige or remnant of an organism that lived in the past. Fossils may be formed from mineralized body parts, such as shells, bones and teeth, or from molds or casts of organisms or parts of organisms.

Founder effect – A change in allele frequencies in a newly established population, relative to an ancestral population, due to the chance of which individuals were part of the founding ancestors of the new population.

Ganglia – Small groupings of nerve cells.

Gene overexpression – The artificial creation of increased expression of specific alleles, usually caused by insertion into an individual of multiple copies of the allele.

Gene regulatory proteins – Molecules that bind to specific sites on DNA molecules and determine whether certain alleles are transcribed at a given time.

Genetic code – The sequence of nucleotides of messenger RNA, and ultimately of DNA, that codes for specific sequences of amino acids that are formed during protein synthesis.

Genetic drift – Changes in allele frequencies seen in natural populations from generation to generation in circumstances for which selective, mutational, and gene-flow effects are otherwise accounted.

Genetic load – The degree to which the average genetic fitness of a population is below the optimum, usually due to the presence of deleterious mutations.

Genetics – The study of inheritance of biological traits through the passing on of DNA, or in some viruses RNA, from parents to offspring.

Genome – The total genetic information found in an individual, population, or species.

Genotype – The genetic makeup of an individual in terms of specific alleles, or of the ordering of the nucleotide sequence in DNA.

Genotype frequency – Within a biological population, the proportion of combinations of paired alleles that are found at a given genetic locus.

Genotypic traits – Those characteristics of an individual that vary from other individuals due to simple genetic differences.

Genus – A group of related species that share a recent common ancestor.

Geographic isolation – A condition whereby populations within a species are spatially separated from each other.

Gloger's rule – Idea that there is a general tendency for darker-skinned peoples to be found nearer to the equator than light-skinned populations.

Glucose-6-phosphate dehydrogenase (G6PD) deficiency – A sex-linked trait in which people who are exposed to certain drugs or food products develop a temporary anemia due to the breakdown of hemoglobin; the condition is caused by a deficiency of an enzyme that is involved in glucose metabolism.

Goiter – An enlargement of the thyroid gland caused by low levels of dietary iodine.

Great Chain of Being – The notion that God created all possible entities and that these form a gradation from the most base (such as inorganic forms) to the most exalted (for example, angels), with humans occupying a central rank between earthly and heavenly entities.

Habitat – An area or environment in which a population is located.

Habituation – The process by which an organism becomes less responsive to a stimulus or stress.

Haplogroup – A collection of related haplotypes that share a common ancestor with a given SNP.

Haplotype – A combination of closely linked loci that function as a single unit for some purposes.

Hardy-Weinberg equilibrium – A mathematical formulation for computing allele frequencies from genotype frequencies and vice versa; the formulation assumes that no evolutionary change is occurring.

Harris lines – Lines on long bones that represent growth disruptions due to stress.

Heat shock proteins – Proteins that are produced by cells when under many kinds of stress.

Hemoglobin – A protein that is located in red blood cells and serves to carry oxygen from the lungs to the body's tissues.

Heritability – The degree to which a population's variability in some trait is determined by genetics. The Heritability Index is measured from 0 (no genetic contribution to the trait's variability) to 1 (all of the variability in the trait is accounted for by genetics).

Heterozygote – An organism with two different alleles at a given locus.

HIV (human immunodeficiency virus) – A retrovirus that causes AIDS (acquired immunodeficiency disease) in humans by infecting the victim's immune cells.

Homeostasis – The relative constancy of internal body conditions.

Hominids – The taxonomic family of primates that includes humans and all human ancestors descended from the common ancestor of humans and chimpanzees.

Hominoids – The taxonomic grouping of primates that includes the apes and humans.

Homo erectus – A species of human ancestor, dating back as early as 1.8 million years ago, that spread from Africa throughout much of the Old World.

Homo habilis – A species of early human that may have been the earliest toolmaker among the hominids.

Homo sapiens – The formal species name of modern humans.

Homologous structures – Anatomical or biochemical traits that are structurally similar in different organisms due to shared evolutionary ancestry.

Homoplasy – A similarity in characteristics of different species due to convergent evolution; the similarities are due to independent evolutionary events, not due to common ancestry.

Homozygote – An organism with two of the same alleles at a given locus.

Human adaptability – The flexibility of responses that permits humans to live successfully in disparate environments throughout the world; or the study of this flexibility.

Human population biology – A branch of biological anthropology that studies the biological diversity of contemporary humans, examining similarities and differences among humans, and among human groups.

Huntington's disease – A genetically based neurological disorder caused by a dominant allele.

Hybrid breakdown – The process by which descendants of an interspecies mating become steadily less viable over generations, often due to the poor coadaptation of different genes from the two ancestral species.

Hypertension – Chronically elevated blood pressure.

Hypoelectrolytemia – Condition caused by having deficient concentrations of sodium, potassium, and chloride in the body.

Hyponatremia – Condition caused by deficient concentrations of sodium in the body.

Hypoplasias – Areas of thinned enamel on teeth, present as irregular grooves or pits in the enamel surface, that demark periods of developmental disruptions due to stress.

Hypoxia – A condition of low oxygen availability.

Illness – A condition that is subjectively defined by members of a community as deviating from a healthy state.

Immune system – The parts of the body that function to detect and neutralize pathogens.

Imprinting (of DNA) – A chemical modification of a gene that affects whether or how it is expressed; these modifications can be inherited.

Incidence – The rate at which a disease or illness occurs among individuals in a population over a given time period.

Independent Assortment, Principle of – One of the principles of Mendelian genetics: whichever one of an allele pair at a locus goes into a gamete (through segregation) has no effect on which of *another* pair of alleles at a different locus will go into that gamete.

Infection – The colonization of a host organism by an invading and reproducing pathogen, causing harm to the host.

Infectivity – A pathogen's ability to establish an infection in a host.

Innate immunity – The portion of the body's immune system that is nonspecific, directed towards any pathogen; this is the initial immune response to contact with a pathogen.

Intelligence – The mental ability to acquire and apply knowledge.

Intelligent Design – The notion that certain features of the universe were purposefully created by an intelligent being as opposed to being formed by chance or natural processes.

Intrinsic rate of natural increase – The maximum specific growth rate of a species measured under ideal circumstances.

Intron – A portion of a messenger RNA molecule that is excised from the molecule before protein synthesis occurs and therefore is not used to code for the amino acid sequence of a protein. The corresponding sequence of nucleotides in the intron is also found in the DNA molecule.

IQ – The score on a test designed to measure intelligence, but which is affected by socioeconomic, ethnic, and cultural factors.

Key resources – Required materials that are expensive, rare, or simply difficult to acquire.

Kingdom – In taxonomy, a group of related phyla that share a common ancestor.

Kwashiorkor – A malnutrition disease usually found in recently weaned children that involves protein deficiency and results in muscle wasting, skin and hair discoloration, and edema, among other symptoms.

Lactation amenorrhea – Cessation of menses caused by breast feeding.

Lamarck's theory of evolution – A science-based theory of evolution that includes the notion that succeeding generations of organisms climb the Great Chain of Being based upon biological changes due to use and disuse of body parts, as well as upon the inheritance of acquired characteristics by descendants.

Life expectancy – The estimated remaining years of life for an individual of a given age based upon population averages.

Life tables – Tabulations of mortality rates by age group within a population.

Limiting factor – An environmental condition that places constraints either on a species's population size or on its range.

Linkage – The tendency for some alleles from different loci to be inherited together because they are found on the same chromosome.

Locus – The place on a chromosome where a specific gene type is found.

Longitudinal study – Research carried out over a given time span and incorporating multiple measurements over time.

Macroenvironment – The general environmental conditions in which a species lives.

Macroevolution – Process by which large-scale changes over time occur in the biology of organisms making up populations; these changes usually involve major structural alterations.

Malaria – Parasitic disease passed by mosquito vectors in which the pathogen attacks red blood cells.

Malnutrition – A condition due to a deficiency or excess in one or more essential nutrients in the diet or in the ability to process foods in the diet.

Mammals – The class of vertebrates that are characterized by mammary glands, hair or fur, and homeothermy, the ability to keep internal conditions relatively constant despite varying external temperatures.

Marasmus – A malnutrition disease of children that results from low levels of protein and calorie intake.

Maternal-fetal incompatability – A condition in which a genetic difference between a mother and her fetus can lead to an attack on the fetus by the mother's immune system.

Maximum life span – The maximum length of time that any individual of a given species can be expected to live.

Meiosis – The process by which gametes, or reproductive cells, are produced by division of a cell into four cells (gametes).

Melanesia – Regional grouping of Pacific islands stretching from New Guinea to Fiji, named due to the dark skin color of indigenous peoples on the islands.

Melanin – A dark pigment that provides the major aspect of skin and hair color in humans. It comes in two forms, eumelanin and phaeomelanin.

Melanocyte – Cells found in the skin that produce melanin pigment.

Melanosome – Vesicle found in skin cells that contains melanin pigment.

Menarche – The onset of menstruation, identified by the first menstrual period; it defines the onset of the reproductive stage in a woman's life.

Menopause – The end of menstruation, identified by the last menstrual period; it defines the conclusion of the reproductive stage in a woman's life.

Mesenchyme – Cells derived from the mesoderm that develop into bone and teeth.

Mesoderm – The middle layer of the three embryonic germ layers.

Messenger RNA – A form of ribonucleic acid that is transcribed from DNA and serves as the model from which amino acids are aligned in a specific order during protein synthesis.

Metabolic syndrome – A set of characteristics that are often associated with each other, including: obesity, a poor blood lipid profile, high blood pressure, high levels of generalized inflammation, and insulin resistance.

Microenvironment – The external conditions next to an organism's body; the organism's behavior can change its microenvironment.

Microevolution – Process by which small-scale changes over time occur in a population, such as can be explained by Mendelian genetics, short-term selection, or mutations.

Micronesia – Regional grouping of small Pacific islands and atolls located to the north of Melanesia.

Microsatellites – Repetitive sequences of DNA that are usually only two to three nucleotides long for each repeated sequence unit.

Mimicry – A type of adaptation in which individuals of one species duplicate the behavior and/or appearance of a different species of organism.

Minisatellites – Repetitive sequences of DNA that are from six to hundreds of nucleotides in length for each repeated sequence unit.

Mitochondria – Organelles in the cells of eukaryotic organisms where much of the cell metabolism occurs.

Mitosis – The process of cell division whereby a cell divides into two nearly identical cells.

Mitotic or meiotic spindles – Fibers that form during mitosis and meiosis and serve to pull apart homologous chromosomes into separate portions of the cell immediately prior to the cell dividing into two "daughter" cells.

Modernization – The process by which societies are transformed from a traditional lifestyle to a high technology, industrial-based lifestyle.

Molecular clock – The use of a quantitative measure of molecular differences between living species to estimate the time of speciation from a common ancestor of the two species.

Monogenists – Those who believe that modern humans form a single species. This notion was debated in the eighteenth century.

Mortality rate – The number of deaths in a population during a given time period; the infant mortality rate is defined as the number of deaths per 1,000 individuals between birth and one year of age in a given year.

Muscular strength – The maximal amount of force a muscle can exert.

Mutagens – Environmental agents that cause mutations.

Mutations – Errors in the structure of DNA such that nucleotide sequence differences occur due to the effects of environmental agents or to mistakes during either mitosis or meiosis. Mutations may be due to substitution, deletion, or insertion of nucleotides in a portion of DNA.

Myoglobin – A protein that binds to oxygen and functions to aid in the transport of oxygen from blood into tissues and to store oxygen within muscle tissue.

Myopia – The inability to focus one's vision properly on distant objects due to refractive errors in the eyes; nearsightedness.

Myxedema – Severe loss of thyroid function, often due to iodine deficiency, that leads to widespread edema.

Natural experiments – Research conducted where normal scientific protocols are impossible or unethical; studies are done by finding conditions in the natural world that provide a means for controlling factors, usually by comparisons of populations under different natural conditions.

Natural selection – The process by which adaptive traits predominate in biological populations due to a differential reproductive rate; natural selection forms the basis for evolutionary change.

Nature versus nurture – Refers to the debate over whether biological traits are due entirely to inheritance ("nature") or to environmental effects ("nurture"). Traits are now seen to result from both nature and nurture.

Neanderthals – A grouping, commonly thought to constitute a separate species, of archaic Homo sapiens.

Net reproductive rate – The average number of female offspring produced by each female in a population.

Neurotransmitters – Chemicals that are released at nerve endings to permit communication between nerve cells.

Niche – In ecology, the function of a population of organisms within an environmental area; how a type of organism obtains resources, finds mates, avoids predators, and otherwise adapts to its surroundings.

Nitric oxide – A chemical that induces vasodilation.

Non-shivering thermogenesis – An increase in metabolic rate that is not due to increased muscular activity, whether voluntary or involuntary, such as shivering.

Norepinephrine – A neurotransmitter that is produced in the brain and in the sympathetic nervous system; it is involved in general stress responses.

Normality – A condition that is both common and considered "proper" within a population.

Nucleic Acids – Forms of biochemicals made up of a repeated structure of subunits composed of nucleotide bases, sugars, and phosphates; nucleic acids are structural components of DNA and RNA.

Nucleotide base – Part of the subunits of nucleic acids; there are four forms of nucleotide bases, and the order in which they are arranged in a nucleic acid determines the molecule's function .

Nucleus – Organelle found in eukaryotic organisms where DNA is present and where transcription of messenger RNA from the DNA occurs.

Nutrients – Substances that provide nourishment required by our bodies for reproduction, function, and survival.

Obesity – Having excess body fat to the extent that health may be negatively affected; sometimes defined as having a BMI in excess of 30 kg/m^2.

Oligonucleotides – Short stretches of single-stranded DNA that are synthesized in laboratories.

Oncogenes – Alleles that increase the risk of developing cancer.

Order – In taxonomy, a group of related families that share a common ancestor.

Organelles – Structures found within the cells of eukaryotes that are associated with different functions. Organelles include the nucleus (where the DNA is located and where transcription takes place), and mitochondria (where much of the cell's aerobic metabolism occurs).

Osteichthyes – The taxonomic class of bony fish.

Osteoblasts – Specialized mesenchymal cells that form bone.

Benedict, R., 1934. Anthropology and the abnormal. *Journal of General Psychology* 10:59–82.

Benyshek, D. C. and J. T. Watson, 2006. Exploring the thrifty genotype's food-shortage assumptions: a cross-cultural comparison of ethnographic accounts of food security among foraging and agricultural societies. *American Journal of Physical Anthropology* 131:120–126.

Bernstein, F., 1924. Ergebnisse einer biostatistischen zusammenfassenden Betrachtung über die erbichen Blutstrukturen des Menschen. *Klinische Wochenschrift*, 3:1495–1497.

Bertranpetit, J., F. Calafell, D. Comas, A. Perez-Lezaun and E.Mateu, 1996. Mitochondrial DNA sequences in Europe: an insight into population history. In: *Molecular Biology and Human Diversity*, eds. A. J. Boyce and C. G. N. Mascie-Taylor, Cambridge: Cambridge University Press, pp. 112–129.

Biasutti, R. 1959. *Razze e Popoli della Terra*. 2d ed. Torino: Unione Tipografico-Editrice Torinese.

Birdsell, J. B., 1953. Some environmental and cultural factors influencing the structuring of Australian aboriginal populations. *American Naturalist*, 87:171–207.

Birdsell, J. B., 1972. *Human Evolution*. Chicago: Rand McNally & Company.

Birdsell, J. B., 1993. *Microevolutionary Patterns in Aboriginal Australia: A Gradient Analysis of Clines*. New York: Oxford University Press.

Black, D. L., 2003. Mechanisms of alternative pre-messenger RNA splicing. *Annual Review of Biochemistry* 72:291–336.

Black, F. L., 1992.Why did they die? *Science* 258:1739–1740.

Blass, E. M., D. R. Anderson, H. L. Kirkorian, T. A. Pempek, I. Price and M. F. Koleini, 2006. On the road to obesity: television viewing increases intake of high-density foods. *Physiology & Behavior* 88:597–604.

Bloch, J.I. and M.T. Silcox, 2001. New basicrania of Paleocene-Eocene *Ignacius*: Re-evaluation of the Plesiadapiform-Dermopteran link. *American Journal of Physical Anthropology*, 116:184–198.

Block, N., 1995. How heritability misleads about race. *Cognition* 56:99–128.

Bloom, B. L., 1988. *Health Psychology: A Psychosocial Perspective*. Englewood Cliffs, N.J.: Prentice Hall.

Blumenfeld, O. O. and A. M. Adamany, 1978. Structural polymorphism within the amino-terminal region of MM, NN, and MN glycoproteins (glycophorins) of the human erythrocyte membrane. *Proceedings of the National Academy of Sciences* 75:2727–2731.

Bodmer, W.F. and L.L. Cavalli-Sforza, 1976. *Genetics, Evolution, and Man*. San Francisco: W. H. Freeman and Company.

Bogin, B., 1999. Evolutionary perspective on human growth. *Annual Review of Anthropology*, 28:109–153.

Bogin, B., R. Keep and R. Edwards, 1996. Negative secular trend in stature for high SES Guatemalan boys. *American Journal of Human Biology*, 8:110–111 [Abstract].

Bohonak, A. J., 1999. Dispersal, gene flow, and population structure. *Quarterly Review of Biology* 74:21–45.

Bolnick, D. A., B. A. Shook, L. Campbell and I. Goddard, 2004. Problematic use of Greenberg's linguistic classification of the Americas in studies of Native American genetic variation. *American Journal of Human Genetics* 75:519–522.

Borecki, I. B., K. C. Malhotra, S. Mathew, M. Vijayakumar, D. V. R. Poosha and C. Rao, 1985. A family study of dermatoglyphic traits in India: resolution of genetic and uterine environmental effects of palm-pattern ridge counts. *American Journal of Physical Anthropology* 68:417–424.

Bouchard, C., F. T. Dionne, J.-A. Simoneau and M. R. Boulay, 1992. Genetics of aerobic and anaerobic performances. *Exercise and Sport Sciences Reviews* 20:27–58.

Bowcock, A. and V. Sartorelli, 1990. Polymorphism and mapping of the IGF1 gene, and absence of association with stature among African Pygmies. *Human Genetics*, 85:349–354.

Bowler, P. J., 1989. *Evolution: The History of an Idea*. Berkeley: University of California Press.

Boyd, W. C., 1963. Four achievements of the genetical method in physical anthropology. *American Anthropologist*, 65:243–252.

Boyden, S., 1970. Cultural adaptation to biological maladjustment. In: *The Impact of Civilisation on the Biology of Man*, ed. S. Boyden, Toronto: University of Toronto Press, pp. 190–218.

Brace, C. L. 2005. *Race is a Four Letter Word: The Genesis of the Concept*. New York: Oxford University Press.

Brace, C. L., D. P. Tracer, L. A. Yaroch, J. Robb, K. Brandt and A. R. Nelson, 1993. Clines and clusters versus "race": A test in ancient Egypt and the case of a death on the Nile. *Yearbook of Physical Anthropology*, 36:1–31.

Brandes, R. P., I. Fleming and R. Busse, 2005. Endothelial aging. *Cardiovascular Research*, 66:286–294.

Bräuer, G. and V. P. Chopra, 1980. Estimating the heritability of hair color and eye color. *Journal of Human Evolution*, 9:625–630.

Brewis, A. A., 1992. Sexually transmitted disease risk in a Micronesian atoll population, *Health Transition Review*, 2:195–211.

Brockmann, G. A. and M. R. Bevova, 2002. Using mouse models to dissect the genetics of obesity. *Trends in Genetics*, 18:367–376.

Brody, N., 1992. *Intelligence*. 2d ed. San Diego: Academic Press.

Brody, S., 1945. *Bioenergetics and Growth*. New York: Reinhold Publishing Corporation.

Brown, D. E., 1981. General stress in anthropological fieldwork. *American Anthropologist* 83:74–92.

Brown, D. E., 1982. Physiological stress and culture change in a group of Filipino-Americans: a preliminary investigation. *Annals of Human Biology* 9:553–563.

Brown, D. E. and G. D. James, 2000. Physiological stress responses in Filipino-American immigrant nurses: the effects of residence time, life-style, and job strain. *Psychosomatic Medicine* 62:394–400.

Brown, D. E., G. D. James and P. S. Mills, 2006. Occupational differences in job strain and physiological stress: female nurses and school teachers in Hawaii. *Psychosomatic Medicine* 68:524–530.

Brown, D. E., J. L. Johnson and C. J. Severance, 1991. Growth of native Hawaiian school children: I. Research design, stature and weight measurements. *American Journal of Human Biology*, 3:677–688.

Brown, D. E., T. V. Koenig, A. M. Demorales, K. McGuire and C. T. Mersai, 1996. Menarche age, fatness, and fat distribution in Hawaiian adolescents. *American Journal of Physical Anthropology*, 99:239–247.

Brown, H., 1954. *The Challenge of Man's Future*. New York: The Viking Press.

Brown, J. L. and E. Pollitt, 1996. Malnutrition, poverty and intellectual development. *Scientific American* 274(2):38–43.

Brown, T. A., 1999. *Genomes*. New York: Wiley-Liss.

Brown, W. J., J. F. Donohue, N. W. Axnick, J. H. Blount, N. H. Ewen and O. G. Jones, 1970. *Syphilis and Other Venereal Diseases*. Cambridge, Massachusetts: Harvard University Press.

Brown, W. M., 1980. Polymorphism in mitochondrial DNA of human as revealed by restriction endonuclease analysis. *Proceedings of the National Academy of Sciences*, 77:3605–3609.

Brucker, M. J., J. Patel, and P. K. Sullivan, 2003. A Morphometric Study of the External Ear: Age- and Sex-Related Differences. *Plastic & Reconstructive Surgery*, 112:647–652.

Brues, A., 1977. *People and Races*. New York: Macmillan Publishing Company.

Buono, M. J., K. D. Ball and F. W. Kolkhorst, 2007. Sodium ion concentration vs. sweat rate relationship in humans. *Journal of Applied Physiology* 103:990–994.

Burger, G., M. W. Gray and B. F. Lang, 2003. Mitochondrial genomes: anything goes. *Trends in Genetics* 19:709–716.

Burnet, M. and D. O. White, 1972. *Natural History of Infectious Disease*. 4th ed. Cambridge: Cambridge University Press.

Bury, J. B., 1932. *The Idea of Progress*. New York: Dover Publications, Inc.

Bushnell, O. A., 1993, *The Gifts of Civilization: Germs and Genocide in Hawai'i*, Honolulu: University of Hawaii Press.

Buvé, A., K. Bishikwabo-Nsarhaza and G. Mutangadura, 2002. The spread and effect of HIV-1 infection in sub-Saharan Africa. *The Lancet* 359:2011–2017.

Cahill, G. F., Jr., 1970. Starvation in man. *New England Journal of Medicine* 282:668–675.

Calogero, A.E., W. T. Galluci, G. P. Chrousos, and P. W. Gold, 1988. Catecholamine effects upon rat hypothalamic corticotropin-releasing hormone secretion in vitro. *Journal of Clinical Investigation* 82:839–846.

Campbell, B. 1985. *Human Evolution*. 3d ed. New York: Aldine Publishing Company.

Campbell, H., N. Andrews, K. E. Brown and E. Miller, 2007. Review of the effects of measles vaccination on the epidemiology of SSPE. *International Journal of Epidemiology* 36:1334–1348.

Campbell, L., 1997. *American Indian Languages: The Historical Linguistics of Native America*. Oxford University Press, New York.

Campisi, J., 2001. Cellular senescence as a tumor-suppressor mechanism. *Trends in Cell Biology*, 11:S27–S31.

Cann, R. L., 2001. Genetic clues to dispersal in human populations: retracing the past from the present. *Science*, 291:1742–1748.

Cann, R. L. and J. K. Lum, 2004. Dispersal ghosts in Oceania. *American Journal of Human Biology*. 16:440–451.

Cann, R. L., M. Stoneking and A. C. Wilson, 1987. Mitochondrial DNA and human evolution. *Nature*, 325:31–36.

Carlsen, E., A. Giwercman, N. Keiding, and N. Skakkebaek, 1992. Evidence for decreasing quality of semen during past 50 years. *British Medical Journal*, 305:609–613.

Carroll, J. B., 1997. Theoretical and technical issues in identifying a factor of general intelligence. In: *Intelligence, Genes, and Success: Scientists Respond to the Bell Curve. eds*. B. Devlin, S. E. Fienberg, D. P. Resnick and K. Roeder, New York: Springer-Verlag, pp. 125–156.

Cavalli-Sforza, L. L. and W. F. Bodmer, 1971. *The Genetics of Human Populations*. San Francisco: W. H. Freeman and Company.

Cavalli-Sforza, L. L., P. Menozzi and A. Piazza, 1994. *The History and Geography of Human Genes*. Princeton: Princeton University Press.

Chakraborty, R., 1991. The role of heredity and environment on dermatoglyphic traits. In: *Dermatoglyphics: Science in Transition.* eds. C. C. Plato, R. M. Garruto, and B. A. Schaumann, New York: Wiley-Liss, pp. 151–191.

Charmandari, E., T. Kino, E. Souvatzoglou, and G. P. Chrousos, 2003. Pediatric stress: hormonal mediators and human development. *Hormone Research* 59:161–179.

Charrow, J., 2004. Ashkenazi Jewish genetic disorders. *Familial Cancer* 3:201–206.

Cheek, D. B., D. E. Hill, A. Cordano and G. G. Graham, 1970. Malnutrition in infancy, changes in muscle mass and adipose tissue before and after rehabilitation. *Paediatric Research* 4:135–144.

Chien K. R. and G. Kersenty, 2005. Longevity and lineages: toward the integrative biology of degenerative diseases in heart, muscle, and bone. *Cell*, 120:533–544.

Chikhi, L., G. Destro-Bisol, G. Bertorelle, V. Pascali and G. Barbujani, 1998. Clines of nuclear DNA markers suggest a largely Neolithic ancestry of the European gene pool. *Proceedings of the National Academy of Science* 95: 9053–9058.

Cho, H., S. D. Stout and T. A. Bishop, 2006. Cortical bone remodeling rates in a sample of African American and European American descent groups from the American Midwest: Comparisons of age and sex in ribs. *American Journal of Physical Anthropology*, 130:214–226.

Chobanian A. V., G. L. Bakris, H.R. Black, W. C. Cushman, L. A. Green, J. L. Izzo Jr, D. W. Jones, B. J. Materson, S. Oparil, J. T. Wright Jr, E. J. Roccella, Joint National Committee on Prevention, Detection, Evaluation, and Treatment of High Blood Pressure, and National High Blood Pressure Education Program Coordinating Committee, 2003. The seventh report of the joint national committee on prevention, detection, evaluation, and treatment of high blood pressure: the JNC 7 report. *JAMA* 289:2560–2572.

Chrousos, G.P. and P. W. Gold, 1992. The concepts of stress and stress system disorders: overview of physical and behavioral homeostasis. *JAMA* 267:1244–1252.

Chumlea, W. C., S. S. Guo, R. J. Kuczmarski, K. M. Flegal, C. L. Johnson, S. B. Heymsfield, H. C. Lukaski, K. Friedl and V. S. Hubbard, 2002. Body composition estimates from NHANES III bioelectrical impedance data. *International Journal of Obesity* 26:1596–1609.

Clavano-Harding, A. B., G. R. Ambler, C. T. Cowell, S. P. Garnett, B. Al- Toumah, J. C. Coakley, K. K. Y. Ho and R. C. Baxter, 1999. Initial characterization of the GH-IGF axis and nutritional status of the Ati negritos of the Philippines. *Clinical Endocrinology*, 51:741–747.

Clegg, E. J., I. G. Pawson, E. H. Ashton and R. W. Flinn, 1972. The growth of children at different altitudes in Ethiopia. *Philosophical Transactions of the Royal Society of London (Biology)*, 264:403–437.

Cliff, A. and P. Haggett, 1984. Island epidemics. *Scientific American* 250(5):138–147.

Cloninger, C. R., M. Bohman and S. Sigvardsson, 1981. Inheritance of alcohol abuse: Cross-fostering analysis of adopted men. *Archives of General Psychiatry* 36:861–868.

Clutton-Brock, T. H., S. D. Albon and F. E. Guinness, 1984. Maternal dominance, breeding success and birth sex ratios in red deer. *Nature*, 308:358–60.

Cogan, J. D., J. A. Phillips III, S. S. Schenkman, R. D. Milner and N. Sakati, 1994. Familial growth hormone deficiency: a model of dominant and recessive mutations affecting a monomeric protein. *Journal of Clinical Endocrinology and Metabolism* 79:1261–1265.

Cohen, J. E., 1975. Human population grows up. *Scientific American* 293(3):48–55.

Colin, Y., B. Chérif-Zahar, C. L.V. Kim,V. Raynal, V. Van Huffel and J.-P. Cartron, 1991. Genetic basis of the RhD-Positive and RhD-negative blood group polymorphism as determined by Southern analysis. *Blood*, 78:2747–2752.

Collard, M. and B. Wood, 2000. How reliable are human phylogenetic hypotheses? *Proceedings of the National Academy of Sciences*, 97(9):5003–5006.

Collings, D. A., S. D. Sithole and K. S. Martin, 1990. Indoor woodsmoke pollution causing lower respiratory disease in children. *Tropical Doctor* 20:151–155.

Colom, R., F. J. Abad, L. F. Garcia and M. Juan-Espinoza, 2002. Education, Wechsler's full scale IQ, and *g*. *Intelligence*, 30:449–462.

Commo, S., O. Gaillard and B. A. Bernard, 2004. Human hair graying is linked to a specific depletion of hair follicle melanocytes affecting both the bulb and the outer root sheath. *British Journal of Dermatology*, 150:435–443.

Comuzzie, A. G., 2002. The emerging pattern of the genetic contribution to human obesity. *Best Practice & Research. Clinical Endocrinology and Metabolism* 16:611–621.

Conway, D. L. and P. T. Baker, 1972. Skin reflectance of Quechua Indians: the effects of genetic admixture, sex and age. *American Journal of Physical Anthropology*, 36:267–282.

Coon, C. S., 1962. *The Origin of Races.* New York: Random House.

Coon, C. S., S.M. Garn and J. B. Birdsell, 1950. *Races: A Study of the Problem of Race Formation in Man.* Springfield, Illinois: Charles C. Thomas.

Cooper, R. S., A. G. Amoah and G. A. Mensah, 2003. High blood pressure: the foundation for epidemic cardiovascular disease in African populations. *Ethnicity and Disease* 13(Suppl 2):S48–S52.

Corliss, C. E., 1976. *Patten's Human Embryology: Elements of Clinical Development*. New York: McGraw-Hill Book Company.

Corsi, P., 1988. *The Age of Lamarck: Evolutionary Theories in France 1790–1830*. Berkeley: University of California Press.

Cosgrove, M., 2004. Do stressful life events cause type 1 diabetes? *Occupational Medicine* 54:250–254.

Cowles, R. B., 1959. Some ecological factors bearing on the origin and evolution of pigment in the human skin. *American Naturalist*, 93:283–293.

Crews, D. E., 2003. *Human Senescence: Evolutionary and Biocultural Perspectives*. Cambridge: Cambridge University Press.

Crews, D. E. and R. M. Garruto (eds.), 1994. *Biological Anthropology and Aging*. New York: Oxford University Press.

Crews, D. E. and L. M. Gerber, 1994. Chronic degenerative diseases and aging. In: *Biological Anthropology and Aging*. eds. D. E. Crews and R. M. Garruto, New York: Oxford University Press, pp. 174–208.

Cruikshank, J. K., J. C. Mbanya, R. Wilks, B. Balkau, N. McFarlane-Anderson and T. Forrester, 2001. Sick genes, sick individuals or sick populations with chronic disease? The emergence of diabetes and high blood pressure in African-origin populations. *International Journal of Epidemiology*, 30:111–117.

Cuervo, A.M., 2004. Autophagy: in sickness and in health. *Trends in Cell Biology*, 14:70–77.

Cutler, R. G., 1978. Evolutionary biology of senescence. In: Behnke, J. A., C. E. Finch and G. B. Moment (eds.), *The Biology of Aging*. New York: Plenum Press.

Dagan, T., R. Sorek, E. Sharon, G. Ast and D. Graur, 2004. *Alu*Gene: a database of *Alu* elements incorporated within protein-coding genes. *Nucleic Acids Research* 32:D489–D492.

Dai, S., D. R. Labarthe, J. Grunbaum, R. B. Harrist and W. H. Mueller, 2002. Longitudinal analysis of changes in indices of obesity from age 8 years to age 18 years: Project HeartBeat! *American Journal of Epidemiology*, 156:720–729.

Daniels, M., B. Devlin and K. Roeder, 1997. Of genes and IQ. In: *Intelligence, Genes, and Success: Scientists Respond to the Bell Curve*. eds. B. Devlin, S. E. Fienberg, D. P. Resnick and K. Roeder, New York: Springer-Verlag, pp.45–70.

Davies, J. L., Y. Kawaguchi, S. T. Bennett, J. B. Copeman, H. J. Cordell, L. E. Pritchard, P. W. Reed, S. C. L. Gough, S. C. Jenkins, S. M. Palmer, K. M. Balfour, B. R. Rowe, M. Farrall, A. H. Barnett, S. C. Bain and J. A. Todd, 2002. A genome-wide search for human type 1 diabetes susceptibility genes. *Nature* 371:130–136.

Davila, N., B. T. Shea, K. Omoto, M. Mercado, S. Misawa and G. Baumann, 2002. Growth hormone binding protein, insulin-like growth factor-I and short stature in two pygmy populations from the Philippines. *Journal of Pediatric Endocrinology and Metabolism*, 15:269–276.

Davis, K. (1974) The migrations of human populations. *Scientific American*, 231:92–107.

Davison, K. K., S. J. Marshall and L. L. Birch, 2006. Cross-sectional and longitudinal associations between TV viewing and girls' body mass index, overweight status, and percentage of body fat. *Journal of Pediatrics* 149:32–37.

De la Mettrie, R., D. Saint-Léger, G. Loussouarn, A. Garcel, C. Porter and A. Langaney, 2007. Shape variability and classification of human hair: a worldwide approach. *Human Biology* 79:265–281.

Dean, M., M. Carrington and S. J. O'Brien, 2002. Balanced polymorphism selected by genetic versus infectious human disease. *Annual Review of Genomics and Human Genetics* 3:263–292.

Deiana, L., L. Ferrucci, G. M. Pes, C. Carru, G. Delitala, A. Ganau, S. Mariotti, A. Nieddu, S. Pettinato, P. Putzu, C. Franceschi and G. Baggio, 1999. AKEntAnnos. The Sardinia study of extreme longevity. *Aging (Milano)* 11:142–149.

Denaro, M., H. Blanc, M. J. Johnson, K. H. Chen, F. Wilmsen, L. L. Cavalli-Sforza and D. C. Wallace, 1981. Ethnic variation in *HpaI* endonuclease cleavage patterns of human mitochondrial DNA. *Proceedings of the National Academy of Sciences*, 78:5768–5772.

Deschenes, M. R., 2004. Effects of aging on muscle fibre type and size. *Sports Medicine*, 34:809–824.

Dessein, A. J., C. Chevillard, S. Marquet, S. Henri, D. Hillaire and H. Dessein, 2001. Genetics of parasitic infections. *Drug Metabolism and Disposition* 29:484–488.

Dettwyler, K. A., 1994. *Dancing Skeletons: Life and Death in West Africa*. Prospect Heights, Illinois: Waveland Press.

de Zwaan, M., Z. Aslam and J. E. Mitchell, 2002. Research on energy expenditure in individuals with eating disorders: A review. *International Journal of Eating Disorders* 32:127–134.

Diamond, J. M., 1988. Express train to Polynesia. *Nature*, 336:307–308.

Diamond, J. M., 1991. Why are Pygmies small? *Nature* 354:111–112.

Dietz, W. H., B. Marino, N. R. Peacock and R. C. Bailey, 1989. Nutritional status of Efe pygmies and Lese horticulturalists. *American Journal of Physical Anthropology*. 78:509–518.

Dittus, W. P. J., 1980. The social regulation of primate populations: a synthesis. In: *The Macaques*, ed. D.G. Lindburg, New York: Van Nostrand, pp. 263–286.

Dobzhansky, T., 1970. *Genetics of the Evolutionary Process*. New York: Columbia University Press.

Dobyns, H. F., 1983. *Their Number Become Thinned*. Knoxville, Tennessee: University of Tennessee Press.

Dockery, D. W., C. A. Pope, X. Xu, J. D. Spengler, J. H. Ware, M. E. Fay, B. G. Ferris and F. E. Speizer, 1993. An association between air pollution and mortality in six U.S. cities. *New England Journal of Medicine* 329:1753–1759.

Doull, I. J. M., 2001. Recent advances in cystic fibrosis. *Archives of Disease in Childhood* 85:62–66.

Downward, J., 2004. RNA interference. *British Medical Journal* 328:1245–1248.

Dreizen, S., C. N. Spirakis and R. E. Stone, 1964. The retarding effect of protracted undernutrition on the appearance of the postnatal ossification centers in the hand and wrist. *American Journal of Diseases of Children*, 108:44–52.

Dreyfus, P. M., 1979. Nutritional disorders of the nervous system. In *Nutrition: Metabolic and Clinical Applications*, ed. R. E. Hodges, New York: Plenum Press, pp. 53–81.

Dubos, R., 1965. *Man Adapting.* New Haven: Yale University Press.

Dudas, S. P. and R. Arking, 1995. A coordinate upregulation of antioxidant gene activities is associated with the delayed onset of senescence in a long lived strain of *Drosophila*. *Journals of Gerontology. Series A: Biological Sciences and Medical Sciences*, 50:B117–127.

Dunn, F. L., 1968. Epidemiological factors: Health and disease in hunter gatherers. In *Man the Hunter*, eds. R. B. Lee and I. DeVore, Chicago: Aldine-Atherton, pp. 221–228.

Duxbury, M. S. and E. E. Whang, 2004. RNA interference: a practical approach. *Journal of Surgical Research* 117: 339–344.

Edelstein, S. J., 1986. *The Sickled Cell: From Myths to Molecules.* Cambridge, Massachusetts: Harvard University Press.

Edholm, O. G. and J. S. Weiner, 1981. Thermal physiology. In *The Principles and Practice of Human Physiology*, eds. O. G. Edholm and J. S. Weiner. London: Academic Press, pp. 111–190.

Effros, R. B., 2001. Ageing and the immune system. *Novartis Foundation Symposium*, 235:130–149.

Ehrlich, P. R. and A. H. Ehrlich, 1970. *Population, Resources, Environment: Issues in Human Ecology.* San Francisco: W. H. Freeman and Company.

Eiseley, L., 1958. *Darwin's Century.* Garden City, NY: Doubleday & Co.

Ekvall, R. B., 1968. *Fields on the Hoof: Nexus of Tibetan Nomadic Pastoralism.* Prospect Heights, Illinois: Waveland Press.

Eldredge, N. and S. J. Gould, 1972. Punctuated equilibria: an alternative to phyletic gradualism. In *Models in Paleobiology*, ed. T. J. M. Schopf, San Francisco: Freeman, Cooper and Co., pp. 82–115.

Ellison, P. T., 1995. Breastfeeding, fertility, and maternal condition. In: *Breastfeeding:Biocultural Perspectives,* eds. P. Stuart-Macadam and K. A. Dettwyler, New York: Aldine de Gruyter, pp. 305–346.

Ellison, P. T. and M. T. O'Rourke, 2000. Population growth and fertility regulation. In: *Human Biology: An Evolutionary and Biocultural Perspective*, eds. S. Stinson, B. Bogin, R. Huss-Ashmore and D. O'Rourke, New York: Wiley-Liss, pp. 553–586.

Endicott, P., M. T. P. Gilbert, C. Stringer, C. Lalueza-Fox, E. Willerslev, A. J. Hansen and A. Cooper, 2003. The genetic origins of the Andaman Islanders. *American Journal of Human Genetics*, 72:178–184.

Endocrine Society, 2000. Endocrinology and male infertility. Fact sheet on society's web site: www.endo-society.org/pubaffai/factshee/maleinf.htm.

England, M. A., 1996. *Life Before Birth.* 2d ed. London: Mosby-Wolfe.

EPA, 2006. *Municipal Solid Waste in the United States: 2005 Facts and Figures.* U.S. Environmental Protection Agency, Office of Solid Waste.

Etkin, N. L. and P. J. Ross, 1991. Recasting malaria, medicine, and meals: A perspective on disease adaptation. In *The Anthropology of Medicine: From Culture to Method*, eds. L. Romanucci-Ross, D. E. Moerman and L. R. Trancredi, New York: Bergin and Garvey, pp. 230–258.

Eveleth, P. B. and J. M. Tanner, 1990. *Worldwide Variation in Human Growth.* 2d ed. Cambridge: Cambridge University Press.

Ewald, P. W., 1993. The evolution of virulence. *Scientific American* 268(4):86–93.

Ewald, P. W., 1994. *Evolution of Infectious Disease.* Oxford: Oxford University Press.

Ezzell, C., 2002. Proteins rule. *Scientific American* 286(4):40–47.

Farb, P. and G. Armelagos, 1980. *Consuming Passions: The Anthropology of Eating.* Boston: Houghton Mifflin.

Faust, I. M., 1986. Adipose tissue growth and obesity. In: *Human Growth: A Comprehensive Treatise, Volume II*, eds. F. Falkner and J. M. Tanner, New York: Plenum Press, pp. 61–75.

Faustino, N. A. and T. A. Cooper, 2003. Pre-mRNA splicing and human disease. *Genes and Development* 17:419–437.

Feder, J. L., C. A. Chilcote and G. L. Bush, 1988. Genetic differentiation between sympatric host races of *Rhagoletis pomonella*. *Nature*, 336:61–64.

Feldman, R. A., 1994. *Molecular evolution, genetic diversity, and avian malaria in the Hawaiian honeycreepers.* Ph.D. dissertation, University of Hawaii at Manoa.

Ferris, S. D., W. M. Brown, W. S. Davidson and A. C. Wilson, 1981. Extensive polymorphism in the mitochondrial DNA of apes. *Proceedings of the National Academy of Sciences*, 78:6319–6323.

Filchak, K. E., J. B. Roethele and J. L. Feder, 2000. Natural selection and sympatric divergence in the apple maggot *Rhagoletis pomonella.* Nature 407:739–742.

Finch, C. E., 2005. Developmental origins of aging in brain and blood vessels: an overview. *Neurobiology of Aging,* 26:281–291.

Fitzpatrick, E. A., 1979. Radiation. In *Arid-Land Ecosystems: Structure, Functioning and Management,* eds. D. W. Goodall and R. A. Perry, Cambridge: Cambridge University Press, pp. 347–372.

Flegal, K. M., M. D. Carroll, C. L. Ogden and C. L. Johnson, 2002. Prevalence and trends in obesity among U.S. adults, 1999-2000. *Journal of the American Medical Association* 288:1723–1727.

Folk, G. E., 1974. *Textbook of Environmental Physiology,* 2d ed., Philadelphia: Lea & Febiger.

Fost, N., 1992. Ethical implications of screening asymptomatic individuals. *FASEB Journal* 6:2813–2817.

Foulks, E. F., 1972. *The Arctic Hysterias of the North Alaskan Eskimo.* Anthropological Studies no. 10. Washington, D.C.: American Anthropological Association.

Frankenhaeuser, M., 1973. Experimental approaches to the study of human behavior as related to neuroendocrine functions. In *Society, Stress and Disease, Volume I: The Psychosocial Environment and Psychosomatic Diseases,* ed. L. Levi, London: Oxford University Press, pp. 22–35.

Fraser, F. C. and J. J. Nora, 1975. *Genetics of Man.* Philadelphia: Lea & Febiger.

Frayling TM, N. J. Timpson, M. N. Weedon, E. Zeggini, R. M. Freathy, C. M. Lindgren, J. R. B. Perry, K. S. Elliott, H. Lango, N. W. Rayner, B. Shields, L. W. Harries, J. C. Barrett, S. Ellard, C. J. Groves, B. Knight, A.-M. Patch, A. R. Ness, S. Ebrahim, D. A. Lawlor, S. M. Ring, Y. Ben-Shlomo, M.-R. Jarvelin, U. Sovio, A. J. Bennett, D. Melzer, L. Ferrucci, R. J. F. Loos, I. Barroso, N. J. Wareham, F. Karpe, K. R. Owen, L. R. Cardon, M. Walker, G. A. Hitman, C. N. A. Palmer, A. S. F. Doney, A. D. Morris, G. Davey Smith, T. Hattersley and M. I. McCarthy, 2007. A common variant in the FTO gene is associated with body mass index and predisposes to childhood and adult obesity. *Science* 316:889–894.

Freed, L. A., S. Conant and R. C. Fleischer, 1987. Evolutionary ecology and radiation of Hawaiian passerine birds. *Trends in Ecology and Evolution,* 2:196–203.

Freeland, S. J. and L. D. Hurst, 2004. Evolution encoded. *Scientific American,* 290(4):84–91.

Freeman, S. and J. C. Herron, 2004. *Evolutionary Analysis.* 3d ed. Upper Saddle River, N.J.: Prentice Hall.

Friedmann, T., 1997. Overcoming the obstacles to gene therapy. *Scientific American* 276(6):95–101.

Frisancho, A.R., 1994. *Human Adaptation and Accommodation.* Ann Arbor: University of Michigan Press.

Frisancho, A. R. and P. T. Baker, 1970. Altitude and growth: a study of the patterns of physical growth of a high altitude Peruvian Quechua population. *American Journal of Physical Anthropology,* 32:279–292.

Frisancho, A. R., G. A. Borkan and J. E. Klayman, 1975. Patterns of growth of lowland and highland Peruvians of similar genetic composition. *Human Biology,* 47:233–243.

Frisancho, A. R., S. M. Garn and W. Ascoli, 1970. Unequal influence of low dietary intakes on skeletal maturation during childhood and adolescence. *American Journal of Clinical Nutrition,* 23:1220–1227.

Frisancho, A. R., H. G. Frisancho, M. Milotich, T. Brutsaert, H. Spielvogel, M. Villena, E. Vargas and R. Soria, 1994. Influence of developmental acclimatization and activity level on bioenergetic adaptation to high altitude hypoxia. *American Journal of Physical Anthropology* Supplement 18:89–90 [abstract].

Frisancho, A. R. and L. P. Greksa, 1989. Developmental responses in the acquisition of functional adaptation to high altitude. In *Human Population Biology,* eds. M. A. Little and J. D. Haas, New York: Oxford University Press, pp. 203–221.

Frisch, R., 1978. Population, food intake, and fertility. *Science,* 199:22–30.

Frisch, R. and R. Revelle, 1970. Height and weight at menarche and a hypothesis of critical body weights and adolescent events. *Science,* 169:397–399.

Froehlich, J. W. and E. Giles 1981. A multivariate approach to fingerprint variation in Papua New Guinea: implications for prehistory. *American Journal of Physical Anthropology,* 54:93–106.

Futuyma, D. J., 1983. Evolutionary interactions among herbivorous insects and plants. In *Coevolution,* eds. D. J. Futuyma and M. Slatkin, Sunderland, Massachusetts: Sinauer Associates Inc., pp. 207–231.

Gage, T. B., 2000. Demography. In: *Human Biology: An Evolutionary and Biocultural Perspective,* eds. S. Stinson, B. Bogin, R. Huss-Ashmore and D. O'Rourke, New York: Wiley-Liss, pp. 507–551.

Gagneux, P., 2002. The genus Pan: population genetics of an endangered outgroup. *Trends in Genetics,* 18:327–330.

Gagneux, P., C. Wills, U. Gerloff, D. Tautz, P. A. Morin, C. Boesch, B. Fruth, G. Hohmann, O. A. Ryder and D. S. Woodruff, 1999. Mitochondrial sequences show diverse evolutionary histories of African hominoids. *Proceedings of the National Academy of Sciences,* 96:5077–5082.

Galvani, A. P. and M. W. Slatkin, 2003. Evaluating plague and smallpox as historical selective pressures for the CCR5-delta32

HIV-resistance allele. *Proceedings of the National Academy of Sciences* 100:15276–15279.

Gao, W., Y. Gao, G. Zhang, L. Song, B. Sun and J. Q. Shi, 2005. Hypoxia-induced expression of HIF-1α and its target genes in umbilical venous endothelial cells of Tibetans and immigrant Han. *Comparative Biochemistry and Physiology*, Part C 141:93–100.

Garn, S. M., 1961 *Human Races*. Springfield, Illinois: Charles C. Thomas.

Garn, S. M., 1980. Continuities and change in maturational timing. In: *Constancy and Change in Human Development*, eds. O. G. Brim and J. Kagan, Cambridge: Harvard University Press, pp. 113–162.

Garn, S. M. and C. G. Rohmann, 1960. Variability in the order of ossification of the bony centers of the hand and wrist. *American Journal of Physical Anthropology*, 18:219–228.

Garruto, R.M., 2006. A commentary on neuronal degeneration and cell death in Guam ALS and PD: An evolutionary process of understanding. *Current Alzheimer Research* 3:397–401.

Garssen, B., 2004. Psychological factors and cancer development: evidence after 30 years of research. *Clinical Psychology Review* 24:315–338.

Gärtner, K., H. Resnik-Schueller and G. Reznik, 1973. The influence of overcrowding on spermatogenesis, size of Leydig-cell nuclei (histometrical investigation), and the adrenal corticosterone contents in mice. *Acta Endocrinologica* 74:783–791.

Gasser, T., A. Kneip, P. Ziegler, R. Largo, L. Molinari and A. Prader, 1991. The dynamics of growth of width in distance, velocity and acceleration. *Annals of Human Biology*, 18:449–461.

Gates, D. M., 1980. *Biophysical Ecology*. New York: Springer.

Geffner, M. E., N. Bersch, R. C. Bailey and D. W. Golde, 1995. Insulin-like growth factor I resistance in immortalized T cell lines from African Efe Pygmies. *Journal of Clinical Endocrinology and Metabolism*, 80:3732–3738.

Giacomoni, P. U. and G. Rein, 2004. A mechanistic model for the aging of human skin. *Micron*, 35:179–184.

Gibbons, A., 1998. Genes put mammals in age of dinosaurs. *Science*, 280:675–676.

Gibbons, A., 2002. In search of the first hominids. *Science*, 295:1214–1219.

Gilbert, L. E., 1983. Coevolution and mimicry. In *Coevolution*, eds. D. J. Futuyma and M. Slatkin, Sunderland, Massachusetts: Sinauer Associates Inc., pp. 263–281.

Gilbert, W. H., T. D. White and B. Asfaw, 2003. *Homo erectus*, *Homo ergaster*, *Homo "cepranensis,"* and the Daka cranium. *Journal of Human Evolution* 45:255–259.

Gilchrest, B. A., F. B. Blog, and G. Szabo, 1979. Effects of aging and chronic sun exposure on melanocytes in human skin. *Journal of Investigative Dermatology*, 73:141–143.

Gillespie, K. M., 2006. Type I diabetes: pathogenesis and prevention. *Canadian Medical Association Journal* 175:165–170.

Gilley, D., H. Tanaka and B. Brittney-Shea, 2005. Telomere dysfunction in aging and cancer. *International Journal of Biochemistry and Cell Biology*, 37:1000–1013.

Giussani, D. A., P. S. Phillips, S. Anstee and D. J. P. Barker, 2001. Effects of altitude versus economic status on birth weight and body shape at birth. *Pediatric Research*, 49:490–494.

Glazko, G. V. and M. Nei, 2003. Estimation of divergence times for major lineages of primate species. *Molecular Biology and Evolution*, 20:424–434.

Gluckman, P. D., M. A. Hanson and A. S. Beedle, 2007. Non-genomic transgenerational inheritance of disease risk. *BioEssays* 29:145–154.

Godfrey, L. R. (ed.), 1983. *Scientists Confront Creationism*. New York: W. W. Norton.

Goldman, N. and M. Montgomery, 1989. Fecundability and husband's age. *Social Biology*, 36:146–66.

Goldstein, M. C., P. Tsarong and C. M. Beall, 1983. High altitude hypoxia, culture, and human fecundity/fertility: a comparative study. *American Anthropologist*, 85:28–49.

González-Pérez, E., E. Esteban, M. Via, C. García-Moro, M. Hernández and P. Moral, 2006. Genetic change in the Polynesian population of Easter Island: evidence from Alu insertion polymorphisms. *Annals of Human Genetics* 70:829–840.

Goodman, A. H., G. J. Armelagos and J. C. Rose, 1980. Enamel hypoplasias as indicators of stress in three prehistoric populations from Illinois. *Human Biology*, 52:515–528.

Gopalan, C., 1992. The contribution of nutrition research to the control of undernutrition: the Indian experience. *Annual Review of Nutrition* 12:1–17.

Goss, D. A., M. J. Hampton and M. G. Wickham, 1988. Selected review of genetic factors in myopia. *Journal of the American Optometric Association* 59:875–884.

Gotlieb, A. I. And M. D. Silver, 2001. Atherosclerosis: morphology and pathogenesis in cardiovascular pathology. In: *Cardiovascular Pathology*, eds. M. D. Silver, A. I. Gotlieb and F. J. Schoen, New York: Churchill-Livingstone, pp. 68–106.

Gould, S. J., 1980. *The Panda's Thumb: More Reflections in Natural History*. New York: Norton.

Gould, S. J., 1981. *The Mismeasure of Man*. New York: W.W. Norton & Company.

Gould, S. J., 1987. *Time's Arrow, Time's Cycle: Myth and Metaphor in the Discovery of Geological Time.* Cambridge, MA: Harvard University Press.

Gould, S.J. 1989. *Wonderful Life: The Burgess Shale and the Nature of History.* New York: Norton.

Gourlay, C. W. and K. R. Ayscough, 2005. A role for actin in aging and apoptosis. *Biochemical Society Transactions,* 33:1260–1264.

Gracey, M., 1991. Nutrition and physical growth. In: *Anthropometric Assessment of Nutritional Status,* ed. J. H. Himes, New York: Wiley-Liss, pp. 29–49.

Grande, F., J. T. Anderson and A. Keys, 1958. Changes of basal metabolic rate in man in semistarvation and refeeding. *Journal of Applied Physiology* 12:230–238.

Gravlee, C. C., H. R. Bernard and W. R. Leonard, 2003. Heredity, environment, and cranial form: a reanalysis of Boas' immigrant data. *American Anthropologist,* 105: 125–138.

Gray, M. W., G. Burger and B. F. Lang, 1999. Mitochondrial evolution. *Science* 283:1476–1481.

Green, R. E., J. Krause, S. E. Ptak, A.W. Briggs, M. T. Ronan, J. F. Simons, L. Du, M. Egholm, J. M. Rothberg, M. Paunovic and S. Pääbo, 2006. Analysis of one million base pairs of Neanderthal DNA. *Nature* 444:330–336.

Greenberg, J. H., 1987. *Language in the Americas.* Palo Alto: Stanford University Press.

Greene, J. C., 1959. *The Death of Adam.* Ames: The Iowa State University Press.

Greene, L. S., 1993. G6PD deficiency as protection against *falciparum* malaria: an epidemiological critique of population and experimental studies. *Yearbook of Physical Anthropology,* 36:153–178.

Greenwood, N. H. and J. M. B. Edwards, 1973. *Human Environments and Natural Systems: A Conflict of Dominion.* North Scituate, Massachusetts: Duxbury Press.

Greider, C. W. and E. H. Blackburn, 1996. Telomeres, telomerase and cancer. *Scientific American* 274(2):92–97.

Greksa, L. P., H. Spielvogel, L. Paredes-Fernandez, M. Paz-Zamora and E. Caceres, 1984. The physical growth of urban children at high altitude. *American Journal of Physical Anthropology,* 65:315–322.

Greksa, L. P., H. Spielvogel and L. Paredes-Fernandez, 1985. Maximal exercise capacity in adolescent European and Amerindian high altitude natives. *American Journal of Physical Anthropology* 67:209–216.

Gresham, D., B. Morar, P. A. Underhill, G. Passarino, A. A. Lin, C. Wise, D. Angelicheva, F. Calafell, P. J. Oefner, P. Shen, I. Tournev, R. de Pablo, V. Kûcinskas, A. Perez-Lezaun, E. Marushiakova, V. Popov and L. Kalaydjieva, 2001. Origins and divergence of the Roma (gypsies). *American Journal of Human Genetics,* 69:1314–1331.

Greulich, W. W., 1976. Some secular changes in the growth of American-born and native Japanese children. *American Journal of Physical Anthropology,* 45:553–568.

Grim, C. E., J. P. Henry and H. Myers, 1995. High blood pressure in blacks: salt, slavery, survival, stress, and racism. In: *Hypertension: Pathophysiology, Diagnosis, and Management.* 2d ed., eds. J. H. Laragh and B. M. Brenner, New York: Raven Press, pp. 171–207.

Grisk, O. and R. Rettig, 2004. Interactions between the sympathetic nervous system and the kidneys in arterial hypertension. *Cardiovascular Research* 61:238–246.

Groube, L., J. Chappell, J. Muke and D. Price, 1986. A 40,000 year old human occupation site at Huon Peninsula, Papua New Guinea. *Nature,* 324:453–455.

Gryseels, B., K. Polman, J. Clerinx and L. Kestens, 2006. Human schistosomiasis. *Lancet* 368:1106–1118.

Guinovart, C., M. M. Navia, M. Tanner and P. L. Alonso, 2006. Malaria: burden of disease. *Current Molecular Medicine* 6:137–140.

Haas, J. D., 1976. Prenatal and infant growth and development. In: *Man in the Andes: A Multidisciplinary Study of High-Altitude Quechua Natives,* eds. P. T. Baker and M. A. Little, Stroudsburg, Pennsylvania: Dowden, Hutchinson and Ross, pp. 161–179.

Haas, J. D. and D. L. Pelletier, 1989. Nutrition and human population biology. In *Human Population Biology: A Transdisciplinary Science,* eds. M. A. Little and J. D. Haas, New York: Oxford University Press, pp. 152–167.

Hackshaw, A. K., M. R. Law and N. J. Wald, 1997. The accumulated evidence on lung cancer and environmental tobacco smoke. *British Medical Journal* 315:980–988.

Haenszel, W., M. Kurihara, M. Segi and R. C. K. Lee, 1972. Stomach cancer among Japanese in Hawaii. *Journal of the National Cancer Institute* 49:969–988.

Haffner, S. M., 2003. Insulin resistance, inflammation, and the prediabetic state. *American Journal of Cardiology* 92 (Suppl.):18J–26J.

Hales, C. N. and D. J. P. Barker, 1992. Type II (non-insulin dependent) diabetes mellitus: the thrifty phenotype hypothesis. *Diabetologia* 35:595–601.

Hales, C. N., D. J. P. Barker, P. M. S. Clark, L. J. Cox, C. H. D. Fall, C. Osmond and P. D. Winter, 1993. Fetal and infant growth and impaired glucose tolerance at age 64. *British Medical Journal,* 303:1019–1022.

Hamilton, W. D., 1966. The moulding of senescence by natural selection. *Journal of Theoretical Biology,* 12:12–45.

Hamilton, W. J., 1973. *Life's Color Code.* New York: McGraw-Hill.

Hamlin, C. R. and R. R. Kohn, 1972. Determination of human chronological age by study of a collagen sample. *Experimental Gerontology*, 7:377–379.

Hanna, J. M. and D. E. Brown, 1979. Human heat tolerance: Biological and cultural adaptations. *Yearbook of Physical Anthropology* 22:163–186.

Hanna, J. M. and D. E. Brown, 1983. Human heat tolerance: An anthropological perspective. *Annual Review of Anthropology* 12:259–284.

Hanna, J. M., M. A. Little and D. M. Austin, 1989. Climatic physiology. In *Human Population Biology: A Transdisciplinary Science*, eds. M. A. Little and J. D. Haas, New York: Oxford University Press, pp. 132–151.

Hanna, J. M., M. H. Fitzgerald, J. D. Pearson, A. Howard and J. Martz-Hanna, 1990. Selective migration from Samoa: a longitudinal study of pre-migration differences in social and psychological characteristics. *Social Biology*, 37: 204–214.

Hanson, R. L., M. G. Ehm, D. J. Pettitt, M. Prochazka, D. B. Thompson, D. Timberlake, T. Foroud, S. Kobes, L. Baier, D. K. Burns, L. Almasy, J. Blangero, W. T. Garvey, P. H. Bennett and W. C. Knowler, 1998. An autosomal genomic scan for loci linked to type II diabetes mellitus and body-mass index in Pima Indians. *American Journal of Human Genetics*, 63:1130–1138.

Harman, D., 1956. Aging: a theory based on free radical and radiation chemistry. *Journal of Gerontology*, 11:298–300.

Harman, D., 1962. Role of free radicals in mutation, cancer, aging and the maintenance of life. *Radiation Research*, 16:753–763.

Harris, A., 1933. *Bone Growth in Health and Disease.* London: Oxford University Press.

Harris, J. B., A. I. Khan, R. C. LaRocque, D. J. Dorer, F. Chowdhury, A. S. G. Faruque, D. A. Sack, E. T. Ryan, F. Qadri and S. B. Calderwood, 2005. Blood group, immunity, and risk of infection with *Vibrio cholerae* in an area of endemicity. *Infection and Immunity* 73:7422–7427.

Harris, M., 1968. *The Rise of Anthropological Theory: A History of Theories of Culture.* New York: Thomas Y. Crowell Company.

Harrison, G. A., J. S. Weiner, J. M. Tanner, and N. A. Barnicot, 1964. *Human Biology: An Introduction to Human Evolution, Variation and Growth.* New York: Oxford University Press.

Hasselbalch, S. G., G. M. Knudsen, J. Jakobsen, L. P. Hageman, S. Holm and O. B. Paulson, 1994. Brain metabolism during short-term starvation in humans. *Journal of Cerebral Blood Flow and Metabolism* 14:125–131.

Hattori, Y., J. C. Vera, C. I. Rivas, N. Bersch, R. C. Bailey, M. E. Geffner and D. W. Golde, 1996. Decreased insulin-like growth factor I receptor expression and function in immortalized African Pygmy T cells. *Journal of Clinical Endocrinology and Metabolism*, 81:2257–2263.

Haverkos, H. W., N. Battula, D. P. Drotman and O. M. Rennert, 2003. Enteroviruses and type 1 diabetes mellitus. *Biomedicine and Pharmacotherapy* 57:379–385

Hawkes, K., 2003. Grandmothers and the evolution of human longevity. *American Journal of Human Biology*, 15:380–400.

Hayasaka, K., T. Gojobori and S. Horai, 1988. Molecular phylogeny and evolution of primate mitochondrial DNA. *Molecular Biology and Evolution*, 5:626–644.

Hayflick, L., 1965. The limited *in vitro* lifetime of human diploid cell strains. *Experimental Cell Research*, 37:614–636.

Hayflick, L., 1987. Origins of longevity. In: *Modern Biological Theories of Aging*, eds. H. R. Warner, R. N. Butler and R. L. Sprott, New York: Raven Press, pp. 21–34.

Hayflick, L., 1994. *How and Why We Age.* New York: Ballantine Books.

Hayflick, L. and P. S. Moorhead, 1961. The serial cultivation of human diploid cell strains. *Experimental Cell Research*, 25:585–621.

Hayward, A. R., 1986. Immunity development. In: *Human Growth: A Comprehensive Treatise, Volume I*, eds. F. Falkner and J. M. Tanner, New York: Plenum Press, pp. 377–390.

He, H., A. Isnard, B. Kouriba, S. Cabantous, A. Dessein, O. Doumbo and C. Chevillard, 2008. A STAT6 gene polymorphism is associated with high infection levels in urinary schistosomiasis. *Genes and Immunity* 9:195–206.

Heath, D. and D. R. Williams, 1977. *Man at High Altitude.* Edinburgh: Churchill Livingstone.

Hebsgaard, M. B., C. Wiuf, M. T. Gilbert, H. Glenner and E. Willerslev, 2007. Evaluating Neanderthal genetics and phylogeny. *Journal of Molecular Evolution* 64:50–60.

Heeney, J. L., A. G. Dalgleish and R. A. Weiss, 2006. Origins of HIV and the evolution of resistance to AIDS. *Science* 313:462–466.

Hegyi, J., R. A. Schwartz and V. Hegyi, 2004. Pellagra: dermatitis, dementia and diarrhea. *International Journal of Dermatology* 43:1–5.

Henderson, J., J. M. Withford-Cave, D. L. Duffy, S. J. Cole, N. A. Sawyer, J. P. Gulpin, A. Hahn, R. J. Trent and B. Yu, 2005. The EPAS1 gene influences the aerobic-anaerobic contribution in elite athletes. *Human Genetics* 118:416–423.

Henry, J. P., 1983. Coronary heart disease and arousal of the adrenal cortical axis. In: *Biobehavioral Basis of Coronary Heart Disease*, eds. T. M. Dembroski, T. H. Schmit and G. Blumchen, Basel: Karger, pp. 365–381.

Herd, J. A., 1981. Behavioral factors in the physiologic mechanisms of cardiovascular disease. In: *Perspectives on Behavioral Medicine*, eds. S. M. Weiss, J. A. Herd, and B. H. Fox, New York: Academic Press, pp. 55–66.

Herlenius, E. and H. Lagercrantz, 2004. Development of neurotransmitter systems during critical periods. *Experimental Neurology*, 190 (Suppl. 1):8–21.

Herrnstein, R. J. and C. Murray, 1994. *The Bell Curve: Intelligence and Class Structure in American Life*. New York: The Free Press.

Hertzberg, M., K. N. P. Mickleson, S. W. Serjeantson, J. F. Prior and R. J. Trent, 1989. An Asian-specific 9-bp deletion of mitochondrial DNA is frequently found in Polynesians. *American Journal of Human Genetics*, 44:504–510.

Heyerdahl, T., 1984. *Kon-Tiki, a True Adventure of Survival at Sea*. New York: Random House.

Heywood, P. F. and C. Jenkins, 1992. Nutrition in Papua New Guinea. In: *Human Biology in Papua New Guinea: The Small Cosmos*, ed. D. Attenborough and M. P. Alpers, Oxford: Clarendon Press, pp. 249–267.

HGDP, 1993. *HGDP Alghero Summary Report*. www.stanford.edu/group/morrinst/hgdp/summary93.html.

Hodgen, M. T., 1964. *Early Anthropology in the Sixteenth and Seventeenth Centuries*. Philadelphia: University of Pennsylvania Press.

Hof, P. R. and J. H. Morrison, 2004. The aging brain: morpho-molecular senescence of cortical circuits. *Trends in Neurosciences*, 27:607–613.

Hoff, C., 1974. Altitudinal variations in the physical growth and development of Peruvian Quechua. *Homo*, 24:87–99.

Hoff, C. J. and A. E. Abelson, 1976. Fertility. In: *Man In the Andes*, eds. P. T. Baker and M. A. Little, Stroudsburg, Pennsylvania: Hutchinson and Ross, pp. 138–146.

Hoffmann, A. A. and P. A. Parsons, 1991. *Evolutionary Genetics and Environmental Stress*. Oxford: Oxford University Press.

Hofler, W., 1968. Changes in the regional distribution of sweating during acclimatization to heat. *Journal of Applied Physiology* 25:503–506.

Holden, C., 2004. Peering under the hood of Africa's runners. *Science* 305:637–639.

Holick, M. F., 2003. Vitamin D: a millennium perspective. *Journal of Cellular Biochemistry* 88:296–307.

Hong, S. K., 1973. Pattern of cold adaptation in women divers of Korea. *Federation Proceedings* 32:1614–1622.

Hosaka, A., 1988. Population studies – myopia experience in Japan. *Acta Ophthalmology Supplement* 185:37–40.

Howe, C. J., A. C. Barbrook, V. L. Koumandou, R. E. R. Nisbet, H. A. Symington and T. F. Wightman, 2003. Evolution of the chloroplast genome. *Philosophical Transactions of the Royal Society of London B* 358:99–107.

Howell, N., 2000. *Demography of the Dobe !Kung*. 2d ed. New York: Academic Press.

Howells, W., 1973. *The Pacific Islanders*. New York: Charles Scribner's Sons.

Hughes, K. A. and R. M. Reynolds, 2005. Evolutionary and mechanistic theories of aging. *Annual Review of Entomology*, 50:421–445.

Hurles, M. E., J. Nicholson, E. Bosch, C. Renfrew, B. C. Sykes and M. A. Jobling, 2002. Y chromosomal evidence for the origins of Oceanic-speaking peoples. *Genetics*, 160:289–303.

Hurst, W., 2002. *The Heart, Arteries and Veins*. 10th ed. New York: McGraw-Hill.

Hutagalung, R., P. Wilairatana, S. Looareesuwan, G. M. Brittenham, M. Aikawa and V. R. Gordwuk, 1999. Influence of hemoglobin E trait on the severity of falciparum malaria. *Journal of Infectious Diseases*, 179:283–286.

Huxley, A., 1932. *Brave New World*. London: Chatto & Windus.

Ilkilic, I. and N. W. Paul, 2009. Ethical aspects of genome diversity research: Genome research into cultural diversity or cultural diversity in genome research? *Medicine, Health Care, and Philosophy* 12:25–34.

Jablonski, N. G. and G. Chaplin, 2000. The evolution of human skin coloration. *Journal of Human Evolution*, 39:57–106.

Jackson, F. L. C., 1990. Two evolutionary models for the interactions of dietary organic cyanogens, hemoglobins, and falciparum malaria. *American Journal of Human Biology*, 2:521–532.

Jackson, F. L. C., 1992. Race and ethnicity as biological constructs. *Ethnicity and Disease*, 2:120–125.

Jacobi, F. K., E. Zrenner, M. Broghammer and C. M. Pusch, 2005. A genetic perspective on myopia. *Cellular and Molecular Life Sciences* 62:800–808.

Jain, S., D. W. Golde, R. Bailey and M. E. Geffner, 1998. Insulin-like growth factor-I resistance. *Endocrine Reviews*, 19:625–646.

James, G. D. and D. E. Brown, 1997. The biological stress response and lifestyle: Catecholamines and blood pressure. *Annual Review of Anthropology* 26:313–335.

James, G. D., P. T. Baker, D. A. Jenner, and G. A. Harrison, 1987. Variation in lifestyle characteristics and catecholamine excretion rates among young Western Samoan men. *Social Science and Medicine* 25:981–986.

James, G. D., D. E. Crews and J. Pearson, 1989. Catecholamines and stress. in *Human Population Biology*, eds. M. A. Little and J. D. Haas, New York: Oxford University Press, pp. 280–295.

James, G. D., D. A. Jenner, G. A. Harrison and P. T. Baker, 1985. Differences in catecholamine excretion rates, blood pressure and lifestyle among young Western Samoan men. *Human Biology* 57:635–647.

Janssens, P. A., 1970. *Paleopathology: Diseases and Injuries of Prehistoric Man*. London: John Baker.

Jantz, R. L., 1997. Variation among European populations in summary finger ridge-count variables. *Annals of Human Biology*, 24:97–106.

Janvier, D., Y. Lam and J. Maury, 2002. Anti-U-like: a common antibody in Black individuals. *Vox Sanguinis*, 83:51–54.

Jasieńska, G. and P. T. Ellison, 1998. Physical work causes suppression of ovarian function in women. *Proceedings of the Royal Society of London B*, 265:1847–1851.

Jelliffe, D. B., 1968. *Child Nutrition in Developing Countries*. Washington, D.C.: Agency for International Development, U.S. Department of State.

Jensen-Seaman, M. I., A. S. Deinard and K. K. Kidd, 2001. Modern African ape populations as genetic and demographic models of the last common ancestor of humans, chimpanzees, and gorillas. *The Journal of Heredity*, 92:475–480.

Jiroutek, M. R., M. H. Chen, C. C. Johnston and C. Longcope, 1998. Changes in reproductive hormones and sex hormone-binding globulin in a group of postmenopausal women measured over 10 years. *Menopause*, 5:90–94.

Johnson, N. K., J. A. Martin and C. J. Ralph, 1989. Genetic evidence for the origin and relationships of Hawaiian honeycreepers (Aves: Fringillidae). *The Condor*, 91:379–396.

Johnson, N.W., G. S. Griffiths, J. M.Wilton, M. F. Maiden, M. A. Curtis, I. R. Gillett, D. T. Wilson and J. A. Sterne, 1988. Detection of high-risk groups and individuals for periodontal diseases. Evidence for existence of high-risk groups and individuals and approaches to their detection. *Journal of Clinical Periodontology* 15:276–282.

Jolly, Alison, 1985. *The Evolution of Primate Behavior*, 2d ed., New York: Macmillan Publishing Company.

Jones, M. P., 2006. The role of psychosocial factors in peptic ulcer disease: beyond Helicobacter pylori and NSAIDS. *Journal of Psychosomatic Research* 60:407–412.

Jones, R. H. and S. E. Ozanne, 2007. Intra-uterine origins of type 2 diabetes. *Archives of Physiology and Biochemistry* 113:25–29.

Jost, A., B. Vigier, J. Prepin and J. P. Perchellet, 1973. Studies on sex differentiation in mammals. *Recent Progress in Hormone Research*, 29:1–41.

Jurewicz, J. and W. Hanke, 2006. Exposure to pesticides and childhood cancer risk: has there been any progress in epidemiological studies? *International Journal of Occupational Medicine and Environmental Health* 19:152–169.

Jurmain, R., L. Kilgore and W. Trevathan, 2005. *Introduction to Physical Anthropology*. 10th ed. Belmont, California: Thomson Wadsworth.

Kaessmann, H., V. Wiebe and S. Pääbo, 2001. Extensive nuclear DNA sequence diversity among chimpanzees. *Science*, 286:1159–1162.

Kagame, A., 1976. The empirical apperception of time and the conception of history in Bantu thought. In *Cultures and Time*, eds. L. Gardet, et al., Paris: The UNESCO Press, pp. 89–116.

Kaij, L., 1960. *Alcoholism in Twins: Studies on the Etiology and Sequels of Abuse of Alcohol*. Stockholm: Almquist and Wiksell.

Kano, K. and C. S. Chung, 1975. Do American born Japanese children still grow faster than native Japanese? *American Journal of Physical Anthropology*, 43:187–194.

Karakelides, H. and K. S. Nair, 2005. Sarcopenia of aging and its metabolic impact. *Current Topics in Developmental Biology*, 68:123–148.

Karvonen, M., J. Tuomilehto, I. Libman and R. LaPorte, 1993. A review of the recent epidemiological data on the worldwide incidence of type I (insulin-dependent) diabetes mellitus. *Diabetologia* 36:883–892.

Katz, S. L. and J. F. Enders, 1965. Measles virus. In *Viral and Rickettsial Infections of Man*, 4th ed., eds. F. L. Horsfall and I. Tamm, Philadelphia: J. B. Lippincott Company, pp. 784–801.

Kaufman, J. S., E. E. Owoaje, S. A. James, C. N. Rotimi and R. S. Cooper, 1996. Determinants of hypertension in West Africa: Contribution of anthropometric and dietary factors to urban-rural and socioeconomic gradients. *American Journal of Epidemiology* 143:1203–1218.

Kay, R. F., R. W. Thorington, Jr. and P. Houde, 1990. Eocene plesiadapiform shows affinities with flying lemurs not primates. *Nature*, 345:342–344.

Kay, R. F., C. Ross and B. A. Williams, 1997. Anthropoid origins. *Science*, 275:797–804.

Keller, J. N., 2006. Age-related neuropathology, cognitive decline, and Alzheimer's disease. *Ageing Research Reviews*, 5:1–13.

Kerslake, D. M., 1972. *The Stress of Hot Environments*. Cambridge: Cambridge University Press.

Keys, A., J. Brozek, A. Henschel, O. Mickelsen and H. L. Taylor, 1950. *The Biology of Human Starvation*. Minneapolis: University of Minnesota Press.

Khoo, K. L., H. Tan, Y. M. Liew, J. P. Deslypere and E. Janus, 2003. Lipids and coronary heart disease in Asia. *Atherosclerosis* 169:1–10.

Khuroo, M. S., 1996. Ascariasis. *Gastroenterology Clinics of North America.* 25:553–577.

Kidd, J. R., A. J. Pakstis, H. Zhao, R. B. Lu, F. E. Okonofua, A. Odunsi, E. Grigorenko, B. B. Tamir, J. Friedlaender, L. O. Schulz, J. Parnas and K. K. Kidd, 2000. Haplotypes and linkage-disequilibrium at the phenylalanine hydroxylase locus, PAH, in a global representation of populations. *American Journal of Human Genetics* 66:1882–1899.

Kieburtz, K., M. Macdonald, C. Shih, A. Feigin, K. Steinberg, K. Bordwell, C. Zimmerman, J. Srinidhi, J. Sotack, J. Gusella, et al., 1994. Trinucleotide repeat length and progression of illness in Huntington's disease. *Journal of Medical Genetics* 31:872–874.

Kim, U. K. and D. Drayna, 2004. Genetics of individual differences in bitter taste perception: lessons from the PTC gene. *Clinical Genetics* 67:275–80.

Kinane, D. F. and T. C. Hart, 2003. Genes and gene polymorphisms associated with periodontal disease. *Critical Reviews in Oral Biology and Medicine* 14:430–449.

Kirchman, D., H. Ducklow, and R Mitchell, 1982. Estimates of bacterial growth from changes in uptake rates and biomass. *Applied Environmental Microbiology*, 44:1296–1307.

Kirk, R. L., 1990. Population genetic studies in the Pacific: red cell antigen, serum protein, and enzyme systems. In: *The Colonization of the Pacific: A Genetic Trail*, eds. A. V. S. Hill and S. Serjeantson, Oxford: Oxford University Press, pp. 60–117.

Kirkwood, T. B. and R. Holliday, 1979. The evolution of ageing and longevity. *Proceedings of the Royal Academy of Science, Series B*, 205:531–546.

Klingenspor, M., 2003. Cold-induced recruitment of brown adipose tissue thermogenesis. *Experimental Physiology* 88:141–148.

Klug, W. S. and M. R. Cummings, 2000. *Concepts of Genetics.* 6th ed. Upper Saddle River, N.J.: Prentice Hall.

Knower, K. C., S. Kelly and V. R. Harley, 2003. Turning on the male - SRY, SOX9 and sex determination in mammals. *Cytogenetic and Genome Research*, 101:185–198.

Knowler, W. C., P. H. Bennett, R. F. Hamman and M. Miller, 1978. Diabetes incidence and prevalence in Pima Indians: a 19-fold greater incidence than in Rochester, Minnesota. *American Journal of Epidemiology* 108:497–505.

Koenig, R., 2001. Sardinia's mysterious male Methuselahs. *Science*, 291:2074–2076.

Kollias, N. and J. L. Bykowski, 1999. Immediate pigment darkening thresholds of human skin to monochromatic (362 nm) ultraviolet A radiation are fluence rate dependent. *Photodermatology, Photoimmunology & Photomedicine*, 15:175–178.

Kormondy, E. J. and D. E. Brown, 1998. *Fundamentals of Human Ecology.* Upper Saddle River, N.J.: Prentice Hall.

Kostek, M. C., M. J. Delmonico, J. B. Reichel, S. M. Roth, L. Douglass, R. E. Ferrell and B. F. Hurley, 2005. Muscle strength response to strength training is influenced by insulin-like growth factor 1 genotype in older adults. *Journal of Applied Physiology*, 98:2147–2154.

Kowarski, A., V. V. Weldon and C. J. Migeon, 1968. Adrenal cortical function. In: *Human Growth*, ed. D. B. Cheek, Philadelphia: Lea and Febiger, pp. 274–286.

Krantz, D. S. and S. B. Manuck, 1984. Acute psychophysiologic reactivity and risk of cardiovascular disease, a review and methodologic critique. *Psychological Bulletin* 96:434–464.

Krings, M., A. Stone, R. W. Schmitz, H. Krainitzki, M. Stoneking and S. Pääbo, 1997. Neanderthal DNA sequences and the origin of modern humans. *Cell*, 90:19–30.

Krog, J., B. Folkow, R. H. Fox and K. L. Andersen, 1960. Hand circulation in the cold of Lapps and north Norwegian fishermen. *Journal of Applied Physiology* 15:654–658.

Kültz, D., 2005. Molecular and evolutionary basis of the cellular response. *Annual Review of Physiology* 67:225–257.

Kuhnlein, H.V. and M. J. Turner, 1991. *Traditional Plant Foods of Canadian Indigenous Peoples: Nutrition, Botany and Use.* Gordon and Breach Science Publishers, Philadelphia.

Kura, F., J. Amemura-Maekawa, K. Yagita, T. Endo, M. Ikeno, H. Tsuji, M. Taguchi, K. Kobayashi, E. Ishii and H. Watanabe, 2006. Outbreak of Legionnaire's disease on a cruise ship linked to spa-bath filter stones contaminated with Legionella pneumophila serogroup 5. *Epidemiology and Infection* 134:385–391.

Kuzawa, C. W., 1998. Adipose tissue in human infancy and childhood: an evolutionary perspective. *Yearbook of Physical Anthropology*, 41:177– 209.

Lackland, D. T., H. E. Bendall, C. Osmond, B. M. Egan and D. J. P. Barker, 2000. Low birth weights contribute to high rates of early-onset chronic-renal failure in the Southeastern United States. *Archives of Internal Medicine*, 160:1472–1476.

Lampl, M., K. Ashizawa, M. Kawabata and M. L. Johnson, 1998. An example of variation and pattern in saltation and stasis growth dynamics. *Annals of Human Biology*, 25:203–219.

Lampl, M., N. Cameron, J. D. Veldhuis and M. L. Johnson, 1995. Response. patterns of human growth. Technical comment. *Science*, 268:442–444.

Lampl, M., J. D. Veldhuis and M. L. Johnson, 1992. Saltation and stasis: a model of human growth. *Science*, 258:801–803.

Landsteiner, K., 1900. Zur Kenntnis der antifermentativen, lytischen, und agglutinierenden Werkungen des Blutserums und der Lymphe. *Zentralblatt fur Bacteriologie, Parasitenkunde, Infectionskrankheiten und Hygiene*, 27:357–362.

Larsen, H. B., 2003. Kenyan dominance in distance running. *Comparative Biochemistry and Physiology* Part A 136: 161–170.

LeBlanc, J., 1978. Adaptation of man to cold. In *Strategies in Cold, Natural Torpidity and Thermogenesis*, eds. L. C. H. Wang and J. W. Hudson, London: Academic Press, pp. 695–715.

Lederberg, J., 1963. Molecular biology, eugenics and euphenics. *Nature* 198:428–429.

Leidy, L. E., 1994. Biological aspects of menopause: across the life span. *Annual Review of Anthropology*, 23:231–253.

Lenfant, C. and K. Sullivan, 1971. Adaptation to high altitude. *New England Journal of Medicine* 284:1298–1309.

Leon-Del-Rio, A., 2005. Biotin-dependent regulation of gene expression in human cells. *Journal of Nutritional Biochemistry* 16:432–434.

Leonard, W. R., 1989. Nutritional determinants of high-altitude growth in Nunoa, Peru. *American Journal of Physical Anthropology*, 80:341–352.

Leonard, W. R., M. V. Sorensen, V. A. Galloway, G. J. Spencer, M. J. Mosher, L. Osipova and V. A. Spitsyn, 2002. Climatic influences on basal metabolic rates among circumpolar populations. *American Journal of Human Biology* 14:609–620.

Leppäluoto, J., T. Pääkkönen, I. Korhonen and J. Hassi, 2005. Pituitary and autonomic responses to cold exposures in man. *Acta Physiologica Scandanavia* 184:255–264.

Lescano-Ponce, E., J. Tamayo, A. Cruz-Valdez, R. Diaz, B. Hernández, R. Del Cueto and M. Hernández-Avila, 2003. Peak bone mineral area density and determinants among females ages 9 to 24 years in Mexico. *Osteoporosis International*, 14:539–547.

Leslie, P. W. and P. H. Fry, 1989. Extreme seasonality of births among Nomadic Turkana pastoralists. *American Journal of Physical Anthropology*, 79:103–115.

Leslie, P. W. and M. A. Little, 2003, Human biology and ecology: variation in nature and the nature of variation. *American Anthropologist*, 105:28–37.

Lesná, I., S. Vybíral, L. Janský and V. Zeman, 1999. Human non-shivering thermogenesis. *Journal of Thermal Biology* 24:63–69.

Le Souëf, P. N., P. Candelaria and J. Goldblatt, 2006. Evolution and respiratory genetics. *European Respiratory Journal* 28:1258–1263.

Le Souëf, P. N., J. Goldblatt and N. R. Lynch, 2000. Evolutionary adaptation of inflammatory immune responses in human beings. *Lancet* 356:242–244.

Levy-Marchal, C. and D. Jacquet, 2004. Long term metabolic consequences of being born small for gestational age. *Pediatric Diabetes*, 5:147–153.

Lewin, R., 1980. Is your brain really necessary? *Science* 210:1232–1234.

Lewis, B., 1971. *Race and Color in Islam*. New York: Harper & Row.

Lewontin, R. C., 1974. *The Genetic Basis of Evolutionary Change*. New York: Columbia University Press.

Lewontin, R. C., S. Rose and L. J. Kamin, 1984. *Not in Our Genes: Biology, Ideology, and Human Nature*. New York: Pantheon Books.

Lichty, J. A., R. Y. Ting, P. D. Burns and E. Dyar, 1957. Studies of babies born at high altitude. Part I. Relation of altitude to birth weight. *American Journal of Diseases of Childhood*, 93:666–669.

Ling, X., S. R. Cummings, Q. Mingwei, Z. Xihe, C. Xioashu, M. Nevitt and K. Stone, 2000. Vertebral fractures in Beijing, China: The Beijing Osteoporosis Project. *Journal of Bone and Mineral Research*, 15:2019–2025.

Lippmann, M. and R. B. Schlesinger, 1979. *Chemical Contamination in the Human Environment*. New York: Oxford University Press.

Little, M. A. and J. D. Haas, 1989. Introduction: human population biology and the concept of transdisciplinarity. In: *Human Population Biology*, eds. M.A. Little and J. D. Haas, New York: Oxford University Press, pp. 113–131.

Little, M. A. and J. M. Hanna, 1978. The response of high-altitude populations to cold and other stresses. In *The Biology of High-Altitude Peoples*, ed. P. T. Baker, London: Cambridge University Press, pp. 251–298.

Livingstone, F. B., 1962. On the non-existence of human races. *Current Anthropology*, 3:533–562.

Livshits, G., M. Vainder, O. Pavlovsky and E. Kobyliansky, 1996. Population biology of human aging: ethnic and climatic variation of bone age scores. *American Journal of Human Biology*, 68:293–314.

Lloyd, G. E. R., 1976. Views on time in Greek thought. In *Cultures and Time*, eds. L. Gardet, et al., Paris: The UNESCO Press, pp. 117–148.

Loehlin, J. C., 1972. An analysis of alcohol-related questionnaire items from the National Merit Twin Study. *Annals of the New York Academy of Science* 197:117–120.

Loos R. J., C, M. Lindgren, S. Li, E. Wheeler, J.H. Zhao, I. Prokopenko, M. Inouye, R. M. Freathy, A. P. Attwood, J. S. Beckmann, S. I. Berndt, et al., 2008. Common variants near

MC4R are associated with fat mass, weight and risk of obesity. *Nature Genetics* 40:768–775.

Lovejoy, A. O., 1957. *The Great Chain of Being: A Study of the History of an Idea.* Cambridge, MA: Harvard University Press.

Lucentini, J., 2004. Silencing cancer. *The Scientist* 18 (17):14–15.

Lucey, J. F., C. A. Rowan, P. Shiono, A. R. Wilkinson, S. Kilpatrick, N. R. Payne, J. Horbar, J. Carpenter, J. Rogowski and R. F. Soll, 2004. Fetal infants: the fate of 4172 infants with birth weights of 401 to 500 grams – the Vermont Oxford network experience (1996-2000). *Pediatrics*, 113:1559–1566.

Lum, J. K. and R. L. Cann, 1998. mtDNA and language support a common origin of Micronesians and Polynesians in Island Southeast Asia. *American Journal of Physical Anthropology*, 105:109–119.

Lum, J. K., R. L. Cann, J. J. Martinson and L. B. Jorde, 1998. Mitochondrial and nuclear genetic relationships among Pacific island and Asian populations. *American Journal of Human Genetics*, 63:613–624.

Lundberg, U., 1976. Urban commuting, crowdedness and catecholamine excretion. *Journal of Human Stress* 2:26–34.

Lynch, M. and A. Kewalramani, 2004. Messenger RNA surveillance and the evolutionary proliferation of introns. *Molecular Biology and Evolution* 20:563–571.

Madati, P. and E. Kormondy. 1989. Introduction. In *International Handbook of Pollution Control*, ed. E. J. Kormondy, Westport, CT: Greenwood Press, pp. 1–17.

Maeda, T., T. Fukushima, K. Ishibashi and S. Higuchi, 2007. Involvement of basal metabolic rate in determination of type of cold tolerance. *Journal of Physiological Anthropology* 26:415–418.

Malotki, E., 1983. *Hopi Time.* Berlin: Mouton Publishers.

Margulis, L. 1970. *Origin of Eukaryotic Cells.* New Haven: Yale University Press.

Margulis, L., 1971. The origin of plant and animal cells. *American Scientist* 59:230–235.

Margulis, L., 1982. *Early Life.* New York: Van Nostrand Reinhold.

Margulis, L. and K. V. Schwartz, 1988. *Five Kingdoms: An Illustrated Guide to the Phyla of Life on Earth.* 2d ed. New York: W. H. Freeman and Company.

Marieb, E. N., 2009. *Essentials of Human Anatomy & Physiology.* 9th ed., San Francisco: Pearson Education.

Markow, T. A. and K. Wandler, 1986. Fluctuating dermatoglyphic asymmetry and the genetics of liability to schizophrenia. *Psychiatry Research*, 19:323–328.

Marks, J., 1995. *Human Biodiversity: Genes, Race, and History.* New York: Aldine De Gruyter.

Marmot, M. G., S. L. Syme, A. Kagan, H. Kato, J. B. Cohen and J. Belsky, 1975. Epidemiologic studies of coronary heart disease and stroke in Japanese men living in Japan, Hawaii and California: Prevalence of coronary and hypertensive heart disease and associated risk factors. *American Journal of Epidemiology* 102:514–525.

Massé, G. and E. E. Hunt, Jr., 1963. Skeletal maturation of the hand and wrist in West African children. *Human Biology*, 35:3–25.

Martin, R. D., 1990. *Primate Origins and Evolution: A Phylogenetic Reconstruction.* Princeton: Princeton University Press.

Martinson, J. J., 1996. Molecular perspectives on the colonization of the Pacific. In: *Molecular Biology and Human Diversity*, eds. A. J. Boyce and C. G. N. Maycie-Taylor, London: Cambridge University Press, pp. 171–195.

May, R. L., A. H. Goodman and R. S. Meindl, 1993. Response of bone and enamel formation to nutritional supplementation and morbidity among malnourished Guatemalan children. *American Journal of Physical Anthropology*, 92:37–51.

Maynard, A. D., R. J. Aitken, T. Butz, V. Colvin, K. Donaldson, G. Oberdörster, M. A. Philbert, J. Ryan, A. Seaton, V. Stone, S. S. Tinkle, L. Tran, N. J. Walker and D. B. Warheit, 2006. Safe handling of nanotechnology. *Nature* 444:267–269.

Mayr, E., 1970. *Populations, Species, and Evolution.* Cambridge, Massachusetts: Belknap Press (Harvard University Press).

McAfee, K., 1990. Why the third world goes hungry. *Commonweal* (June 15):380– 385.

McAlester, A.L., 1968. *The History of Life.* Englewood Cliffs, N.J.: Prentice-Hall.

McArthur, M., 1977. Nutritional research in Melanesia: a second look at the Tsembaga. In: *Rural Ecology in the Pacific*, eds. T. P. Bayliss-Smith and R. G. Feachem, London: Academic Press, pp. 91–128.

McCown, T. D. and K. A. R. Kennedy (eds.), 1972. *Climbing Man's Family Tree.* Englewood Cliffs, N.J.: Prentice-Hall.

McElroy, A. and P. K. Townsend, 1989. *Medical Anthropology in Ecological Perspective.* 2d ed. Boulder, Colorado: Westview Press.

McFalls, J. A., Jr. and M. H. McFalls, 1984. *Disease and Fertility.* Orlando: Academic Press.

McManamon, F. P., 1999. The initial scientific examination, description, and analysis of the Kennewick Man human remains. In: Department of the Interior, *Report on the Non-Destructive Examination, Description, and Analysis of the Human Remains from Columbia Park, Kennewick, Washington*, http://www.cr.nps.gov/aad/kennewick/mcmanamon.htm.

McNeill, W. H., 1976. *Plagues and Peoples.* New York: Doubleday.

Meier, R. J., 1975. Dermatoglyphics of Easter Islanders analyzed by pattern type, admixture effect, and ridge count variation. *American Journal of Physical Anthropology*, 42:269–276.

Meier, R. J., 1991. Applications of dermatoglyphics to anthropological populations. In: *Dermatoglyphics: Science in Transition*. eds. C. C. Plato, R. M. Garruto, and B. A. Schaumann, New York: Wiley-Liss, pp. 253–265.

Melov, S., J. Ravenscroft, S. Malik, M. S. Gill, D. W. Walker, P. E. Clayton, D. C. Wallace, B. Malfroy, S. R. Doctrow and G. J. Lithgow, 2000. Extension of life-span with superoxide dismutase/catalase mimetics. *Science* 289:1567–1569.

Menzel, D. B., 1984. Ozone: an overview of its toxicity in man and animals. *Journal of Toxicology and Environmental Health* 13:183–204.

Merimée, T. J., J. Zapf, B. Hewlett and L. L. Cavalli-Sforza, 1987. Insulin-like growth factors in pygmies. *New England Journal of Medicine*, 15:906–911.

Merimée, T.J., G. Baumann and W. Daughaday, 1990. Growth hormone-binding protein: II. Studies in pygmies and normal statured subjects. *Journal of Clinical Endocrinological Metabolism*, 71:1183–1188.

Mervis, J., 1995. China's unique environment favors large intervention trials. *Science* 270:1149–1151.

Miles, R. and L. Panton, 2006. The influence of the perceived quality of community environments on low-income women's efforts to walk more. *Community Health* 31:379–392.

Miller, K. R., 2000. *Finding Darwin's God: A Scientist's Search for Common Ground Between God and Evolution*. New York: HarperCollins.

Miller, K. R., 2002. The flaw in the mousetrap. *Natural History*, April, p. 75.

Molnar, S., 2002. *Human Variation: Races, Types, and Ethnic Groups*. 5th ed. Upper Saddle River, N.J.: Prentice-Hall.

Monod, J., 1971. *Chance and Necessity: An Essay on the Natural Philosophy of Modern Biology*. New York: Knopf.

Montagu, A., 1963. On Coon's *The Origin of Races. Current Anthropology*, 4:361–364.

Montgomery, R. D., Muscle morphology in infantile protein malnutrition. *Journal of Clinical Pathology* 15:511–521.

Moore, L. G., P. W. Van Arsdale, J. E. Glittenberg and R. A. Aldrich, 1980. *The Biocultural Basis of Health: Expanding Views of Medical Anthropology*. St. Louis: The C. V. Mosby Company.

Moore, L. G., S. Niermeyer, and S. Zamudio, 1998. Adaptation to high altitude: Regional and life-cycle perspectives. *Yearbook of Physical Anthropology*, 41:25–64.

Moore, L. G., S. Zamudio, J. Zhuang, S. Sun and T. Droma, 2001. Oxygen transport in Tibetan women during pregnancy at 3,658 m. *American Journal of Physical Anthropology*, 114:42–53.

Moore, J. A., 1949. Patterns of evolution in the genus *Rana*. In: *Genetics, Paleontology and Evolution*, eds. G. L. Jepsen, G. G. Simpson and E. Mayr, New York: Atheneum, pp. 315–338.

Moore, J. A., 1950. Further studies on *Rana pipiens* racial hybrids. *American Naturalist*, 84:247–254.

Morar, B., D. Gresham, D. Angelicheva, I Tournev, R. Gooding, V. Guergueltcheva, C. Schmidt, A. Abricht, H. Lochmüller, A. Tordai, L. Kalmar, M. Nagy, V. Karcagi, M. Jeanpierre, A. Herczegfalvi, D. Beeson, V. Venkataraman, K. W. Carter, J. Reeve, R. de Pablo, V. Kucinskas and L. Kalaydjieva, 2004. Mutation history of the Roma/Gypsies. *American Journal of Human Genetics*, 75:596–609.

Morehouse, L. E. and A. T. Miller, Jr., 1967. *Physiology of Exercise*. 5th ed. St. Louis: The C. V. Mosby Company.

Morin, P. A., J. J. Moore, R. Chakraborty, L. Jin, J. Goodall and D. S. Woodruff, 1994. Kin selection, social structure, gene flow, and the evolution of chimpanzees. *Science*, 265:1193–1201.

Morris, K., M. Morganlander, J. L. Coulehan, S. Gahagen and V. C. Arena, 1990. Wood-burning stoves and lower respiratory tract infection in American Indian children. *American Journal of Diseases of Children* 144:105–108.

Muir, C. S., 1976. The evidence from epidemiology. In *Health and the Environment*, eds. J. Lenihan and W. W. Fletcher, New York: Academic Press, pp. 88–115.

Müller, O. and M. Krawinkel, 2005. Malnutrition and health in developing countries. *Canadian Medical Association Journal* 173:279–286.

Mulligan, C. J., K. Hunley, S. Cole and J. C. Long, 2004. Population genetics, history, and health patterns in Native Americans. *Annual Review of Genomics and Human Genetics*, 5:295–315.

Myburgh, K. H., 2003. What makes an endurance athlete world-class? Not simply a physiological conundrum. *Comparative Biochemistry and Physiology* Part A 136:171–190.

Naeher, L. P., M. Brauer, M. Lipsett, J. T. Zelikoff, C. D. Simpson, J. Q. Koenig and K. R. Smith, 2007. Woodsmoke health effects: a review. *Inhalation Toxicology* 19:67–106.

Nagasaki, K., T. Kikuchi, M. Hiura and M. Uchiyama, 2004. Obese Japanese children have low bone mineral density after puberty. *Journal of Bone and Mineral Metabolism*, 22:376–381.

Napier, P. J. and J. B. West, 1998. High-altitude medical and operations problems and solutions for the Millimeter Array. *Proceedings of the International Society for Optical Engineering* 3349:456–465.

National Academy of Sciences, *Science and Creationism: A View from the National Academy of Sciences*. Washington, D.C.: National Academy Press.

National Research Council, 1989. *Diet and Health: Implications for Reducing Chronic Disease Risk*. Washington, D.C.: National Academy Press.

Nebert, D. W., 2005. Inter-individual susceptibility to environmental toxicants: a current assessment. *Toxicology and Applied Pharmacology* 207:S34–S42.

Neel, J. V., 1962. Diabetes mellitus: a "thrifty" genotype rendered detrimental by "progress"? *American Journal of Human Genetics*, 14:353–362.

Neel, J. V., 1982. The thrifty genotype revisited. In: *The Genetics of Diabetes Mellitus*, eds. J. Kobberling and J. Tattersall, New York: Academic Press, pp. 283–293.

Neel, J. V., 1999. The "thrifty genotype" in 1998. *Nutrition Reviews*, 57:S2–S9.

Nelms, J. D. and D. J. G. Soper, 1962. Cold vasodilation and cold acclimatization in the hands of British fish filleters. *Journal of Applied Physiology* 17:444–448.

Newcomb, R. D., P. M. Campbell, D. L. Ollis, E. Cheah, R. J. Russell, and J. G. Oakeshott, 1997. A single amino acid substitution converts a carboxylesterase to an organophosphorus hydrolase and confers insecticide resistance on a blowfly. *Proceedings of the National Academy of Sciences*, 94:7464–7468.

Newman, M. T., 1962. Ecology and nutritional stress in man. *American Anthropologist* 64:22–34.

Newman, R. W., 1970. Why man is such a sweaty and thirsty naked animal: A speculative review. *Human Biology* 42: 12–27.

Newman, R. W., 1975. Human adaptation to heat. In *Physiological Anthropology*, ed. A. Damon, New York: Oxford University Press, pp. 80–92.

Nikolic, M., S. Bajek, D. Bobinac, T. S. Vranic and R. Jerkovic, 2005. Aging of human skeletal muscles. *Collegium Antropologium*, 29:67–70.

Nilsen, T. W., 2003. The spliceosome: the most complex macromolecular machine in the cell? *BioEssays* 25:1147–1149.

Noonan, J. P., G. Coop, S. Kudaravalli, D. Smith, J. Krause, J. Alessi, F. Chen, D. Platt, S. Pääbo, J. K. Pritchard and E. M. Rubin, 2006. Sequencing and analysis of Neanderthal genomic DNA. *Science* 314:1113–1118.

Norgan, N. G., 1995. Changes in patterns of growth and nutritional anthropometry in two rural modernizing Papua New Guinea communities. *Annals of Human Biology* 22:491–513.

Norton, H. L., J. S. Friedlaender, D. A. Merriwether, G. Koki, C. S. Mgone and M. D. Shriver. 2006. Skin and hair pigmentation variation in island Melanesia. *American Journal of Physical Anthropology* 130:254–268.

Novitski, E., 1982. *Human Genetics*. 2d ed. New York: Macmillan Publishing Company, Inc.

Nowak, O. and J. Piontek, 2002. The frequency of appearance of transverse (Harris) lines in the tibia in relationship to age at death. *Annals of Human Biology*, 29:314–325.

Numbers, R. L., 1992. *The Creationists*. New York: A. A. Knopf.

Nystrom, T., 2003. The free-radical hypothesis of aging goes prokaryotic. *Cell and Molecular Life Sciences*, 60:1333–1341.

O'Brien, S. J. and G. W. Nelson, 2004. Human genes that limit AIDS. *Nature Genetics* 36:565–574.

O'Brien, S. J., D. E. Wildt, and M. Bush, 1986. The cheetah in genetic peril. *Scientific American*, 254(5):84–92.

Onkamo, P., S. Vaananen, M. Karvonen, and J. Tuomilehto, 1999. Worldwide increase in incidence of type I diabetes – the analysis of the data on published incidence trends. *Diabetologia* 42:1395–1403.

Ovchinnikov, I. V., A. Götherström, G. P. Romanova, V. M. Kharitonov, K. Lidén and W. Goodwin, 2000. Molecular analysis of Neanderthal DNA from the northern Caucasus. *Nature*, 404:490–493.

Ovid, 2000. *Metamorphoses. Book II*. Translated by A. S. Kline. http://etext.virginia.edu/latin/ovid/trans/Ovhome.htm.

Owen, J. B., 1999. Genetic aspects of body composition. *Nutrition* 15:609–613.

Owen, O. S. and D. D. Chiras, 1995. *Natural Resource Conservation: Management for a Sustainable Future*. 6th ed. Englewood Cliffs, N.J.: Prentice-Hall.

Page, L. B., A. D. Damon and R. C. Moellering, 1974. Antecedents of cardiovascular disease in six Solomon Islands societies. *Circulation* 49:1132–1147.

Pandey, M. R., R. P. Neupane, A. Gautam and I. B. Shrestha, 1989. Domestic smoke pollution and acute respiratory infections in a rural community of the hill region of Nepal. *Environment International* 15:337–540.

Panter-Brick, C., D. S. Lotstein and P. T. Ellison, 1993. Seasonality of reproductive function and weight loss in rural Nepali women. *Human Reproduction*, 8:684–690.

Park, E.-S., J.-H. Seo, J.-Y. Lim, C.-H. Park, H.-O. Woo and H.-S. Youn, 2006. Hypoelectrolytemia due to inadequate diet. *Pediatric Nephrology* 21:430–432.

Parr, L. A., J. T. Winslow, W. D. Hopkins and F. B. M. de Waal 2000 Recognizing facial cues: Individual discrimination by chimpanzees (Pan troglodytes) and Rhesus monkeys (Macaca mulatta). *Journal of Comparative Psychology*, 114:47–60.

Parra, E. J., 2007. Human pigmentation variation: evolution, genetic basis, and implications for public health. *Yearbook of Physical Anthropology* 50:85–105.

Parra, E. J., A. Mancini, J. Akey, J. Martinson, M. A. Batzer, R. Cooper, T. Forrester, D. B. Allison, R. Deka, R. E. Ferrell and M. D. Shriver, 1998. Estimating African American admixture proportions by use of population-specific alleles. *American Journal of Human Genetics*, 63:1839–1851.

Parra, E. J., R. A. Kittles, G. Argyropoulos, C. L. Pfaff, K. Hiester, C. Bonilla, N. Sylvester, D. Garrish-Gause, W. T. Garvey, L. Jin, P. M. McKeigue, M. I. Kamboh, R. E. Ferrell, W. S. Pollitzer and M. D. Schriver, 2001. Ancestral proportions and admixture dynamics in geographically defined African Americans living in South Carolina. *American Journal of Physical Anthropology*, 114:18–29.

Partanen, J., K. Bruun, and T. Markkanen, 1966. *Inheritance of Drinking Behavior.* New Brunswick, New Jersey: Rutgers Center of Alcohol Studies.

Passarino, G., G. L. Cavalleri, R. Stecconi, C. Franceschi, K. Altomare, S. Dato, V. Greco, L. L. Cavalli-Sforza, P. A. Underhill and G. de Benedictis, 2003. Molecular variation of human HSP90alpha and HSP90beta genes in Caucasians. *Human Mutation* 21:554–555.

Pasvol, G., M. Jungery, D. J. Weatherall, S. F. Parsons, D. J. Anstee and M. J. A. Tanner, 1982. Glycophorin as a possible receptor for Plasmodium falciparum. *The Lancet*, 320:947–950.

Patterson, C. C., G. Dahlquist, G. Soltész and A. Green, 2001. Is childhood-onset type I diabetes a wealth-related disease? An ecological analysis of European incidence rates. *Diabetologia* 44[Suppl 3]:B9–B16.

Pearl, R., 1928. *The Rate of Living Theory.* New York: A. A. Knopf.

Plato, C., K. M. Fox and J. D. Tobin, 1994. Skeletal changes in human aging. In: *Biological Anthropology and Aging: Perspectives on Human Variation Over the Life Span,* eds. D. E. Crews and R. M. Garruto, New York: Oxford University Press, pp. 272–300.

Pennisi, E., 1998. Sifting through and making sense of genome sequences. *Science* 280:1692–1693.

Pennisi, E., 2007. Breakthrough of the year: human genetic variation. *Science* 318:1842–1843.

Perna, N. T., M. Batzer, P. Deininger and M. Stoneking, 1992. *Alu* insertion polymorphism: a new type of marker for human population studies. *Human Biology*, 64:641–648.

Petit, L., L. Fougouang, I. Uhoda, S. Smitz, C. Piérard-Franchimont and G. E. Piérard, 2003. Regional variability in mottled subclinical melanoderma in the elderly. *Experimental Gerontology*, 38:327–331.

Pitkäniemi, J., P. Onkamo, J. Tuomilehto and E. Arjas, 2004. Increasing incidence of Type I diabetes – role for genes? *BMC Genetics* 5:5.

Planalp, J. M., 1971. *Heat Stress and Culture in North India.* Special Technical Report, U.S. Army Institute of Environmental Medicine, Natick, Massachusetts.

Pocock, D. F., 1964. The anthropology of time-reckoning. *Contributions to Indian Sociology*, 7:18–29.

Pollard, T. M., 2008. *Western Diseases: An Evolutionary Perspective.* Cambridge: Cambridge University Press.

Pollitzer, W. S., 1999. *The Gullah People and Their African Heritage.* Athens, Georgia: University of Georgia Press.

Porter, K. R., 1941. Developmental variations resulting from the androgenetic hybridization of four forms of *Rana pipiens. Science*, 93:439.

Poulain, M., G. M. Pes, C. Grasland, C. Carru, L. Ferrucci, G. Baggio, C. Franceschi and L. Deiana, 2004. Identification of a geographic area characterized by extreme longevity in the Sardinia island: the AKEA study. *Experimental Gerontology*, 39:1423–1429.

Pourrut, X., A. Délicat, P. E. Rollin, T. G. Ksiazek, J. P. Gonzalez and E. M. Leroy, 2007. Spatial and temporal patterns of Zaire ebolavirus antibody prevalence in the possible reservoir bat species. *Journal of Infectious Diseases* 196 (Suppl 2): S176–S183.

Prader, A., J. M. Tanner and G. A. Von Harnack, 1963. Catch-up growth following illness or starvation. *Journal of Pediatrics*, 62:646–659.

Pray, L. A., 2004. Epigenetics: genome, meet your environment. *The Scientist* 18 (13):14–20.

Price, P. W., 1996. *Biological Evolution.* Fort Worth: Saunders College Publishing.

Proctor, D. N., P. C. O'Brien, E. J. Atkinson and K. S. Nair, 1999. Comparison of techniques to estimate total body skeletal muscle mass in people of different age groups. *American Journal of Physiology*, 277:E489–E495.

Prothero, J. and K. D. Jurgens, 1987. Scaling of maximal lifespan in mammals: a review. In: *Evolution of Longevity in Animals: A Comparative Approach,* eds. A.D.Woodhead and K. H. Thompson, New York: Plenum Press, 44–74.

Quevedo, W. C., G. Szabo and J. Virks, 1969. Influence of age and UV on the population of dopa-positive melanocytes in human skin. *Journal of Investigative Dermatology*, 52:287–290.

Raab, W., 1966. Emotional and sensory stress factors in myocardial pathology. *American Heart Journal* 72:538–564.

Rabinowicz, T., 1986. The differentiated maturation of the cerebral cortex. In: *Human Growth: A Comprehensive Treatise, Volume II,* eds. F. Falkner and J. M. Tanner, New York: Plenum Press, pp. 385–410.

Rapoport, A., 1969. *House Form and Culture.* Englewood Cliffs, New Jersey: Prentice-Hall.

Raup, D.M., 1991. *Extinction: Bad Genes or Bad Luck?* New York: W.W. Norton & Company.

Raup, D. M. and J. J. Sepkoski, Jr., 1982. Mass extinctions in the marine fossil record. *Science*, 215:1501–1503.

Reame, N. E., R. P. Kelche, I. Z. Beitins, M. Y. Yu, C. M. Zawacki and V. Padmanabhan, 1996. Age effects of follicle-stimulating hormone and pulsatile luteinizing hormone secretion across the menstrual cycle of premenopausal women. *Journal of Clinical Endocrinology and Metabolism*, 81:1512–1518.

Redfield, R., 1941. *The Folk Culture of Yucatan*. Chicago: University of Chicago Press.

Reed, K. E., 1997. Early hominid evolution and ecological change through the African Plio-Pleistocene. *Journal of Human Evolution* 32:289– 322.

Rees, J. L., 2004. The genetics of sun sensitivity in humans. *American Journal of Human Genetics* 75:739–751.

Refshauge, W. F. and R. J. Walsh, 1981. Pitcairn island: fertility and population growth, 1790-1856. *Annals of Human Biology*, 8(4):303–312.

Rehman, H. U. and E. A. Masson, 2005. Neuroendocrinology of female aging. *Gender Medicine*, 2:41–56.

Reiner, A. P., E. Ziv, D. L. Lind, C. M. Nievergelt, N. J. Schork, S. R. Cummings, A. Phong, E. G. Burchard, T. B. Harris, B. M. Psaty and P.-Y. Kwok, 2005. Population structure, admixture, and aging-related phenotypes in African American adults: the cardiovascular health study. *American Journal of Human Genetics*, 76:463–477.

Reuter-Lorenz, P. A. and C. Lustig, 2005. Brain aging: reorganizing discoveries about the aging mind. *Current Opinion in Neurobiology*, 15:245–251.

Reynolds, L. F., I. B. Mekjavic and S. S. Cheung, 2007. Cold-induced vasodilatation in the foot is not homogeneous or trainable over repeated cold exposure. *European Journal of Applied Physiology* 102:73– 78.

Richards, M. and V. Macaulay, 2001. The mitochondrial tree comes of age. *American Journal of Human Genetics*, 68:1315–1320.

Riddle, D. R., W. E. Sonntag and R. J. Lichtenwalner, 2003. Microvascular plasticity in aging. *Ageing Research Reviews*, 2:149–168.

Riley, B.W. and D. Brokensha, 1988. *The Mbeere of Kenya, Volume 1: Changing Rural Ecology*. Institute for Development Anthropology, Lanham, Maryland: University Press of America,.

Roberts, D. F., 1978. *Climate and Human Variability*. 2d ed. Menlo Park, California: Cummings.

Robins, A. H., 1991. *Biological Perspectives on Human Pigmentation*. Cambridge: Cambridge University Press.

Roche, A. F., 1986. Bone growth and maturation. In: *Human Growth: A Comprehensive Treatise, Volume II*, eds. F. Falkner and J. M. Tanner, New York: Plenum Press, pp. 25–60.

Roche, A. F., 1992. *Growth, Maturation, and Body Composition: The Fels Longitudinal Study 1929–1991*. Cambridge: Cambridge University Press.

Rode, A. and R. J. Shephard, 1995. Basal metabolic rate of Inuit. *American Journal of Human Biology* 7:723–729.

Rogan, W. J. and A. Chen, 2005. Health risks and benefits of bis(4-chlorophenyl)-1,1,1-trichloroethane (DDT). *Lancet* 366:763–773.

Romer, A.S., 1970. *The Vertebrate Body*. 4th ed. Philadelphia: W. B. Saunders Company.

Rota M. C., R. Cano Portero, D. Che, M. G. Caporali, V. Hernando and C. Campese, 2007. Clusters of travel-associated Legionnaire's disease in Italy, Spain and France, July 2002 – June 2006. *Euro Surveillance* 12:E3–E4.

Rotter, N., G. Tobias, M. Lebl, A. K. Roy, M. C. Hansen, C. A. Vacanti and L. J. Bonassar, 2002. Age-related changes in the composition and mechanical properties of human nasal cartilage. *Archives of Biochemistry and Biophysics*, 403:132–140.

Ruff, C., 2002. Variation in human body size and shape. *Annual Review of Anthropology*, 31:211–232.

Ruse, M., 1979. *The Darwinian Revolution: Science Red in Tooth and Claw*. Chicago: University of Chicago Press.

Saccone, C., C. Gissi, C. Lanave, A. Larizza, G. Pesole and A. Reyes, 2000. Evolution of the mitochondrial genetic system: an overview. *Gene* 261:153–159.

Sahlin, K., M. Tonkonogi and K. Söderlund, 1998. Energy supply and muscle fatigue in humans. *Acta Physiologica Scandinavica* 162:261–266.

Salzano, F. M., 1985. The peopling of the Americas as viewed from South America. In: *Out of Asia: Peopling the Americas and the Pacific*, eds. R. Kirk and E. Szathmary, Canberra: The Journal of Pacific History, Inc., pp. 19–29.

Santoro, N., J. R. Brown, T. Adel and J. H. Skurnick, 1996. Characterization of reproductive hormonal dynamics in the perimenopause. *Journal of Clinical Endocrinology and Metabolism*, 81:1495–1501.

Sarinas, P. S. and R. K. Chitkara, 1997. Ascariasis and hookworm. *Seminars in Respiratory Infections* 12:130–137.

Sattenspiel, L., 1990. Modeling the spread of infectious disease in human populations. *Yearbook of Physical Anthropology* 33:245–276.

Saw, S. M., G. Gazzard, D. Koh, M. Farook, D. Widjaja, J. Lee and D. T. Tan, 2002. Prevalence rates of refractive errors in Sumatra, Indonesia. *Investigative Ophthalmology and Visual Science* 43:3174–3180.

Sawka, M. N. and C. B. Wenger, 1988. Physiological responses to acute exercise-heat stress. In *Human Performance Physiology and Environmental Medicine at Terrestrial Extremes*, eds. K. B. Pandolf, M. N. Sawka and R. R. Gonzalez, Indianapolis: Benchmark Press, pp. 97–151.

Schell, L. M., 1991. Pollution and human growth: lead, noise, polychlorobiphenyl compounds and toxic wastes. In: *Applications of Human Biology to Human Affairs*, eds. C. G. N. Mascie-Taylor and G. W. Lasker, Cambridge: Cambridge University Press, pp. 83–116.

Schleif, R., 1993. *Genetics and Molecular Biology.* 2d ed. Baltimore: The John Hopkins University Press.

Scholander, P. F., H. T. Hammel, J. S. Hart, D. H. LeMessurier and J. Steen, 1958. Cold adaptation in Australian aborigines. *Journal of Applied Physiology* 13:211–218.

Schulz, L. O., P. H. Bennett, E. Ravussin, J. R. Kidd, K. K. Kidd, J. Esparza and M. E. Valencia, 2006. Effects of traditional and Western environments on prevalence of type II diabetes in Pima Indians in Mexico and the U.S. *Diabetes Care* 29:1866–1871.

Schurr, T. G. and S. T. Sherry, 2004. Mitochondrial DNA and Y chromosome diversity and the peopling of the Americas: Evolutionary and demographic evidence. *American Journal of Human Biology*, 16:420–439.

Schwartz, J., R. C. Brumbaugh and M. Chiu, 1987. Short stature, growth hormone, insulin-like growth factors, and serum proteins in the mountain Ok people of Papua New Guinea. *Journal of Clinical Endocrinological Metabolism*, 65:901–905.

Schwela, D., 2000. Air pollution and health in urban areas. *Reviews on Environmental Health* 15:13–42.

Scott, S. and C. J. Duncan, 2004. *Return of the Black Death.* Chichester: John Wiley.

Scrimshaw, N. S., 1991. Iron deficiency. *Scientific American* 265(4):46–52.

Scupin, R., 2006. *Cultural Anthropology: A Global Perspective.* 6th ed. Upper Saddle River, N.J.: Prentice Hall.

Sebastián, C., M. Espia, M. Serra, A. Celada and J. Lloberas, 2005. MacrophAging: a cellular and molecular review. *Immunobiology*, 210:121–126.

Selye, H., 1956. *The Stress of Life.* New York: McGraw-Hill.

Selye, H., 1973. The evolution of the stress concept. *American Scientist* 61:692–699.

Semenza, G. L., 2001. HIF-1, O_2, and the 3 PHDs: how animal cells signal hypoxia to the nucleus. *Cell* 107:1–3.

Semenza, G. L., 2004. Hydroxylation of HIF-1: oxygen sensing at the molecular level. *Physiology* 19:176–182.

Senut, B., M. Pickford, D. Gommery, P. Mein, K. Cheboi and Y. Coppens, 2001. First hominid from the Miocene (Lukeino Formation, Kenya). *Comptes Rendus de l'Academie des Sciences, Series IIA - Earth and Planetary Science*, 332:137–144.

Serjeant, G. R., 1985. *Sickle Cell Disease.* Oxford: Oxford University Press.

Serjeantson, S. W., 1985. Migration and admixture in the Pacific: insights provided by human leukocyte antigens. In: *Out of Asia: Peopling the Americas and the Pacific,* eds. R. Kirk and E. Szathmary, Canberra: The Journal of Pacific History, Inc., pp. 133–145.

Seth, S. and P. K. Seth, 1986. A review of evolutionary and genetic differentiation in primates. In: *Primate Evolution,* eds. J. G. Else and P. C. Lee, Cambridge: Cambridge University Press, pp. 291–306.

Sgró, C. M. and L. Partridge, 1999. A delayed wave of death from reproduction in *Drosophila. Science,* 286:2521–2524.

Shea, B. T. and R. C. Bailey, 1996. Allometry and adaptation of body proportions and stature in African pygmies. *American Journal of Physical Anthropology*, 100:311–340.

Shipman, P., A. Walker and D. Bichell, 1985. *The Human Skeleton.* Cambridge, Massachusetts: Harvard University Press.

Simmons, I. G., 1979. *Biogeography: Natural and Cultural.* North Scituate, Massachusetts: Duxbury Press.

Simon, C., J. Tang, S. Dalwadi, G. Staley, J. Deniega and T. R. Unnasch, 2000. Genetic evidence for assortative mating between 13-year cicadas and sympatric "17-year cicadas with 13 year life cycles" provides support for allochronic speciation. *Evolution,* 54:1326–1336.

Simpson, G. G., 1944. *Tempo and Mode in Evolution.* New York: Columbia University Press.

Simpson, G. G., C. S. Pittendrigh and L. H. Tiffany, 1957. *Life: An Introduction to Biology.* New York: Harcourt, Brace & World.

Sinclair, R., A. Chapman and J. Magee, 2005. The lack of significant changes in scalp hair follicle density with advancing age. *British Journal of Dermatology*, 152:646–649.

Sizonenko, P. C. and M. L. Aubert, 1986. Pre- and perinatal endocrinology. In: *Human Growth: A Comprehensive Treatise, Volume I*, eds. F. Falkner and J. M. Tanner, New York: Plenum Press, pp. 339–376.

Slobodkin, L. B. and A. Rapoport, 1974. An optimal theory of evolution. *Quarterly Review of Biology*, 49:181–200.

Snodgrass, J. J., M. V. Sorensen, L. A. Tarskaia and W. R. Leonard, 2007. Adaptive dimensions of health research among indigenous Siberians. *American Journal of Human Biology* 19:165–180.

Snowden, F. M., Jr., 1983. *Before Color Prejudice: The Ancient View of Blacks*. Cambridge: Harvard University Press.

Snowden, F. M., Jr., 1996. Bernal's "blacks" and the Afrocentrists. In: *Black Athena Revisited*, eds. M. R. Lefkowitz and G. M. Rogers, Chapel Hill: University of North Carolina Press, pp. 112–128.

Sohal, R. S., B. H. Sohal and W. C. Orr, 1995. Mitochondrial superoxide and hydrogen peroxide generation, protein oxidative damage, and longevity in different species of flies. *Free Radical Biology and Medicine*, 19:499–504.

Sparks, C. S. and R. L. Jantz, 2002. A reassessment of human cranial plasticity: Boas revisited. *Proceedings of the National Academy of Sciences*, 99:14636–14639.

Spearman, C., 1904. "General intelligence" objectively determined and measured. *American Journal of Psychology*, 15:201–293.

Spence A. P., 1989. *Biology of Human Aging*. Englewood Cliffs, N.J.: Prentice Hall.

Spiteller, G., 2001. Lipid peroxidation in aging and age-dependent diseases, *Experimental Gerontology*, 36:1425–1457.

Srb, A. M., R. D. Owen, and R. S. Edgar, 1965. *General Genetics*. 2d ed. San Francisco: W. H. Freeman and Company.

Stannard, D. E., 1989. *Before the Horror: The Population of Hawaii on the Eve of Western Contact*. Honolulu: University of Hawaii Press.

Stebbins, G. L., 1966. *Processes of Organic Evolution*. Englewood Cliffs, New Jersey: Prentice-Hall.

Steketee, R. W., 2003. Pregnancy, nutrition and parasitic diseases. *Journal of Nutrition*, 133:1661S–1667S.

Stein, A. D. and L. H. Lumey, 2000. The relationship between maternal and offspring birth weights after maternal prenatal famine exposure: the Dutch Famine Birth Cohort Study. *Human Biology* 72:641–654.

Stephens, J. C., D. E. Reich, D. B. Goldstein, H. D. Shin, M. W. Smith, M. Carrington, C. Winkler, G. A. Huttley, R. Allikmets, L. Schriml, B. Gerrard, et al., 1998. Dating the origin of the CCR5-delta32 AIDS-resistance allele by the coalescence of haplotypes. *American Journal of Human Genetics* 62:1507–1515.

Stern, M., M. Bartley, R. Duggirala and B. Bradshaw, 2000. Birth weight and the metabolic syndrome: thrifty phenotype or thrifty genotype? *Diabetes Metabolism Research Reviews*, 16:88–93.

Stini, W. A., 1969. Nutritional stress and growth: sex difference in adaptive response. *American Journal of Physical Anthropology* 31:417–426.

Stini, W.A., 1971. Evolutionary implications of changing nutritional patterns in human populations. *American Anthropologist*, 73:1019–1030.

Stini, W. A., 1972. Reduced sexual dimorphism in upper arm muscle circumference associated with protein-deficient diet in a South American population. *American Journal of Physical Anthropology* 36:341–352.

Stini, W. A., 1975. *Ecology and Human Adaptation*. Dubuque, Iowa: Wm. C. Brown Company Publishers.

Stinson, S., 2000. Growth variation: biological and social factors. In: *Human Biology: An Evolutionary and Biocultural Perspective*, eds. S. Stinson, B. Bogin, R. Huss-Ashmore and D. O'Rourke, New York: Wiley- Liss, Inc., pp. 425–463.

Stix, G., 2008. Traces of a distant past. *Scientific American* 299(1):56–63.

Stoltzfus, R. J., M. Albonico, J. M. Tielsch, H. M. Chwaya and L. Savioli, 1997. Linear growth in Zanzibari school children. *Journal of Nutrition*, 127:1099–1105.

Stolzel, M., S. Breitner, J. Cyrys, M. Pitz, G. Wolke, W. Kreyling, J. Heinrich, H. E. Wichmann and A. Peters, 2006. Daily mortality and particulate matter in different size classes in Erfurt, Germany. *Journal of Exposure Science and Environmental Epidemiology* 17:458–467.

Strickland, G. T., 2006. Liver disease in Egypt: hepatitis C superceded schistosomiasis as a result of iatrogenic and biological factors. *Hepatology* 43:915–922.

Sturm, R. A., R. D. Teasdale and N. F. Box, 2001. Human pigmentation genes: identification, structure and consequences of polymorphic variation. *Gene*, 277:49–62.

Suji, G. and S. Sivakami, 2004. Glucose, glycation and aging. *Biogerontology*, 5:365–373.

Sullivan, J., M. Ndekha, D. Maker, C. Hotz and M. J. Manary, 2006. The quality of the diet in Malawian children with kwashiorkor and marasmus. *Maternal and Child Nutrition*, 2:114–122.

Sullivan, R.M., D. A. Wilson, C. Lemon, and G. A. Gerhardt, 1994. Bilateral 6-OHDA lesions of the locus coeruleus impair associative olfactory learning in newborn rats. *Brain Research* 643:306–309.

Surwit, R. S. and M. S. Schneider, 1993. Role of stress in the etiology and treatment of diabetes mellitus. *Psychosomatic Medicine* 55:380–393.

Surwit, R. S., M. S. Schneider and M. N. Feinglos, 1992. Stress and diabetes mellitus. *Diabetes Care* 15:1413–1422.

Sussman, M. A. and P. Anversa, 2004. Myocardial aging and senescence: where have all the stem cells gone? *Annual Review of Physiology*, 66:29–48.

Suzuki, K., T. Kizaki, Y. Hitomi, M. Nukita, K. Kimoto, N. Miyazawa, K. Kobayashi, Y. Ohnuki and H. Ohno, 2003. Genetic variation in hypoxia-inducible factor 1 alpha and its possible association with high altitude adaptation in Sherpas. *Medical Hypotheses* 61:385–389.

Swan, S. H., E. E. Elkin and F. Fenster, 2000. The question of declining sperm density revisited: an analysis of 101 studies published 1934-1996. *Environmental Health Perspectives*, 108:961–966.

Sykes, B., A. Leiboff, J. Low-Beer, S. Tetzner and M. Richards, 1995. The origins of the Polynesians: an interpretation from mitochondrial lineage analysis. *American Journal of Human Genetics*, 57:1463–1475.

Szabo, G., A. R. Pathak and T. B. Fitzpatrick, 1969. Racial differences in the fate of melanosomes in human epidermis. *Nature*, 222:1081–1082.

Szathmáry, E. J. E., 1994. Non-insulin dependent diabetes mellitus among aboriginal North Americans. *Annual Review of Anthropology* 23:457–482.

Takai, M., F. Anaya, N. Shigehara and T. Setoguchi, 2000. New fossil materials of the earliest New World monkey, *Branisella boliviana*, and the problem of platyrrhine origins. *American Journal of Physical Anthropology*, 111:263–281.

TallBear K., 2007. Narratives of race and indigeneity in the Genographic Project. *Journal of Law, Medicine and Ethics* 35:412–424.

Tanner, J. M., 1962. *Growth at Adolescence*. 2d ed. Oxford: Blackwell Science Limited.

Tanner, J. M., 1988. Human growth and constitution. In: *Human Biology: An Introduction to Human Evolution, Variation, Growth, and Adaptability*. 3d ed., eds. G. A. Harrison, J. M. Tanner, D. R. Pilbeam and P. T. Baker, Oxford: Oxford University Press, pp. 337–435.

Tariq, S. H., M. T. Haren, M. J. Kim and J. E. Morley, 2005. Andropause: is the emperor wearing any clothes? *Reviews in Endocrine and Metabolic Disorders*, 6:77–84.

Taylor, H. L. and A. Keys, 1950. Adaptation to caloric restriction. *Science* 112:215–218.

Taylor, S. C., 2002. Skin of color: biology, structure, function, and implications for dermatologic disease. *Journal of the American Academy of Dermatology*, 46:S41–S62.

Te Velde, E. R., G. J. Scheffer, M. Dorland, F. J. Broekmans and B. C. J. M. Fauser, 1998. Developmental and endocrine aspects of normal ovarian aging. *Molecular and Cellular Endocrinology*, 145:67–73.

Terrell, J., 1988. History as a family tree, history as an entangled bank: constructing images and interpretations of prehistory in the South Pacific. *Antiquity*, 62:642–657.

Thangaraj, K., L. Singh, A. G. Reddy, V. R. Rao, S. C. Sehgal, P. A. Underhill, M. Pierson, I. G. Frame and E. Hagelberg, 2003. Genetic affinities of the Andaman Islanders, a vanishing human population. *Current Biology*, 13:86–93.

Thayer, R., J. Collins, E. G. Noble and A. W. Taylor, 2000. A decade of aerobic endurance training: histological evidence for fibre type transformation. *Journal of Sports Medicine and Physical Fitness* 40:284–289.

Thomas, R. B., 1975. The ecology of work. In *Physiological Anthropology*, ed. A. Damon, New York: Oxford University Press, pp. 59–79.

Thomas, R. B., T. B. Gage and M. A. Little, 1989. Reflections on adaptive and ecological models. In *Human Population Biology: A Transdisciplinary Science*, eds. M. A. Little and J. D. Haas, New York: Oxford University Press, pp. 296–319.

Tilkins, M. J., C. Wall-Scheffler, T. D. Weaver and K. Steudel-Numbers, 2007. The effects of body proportions on thermoregulation: An experimental assessment of Allen's Rule. *Journal of Human Evolution* 53:286–291.

Tissières, A., H. K. Mitchell and U. M. Tracy, 1974. Protein synthesis in salivary glands of *Drosophila melanogaster*: relation to chromosome puffs. *Journal of Molecular Biology* 84:389–398.

Tobias, P. V., 1985. The negative secular trend. *Journal of Human Evolution*, 14:347–356.

Tobin, D. J. and R. Paus, 2001. Graying: gerontobiology of the hair follicle pigmentary unit. *Experimental Gerontology*, 36:29–54.

Tolmasoff, J. M., T. Ono and R. G. Cutler, 1980. Superoxide dismutase: Correlation with life-span and specific metabolic rate in primate species. *Proceedings of the National Academy of Sciences* 77:2777–2781.

Townsend, G. C. and N. G. Martin, 1992. Fitting genetic models to Carabelli trait data in South Australian twins. *Journal of Dental Research*, 71:403–409.

Tracy, J. K., W. A. Meyer, R. H. Flores, P. D. Wilson and M. C. Hochberg, 2005. Racial differences in rate of decline in bone mass in older men: the Baltimore men's osteoporosis study. *Journal of Bone Mineral Research*, 20:1228–1234.

Trivers, Robert, 1985. *Social Evolution*. Menlo Park, California: Benjamin/Cummings Publishing Co.

Ulijaszek, S. J., 2000. Work and energetics. In *Human Biology: An Evolutionary and Biocultural Perspective*, eds. S. Stinson, B. Bogin, R. Huss-Ashmore and D. O'Rourke, New York: John Wiley and Sons, Inc., pp. 345–376.

UNESCO, 1952. *The Race Concept: Results of an Inquiry*. Westport, Connecticut: Greenwood Press, Publishers.

UNESCO, 1969. *Race and Science*. New York: Columbia University Press.

UNICEF, 2006. *The State of the World's Children 2007*. Oxford: Oxford University Press.

Upadhyay, A., B. L. Jaber and N. E. Madias, 2006. Incidence and prevalence of hyponatremia. *American Journal of Medicine* 119:S30–S35.

Upton, A.C., 1982. The biological effects of low-level ionizing radiation. *Scientific American*, 246(2):41–49.

Van Neste, D. and D. J. Tobin, 2004. Hair cycle and hair pigmentation: dynamic interactions and changes associated with aging. *Micron*, 35:193–200.

van Oel, C. J., W. F. C. Baaré, H. E. Hulshoff Pol, J. Haag, J. Balazs, A. Dingemans, R. S. Kahn and M. M. Sitskoorn, 2001. Differentiating between low and high susceptibility to schizophrenia in twins: the significance of dermatoglyphic indices in relation to other determinants of brain development. *Schizophrenia Research*, 52:181–193.

Vanhaesebrouck, P., K. Allegaert, J. Bottu, C. Debauche, H. Devlieger, M. Docx, A. François, D. Haumont, J. Lombet, J. Rigo, K. Smets, I. Vanherreweghe, B. Van Overmeire and P. Van Reempts, 2004. The EPIBEL study: outcomes to discharge for extremely preterm infants in Belgium. *Pediatrics*, 114:663–675.

Van Rossum, E. F. and S. W. Lamberts, 2004. Polymorphisms in the glucocorticoid receptor gene and their associations with metabolic parameters and body composition. *Recent Progress in Hormone Research* 59:333–357.

Vasudevan, S. and S. W. Peltz, 2003. Nuclear mRNA surveillance. *Current Opinion in Cell Biology* 15:332–337.

Vaughn, M., R. Van Oorschot and S. Baindur-Husdon, 2008. Hair color measurement and variation. *American Journal of Physical Anthropology* 137:91–96.

Verano, J. W. and D. H. Ubelaker (eds.), 1992. *Disease and Demography in the Americas*. Washington, D.C.: Smithsonian Institution Press.

Vermeij, G. J., 1987. *Evolution and Escalation*. Princeton: Princeton University Press.

Vitzthum, V. J., 1995. Comparative study of breastfeeding structure and its relation to human reproductive ecology. *Yearbook of Physical Anthropology*, 37:307–349.

Vitzthum, V. J., P. T. Ellison, S. Sukalich, E. Caceres and H. Spielvogel, 2000. Does hypoxia impair ovarian function in Bolivian women indigenous to high altitude? *High Altitude Medicine & Biology*, 1:39–49.

Vorster, H. H., 2002. The emergence of cardiovascular disease during urbanisation of Africans. *Public Health Nutrition* 5:239–243.

Vybíral, S., I. Lesná, L. Janský and V. Zeman, 2000. Thermoregulation in winter swimmers and physiological significance of human catecholamine thermogenesis. *Experimental Physiology* 85:321–326.

Waddington, C. H., 1966. *Principles of Development and Differentiation*. New York: Macmillan.

Walker, A. R. and P. Sareli, 1997. Coronary heart disease: outlook for Africa. *Journal of the Royal Society of Medicine* 90:23–27.

Walker, F. O., 2007. Huntington's disease. *Lancet* 369:218–228.

Wallace, B., 1970. *Genetic Load: Its Biological and Conceptual Aspects*. Englewood Cliffs, N.J.: Prentice-Hall.

Walsh, J. 1977. Seveso: the questions persist where dioxin created a water-shed. *Science* 197:1064–1067.

Wang, D. G., J.-B. Fan, C.-J. Siao, A. Berno, P. Young, R. Sapolsky, G. Ghandour, N. Perkins, E. Winchester, J. Spencer, L. Kruglyak, et al., 1998. Large scale identification, mapping, and genotyping of single-nucleotide polymorphisms in the human genome. *Science* 280:1077–1082.

Wang, Q., P. Ravn, S. Wang, K. Overgaard, C. Hassager and C. Christiansen, 1996. Bone mineral density in immigrants from southern China to Denmark. A cross-sectional study. *European Journal of Endocrinology*, 134:163–167.

Warner, M., B. Eskenazi, P. Mocarelli, P. M. Gerthoux, S. Samuels, L. Needham, D. Patterson and P. Brambilla, 2002. Serum dioxin concentrations and breast cancer risk in the Seveso Women's Health Study. *Environmental Health Perspectives* 110:625–628.

Watkins, W. S., C. E. Ricker, M. J. Bamshad, M. L. Carroll, S. V. Nguyen, M. A. Batzer, H. C. Harpending, A. R. Rogers and L. B. Jorde, 2001. Patterns of ancestral human diversity: an analysis of *Alu*-insertion and restriction-site polymorphisms. *American Journal of Human Genetics* 68:738–752.

Weismann, A., 1889. The duration of life. In: *Essays Upon Heredity and Kindred Biological Problems*, eds. E. B. Poulton, S. Schonland and A. E. Shipley, Oxford: Clarendon Press, pp. 1–66.

Weitz, C. A., I. G. Pawson, M. V. Weitz, S. D. R. Lang and A. Lang, 1978. Cultural factors affecting the demographic structure of a high altitude Nepalese population. *Social Biology*, 25:179–195.

Wenger, C. B., 1988. Human heat acclimatization. In *Human Performance Physiology and Environmental Medicine at Terrestrial Extremes*, eds. K. B. Pandolf, M. N. Sawka and R. R. Gonzalez, Indianapolis: Benchmark Press, pp. 153–197.

West, J. B., 1979. *Respiratory Physiology*. 2d ed. Baltimore: Williams and Wilkins.

West. J. B., 2006. Human responses to extreme altitudes. *Integrative & Comparative Biology* 46:25–34.

Whittemore, A. T. and B. A. Schaal, 1991. Interspecific gene flow in sympatric oaks. *Proceedings of the National Academy of Sciences*, 88:2540–2544.

Whorf, B. L., 1950. An American Indian model of the universe. *International Journal of American Linguistics,* 16:67-72. Reprinted in *The Philosophy of Time: A Collection of Essays,* ed. R. M. Gale, Garden City, NY: Doubleday & Company, Inc., pp. 377–385.

Wickler, S. and M. Spriggs, 1988. Pleistocene human occupation of the Solomon Islands, Melanesia. *Antiquity,* 62:703–706.

Wills, C., 1970. Genetic load. *Scientific American,* 222(3):98–107.

Williams, G. C., 1996. *Plan and Purpose in Nature.* London: Weidenfeld & Nicolson.

Williams-Blangero, S., J. L. VandeBerg, J. Subedi, M. J. Aivaliotis, D. R. Rai, R. P. Upadhayay, B. Jha and J. Blangero. 2002. Genes on chromosomes 1 and 13 have significant effects on *Ascaris* infection. *Proceedings of the National Academy of Sciences* 99:5533–5538.

Wilson, E.O., 1992. *The Diversity of Life.* New York: W. W. Norton & Company.

Wilson, J.D., M. W. Leihy, G. Shaw and M. B. Renfree, 2002. Androgen physiology: unsolved problems at the millennium. *Molecular and Cellular Endocrinology,* 198:1–5.

Wise, C. A., M. Srami, D. C. Rubinsztein and S. Easteal, 1997. Comparative nuclear and mitochondrial genome diversity in humans and chimpanzees. *Molecular Biology and Evolution,* 14:707–716.

Wolf, S. and H. Goodell (eds.), 1968. *Harold G. Wolff's Stress and Disease.* 2d ed. Springfield, Illinois: Charles C. Thomas.

Woo, J., M. Li, and E. Lau, 2001. Population bone mineral density measurements for Chinese women and men in Hong Kong. *Osteoporosis International,* 12:289–295.

Wood, B., 1992. Early hominid species and speciation. *Journal of Human Evolution* 22:351–365.

Wood, C. S., 1979. *Human Sickness and Health.* Palo Alto: Mayfield Publishing Company.

Wood, J. W., 1994. *Dynamics of Human Reproduction: Biology, Biometry, Demography.* New York: Aldine De Gruyter.

World Health Organization, 1972. *Vector Ecology.* WHO Technical Report Series, No. 501. Geneva: World Health Organization.

World Health Organization, 1993. *World Health Statistics Annual.* Geneva: World Health Organization.

World Health Organization, 2004. *Global Burden of Disease Estimates, 2002.* Geneva: World Health Organization.

Wyndham, C. H. and J. F. Morrison, 1958. Adjustment to cold of Bushman in the Kalahari desert. *Journal of Applied Physiology* 13:219–225.

Xing, J., D. J. Witherspoon, D. A. Ray, M. A. Batzer and L. B. Jorde, 2007. Mobile DNA elements in primate and human evolution. *Yearbook of Physical Anthropology* 50:2–19.

Xu, Z.-Y., W. J. Blot, H.-P. Xiao, A. Wu, Y.-P. Feng, B. J. Stone, J. Sun, A. G. Ershow, B. E. Henderson and J. F. Fraumeni, Jr., 1989. Smoking, air pollution, and the high rates of lung cancer in Shenyang, China. *Journal of the National Cancer Institute* 81:1800–1806.

Yoshida, N., K. Okumura and Y. Aso, 2005. High serum pentosidine concentrations are associated with increased arterial stiffness and thickness in patients with type 2 diabetes. *Metabolism Clinical and Experimental,* 54:345–350.

Young, A. J., 1988. Human adaptation to cold. In *Human Performance Physiology and Environmental Medicine at Terrestrial Extremes,* eds. K. B. Pandolf, M. N. Sawka and R. R. Gonzalez, Indianapolis: Benchmark Press, pp. 401– 434.

Yu, B. P., 2005. Membrane alteration as a basis of aging and the protective effects of calorie restriction. *Mechanisms of Ageing and Development,* 126:1003–1010.

Yu, N., M. I. Jensen-Seaman, L. Chemnick, J. R. Kidd, A. S. Deinard, O. Ryder, K. K. Kidd and W.-H. Li, 2003. Low nucleotide diversity in chimpanzees and bonobos. *Genetics,* 164:1511–1518.

Yuan, H., L. S. Wong, M. Bhattacharya, C. Ma, M. Zafarani, M. Yao, M. Schneider, R. E. Pitas and M. Martins-Green, 2007. The effects of second-hand smoke on biological processes important in atherogenesis. *BMC Cardiovascular Disorders* 7:1.

Zahm, S. H. and M. H. Ward, 1998. Pesticides and childhood cancer. *Environmental Health Perspectives* 106 (Suppl 3): 893–908.

Zegura, S. L., 1985. The initial peopling of the Americas: an overview. In: *Out of Asia: Peopling the Americas and the Pacific,* eds. R. Kirk and E. Szathmary,. Canberra: The Journal of Pacific History, pp. 1–18.

Zegura, S. L., T. M. Karafet, L. A. Zhivotovsky and M. F. Hammer, 2004. High-resolution SNPs and microsatellite haplotypes point to a single, recent entry of Native American Y chromosomes into the Americas. *Molecular Biology and Evolution,* 21:164–175.

Zhong, N., X. P. Wu, Z. R. Xu, A. H. Wang, X. H. Luo, X. Z. Cao, H. Xie, P. F. Shan and E. Y. Liao, 2005. Relationship of serum leptin with age, body weight, body mass index, and bone mineral density in healthy mainland Chinese women. *Clinical Chimica Acta,* 351:161–168.

Zimmermann, M. B. and R. F. Hurrell, 2007. Nutritional iron deficiency. *The Lancet* 370:511–520.

Zs-Nagy, I., 1994. *The Membrane Hypothesis of Aging.* Boca Raton, Florida: CRC Press.

Zuckerkandl, E. and L. Pauling, 1962. Molecular disease, evolution and genic heterogeneity. In: *Horizons in Biochemistry,* eds. M. Kasha and B. Pullman, New York: Academic Press,

CREDITS

ART

Chapter 2:   *p. 9:* Courtesy of the Benson Latin American Collection, University of Texas at Austin; *p. 18:* G. C. Williams, 2000. Am J Human Biol. 12(1), Figure 2 p. 15. Permission granted from Wiley-Liss; *p. 21* Illustrator: Elena Brown; *p.* 22 Illustrator: Elena Brown.

Chapter 5:   *p. 72:* C. Woese 1996 Phylogenetic trees: Whither microbiology? Current Biology 6:1060-1063. Courtesy of Elsevier, Ltd.

Chapter 6:   *p. 109:* Courtesy of Robert Meier.

Chapter 7:   *p. 123:* Reprinted Fig. 1a, 1b with permission from M. S. Turner, R. W. Briehl, F. A. Ferrone, and R. Josephs, Twisted Protein Aggregates and Disease: The Stability of Sickle Hemoglobin Fibers, *Physical Review* Lett. Vol. 90, 128103, 2003. Copyright 2003 by the American Physical Society; *p. 131:* Based in part on data from Hayasaka, et al. 1988.

Chapter 8:   *p. 144:* Based in part on data from Kirchman, et al. 1982; *p. 144:* Based in part on data from Carlson 1913 as noted in Pearl 1928; *p. 151:* Modified from table 4-4, page 88 in N. Howell, *Demography of the Dobe !Kung*, Second Edition, New York: Aldine de Gruyter, 2000.

Chapter 9:   *p. 167:* Tanner, J. M., 1988. Human growth and constitution. In: G. A. Harrison, J. M. Tanner, D. R. Pilbeam and P. T. Baker, Human Biology: An Introduction to Human Evolution, Variation, Growth, and Adaptability, Third Edition, Oxford: Oxford University Press, pp. 347; *p. 169:* Abbie, AA, 1964. The factor of timing in the emergence of distinctively human characteristics. Papers and Proceedings of the Royal Society of Tasmania, 98:63-71. Used with permission of the Royal Society of Tasmania; *p. 169:* Based in part on data from Dai, et al. 2002; *p. 170:* Melvyn J. Baer, James E. Harris, "A commentary on the growth of the human brain and skull," American Journal of Physical Anthropology 30: 39-44; *p. 172:* Tanner, JM, 1962, Growth at Adolescence, 2nd edition, figures 13 and 14, pp. 30 and 36; *p. 173:* Weiss, Mark L.; Mann, Alan E., *Human Biology and Behavior: An Anthropological Perspective*, 5th ed., © 1990. Reproduced by permission of Pearson Education, Inc. Upper Saddle River, NJ; *p. 175:* Based in part on data from Norgan 1995.

Chapter 10:   *p. 183:* Based in part on data from Proctor, et al. 1999; *p. 185:* This article was published in American Journal of Obstetrics, 110, T. G. Baker, Radiosensitivity of mammalian oocytes with particular reference to the human female, 746, Copyright Mosby, Inc. 1971; *p. 193:* based in part on data from Arias 2004.

Chapter 11:   *p. 202:* Based on R. E. Ricklefs. 1973. *Ecology.* Newton, Massachusetts: Chiron Press, table 13-1; *p. 205:* Redrawn by permission from The ecology of work by R.B. Thomas. In Physiological Anthropology, by Selma T. Damon, 59-79. Copyright @1975 by Oxford University Press, Inc. Used by permission of Oxford University Press, Inc.

Chapter 12:   *p. 246:* Johnson, Michael D., Human Biology: Concepts and Current Issues, 4th ed., © 2008. Reproduced by permission of Pearson Education, Inc. Upper Saddle River, NJ.

Chapter 13:   *p. 261:* Illustrator: Elena Brown

Chapter 14:   *p. 275:* Illustrator: Elena Brown

PHOTOS

Chapter 1:   *p. 5:* Photo courtesy of Catherine Panter-Brick.

Chapter 2:   *p. 15:* Harry Taylor © Dorling Kindersley, Courtesy of the Natural History Museum, London; *p. 15:* © Dorling Kindersley; *p. 16:* Colin Keates © Dorling Kindersley, Courtesy of the Natural History Museum, London; *p. 18:* Harry Taylor © Dorling Kindersley, Courtesy of the Natural History Museum, London; *p. 19:* Andy Crawford © Dorling Kindersley, Courtesy of the State Museum of Nature, Stuttgart; *p. 20:* Mick Loates © Dorling Kindersley; *p. 24:* © Dorling Kindersley; *p. 25:* Reprint from Scientific America; permission received from estate of Eric Mose; *p. 14:* Photo courtesy of A. Roberto Frisancho.

Chapter 3:   *p. 27:* Phototake/Carolina Biological Supply Company; *p. 32:* © Dorling Kindersley; *p. 41:* Photo courtesy of Rebecca Cann.

Chapter 4:   *p. 49:* Annabel Milne © Dorling Kindersley; *p. 54:* Photo courtesy of Susan Jarvi; *p. 60:* Photo courtesy of Susan Jarvi; *p. 64:* Photo courtesy of J. Koji Lum.

Chapter 5:   *p. 76:* © Dorling Kindersley; *p. 78:* Frank Greenaway © Dorling Kindersley; *p. 79:* Michael & Patricia Fogdon/CORBIS All Rights Reserved; *p. 79:* Simone End © Dorling Kindersley; *p. 80:* © Jerry Young; *p. 80:* © Dorling Kindersley; *p. 81:* Courtesy of Dan Brown; *p. 82:* © Patrick Robert/MPFT/CORBIS All Rights Reserved; *p. 83:* © The Natural History Museum, London; *p. 84:* Carolina Biological Supply Company/Phototake NYC; *p. 85:* Photo courtesy of Ivy L. Pike.

Chapter 6:   *p. 93:* Reproduced from the original held by the Department of Special Collections of the University Libraries of Notre Dame; *p. 106:* Getty Images/De Agostini Editore Picture Library; *p. 108:* Adrian Arbib/CORBIS All Rights Reserved; *p. 108:* Yvette Cardozo/Photolibrary.com; *p. 111:* Photo courtesy of María Eugenia Peña.

Chapter 7: *p. 118:* Jean Claude Revy - ISM/Phototake NYC; *p. 124:* Oliver Meckes & Nicole Ottawa/Photo Researchers, Inc.; *p. 137:* Lebrecht Music & Arts Photo Library; *p. 139:* Min Sapir/Photo Researchers, Inc.; *p. 139:* V Englebert/Robert Harding World Imagery; *p. 139:* G H Metcalf/Black Star; *p. 126:* Photo courtesy of Fatima L. C. Jackson.

Chapter 8: *p. 154:* Photo courtesy of Peter Ellison.

Chapter 9: *p. 162:* Saturn Stills/Photo Researchers, Inc.; *p. 162:* © Petit Format/Nestle/Science Source/Photo Researchers, Inc.; *p. 163:* Courtesy Brad Smith; *p. 164:* Photo Lennart Nilsson/Bonnier Alba AB, A CHILD IS BORN, Dell Publishing Company; *p. 178:* Photo courtesy of Noel Cameron.

Chapter 10: *p. 182:* AP Wide World Photos; *p. 182:* Jane Reed, Harvard News Office/AP Wide World Photos; *p. 188:* Michal Heron/Pearson Education/PH College; *p. 187:* Photo courtesy of Lynnette Leidy Sievert.

Chapter 11: *p. 208:* © Dorling Kindersley; *p. 209:* Photo by Michael Little, Binghamton University; *p. 212:* Cosmo Condina/Stock Connection; *p. 214:* © Dorling Kindersley;

p. 215: Photo courtesy of Ralph Garruto; *p. 217:* Photo courtesy of Dan Brown; *p. 223:* Photo courtesy of William R. Leonard.

Chapter 12: *p. 232:* Omikron/Photo Researchers, Inc.; *p. 232:* P. Pittet/F.A.O. Food and Agriculture Organization of the United Nations; *p. 234:* Courtesy Center for Disease Control; *p. 235:* CORBIS- NY; *p. 236:* Photograph by Dr. J.D.L. Hansen used by permission from: S. Davidson, R. Passmore, J.F. Brock and A.S. Truswell, 1975, Human Nutrition and Dietetics, Sixth Edition, Edinburgh: Churchill Livingstone; *p. 237:* courtesy of Carleton Gajdusek and Ralph M. Garruto, PhD; *p. 243:* Iowa State University Library/University Archives; *p. 249:* Museum of Religion and Atheism, St. Petersburg, Russia/The Bridgeman Art Library; *p. 248:* Photo courtesy of Stephen T. McGarvey.

Chapter 13: *p. 253:* Photo courtesy of Patricia Smith. Source: http://bioanthropology.huji.ac.il; *p. 263:* James Gillray, English, (1757–1815). A Voluptuary under the Horrors of Digestion, Engraving. Metropolitan Museum of Art, New York, New York. Gift of Mrs. Marshall P. Slade, 1940. Art Resource, NY; *p. 268:* UPI/CORBIS- NY; *p. 270:* Maria Stenzel/National Geographic Image Collection; *p. 271:* Courtesy of AT&T Archives and History Center; *p. 267:* Photo courtesy of Tessa Pollard.

Chapter 14: *p. 275:* Photo courtesy of Thomas McDade. Photo Credit: © Mary Hanlon 2007.

INDEX

A

ABO blood groups 116-119, 127, 141, 247
Abortion 150, 156
Acclimatization 203, 205, 211, 213-214, 218, 219, 221, 223, 224-225, 283
Acne 261
Acquired characteristics, inheritance of 10, 54
Actin 182
Adapids 77
Adaptation 1, 3, 4, 6, 15-17, 125, 283
  Behavioral 202-206, 208-217, 220, 221, 224, 226, 250
  Cultural 201, 204-206, 208, 211, 212-217, 220, 221, 224, 226, 275-276
  Demographic 149, 202, 204-205, 211, 215, 216, 220
  Developmental 14, 174, 179, 203, 219, 224
  Effectiveness 206, 216
  Efficiency 206, 217, 221, 225
  Genetic 204, 205, 216, 219, 222, 223, 224, 276
  Imperfect 17-18
  Physiological 202-206, 209-211, 213-224, 230-232, 238, 257, 277
  Riskiness of 206, 255
Adaptive radiation 20, 69-70, 71, 76, 77, 283
Adipocytes 174
Adipose tissue (See Fat)
Adiposity 174, 251, 262-267, 283
Admixture 110, 136, 137-138, 276, 282
Adolescence 161, 165, 168-172, 178, 180, 181, 203, 219, 278
Adolescent growth spurt 165, 168-170, 178, 283
Adoption studies, in human genetics 63, 113, 264
Adrenal gland 257-259
Adrenalin (See Epinephrine)
Adrenocorticotropic hormone (ACTH) 257-258
Adulthood 14, 23, 25, 69, 99-100, 105, 106, 122, 145-146, 148, 153, 156, 161, 165, 167, 170, 171, 173-174, 177, 179, 180, 181, 184, 190, 194, 196, 232, 236, 241
Aegyptopithecus 81
Aerobic capacity 221-222, 283
Aeta 179
Afghanistan 5, 150, 278
Africa 8, 79-80, 81, 83, 85, 91, 92, 95, 101, 102, 125-126, 132-133, 139-140, 148, 151, 154, 176, 178-180, 210, 216, 222, 224, 228, 242, 245, 248, 252
African-Americans 111, 114-115, 126, 137-138, 140, 196

Age 99-100, 103, 110, 112, 113, 145-146, 148, 150-153, 162-180, 181-200, 204, 221, 224, 230, 236
Age structure 156-159, 174
Aging 4, 100, 181-200, 260, 283
Agnatha 75-76
Agouti signaling protein gene (ASIP) 99
Agriculture 149, 150, 154, 159, 223, 226, 238, 241-242, 244, 247, 253, 269-270
AIDS 239, 245
Ainu 135
Akhenaten 91
Alarm reaction 257
Alaska 135
Albinism 99, 101, 104, 283
Albumin 229
Alcohol 209, 211, 233, 234
Aleut 136
Algal blooms 144
Allele frequency 41-44, 46, 73, 117, 119, 125, 126, 249, 255, 283
Alleles 33-47, 48-49, 51, 54, 58-59, 61, 63, 65, 66, 99, 107, 117-122, 124, 126-128, 134, 137-138, 168, 179, 241, 245, 247, 252-256, 260, 264, 272, 277-279, 281, 283
Allen's rule 107-108, 210, 216, 283
Allergy 249, 269
Allochronic speciation 68-69
Allopatric speciation 67-68, 87, 283
Altitude (See High altitude)
Alu transposons 51-52, 127, 133, 135
Alveoli 218, 283
Alzheimer's disease 184
Amenorrhea 149, 176, 283
America 93, 95, 101, 107, 110, 112, 113-114, 133, 135-138, 147, 152
American Anthropological Association 96, 279-280
Amino acids 27, 29, 31-33, 40, 44, 47, 55-56, 117, 120, 122, 227-230, 234, 235, 255, 260, 283
  Essential 228-229, 285
Ammonites 86
Amniote egg 76
Amoeba 155
Anagen 186-187, 283
Anagenesis 70-71, 86, 87, 129, 133, 283
Analogous structures 21-22, 283
Anatomy, comparative 15, 20-22, 25

Andes 14, 148, 177, 194, 203-204, 208-209, 217, 219-220, 223
Andropause 186, 283
Anemia 122-126, 237, 250, 256, 283
Anencephalus 102
Aneurysm 198
Anorexia nervosa 176, 231, 283
Antagonistic pleiotropy 191, 196
Anthropoids 72, 77, 78-79, 81, 283
Anthropology 1, 5, 14, 64, 85, 96, 111, 117, 126, 135, 141, 154, 178, 187, 223, 248, 278, 279-280, 282, 283
Anthropometry 14, 178, 283
Antibiotic resistance 23, 249
Antibiotics 235
Antibodies 117, 121, 283
Anticodons 32
Antigenic drift 243, 283
Antigenic shift 243, 283
Antigens 117-118, 120-121, 184, 283
Antioxidants 189
Antiserum 283
Apartheid 178
Apnea (See: Sleep apnea)
Apoptosis 184, 185, 187, 189, 200, 283
Arch (in dermatoglyphics) 109
Archeology 1, 132, 134, 136, 253, 271, 283
Arctic 19, 154, 201, 208, 209-211, 223, 235, 238
  Hysterias 238
Ardipithecus 82, 283
Argentina 154
Aristotle 9
Arteriosclerosis 197-198, 283
Arthritis 184, 197
Artiodactyls 130
Asbestos 271
Ascaris 247, 283
Ascorbic acid 235
Asia 64, 91, 92, 95, 101, 105-107, 120, 126, 133, 135-136, 138, 140, 187, 197, 234, 247, 248, 253, 267
Asian-Americans 113, 187
Assortative mating 46, 283
Asthma 240, 249, 269
Athabaskans 136, 208
Atherosclerosis 184, 189, 197, 261, 283
Athletes 213, 222, 230, 256
Atresia 185, 283
Australia 19-20, 119
Australian aboriginal people 96, 101, 110, 119, 120, 210

Australopithecus 283
  A. afarensis 82-83
  A .anamensis 82
Austronesian languages 134-135, 283-284
Autophagy 183, 284
Autosomes 129, 138
Auxology 51, 166, 284
Awnings 212, 215
Aztecs 228, 244

B

B-cells 184
Baboons 93, 145-146
Bacteria 27, 32, 40, 48, 50, 58, 71-72, 74-75, 87, 144, 202, 230, 235, 238, 244-245, 247, 253, 255, 260, 262, 270
Balanced polymorphism 123-124, 255, 284
Bangladesh 187
Barker, D. J. P. 165, 174
Barometric pressure 217, 220
Basal metabolic rate (BMR) 194-195, 203, 207, 210, 223, 231, 284
Basques 121
Beans 228-229
Bedding 208-209, 211
Bell Curve, The 114
Bergmann's rule 107-108, 210, 216, 284
Beriberi 233-234, 284
Bering land bridge 135-136
Bible, the 91-92
Big Bang 8
Bile 91-92
Binet, Alfred 112
Biocultural viewpoint 3, 6, 126, 276-277
Biogeography 15, 19-20, 25, 284
Biological anthropology 1, 85, 95-96, 108, 111, 126, 154, 248, 278, 284
Biome 2, 284
Biotic potential 143-144, 160, 284
Biotin 235
Bipedal locomotion 82-84, 88, 274, 277, 284
Birds 68, 69-70, 71, 73, 76-77, 243-244
Birdsell, Joseph 95-96
Birth
  Canal 110, 170
  Control 147
  Rate 147, 158-159
  Weight 165, 167, 174, 177, 219, 220
Biston betularia 15-16, 23, 45
Black bile 91-92

Blackfoot 119
Blastula 163
Blindness 233
Blood 91-92, 99, 116-127, 185, 189, 196, 197, 278
Blood groups 96, 116-127
Blood pressure 14, 258, 260-262, 266, 267, 281
Blow flies, in sheep 44
Blumenbach, Friedrich 93-94
Boas, Franz 95, 108-109
Body
    Fat 98, 105, 107, 111, 168-169, 174, 176, 227, 230-233, 251, 262-267
    Composition 96, 107, 134, 214, 262-267
    Proportions 107-108, 169, 210, 216
    Shape 209-210, 214, 216
    Size 43-44, 107, 111, 194-195, 197, 209-211, 214, 216, 223, 231
    Temperature 231
    Water 231
Body mass index (BMI) 262-264, 284
Bolivia 177, 278
Bone 17, 82, 101, 110-111, 135, 173-178, 184, 196-197, 200, 229, 235, 236, 238, 244
    Density 177, 178, 184, 196-197, 231
Bonobos 81, 129
Bottlenecks, population 45-46
Brain 95, 109, 170-171, 184-185, 196, 213, 218, 219, 223, 230-231, 257-259, 277, 281
    Size 77, 79, 81, 83-84, 86, 88, 170, 192, 194, 229-230, 274, 282
Brazil 276
Breast feeding 5, 150, 171, 174, 228, 237, 244, 254
Britain 20
Bubonic plague 245
Buffon, Comte de 93-94
Burt, Sir Cyril 113

C

Cactus 201
Calcium 196, 227, 235-236, 238
California 105-106
Cambrian Period 75-76
Cameron, Noel 178
Cameroon 126
Canalization 163, 284
Cancer 4, 54, 61, 126, 186, 190, 196, 199, 200, 251, 262, 270, 272, 284
    Bone 184
    Breast 262, 266, 270
    Colon 199

    Lung 199, 268-269
    Skin 99, 101
    Stomach 199
Cann, Rebecca 41
Capillaries 218, 219, 221
Carabelli's cusp 111-112
Carbohydrates 26, 227, 233, 234, 284
Carbon monoxide 269
Cardiovascular
    Disease 4, 138, 165, 174, 184, 186, 189, 196, 197-199, 200, 215, 216, 224, 236, 237, 238, 248, 254, 261-262, 266-267, 284
    System 183, 184, 224, 234, 258, 260-261
Caries, dental 253, 280, 285
Carnegie stages of development 163
Carotene 99
Carrying capacity 144-145, 284
Cartilage 173-174, 184, 188, 197, 235
Casal's collar 234
Case-fatality rate 240, 242, 284
Catagen 186-187, 284
Catarrhines 75, 79-81
Catch-up growth 177-178, 180, 229, 284
Caucasus 194
Celiac disease 176
Cell membrane 182-183, 189
Centenarians 194-195, 284
Central African Republic 139
Centromere 50-51, 284
Cephalic index 108, 284
Cercopithecids 80
Cerebral cortex 184, 257
Chalicotheres 86
Cheetah 46
Chemokine receptor 5 (CCR5) 245
Chiasmata 36-37, 284
Childhood 161, 165-180, 181, 193-194, 203, 219, 221
Children 5, 105-106, 108, 111, 112-114, 165-180, 192, 204, 211, 221, 223, 228, 232, 241-242, 247, 248, 250, 253, 254, 255, 268, 271
    Nutritional diseases 101, 174, 176, 228-229, 232, 235-237, 250
    Obesity 165, 167, 174-177, 178, 238, 248, 263-265
Chile 217
Chimpanzees 1, 80, 81, 82, 84, 93, 119, 120, 129-131, 202-203, 245
China 142-143, 159, 194, 198, 248, 268
Chinese-Americans 113
Chlamydia 149
Chloroplasts 58, 75, 284
Chloride 236, 255

Chloroquinine 64
Cholera 247, 255, 284
Cholesterol 101, 182, 261-262, 266
Chondrichthyes 73, 76, 284
Chordates 71-72, 76
Chromatin 48-49, 181, 284
Chromosomes 27, 33-39, 47, 136, 190, 247, 264, 284
  Mapping 51-53, 58-59, 63, 65
  Structure 48-51
Chronic mountain sickness 219
Cicadas 69
Circulation 213, 218, 219, 224
Cladistics 73, 284
Cladogenesis 67-68, 69, 70, 87, 133, 284
Class (in taxonomy) 71-72, 284
Classification, biological (See Taxonomy)
Clinal distribution 119, 121, 134, 136, 138, 140, 141
Cline 90-91, 101, 102, 107, 115, 284
Clothing 204, 205, 208-209
Clovis sites 136
Cobalamin 235
Coca leaves 209
Codon 32-33, 40
Coelurosaur 19
Coevolution 17, 126, 284
Cognitive function 184-185, 192, 200, 217, 237, 247, 250, 255, 257, 260
Cohort design 166
Coital frequency 148, 149
Cold adaptation 105, 107, 203, 204, 206-212, 216, 223, 224
Cold-induced vasodilatation (CIVD) 211, 284
Collagen 189, 235
Colombia 178
Colostrum 171
Competition 11-12, 24, 47
Complete Replacement Model (see Out of Africa Model)
Concealment 15-16, 102
Conception 145, 147, 148, 161, 165
Conduction 207-208, 224
Confidentiality 279
Consent, informed 166, 277-280
Convection 207-208, 224
Contraception 150
Cooking 209, 211, 216, 268
Coon, Carleton 95
COPD (Chronic obstructive pulmonary disease) 249
Core (in thermoregulation) 206, 209, 211, 213-215, 224, 284
Cori cycle 230-231, 284
Corn (See Maize)

Coronary arteries 197-198
Corticotropin-releasing factor 257
Cortisol 258, 262, 267, 284
Countercurrent heat exchange 209-210, 213, 284
Countershading 15, 284
Cows 23, 130, 226, 254
Coxsackie B virus 254
Cranial capacity 84, 86
Craniometry 95
Creationism 13-15, 17, 19, 93, 285
Cretaceous Period 75, 77, 87
Cretinism 237
Crickets 68
Critical periods of development 123, 161, 171, 178, 181
Cross linkage 189-190, 200
Crossing over 37, 51-52, 58, 65, 285
Cross-sectional design 165, 285
Cultural anthropology 1, 5, 280-281, 285
Culture 1, 3, 5, 90, 95-96, 112, 113-114, 126, 148, 150, 156, 160, 187, 192, 197, 204, 224, 235, 245, 248, 250, 253, 256, 257, 260, 265, 275-278, 280
  As adaptation 4, 201, 204-206, 208, 211, 212-217, 220, 221, 224, 226-227, 253, 276
  Change 256, 260, 267, 272, 277
  Definition 1, 285
Cyanide 125-126
Cystic fibrosis 255-256, 272, 285
Cytoskeleton 182, 190, 285

D

Darwin, Charles 7, 11-13, 15, 17, 23, 24, 26, 94-95, 285
Darwin, Erasmus 7
Datoga 85
Deciduous teeth 172-173
Decline, idea of 7-8, 285
Deep time 8, 9, 13, 24, 204, 285
Deer 130
Dehydration 176, 213, 232, 247
Deletion mutation 40, 44, 59
Demography 4, 6, 96, 116, 129-130, 142, 147-160, 285
Dentition 22, 111-112, 172-173, 175, 235, 238, 253-254
Deoxyribonucleic acid (see DNA)
Depression 186, 187
Dermal bones 173
Dermatoglyphics 109-110, 138, 285
Desert 19, 73, 100, 210, 212-213, 215
Developed countries 106, 132, 142, 145, 147-148, 150, 155-156, 176, 178, 194, 196, 197-199, 200, 233, 236, 238, 251

Developing countries 106, 156, 160, 176, 178, 198, 228, 237
Developmental adaptation (See Adaptation, developmental)
Developmental conversion 203
Devonian Period 73, 75, 76
Diabetes mellitus 4, 55, 149, 240, 251, 272
    Type 1 254-255, 262, 272
    Type 2 14, 107, 165, 167, 174, 176, 189, 238, 248, 262, 264-267, 272
Diaphysis 173-174, 285
Diarrhea 232, 234, 236, 242, 247, 270
Diet 5, 77, 82, 83, 99, 101, 102, 107, 110, 126, 148, 149, 154, 172, 174, 175, 177, 196, 197-199, 226-238, 248, 250, 255, 265, 267
Diffusion 218-219, 222, 285
Dinosaurs 75, 76-77, 87-88, 197
Dioxin 270
Directional selection 43-44, 285
Disability 281-282
Discrimination 279, 281-282
Disease 3-6, 36, 57, 63, 126, 138, 140, 148-150, 158, 159, 160, 176, 179, 180, 219, 248, 277-279, 281
    Chronic 4, 138, 165, 167, 174, 176, 178, 184, 186, 189, 190, 196, 197-199, 200, 215, 216, 224, 238, 248, 254, 261-262, 264-270, 272, 277
    Direct contact 242-244, 250
    Infectious 4, 41, 54, 64, 85, 153, 176, 177, 184, 202, 226, 238-250, 251, 253-256, 258, 261, 265, 276
    Intimate contact 149, 244-247, 250
    Nutritional 101, 176, 227-238, 250
    Poor sanitation 247-249, 250
    Vector-borne 64, 122-125, 126-127, 240-242, 248, 250, 256
Disposable soma 191
Diversifying selection 43-44, 285
DNA 26-47, 73, 77, 86, 189, 243, 245, 285
    Chips 59-60, 127, 285
    Imprinting: 54
    Mitochondrial 41, 57-58, 64, 128-138, 189-190, 200
    Nuclear 27-31, 128-129, 133, 135, 138, 189
    Protein synthesis 29, 31-33
    Regulatory regions 49
    Repair systems 189-190
    Replication of 30-31, 48-50
    Sequencing of 48, 53-54, 63, 65, 77, 116, 128, 129, 132, 141
    Structure of 28-30, 49
Dogs 226-227
Dominance (in behavior) 146
Dominance (in genetics) 35-37, 39, 43, 57, 285

Donora 269
DOPA (dihydroxyphenylalanine) 97-98
Doubling time 144, 155-156, 285
Down's syndrome 109
Droplet route 242, 250
Drosophila 27, 67, 144, 189
Dutch Hunger Winter Study 165

E

Earlobe 117, 188
Easter Island (see Rapa Nui)
Ebola fever 239, 242
Eccrine sweat glands 213-214, 285
Ecology 2, 5
    Population 4
Ectoderm 163, 285
Edema 224, 232, 237
Ecuador 64
Ediacaran fauna 75-76
Efe 106-107, 154, 178-179
Eggs 34, 41, 58, 128, 145, 148, 185
Egg follicles 185, 192
Egypt 91, 126, 137, 242, 281
Elders 1, 11, 100, 142, 145, 150, 161, 181, 184, 186, 192, 194, 196-197
Electrolytes 213, 221, 227, 236-237
Elephants 168, 189, 195
Ellison, Peter 154
Embryo 24, 54, 122, 163, 170, 173, 180, 181, 285
Embryology, comparative 23
Emphysema 269
Endoderm 163, 285
Endometrium 163
Endoscope 161
Endosymbiotic theory 58, 75, 285
Endurance 213, 221, 222, 225, 230, 236, 285
Energy 57, 58, 70, 75, 77, 85, 149, 171, 174, 183, 207, 211, 214, 219, 220, 227-232, 258, 261, 263-264
    Balance 5, 149, 263, 285
Entangled bank hypothesis 135
Environmental
    Determinism 94, 96, 285
    Physiology 96, 201-202, 204, 285
    Resistance 4, 143-145, 155, 160, 285
Enzymes 26-27, 30, 32, 36, 44, 127, 128-129, 183, 189, 190, 227, 233-234, 255, 260, 285
Epicanthic eyefolds 105-106, 285
Epidemics 41, 174, 238, 243, 244, 247, 262-264
Epidemiology 96, 240, 248, 285
Epidermis 97-98, 99, 101, 102

Epigenetics 14, 53-55, 65, 97, 179, 285
Epinephrine 258-259, 262, 267, 285
Epiphysis 173-174, 285
Erythropoietin 219
Eskimo 136
Essential resources 205, 211, 215, 216, 220-222, 286
Estrogen 147-148, 185-186, 196, 286
Ethics 232, 239, 252, 256, 277-282
Ethiopia 5, 91
Ethnic disparities 14, 126, 138, 140, 187, 197, 199
Ethnic group 90, 112, 114, 116, 153-154, 252, 263, 279, 286
Ethnicity 90, 126, 194, 276, 282, 286
Eugenics 252, 255, 286
Eukaryotic cells 27, 48, 49, 55-59, 71, 75, 182, 189, 200, 286
Eumelanin 97, 103
Euphenics 252, 255, 286
Europe 20, 91, 92, 93, 101, 102, 108, 110, 119, 137, 138, 147, 154, 174, 194-196, 198, 244, 245, 252, 255, 279
European-Americans 113-114, 187, 194, 196, 198
Express train hypothesis 135
Evaporation 207-208, 212-216, 224, 225
Evolution 2-3, 7-25
    Definition 7, 286
    History of theory 7-13
    Lamarckian 10-11, 54
    Macroevolution 3, 40, 74-88
    Microevolution 3, 40-46
    Modern synthetic theory 46-47, 282
    Of life 3, 74-84
    Of senescence 181, 187, 190-192, 200
    Rate of 86-87
Exons 55-57, 63, 65, 286
Extinction 3, 66, 69, 76-77, 86-88, 256, 286
Extrachromosomal genetics 55-59
Eye color 37, 103-104

F

Facial features 94, 108, 188
Fallopian tubes 149
Family (in taxonomy) 71-72, 87, 286
Famine 55, 107, 158, 165, 174, 227, 229-233, 249, 264
Fast-twitch muscle fibers 222
Fat 26, 168-169, 176, 227, 230-233, 286
    Brown 174, 210
    White 174
Fayum 80
Fecal-oral route 247, 250

Fecundability 147-148, 154, 160, 286
Fecundity 147-150, 160, 186, 196, 286
Fels study 166
"Feral" people 93
Fertility 147-148, 150, 153, 155-156, 160, 186, 192, 194, 261, 286
Fetus 54, 92, 102, 161-164, 167, 171, 177, 179, 181, 185, 244, 256, 286
Fight or flight response 258, 260
Fingerprints 109-110
Fish 71, 73, 76, 145
Fitness 45, 47
Folate 102, 235
Follicle-stimulating hormone (FSH) 185
Fontanels 173, 286
Forensics 64, 110, 279, 286
Fossils 9, 19, 22, 24, 71, 73-87, 172, 286
Founder effect 46, 286
Frailty 184, 186
Frame-shift mutation 40
Framingham study 198
Frisancho, A. Roberto 14
Fuel 205, 208, 209, 211, 216, 268, 269
Fundus, of eye 103
Fungal cells 239
Fur 22, 203

G

G6PD (glucose-6-phosphate dehydrogenase deficiency) 127
Gambia 5
Gametes 33-36, 38
Gametocytes 241
Ganglia 258, 286
Garn, Stanley 95-96
Gastrulation 163
Gene flow 43, 45
Gene inactivation 59-60, 65
Gene overexpression 61, 286
Gene pool 45
Gene regulation 49, 61, 65, 235, 286
Gene sequencing (See DNA, Sequencing)
Generation time 143
Genetic
    Bottleneck 256
    Code 29, 31-32, 40, 286
    Counseling 252, 277-278
    Drift 43, 45-46, 129, 137, 286
    Engineering 256, 275, 276
    Information Nondiscrimination Act (GINA) 279

Load 45, 286
Penetrance 254, 272
Variation 3, 4, 39, 41, 45-46, 53, 59, 62, 63, 116,
    127, 128, 129-130, 132, 140, 201, 239, 249, 256,
    275-276, 282
Genetics 286
  Mendelian 3, 13, 34-40, 51, 61
  Population 3, 40-43, 96
  Quantitative 61, 264
Genographic project 132
Genome, human 62-63, 65, 128, 129, 131, 132, 286
Genotype 37-39, 43, 45, 47, 48, 116-127, 134, 140, 141,
    264, 286
  Frequency 41-43, 247, 286
Genus 67, 71-72, 83, 87, 286
Geographic isolation 67-68, 73, 79, 87, 276, 286
Geological time 71, 74-75
Germ theory of disease 239
Gestation 164, 165, 171, 174
Gibbons 119, 131
Gill slits 23
Global warming 159
Gloger's rule 100, 102, 286
Glucagon 230
Glucose 57, 230-231, 234, 235, 258, 262
Glucose-6-Phosphate Dehydrogenase (G6PD)
    deficiency 127, 241, 286
Glycation 189, 200
Glycation end products, advanced (AGEs) 189
Glycogen 227, 230, 235
Glycophorin A (GPA) 120
Glycophorin B (GPB) 120
Glycoproteins 117-118, 120, 189, 227
Goiter 237, 286
Gonorrhea 149
"Goose bumps" 22
Gorillas 119, 120, 130-131, 192
Gould, Stephen J. 17
Grandmother hypothesis 192
Great Chain of Being 9-11, 94, 95, 287
Greeks 7, 9, 91-92
Growth
  Acceleration 165-168, 169, 172, 176
  And development 3, 4, 14, 105-107, 110, 111, 161-180,
    223, 229, 261
  Curves 161, 165, 167-168, 170, 175, 178
  Disruption 164-165, 174, 175-179, 229, 231-232, 234,
    237, 247, 261
  Rate 167-168, 169, 171-172, 175, 177, 178, 180, 237
  Spurts 161, 165, 168, 170, 172, 178, 180
  Velocity 166-168

Growth hormone deficiency 57
Guatemala 106, 175, 198
Gullah Sea Islanders 138

H

Habitat 69, 82, 287
Habitat isolation 69
Habituation 210, 287
Hair
  Color 102-104
  Form 94, 104-105, 115, 139
  Graying 186-188
  Loss 186-188
Haplogroups 128, 136, 287
Haplorhines 78-79
Haplotypes 120, 128, 135, 137, 287
Hardy-Weinberg equilibrium 42-43, 46, 287
Harris lines 175, 287
Hawaii 20, 41, 105-106, 140, 153, 187, 199, 217, 276
Hayflick, Leonard 182, 190
Head shape 95, 108-109
Health 1, 5, 85, 91, 106, 111, 126, 129, 140, 177, 178, 196,
    221, 222, 223, 231, 239, 248, 266-267, 269-271,
    278, 281
  Mental 5, 85
  Women's 85, 267
Heart disease (See Cardiovascular disease)
Heat adaptation 103, 105, 107, 174, 204-208, 212-216,
    221, 224, 250
Heat shock proteins 260, 287
Height (See Stature)
Hemoglobin 99, 122-127, 203, 219, 225, 237, 260,
    269, 287
  Hemoglobin A 122, 125, 241
  Hemoglobin E 126-127, 241
  Hemoglobin S 122-123, 126, 241
Hemolytic disease of newborns 118
Heritability 39, 61-62, 63, 65, 97, 108, 109, 113, 255,
    264, 287
Heterozygosity 36-43, 46, 122-124, 126-127, 241, 245,
    255-256, 278, 281, 287
High altitude 4, 14, 17, 148, 177, 180, 203-204, 206, 209,
    211, 216-220, 223, 224, 225, 250, 260
Himalayas 148, 208, 219
Hindus 187
Hippocampus 184
Hippocrates 91
HIV (human immunodeficiency virus) 239, 245-247,
    248, 287
Homeostasis 202, 203, 205, 207, 221, 257, 287

Hominids 72, 75, 81-84, 91, 101, 102, 133, 208, 223, 287
Hominoids 72, 80-81, 119, 133, 235, 287
Homo
  H. antecessor 132
  H. erectus 84, 95, 132-133, 287
  H. ergaster 84, 132
  H. habilis 83-84, 287
  H. heidelbergensis 132
  H. monstrosus 93-94
  H. sapiens 41, 72, 75, 84-85, 91, 93, 95, 129-133, 233, 276-277, 287
Homologous structures 21, 287
Homoplasy 131, 287
Homozygosity 36-37, 41-43, 46, 123-127, 241, 245, 255, 256, 287
Honduras 176
Honeycreepers 20, 41
Hopi 9
Hormone replacement therapy 186
Horses 67, 86
Host 239-242, 250
Hot flashes 186, 187
Human biology, population 2-6, 14, 41, 51, 64, 66, 85, 89-90, 95-96, 99, 102, 108, 115, 116, 141, 152, 154, 159, 161, 165, 166-167, 178, 179, 192-200, 248, 251-252, 267, 274-282, 287
Human Genome Project 63, 97
Human Genome Diversity Project 132
Humors 91-92
Hungary 137
Huntington's disease 36, 277-279, 287
Hybrid breakdown 70, 287
Hybridization, genetic 59-60
Hydrocephaly 281
Hypertension 14, 126, 138, 174, 248, 261-262, 266, 272, 281, 287
Hyperventilation 203, 218
Hypoelectrolytemia 236, 287
Hyponatremia 236, 287
Hypoplasias 175, 287
Hypothalamus 257-258
Hypothalamus-pituitary-adrenal axis (HPA) 257-258, 260
Hypoxia 14, 17, 148-149, 177, 180, 216-220, 224, 225, 250, 256, 260, 287
Hypoxia inducible factor 1 (HIF 1) 219, 260

I

Iceland 150
Igloo 208

Illness 281, 287
Immune system 116-118, 120, 121, 123, 152, 153, 170-171, 179, 180, 183-184, 196, 229, 238, 239, 241, 242-247, 249, 250, 251, 253, 254, 256, 258, 260-261, 265, 269, 278, 287
Immunoglobulin G 171
Impotence 149, 186
Imprinting, of DNA 54, 287
Incas 244
Incidence rates, of disease 240, 243, 248, 254-255, 269, 287
Incubation period 240
Independent assortment 36-38, 46, 287
India 8, 64, 126, 137, 156, 158, 213, 226, 232, 247
Indris 93
Indonesia 134-135, 278
Industrial melanism 15-16, 45
Infancy 99, 101, 146, 147, 150-152, 160, 161, 164-165, 168, 171, 173, 174, 179, 180, 181, 192, 193, 203, 204, 211, 215, 216, 220, 232, 237, 255
Infanticide 150
Infectious disease (See Disease, infectious)
Infectivity 239-240, 287
Infecundability 147-148
Infertility 147
Inflammation 184, 188, 189, 234, 249, 258, 261-262, 265-266
Influenza 240, 242, 243-244, 250
Inheritance
  Acquired characteristics 10-11, 54
  Blending 12, 34
  Maternal 54, 58
  Polygenic 38-39, 43, 47, 65
Insertion mutation 40, 44, 59
Institutional Review Boards (IRBs) 279
Insulation 204, 206, 208-210, 212-214, 224, 225
Insulin 107, 165, 230, 254, 266
Insulin-like growth factor (IGF) 106-107, 179, 197
Insulin resistance 165, 266
Intelligence 4, 112-114, 115, 287
Intelligent design 13-14, 287
Interferon 242
International Biological Programme 2
Intramembrous bones 173
Intrinsic rate of natural increase 143, 287
Introns 55-56, 63, 65, 288
Inuits 208
Iodine 237
IQ tests 112-115, 288
Iran 213
Iris, of the eye 103-104

Iron 237, 250
Islands 20, 242-243
Italy 156-157

J

J-shaped curve 143-145, 155, 160
Jackson, Fatimah L. C. 126
Japan 105-106, 156, 176, 177, 198-199, 210
Japanese-Americans 105-106, 113, 199
Jewish populations 108, 252
"Junk" DNA 128
Juvenile phase of development 145-146, 168

K

Kalahari desert 151
Kallima 16
Kant, Immanuel 94
"Kennewick Man" 135-136
Kenya 85, 149, 222, 278
Keratinocyte 97, 99
Ketones 231
Ketosis 231
Key resources 205-206, 288
Kidney 203, 218, 261, 262
Kingdom (in taxonomy) 71-72, 74, 87, 288
Knockout mice 59
Korea 210
Kwashiorkor 176, 228-229, 232, 288

L

Lactate 222, 230-231
Lactation 148, 150
Lactation amenorrhea 150, 288
Lamarck, Jean Baptiste 10-11, 54, 94, 288
Landfills 270-271
Lapps, or Laplanders (See Saami)
Lazarus, Richard 257
Lead poisoning 271
Leadville, Colorado 177
Legionnaire's disease 239
Lemmings 143-144
Lemurs 77-78, 81
Leonard, William R. 223
Leprosy 149
Lesa 154
Leutinizing hormone (LH) 185
Liberia 126
Life expectancy 150-152, 160, 193-194, 196, 197, 200, 238, 255-256, 277, 288

Life span 146, 160, 161-180, 181-200, 288
Life tables 150-153, 288
Limiting factors 201-202, 204, 288
Line1 transposons 133
Linguistics 1, 9, 110, 134-137
Linkage, genetic 36-37, 51-52, 288
Lipids 227, 235, 237, 261-262, 266
Lipoproteins 227
Litter size 143, 147, 167
Liver 11, 40, 227, 230-231, 233, 235, 241
Locus 34-42, 45-47, 51, 55, 59, 61, 65, 98, 99, 107, 117-122, 138, 242, 245, 252, 255, 288
London 268
Longevity 189, 192, 194, 196
Longitudinal design 166-167, 288
Loops (in dermatoglyphics) 109
Lorises 78
Los Angeles 268
Lucy 83
Lufa 175
Lum, J. Koji 64
Lymphocytes 171
Lysosomes 183

M

Macaque 81, 131-132, 145-146
Macroenvironment 204-206, 207, 211-212, 215, 216, 220, 252, 288
Macroevolution 40, 66, 74-88, 288
Macronutrients 26, 227-233, 250
Macrophages 184
Magnesium 236
Maize 23, 25, 228-229, 234
Malaria 5, 41, 64, 120, 122-127, 141, 240-241, 256, 288
Malay Peninsula 139
Malnutrition 4, 14, 85, 148-149, 154, 159, 165, 174, 175, 176-177, 179, 196, 223, 226-238, 249-250, 288
    Protein 176, 204, 228-229, 250
    Protein-calorie 176, 227-233, 250
Malthus, Thomas 12, 158
Mamanwa 179
Mammals 17, 71-72, 73, 75, 77-78, 86, 87-88, 107, 129, 130, 167-168, 174, 194-195, 203, 210, 211, 213, 235, 241, 249, 288
Mandinka 154
Mangabeys 245
Manioc 228
Marasmus 176, 232, 288
Marsupials 20
Mass extinctions 66, 76-77, 86-87, 286

Massachusetts 187
Mate selection 94-95
Maternal-fetal incompatibility 118, 120, 121, 288
Maternal inheritance 54, 58, 128
Mauna Kea 217
Maupertuis, Pierre du 94
Maya 228
Mayr, Ernst 181-182
McDade, Thomas 278
McGarvey, Stephen T. 248
Measles 242-243, 247
Mechanical isolation 70
Meiosis 33-37, 40, 48, 51-52, 65, 128, 288
Melanesia 64, 101, 103, 110, 120, 126, 133-135, 288
Melanin 97-100, 103-104, 186-188, 288
Melanocortin 1 receptor gene (MC1R) 99
Melanocyte 97-99, 103, 186-188, 288
Melanosome 97, 288
Membrane-associated transporter protein gene
        (MATP) 99
Memory 184, 186, 192
Menarche 148, 171-172, 176, 185, 288
Mendel, Gregor 34-38
Mendelian genetics 3, 12, 34-40, 51, 61
Menopause 148, 184, 185-186, 187, 192, 196, 288
Menses 148, 149, 162, 172, 176
Menstrual cycle 148-149
Mental health 5, 85
Merozoites 241
Mesenchyme 173, 288
Mesoamerica 228
Mesoderm 163, 173, 288
Messenger RNA 31, 33, 55-56, 58, 65, 245, 288
Metabolic syndrome 248, 266-267, 272, 288
Metabolism 40, 44, 57, 75, 122, 127, 174, 176, 189, 190,
        194-195, 200, 203, 206-210, 212, 216, 219, 221-
        224, 230-232, 234-235, 237, 255, 260, 263-265
Methylation of DNA 53-54, 65
Mexico 111, 187, 228, 266
Microenvironment 204-206, 208-209, 211, 215, 216, 220,
        226, 251-252, 273, 276, 288
Microevolution 40-46, 66, 67, 86, 87, 110, 288
Micronesia 64, 101, 133-135, 159, 266, 288
Micronutrients 227, 233-238, 250
Microsatellites 51, 52, 127, 128, 138, 288
Migration 17, 41, 43, 45, 64, 94, 95, 100, 116, 127, 129,
        132-136, 142, 147, 153-156, 159, 197, 199, 260,
        266, 267, 276
"Millennium man" 82
Millet 228
Mimicry 16-17, 288

Minerals, dietary 227, 233, 237
Minisatellites 51, 288
Miocene Epoch 75, 79, 81
Mitochondria 57-58, 72, 75, 183, 189-190, 200, 222, 288
Mitochondrial DNA 41, 57-58, 64, 128-138, 189-190, 200
Mitochondrial Eve 41
Mitosis 33-35, 40, 48, 163, 182, 190, 200, 289
Mixed design 166
MNSs blood group 120, 141
Modern environments 107, 251-273, 276-277, 280
Modernization 4, 6, 174, 176, 214, 224, 248, 249, 252,
        264-267, 272, 289
Molecular clock 130-131, 289
Monkeys 72, 78-81, 130-131, 146, 242, 245
Monogenists 93-95, 289
"Monsters" 93-94
Mortality
    Causes 150, 152-153, 184, 197-200, 224, 239, 249, 250,
        261, 269, 272
    Rates 145-146, 150-153, 155-156, 160, 190, 191, 193,
        194, 219, 243-244, 269, 289
Mosquitoes 5, 64, 240-241
Mother-infant bond 171
Mice 99, 264
mRNA (See Messenger RNA)
mtDNA (See Mitochondrial DNA)
Mucus 255
Muscle 11, 83, 168-169, 172, 176, 183, 197, 200, 207,
        210, 213, 216, 217, 219, 221-222, 225, 227, 229-
        232, 242, 258, 260-262, 266
Musculoskeletal system 183-184, 187
Muslims 92, 187
Mutagens 40, 44, 289
Mutations 12, 24, 39-40, 43-46, 52, 57, 59, 87-88, 117,
        122, 125-126, 130-131, 179, 190-191, 199, 200,
        241, 245, 249, 255, 289
Mutualism 58
Myocin 183
Myoglobin 219, 289
Myopia 252-253, 256, 272, 281, 289
Myxedema 237, 289

N

Na-Dene 136
Native Americans 107, 110, 119, 120, 134, 136, 138, 141,
        264, 266
Natural experiments 62, 239, 289
Natural selection 11-13, 14, 17, 21, 23, 32, 43-44, 47, 67,
        86-88, 126-127, 129, 131, 149, 159, 163, 174, 179,
        181, 188, 190-191, 192, 232, 237, 239, 245, 247,
        249-250, 251-256, 264, 274-276, 289

Nature versus nurture 96-97, 112, 289
Nauru 266
Navaho 136
Neanderthals 84-85, 91, 102, 133, 289
Neel, J. V. 107, 174, 264
Nepal 5, 149, 278
Netherlands 165
Neurological system 164, 170-171, 180, 183, 184-185, 196, 217, 234-235, 237, 244, 258, 270
Neurons 184-185, 196
Neurotransmitters 171, 289
Neutral mutations 130-131
New Guinea 110, 119, 120, 134-135, 139, 175, 179
New World monkeys 79-80
Niacin 234
Niche 69, 81, 289
Niger 5
Nitric oxide 219, 260, 289
Noah 91-92
Noise 259
Nonenzymatic glycation 189
Non-shivering thermogenesis 210, 289
Noradrenalin (See Norepinephrine)
Norepinephrine 210, 257-260, 262, 267, 289
Normality 252, 256, 280-282, 289
Nose 188
Nuclear DNA 27-31, 128-129, 133, 135, 138, 189
Nucleic acids 26-28, 289
Nucleotides 28-32, 34, 39-40, 44, 47, 48-55, 59-60, 63, 65, 117, 122, 125, 127, 128, 130-132, 141, 190, 289
Nucleus 31-33, 55, 289
Nurses 259
Nutrients 226-228, 230, 233-234, 238, 247, 249, 250, 289
Nutrition 226-238, 250

O

Obesity 14, 107, 111, 165, 167, 174, 176-177, 178, 237, 238, 248, 262-266, 272, 289
Occupation 206, 211, 221, 224
Ohio 166
Old World monkeys 75, 79-81
Oligocene Epoch 75, 80-81
Oligonucleotides 59, 289
Omomyids 77
Oncogenes 199, 289
Oocytes (See Eggs)
Orangutans 119, 131, 143
Order (in taxonomy) 71-72, 77, 289
Ordovichian Period 75-76
Organelles 57-58, 183, 189, 289

Ossification 173-174
Osteichthyes 73, 76, 289
Osteoarthritis 184, 197
Osteoblasts 173, 184, 289
Osteoclasts 184, 289
Osteomalacia 236, 289
Osteoporosis 184, 196-197, 236, 238, 289
Out of Africa model 132-133
Ova (See Eggs)
Ovary 168, 171
Overnutrition 176-177, 238, 262-266
Overpopulation 11-12, 24
Overweight 111, 176, 262-265, 289
Ovulation 185, 192
Oxidation 189-190, 221, 234, 260
Ozone 269

P

Pacific Islanders 41, 46, 64, 133-136, 140, 141, 149, 159, 248, 264-265, 266
Pain 258-259, 277
Pakistan 5, 41
Paleoanthropoloogy 132, 290
Paleontology 15, 19, 24, 74-84, 290
Palestine 92
Pancreas 254
Panda's thumb 17-18
Pandemics 243-244
Panter-Brick, Catherine 5
Pantothenic acid 234
Papua New Guinea (See New Guinea)
Papuan languages 134-135, 290
Paraguay 187
Paramecia 67
Parasitic disease 41, 58, 64, 120, 122-127, 141, 176-177, 238, 239-241, 247-250
Parental investment 143
Parkinson's disease 184
Parturition 147, 290
Pathogenicity 240, 290
Pathogens 102, 184, 238-250, 251, 265, 269
Pedomorphism 84, 274, 282, 290
Pellagra 234, 290
Peña, Maria Eugenia 111
Penetrance, of genes 254, 272, 290
Perfusion 218, 225, 290
Perichondrium 173
Periodontal disease 253-254
Periosteum 173
Permian Period 75-76, 86

Personality 91, 97, 153
Perspiration 101, 213-216, 221, 225
Peru 14, 148
pH 201, 203, 218
Phaeomelanin 97, 103
Phaethon 91
Phenotype 4, 37-39, 42-43, 46-47, 48, 53, 59, 60-61, 65,
    95, 96-112, 116, 118, 120, 122, 126, 127, 134, 136,
    140, 141, 252, 254, 255, 256, 290
  Frequency 42
  Plasticity 203, 204, 281, 290
Phenylalanine hydroxylase (PAH) 255
Phenylketonuria (PKU) 255, 290
Philippines 135, 139, 179, 248
Philostratus 91
Phlegm 91-92
Phospholipids 182
Phrenology 95
Phylum 71-72, 76, 290
Physical activity 177, 184, 196, 197, 203, 206-208,
    211-213, 215, 216, 217, 220-225, 262, 264-267
Physical anthropology (See Biological anthropology)
Physical fitness 111, 221-222, 224, 225, 290
Pigs 243-244
Pike, Ivy L. 85
Pima Indians 266
Pinta 244, 290
Pitcairn Island 46
Pituitary gland 100, 257-258
Placenta 167, 177
Placoderms 75-76, 290
Plaque, arterial 261-262, 290
Plasmids 48
Plasmodium 240-241
Platyrrhines 79-80
Pleiotropic effects of genes 39, 191, 196, 290
Pleisiadapids 77
Pliocene Epoch 75, 81
Pokot 85
Pollard, Tessa 267
Pollution 251, 268-273, 290
  Air 251, 268-269, 272, 274
  Solid waste 270-271, 273
  Water 251, 269-270, 272-273, 274
Polycythemia 219-220, 290
Polygenic inheritance 39, 43, 47, 191, 290
Polygenists 93-95, 290
Polymerase chain reaction (PCR) 53, 290
Polymorphisms 52, 58-59, 64, 65, 117, 120, 121, 123,
    127, 136, 290
Polynesia 64, 101, 107, 110, 133-135, 248, 290

Population 2-3, 89-90, 290
  Crashes 143, 145, 244
  Density 159, 160, 202, 204, 242, 251, 272, 274-275, 276
  Distribution 142, 242
  Ecology 142-147
  Genetics 40-43, 96
  Growth 142, 150, 155-160
  Regulation 142, 146-147
  Size 41, 116, 129-130, 135, 142-145, 147, 151-152, 153,
    155, 191, 240, 242, 256
  Structure 142, 145-147, 156-159, 242-243
Potassium 227, 236, 241
Poverty 5, 85, 132, 145, 150, 156, 160, 177, 178, 180, 223,
    233-235, 247, 250, 265-266, 269, 271, 272
Power (muscular) 221, 290
Pregnancy 85, 154, 164, 166, 220
Premature birth 164-165
Prevalence rates, of disease 237, 238, 240-241, 248, 290
Primates 41, 72, 77-79, 82, 129-131, 141, 168, 172,
    223, 290
Pritchard, James Cowles 94
Prodromal period 240
Progesterone 186
Prognathism 84, 290
Progress, idea of 8, 10-11, 94, 290
Prokaryotic cells 27, 48, 55, 182, 290
Prolactin 150
Protein 26-27, 29, 48-50, 55-57, 59, 64-65, 171, 176, 178,
    183, 189, 197, 200, 227-233, 245-246, 250, 290
Protein synthesis 31-33, 49, 55-56, 61, 245
Proteomics 64-65, 290
Puberty 100, 103, 168, 177
Pueblo 212
Punctuated equilibrium 19, 86, 129, 290
Pygmy populations 93, 106-107, 139-140, 154, 178-180,
    215-216
Pygmoid populations 137, 138-140, 179
Pyradoxal 234-235
Pyradoxamine 234-235
Pyradoxine 234-235
Pyruvate 230-231

Q

Quantitative genetics 61, 264
Quechua 209
Quin-zhee 208

R

Race 2, 4, 73, 89-96, 102, 104, 106, 108, 110, 112-114,
    115, 140, 141, 276, 290

Racial profiling 2

Racism 89, 91-92, 94, 95, 108, 112, 114, 132, 138, 178, 252, 279, 290

Radiation (of heat) 207-208, 212, 214, 224

Rafting events 20

Rainforest 81, 102, 201, 214, 216, 223

Rana pipiens 69

Randomization 166-167

Rapa Nui 110

Reactive oxygen species (ROS) 189, 190

Recessive traits 38-39, 42-43, 52

Recombination, genetic 58, 128

Red blood cells 117, 120, 122-124, 127, 241, 260

Reflectometry 99, 290

Regional continuity model 133

Replication, of DNA 30-31

Reproduction 3, 4, 11-12, 32-34, 54, 58, 143, 146-150, 154, 159, 160

Reproductive
  Access 146
  Age 145, 150, 156, 255
  Ecology 154
  Hormones 5, 148, 154
  Isolation 67-68, 73, 290-291
  Rate 143-145, 239, 272, 289
  Season 144
  System 148-149, 170-172, 180, 183, 185-186, 233, 267

Reptiles 73, 75, 76-77

Reservoir, of disease 239-242, 247, 249, 291

Resistance, to disease 239, 241-245, 249, 250

Resources
  Essential 205, 211, 215, 216, 220-222, 286
  Key 205-206, 288

Respiratory
  Alkalosis 203, 218, 291
  System 218, 255-256, 260, 268-269

Restriction endonucleases 52-53, 128-129, 136, 291

Restriction fragment length polymorphisms (RFLPs) 52-53, 128-129, 136, 291

Retinal 233

Retinitis pigmentosa 57

Retinoic acid 233

Retinol 233

Retrovirus 245-246, 248, 291

Rh (Rhesus) blood group system 120-121, 134, 141

Riboflavin 234

Ribonucleic acid (See RNA)

Ribosome 31, 33, 55, 57-58, 291

Rice 233-234, 236

Rickets 101, 236, 291

RNA 27, 29, 31-33, 50-51, 55-57, 245-246, 291
  Interference 60-61, 291
  Processing 55-57, 63, 291

Roma 137, 252

Romans 7, 91-92

Russia 223

S

S-shaped (sigmoid) curve 143-144

Saami 110, 137-139, 154

Sakai 139

Salmonella 255

Salt 213, 221, 236-237

Samburu 85

Samoa 153, 248, 278

Sampling 166-167, 169, 291

San population 101, 151-152, 210

Sanskrit 137

Sarcopenia 183-184, 186, 197, 291

Sardinia 194-196

Saudi Arabia 5, 213

Savanna 81, 83, 215, 216, 224

Scammon curves 170

Scandinavia 222

Schistosomiasis 241-242, 248, 281, 291

Schizophrenia 109

Scurvy 235, 291

Seasonal isolation 68-69

Seasonality 5, 85, 149, 150, 153, 154, 203, 208, 210-211, 223

Sebaceous sweat glands 213-214, 291

Secular trend 106, 111, 175-176, 180, 291

Segregation (in genetics) 35-37, 46, 291

Selection
  Artificial 13, 23, 25
  Natural 11-13, 14, 17, 21, 23, 32, 43-44, 47, 67, 86-88, 126-127, 129, 131, 149, 159, 163, 174, 179, 181, 188, 190-191, 192, 232, 237, 239, 245, 247, 249-250, 251-256, 264, 274-276, 289

Semi-longitudinal design 166

Semi-species 67

Senescence 152-153, 181-200, 291
  Cellular 181-184, 188, 190, 200
  Evolutionary theories of 187, 190-192, 200
  Mechanistic theories of 188-190, 193, 200
  Organismal 183-186

Seveso 270

Sex chromosomes 38, 291

Sex-determining region of Y chromosome (SRY) 168
Sex differences 100, 110, 152, 168-169, 171, 174, 196-197, 224
Sex-linked traits 38, 118
Sex ratios 145-146, 291
Sexual selection 94
Sexually transmitted diseases (STDs) 149, 244-245, 250
Shade 203, 212, 225
Shell (in thermoregulation) 206, 213, 215, 224, 291
Shelter 204, 208-209, 211, 212, 214, 224
Siberia 135-136, 223
Sibling species 67, 291
Sickle cell
    Anemia 122-125, 255
    Hemoglobin 122-126, 281
    Trait 122-126, 141, 241, 249-250, 252, 256, 291
Siestas 212
Sievert, Lynnette Leidy 187
Single nucleotide polymorphisms (See SNPs)
Single-stressor model 204-206, 211, 215, 216, 220, 226, 275-276
Skeletal
    Features 110-111, 136
    Growth 173-174, 177, 178, 238
    System 183-184
Skin 97-98, 102, 109, 186, 188, 200, 214, 233-235, 237, 241, 244
    Color 1, 2, 4, 91, 94, 96-102, 103, 115, 134, 139, 140, 187-188, 236
Slave theory of salt depletion 236-237
Sleep apnea 266, 291
Slovenia 187
Slow-twitch muscle fibers 222
Smallpox 239, 245
Smog 268-269, 272
Smoke 268
Smoking 199, 269, 271, 272
Snails 241, 248
SNPs 59, 63, 65, 242, 291
Socioeconomic status 5, 85, 106, 138, 145, 148, 177, 178, 180, 206, 223, 233, 235, 247, 250, 278
Sodium 227, 236-237
Solomon Islands 134
South Africa 178, 210, 248
Soweto 178
Space colonies 276
Spearman, Charles 112
Speciation 3, 66-71, 74, 82, 86, 87, 129, 131, 141, 276, 291

Species 2-3, 9, 16-17, 20-25, 35, 43, 45-46, 66-73, 86, 87, 129-132, 142-147, 181, 183, 194, 200, 201-202, 204, 210, 256, 276, 291
Species selection 87, 291
Specific growth rate 143, 291
Spectrophotometer 99, 103
Speed 221-222
Sperm 34, 54, 58, 147, 148
Spina bifida 102
Spinal column 170-171, 258
Spindles, mitotic and meiotic 50, 289
Spliceosomes 55-57, 291
Sporozoites 241
Stabilizing selection 43-44, 291
Starvation 227, 229-233
Stature 57, 61, 105-107, 134, 139, 165, 167, 169, 171-172, 175, 179, 180, 229, 291
Stem cells 275
Stratified sample 166, 291
Stratum corneum 99
Strength 172, 176, 206, 221, 222, 289
Strepsirhines 78
Stress 291
    Biological 5, 226-250
    Cellular 260
    Disease 4, 149-150, 226, 238-250
    Environmental 4, 148, 201-206, 210-220, 223, 224, 276-277
    General 251, 256-262, 267, 272, 278, 291
    Nutritional 4, 149, 165, 174, 175, 176-177, 226-238, 248, 249-250, 263
    Physical 4, 148-149, 201-225, 277
    Psychosocial 4, 5, 85, 138, 154, 256-262, 266, 276, 278
Stressors 201-206, 210-220, 223, 224, 251, 258, 291
Strokes 184, 185, 197, 266
Stromatolites 74, 291
Stunting 175, 177-179, 229, 237, 292
Subacute infantile mountain sickness 220
Subcutaneous fat 209, 211, 213, 215, 224, 225
Subsistence 5, 149, 157-158, 232
Subspecies 73, 89, 90, 292
Survivorship patterns 145-146, 153, 192, 194
Sweating 101, 213-214, 221, 225
Sweet potatoes 228
Sympathetic nervous system 210, 257, 258-259, 262
Sympathetic adrenal medullary axis (SAM) 257, 258-259, 260
Sympatric speciation 68-69, 87, 292

Synapses 184, 185
Synthetic theory of evolution 46-47, 292
Syphilis 244-245, 292

T

T-cells 184, 269
Taiwan 135
Tandem repeats 50, 277-278, 292
Tanning 98-99
Tanzania 5, 126
Tarsiers 77-79
Taxonomy 3, 66-73, 87, 292
Tay-Sacks disease 252
Technology 205, 206, 221, 224, 251-253, 265, 271, 272, 275, 276-277, 281
Teeth (See Dentition)
Telogen 187-188, 292
Telomerase 50, 190, 292
Telomere 50-51, 190, 292
Termites 203
Testes 168, 171, 172
Testosterone 154, 186, 196, 292
Thailand 139
Thalassemia 125-126, 141, 241, 292
Thermoregulation 206-208
Threat perception 257, 260-261
Thrifty genotype 107, 174, 233, 264-265, 272, 292
Thrifty phenotype 174, 265, 292
Thyroid function 210, 223, 237, 270
Tibet 17, 217, 220, 260
Time, ideas about 7-9
Tolerance, law of 201-202
Trabeculae 173, 292
Training 221-222
Transcription, genetic 31, 49, 55-56, 58, 60, 61, 260, 292
Transfer RNA (See tRNA)
Translation, genetic 55, 57, 60, 65, 292
Transposable sequences (transposons) 51-52, 292
Treponemal diseases 244-245
Triassic Period 75, 77, 86-87
tRNA 31-33, 58, 292
Tropism 202
Trypanosomiasis 149
Turkana 85, 149
Twins, in human genetics studies 62, 65, 97, 103, 109, 113, 253, 254, 264
Tyndall scattering 103
Tyrosinase gene 99

Tyrosine 97-98
Tyson, Edward 93

U

Ulcers 258, 261, 262
Ultrasound 161-162
Ultraviolet radiation 98-99, 101-102, 103, 105, 115, 212, 216, 235
Umbrellas 212, 215
UNESCO 95
United Kingdom 5, 178, 267, 268
United States 90, 94, 95, 108, 113-115, 126, 137-138, 142-143, 147, 152-153, 157, 165, 169, 175, 177, 178, 193-194, 196, 198, 199, 217, 226, 230, 236, 245, 248, 263-264, 266, 269, 278, 279, 281
Urbanization 176
Use and disuse, theory of 10-11
Uterus 163, 171

V

Vaccination 239, 241, 242-243
Vanuatu 64
Vasoconstriction 205, 209, 211, 218-219, 292
Vasodilation 211, 213, 215, 216, 219, 292
Vectors 64, 240-244, 248, 292
Ventilation
    Of shelters 214, 216
    Respiratory 203, 217-220, 225, 292
Vervet 80
Vestigial structures 22, 24, 292
Virgin soil epidemics 244, 292
Virulence 239-240, 242-245, 292
Viruses 238-239, 242-243, 245-246, 254
Visual recognition 1, 2
Vitamins 227, 233, 250, 292
    Anabolism 101-102, 115
    Ascorbic acid 235
    Catabolism 102
    Folate 102, 235
    Niacin 234
    Riboflavin 234
    Thiamine 233-234
    Vitamin A 233
    Vitamin D 101-102, 196, 235-236, 238

W

Wage labor 142
Wallace, Alfred Russel 11

Warfare 5, 12, 40, 85, 154, 158, 204, 227, 232, 233, 242, 249
Wasting 177, 179, 232, 292
Weaning 168, 171, 174, 228
Wechsler scales 112-114
Weight 5, 17, 107, 164, 170, 176, 177, 194-195, 230-232, 238, 242
Whales 168
Whorls, in dermatoglyphics 109-110
"Wild" people 93
Wind chill 207
Wine 194
Wings 20-22
Wisdom teeth 22
Women's health 85
Work capacity 220, 221, 222-224, 232, 237, 238, 242

Workloads 85, 154, 220-222
Worms 238-239, 241, 247

X

X chromosome 38, 47, 51-52, 168
X-linked traits 38, 51-52
X-rays 174

Y

Y chromosome 38, 47, 128, 129, 132, 135-138, 168
Yaws 244, 292
Yeast 239

Z

Zambia 156, 158
Zygote 163, 292